Infants and Toddlers
in Out-of-Home Care

National Center for
Early Development & Learning

A Series from the National Center
for Early Development & Learning

Series Editor: Don Bailey, Ph.D.

This book is part of a series edited by Don Bailey, Ph.D., and developed in conjunction with the National Center for Early Development & Learning (NCEDL). Books in this series are designed to serve as resources for sharing new knowledge to enhance the cognitive, social, and emotional development of children from birth through 8 years of age. For information on other books in this series, please refer to the Brookes web site at www.brookespublishing.com.

Other Books in this Series

The Transition to Kindergarten
Robert C. Pianta and Martha J. Cox

Infants and Toddlers in Out-of-Home Care

edited by

Debby Cryer, Ph.D.
Frank Porter Graham Child Development Center
University of North Carolina at Chapel Hill

and

Thelma Harms, Ph.D.
Frank Porter Graham Child Development Center
University of North Carolina at Chapel Hill

National Center for
Early Development & Learning

·P·A·U·L·H·
BROOKES
PUBLISHING Cº

Baltimore • London • Toronto • Sydney

Paul H. Brookes Publishing Co.
Post Office Box 10624
Baltimore, Maryland 21285-0624

www.brookespublishing.com

Typeset by Argosy, West Newton, Massachusetts.
Manufactured in the United States of America by
The Maple Press Company, York, Pennsylvania..

The National Center for Early Development & Learning is supported under
the Educational Research and Development Centers Program, PR/Award
Number R307A60004, as administered by the Office of Educational Research
and Improvement, U.S. Department of Education. However, no official
endorsement by the federal government should be inferred.

Library of Congress Cataloging-in-Publication Data
Cryer, Debby.
  Infants and toddlers in out-of-home care/by Debby Cryer and Thelma
Harms.
     p. cm.
  Includes bibliographical references and index.
  ISBN 1-55766-457-9
  1. Child care.   2. Child development.   3. Child care services.   I. Harms,
  Thelma.   II. Title.
HQ778.5 .C79   2000
362.7—dc21

                                                                    00-026375

British Library Cataloguing in Publication data are available from the British
Library.

Contents

About the Editors vii
About the Contributors ix
Foreword xv
Acknowledgments xvii

Chapter 1   Introduction... 1
Thelma Harms

Section I   **Current Knowledge on Early Development**

Chapter 2   Cognitive Development in Infants:
Looking, Listening, and Learning.................................... 7
Judy S. DeLoache

Chapter 3   Language Development in Early Childhood:
The Role of Social Interaction... 49
Jane R. Katz and Catherine E. Snow

Chapter 4   Social Development, Family, and Attachment
Relationships of Infants and Toddlers:
Research into Practice... 87
Carollee Howes

Section II   **Child Care and Intervention Programs**

Chapter 5   New Directions for Studying Quality in
Programs for Infants and Toddlers 117
*John M. Love, Helen Raikes, Diane Paulsell,
and Ellen Eliason Kisker*

Chapter 6   Respiratory Disease in Infants and Toddlers 163
Albert M. Collier and Frederick W. Henderson

Chapter 7   Diarrheal Disease in Infants and Toddlers 179
Robin B. Churchill and Larry K. Pickering

Chapter 8   The Early Intervention System
and Out-of-Home Child Care 207
Michael J. Guralnick

Section III   **Ecological Perspectives on Infant and Toddler Care**

Chapter 9   The Cultural Context of
Infant and Toddler Care 237
Judith K. Bernhard and Janet Gonzalez-Mena

Chapter 10 Supporting Infants and Toddlers:
The Nascent Policy Agenda 269
Sharon Lynn Kagan and Kathryn Taaffe McLearn

Chapter 11 Supporting Families as Primary Caregivers:
The Role of the Workplace 309
Ellen Galinsky and James T. Bond

Chapter 12 The Whole Child: Transdisciplinary
Implications for Infant and Toddler Care 351
Debby Cryer

Index 365

About the Editors

Debby Cryer, Ph.D., Investigator, Frank Porter Graham Child Development Center, University of North Carolina, 137 East Franklin Street, Suite 300, Chapel Hill, North Carolina 27514

Dr. Cryer is Investigator at the Frank Porter Graham (FPG) Child Development Center at the University of North Carolina at Chapel Hill. She has studied and written about early childhood program quality during the last 20 years and directed the child care program at the FPG Center since 1997. Throughout her career, she has combined her interests as an early childhood practitioner with her skills as a researcher, studying real-world issues and translating research findings into practice for early childhood program staff, parents, and policy makers. Dr. Cryer is a coauthor of the *Infant/Toddler Environment Rating Scale* (Harms, Cryer, & Clifford, Teachers College Press, 1990) and the *Early Childhood Environment Rating Scale, Revised Edition* (Harms, Clifford, & Cryer, Teachers College Press, 1998), and she worked as part of a team to develop numerous other quality assessment instruments, such as the National Association for the Education of Young Children (NAEYC) Accreditation instruments and the child development associate (CDA) candidate assessment instruments. She has also developed resources for teachers in early childhood programs, such as the popular *Active Learning Series* (Cryer, Harms, & Bourland, Addison-Wesley Publishing, 1987). Dr. Cryer was Principal Investigator for the national study on Cost, Quality and Child Outcomes in Child Care Centers and continues that research in the International Child Care and Education Study. She is currently Principal Investigator of two studies about the effects of caregiver continuity on infants and toddlers in child care. She is also involved in the development of an instrument to assess the quality of programs delivering services to infants and toddlers with disabilities as part of the quality studies for the National Center for Early Development & Learning.

Thelma Harms, Ph.D., Director of Curriculum Development, Frank Porter Graham Child Development Center, University of North Carolina, 137 East Franklin Street, Suite 300, Chapel Hill, North Carolina 27514

Dr. Harms is Director of Curriculum Development at the Frank Porter Graham Child Development Center and Research Professor in the School of Education at the University of North Carolina at Chapel Hill.

She is lead author of four widely used program assessment instruments: the *Early Childhood Environment Rating Scale, Revised Edition* (Harms, Clifford, & Cryer, Teachers College Press, 1998), the *Family Day Care Rating Scale* (Harms & Clifford, Teachers College Press, 1989), the *Infant/Toddler Environment Rating Scale* (Harms, Cryer, & Clifford, Teachers College Press, 1990), and the *School-Age Care Environment Rating Scale* (Harms, Jacobs, & White, Teachers College Press, 1996). She is also a coauthor of several curriculum series, including the *Active Learning Series* (Cryer, Harms, & Bourland, Addison-Wesley Publishing, 1987) and a 10-part television training series, *Raising America's Children*, for parents, caregivers, and teachers. Dr. Harms has lectured extensively in the United States and in Canada, England, Germany, Portugal, Russia, Sweden, Belgium, Australia, Hong Kong, and Singapore. Her work on environmental assessment and curriculum has been translated and used in many countries.

About the
Contributors

Judith K. Bernhard, Ph.D., Associate Professor, Ryerson Polytechnic University, 350 Victoria Street, Toronto, Ontario, Canada M5B-2K3

Dr. Bernhard, a native of Chile, is a lecturer, author, educator, and parent. Since receiving her doctorate from the University of Toronto, she has addressed the needs of immigrant and refugee children and families through her work with young children, their families, and teachers. Dr. Bernhard teaches child development at Ryerson Polytechnic University and has a particular interest in infants and toddlers in various contexts. Her focus is on pluralistic models that honor the role of culture in determining optimal caregiving practices.

James T. Bond, ABD, Vice President and Director of Child and Family Research, Families and Work Institute, 330 Seventh Avenue, 14th Floor, New York, New York 10001

Mr. Bond is Vice President of the Families and Work Institute with primary responsibility for overseeing and conducting research in the work life and child–family arenas. Before joining the Institute in 1992, he was Deputy Director of the National Center for Children in Poverty at Columbia University, Founding Director of the National Center for the Child, and Director of Research at the High/Scope Educational Research Foundation.

Robin B. Churchill, M.D., Assistant Professor of Pediatrics, Eastern Virginia Medical School, Children's Hospital of The King's Daughters, 601 Children's Lane, Norfolk, Virginia 23507

Dr. Churchill is Assistant Professor of Pediatrics at the Eastern Virginia Medical School and an attending physician in Infectious Diseases at the Children's Hospital of The King's Daughters. She is board-certified in both pediatrics and pediatric infectious diseases. Dr. Churchill has published several articles and book chapters on child care–associated infections and other topics on infectious diseases.

Albert M. Collier, M.D., Professor of Pediatrics, University of North Carolina School of Medicine, CB# 7220, University of North Carolina, Chapel Hill, North Carolina 27599

Dr. Collier has done research on respiratory illness in children in out-of-home care and the effects of indoor air pollution on respiratory illness in children. He is Associate Chairman of Pediatrics for Research, Professor of Pediatrics, Chief of the Pediatric Infectious Diseases Division, and Associate Director of the Center for Environmental Medicine and Lung Biology at the University of North Carolina School of Medicine.

Judy S. DeLoache, Ph.D., Professor of Psychology, University of Illinois, 603 East Daniel Street, Champaign, Illinois 61820

Dr. DeLoache is Professor of Psychology at the Beckman Institute for Advanced Science and Technology at the University of Illinois. Her work focuses on cognitive development in infants and young children, especially their developing understanding of various symbolic media.

Ellen Galinsky, M.S., President, Families and Work Institute, 330 Seventh Avenue, 14th Floor, New York, New York 10001

Ms. Galinsky is President and Co-founder of the Families and Work Institute, a Manhattan-based nonprofit organization conducting research on the changing family, workplace, and community. A leading authority on work–family issues, she has written more than 20 books and reports and has published more than 100 articles and chapters in academic journals, academic books, and magazines. Her newest book, *Ask the Children* (William Morrow & Company, 1999), is a landmark investigation of how America's children feel about their working parents.

Janet Gonzalez-Mena, M.A., Professor (retired), Napa Valley College, Napa, California 94558

Ms. Gonzalez-Mena is author of a number of textbooks, including *Multicultural Issues in Child Care* (Mayfield Publishing, 2000) and *Infants, Toddlers, and Caregivers* (Gonzalez-Mena & Eyer, Mayfield Publishing, 2000). She taught at Napa Valley College for 15 years.

Michael J. Guralnick, Ph.D., Director, Center on Human Development and Disability, Box 357920, University of Washington, Seattle, Washington 98195

Dr. Guralnick is Director of the Center on Human Development and Disability and Professor of Psychology and Pediatrics at the University of Washington at Seattle. Over the years, Dr. Guralnick has conducted research and demonstration projects in the fields of early childhood intervention, inclusion, social skills development, peer relations, and pediatric education. He has edited 6 volumes and published more than 100 articles and book chapters.

Frederick W. Henderson, M.D., Professor of Pediatrics and Pediatric Infectious Diseases, Department of Pediatrics, University of North Carolina School of Medicine, CB# 7220, University of North Carolina, Chapel Hill, North Carolina 27599

Dr. Henderson is Professor of Pediatrics and Pediatric Infectious Diseases at the University of North Carolina School of Medicine and Attending Physician at University of North Carolina Children's Hospital. His research has focused on the epidemiology of respiratory infections, particularly otitis media, among children in group child care and the emergence of drug-resistant respiratory bacteria among children in child care.

Carollee Howes, Ph.D., Professor, Department of Education, Box 951521, University of California, Los Angeles, California 90095

Dr. Howes is a developmental psychologist with a particular interest in social and emotional development within different social contexts. She is Professor of Education at the University of California at Los Angeles. She has been both a child care teacher and a child care parent.

Sharon Lynn Kagan, Ed.D., Senior Associate, Yale University Bush Center in Child Development and Social Policy, 310 Prospect Street, New Haven, Connecticut 06511

Dr. Kagan is Senior Associate at Yale University Bush Center in Child Development and Social Policy. Author of more than 100 articles and 12 books, Dr. Kagan's research focuses on the institutions and policies that affect child and family life. Dr. Kagan consults with numerous federal and state agencies, Congress, governors, and legislators; she is a member of 40 educational boards and is President of the National Association for the Education of Young Children (NAEYC).

Jane R. Katz, M.Ed., Harvard University Graduate School of Education, 309 Larsen Hall, Cambridge, Massachusetts 02138

Ms. Katz is currently a doctoral candidate in Human Development and Psychology at the Harvard University Graduate School of Education, where she earned a master's degree in education in 1994. She has been a teacher of very young children for 12 years.

Ellen Eliason Kisker, Senior Researcher, Mathematica Policy Research, Inc., Post Office Box 2393, Princeton, New Jersey 08543

Ms. Kisker is Senior Researcher at Mathematica Policy Research, Inc. She is a social policy researcher who specializes in evaluations of programs for low-income families and their children and research on child care policy, especially issues related to the supply of child care for low-income families. She is currently Deputy Project Director for the National Early Head Start Research and Evaluation Project.

John M. Love, Senior Fellow, Mathematica Policy Research, Inc., Post Office Box 2393, Princeton, New Jersey 08543

Mr. Love is Senior Fellow at Mathematica Policy Research, Inc. He is a developmental psychologist who specializes in evaluations of programs for low-income families and their children, research on child care quality, and issues related to conceptualizing and measuring children's school readiness. He is Project Director for the National Early Head Start Research and Evaluation Project.

Diane Paulsell, Researcher, Mathematica Policy Research, Inc., Post Office Box 2393, Princeton, New Jersey 08543

Ms. Paulsell is Researcher at Mathematica Policy Research, Inc. She specializes in conducting implementation studies of programs for low-income families and their children and has done research in the areas of child care, early childhood development, and employment retention among former welfare recipients. She is a member of the National Early Head Start Research and Evaluation Project team.

Larry K. Pickering, M.D., Director, Center for Pediatric Research, Children's Hospital of The King's Daughters, 601 Children's Lane, Norfolk, Virginia 23507

Dr. Pickering is Chair of Pediatric Research and Director of the Center for Pediatric Research at the Children's Hospital of The King's Daughters. He is certified in pediatrics and pediatric infectious diseases by the American Board of Pediatrics. Dr. Pickering is the author of more than 340 publications and editor of 9 books relating primarily to pediatric infectious diseases, with an emphasis on infectious diarrhea, child care–related illness, and protective factors in human milk. He is Principal Investigator of an ongoing 19-year National Institute of Health–funded study of human milk as it relates to infant nutrition and health.

Helen Raikes, Ph.D., Early Head Start Research and Evaluation Project Monitor, Administration on Children, Youth, and Families, U.S. Department of Health and Human Services, 330 C Street SW, Room 2411, Washington, D.C. 20201

Dr. Raikes is Special Research Consultant to the Administration on Children, Youth, and Families, U.S. Department of Health and Human Services, and serves as Project Monitor for the National Early Head Start Research and Evaluation Project. She is based at the Gallup Organization in Lincoln, Nebraska, where she was formerly Director of Research and Development and Infant/Toddler Programs. She specializes in infant and toddler development and programs and policy research that relate to young children.

Catherine E. Snow, Ph.D., Henry Lee Shattuck Professor of Education, Harvard University Graduate School of Education, 313 Larsen Hall, Cambridge, Massachusetts 02138

Dr. Snow carries out research on first and second language acquisition and literacy development in monolingual and bilingual children. She chaired the committee that produced the National Research Council report *Preventing Reading Difficulties in Young Children*, and she is President of the American Educational Research Association for 2000–2001. Her research focuses on the social-interactive origins of language and literacy skills and the ways in which oral language skills relate to literacy learning.

Kathryn Taaffe McLearn, Ph.D., Assistant Vice President, The Commonwealth Fund, 1 East 75th Street, New York, New York 10021

Dr. Taaffe McLearn is a public policy expert and scholar in the field of child development and serves as Assistant Vice President at The Commonwealth Fund in charge of the program on child and youth development. She received her doctorate from Yale University and is a visiting research scientist at the Yale University Bush Center in Child Development and Social Policy. Dr. Taaffe McLearn serves on the executive board of the American College of Obstetricians and Gynecologists.

Foreword

One of the biggest changes in the lives of children in the United States today is the increasing number of infants and toddlers younger than 3 years of age who are cared for by someone other than their parents during work hours. A number of factors have led to this change, including financial needs, changes in welfare policies, and, for some families, a perceived need to provide an enhanced educational environment for their child. Regardless of the motivation, the shift in caregiver from a parent to another adult has been variously lauded as an opportunity for working women, heralded as a strategy for promoting the development of children with disabilities or children living in poverty, bemoaned as potentially having negative consequences for children, or viewed with alarm when instances of poor-quality care become evident.

The National Center for Early Development & Learning, funded by the Office of Educational Research and Improvement of the U.S. Department of Education, sponsors an annual synthesis conference on issues of national importance. The purpose of each synthesis conference is to bring together experts around a given topic, share current information about knowledge and practice, engage in wide-ranging discussions, and generate recommendations for future research, policy, practice, and professional development. Out-of-home care for infants and toddlers was a natural topic for one of the first such conferences sponsored by the center. It is timely, of major importance, and complex with no easy solution. It is in our national interest to ensure that every infant has access to high-quality, nurturing, developmentally supportive care, whether that care is provided by a parent or by some other caregiver. Yet, with the exception of state regulations for child care and the establishment of early intervention systems for high-risk children, as a nation we are reluctant to intervene too much in the lives of children, families, or the individuals who make a living caring for young children.

This book represents a compilation of the information presented and the discussions that occurred at this meeting. Debby Cryer and Thelma Harms, organizers of the meeting, did an outstanding job of recruiting leaders across the country in research, policy, and practice related to infants and toddlers. The chapters included in this book articulate the importance of appropriate caregiving during the first years of life, describe current practices and research findings, identify key issues, and propose new directions for researchers, practitioners, and policy makers. This information will be of tremendous use to a variety of audiences as collectively we strive to ensure the well-being of infants and toddlers and to support their families in the process.

Don Bailey, Ph.D.
Director, Frank Porter Graham Child Development Center
University of North Carolina at Chapel Hill

Acknowledgments

This book on infants and toddlers in out-of-home care was written with input from many experts in addition to the authors of the individual chapters. In creating this book, authors were initially given the task of writing their respective chapters and then asked to present their drafts during a synthesis conference. The conference was conducted under the auspices of the National Center for Early Development & Learning, funded by the Office of Educational Research and Improvement of the U.S. Department of Education. Participants read the chapter drafts, responded openly to the authors' work, and generated additional implications that went beyond what had been written. Authors took part in synthesis group meetings and subsequently revised their chapters based on input from the conference participants as well as reviewer comments.

During the synthesis conference, representatives from many areas of early childhood came together, including chapter authors, researchers, practitioners, parents, policy makers, and other constituents in the field. All participants expressed a dedicated interest in ensuring that the lives of infants and toddlers and their families were optimized. They also represented a vast array of beliefs, sometimes conflicting and always thought-provoking and constructive. Without the input of the conference participants, the various chapters would not have been as comprehensive in the ideas they now contain. We greatly appreciate the opinions of all participants who helped to create each chapter included in this book:

Gina Adams
U.S. Division of Child Care
and Development

Don Bailey
University of North Carolina

Robert H. Bradley
University of Arkansas

Donna Bryant
University of North Carolina

Peg Burchinal
University of North Carolina

Camille Catlett
University of North Carolina

Lori Adams Chabay
New Curiosity Shop

Richard Clifford
University of North Carolina

Renatta Cooper
Pacific Oaks College

Martha Cox
University of North Carolina

xviii

ACKNOWLEDGMENTS

Lynette Aytch Darkes
University of North Carolina

George Digsby
Hope for Kids

Diane Early
University of North Carolina

Jim Gallagher
University of North Carolina

Robert Glenn
National Education Association

Jerry Govan
Orangeburg Consolidated Schools

Jim Griffin
U.S. Department of Education

Donna Hinkle
U.S. Department of Education

Alice Honig
Syracuse University

Bev Jackson
Head Start State Collaboration Office

Mary Jenne
University of North Carolina

Naomi Karp
U.S. Department of Education

Ron Lally
WestEd

Gwen Morgan
Wheelock College

Sam Odom
Indiana University

Peter A. Ornstein
University of North Carolina

Carol Brunson Phillips
Council for Early Childhood
Professional Recognition

Suzanne Randolph
University of Maryland

Joanne Roberts
University of North Carolina

Robin Rooney
University of North Carolina

Kate Sanford
Chapel Hill Cooperative School

Paula Scher
Busy Street

Kathy Shepherd
North Carolina Division
for Child Development

Katharine Smith
Family Child Care Provider

Kate Thegen
Smart Start

Pam Winton
University of North Carolina

Mark Wolery
University of North Carolina

Infants and Toddlers in Out-of-Home Care

National Center for
Early Development & Learning

1

Introduction

♦ ❖ ♦

Thelma Harms

Out-of-home care for infants and toddlers is now more the norm than the exception in many countries. This variation from the traditional pattern of early child rearing in the family creates concern for parents, professionals, and policy makers. Infants and toddlers are extremely vulnerable. Their physical, intellectual, emotional, and social skills are developing extremely rapidly, and their requirements for nurturing and stimulation are highly demanding. In addition, a number of studies have raised questions about whether the care generally available to infants and toddlers is of sufficient quality not to compromise their development. The purpose of this book is to present information to bridge the gaps among researchers, practitioners, and policy makers to help ensure that infants and toddlers in out-of-home care receive the care they need for positive development.

In order to present the implications of research for recommended practice in out-of-home care for infants and toddlers, we have had to cast a wide net and include information from a variety of disciplines not often brought together in one volume. In addition to pertinent research in developmental psychology and linguistics, both medical and educational research on the effects of child care on children are included, as well as several different perspectives on the larger ecological context, which influences both the quantity and quality of out-of-home care. The authors in this book have benefited greatly from review by and discussion with people representing different points of view, including parents, early childhood educators, researchers from various fields, and policy makers. These critical reviews were helpful in focusing the authors' attention on the many practical concerns that

1

need to be addressed if we are to make research a pertinent contributor to daily practice.

The book is organized into three sections, each focusing on a major area contributing to our understanding of out-of-home care for infants and toddlers. The first section features three chapters focusing on cognitive, language, and social development. These chapters give insight into the crucial nature of early development. In the chapter, "Cognitive Development in Infants: Looking, Listening, and Learning," DeLoache explains how children learn about the physical and social world by using all of their sensory and motor abilities. During the first 2 years, infants amass a surprising amount of information about objects and people and develop categories, concepts, and symbols based on their experience. The third chapter, by Katz and Snow, "Language Development in Early Childhood: The Role of Social Interaction," not only reviews research about how children develop the ability to communicate, but also introduces the important theme of cultural differences in language development. The effect of the quality of out-of-home care on language development and specific suggestions for improving the language environment in infant/toddler programs is also included. "Social Development, Family, and Attachment Relationships of Infants and Toddlers: Research Into Practice" rounds out the introduction to infant and toddler development. Howes hypothesizes that relationships, principally those experienced in the family and in the child care environment, are central to the child's construction of social interaction. She explores the different types of relationships in which young children engage, including attachment and playmate relationships with adults and peers, as well as the effect of the larger social context on social development.

The second section of the book deals with issues concerning infant and toddler child care programs. Both education and health issues are included. The fifth chapter, "New Directions for Studying Quality in Programs for Infants and Toddlers," proposes an expanded, comprehensive definition of quality in child care programs. Drawing upon extensive research on early childhood programs, Love, Raikes, Paulsell, and Kisker identify four program features particularly in need of further study: relationships, continuity, culture, and context. They also introduce the challenge of finding out how specific features of program quality affect individual children in the program differentially, along with information on average results.

Included in this section are two chapters dealing with the most common health risks to infants and toddlers in group care, namely respiratory infections and diarrhea. These chapters, written by leading medical researchers, give a broad picture of the possible detrimental effects on the health of infants and toddlers who attend group care and provide some suggestions for practice to improve the possibility of healthier outcomes. Health issues in child care are rarely included in discussions of program quality or in policy decisions, despite the long-standing concerns of medical and health professionals. Collier and Henderson in the sixth chapter, "Respiratory Disease in Infants and Toddlers," point out that infants and toddlers are extremely vulnerable to respiratory infections because their immune systems are immature, gradually reaching 80% of adult maturity by the age of 2 years. During the second 6 months of life, the infant's immune system is at its lowest level, and most respiratory tract infections occur at this time. Children younger than 3 years old in child care groups are at substantially greater risk than their home-reared counterparts. Improved hygiene practices and exclusion of infected children have not been shown to reduce the incidence of respiratory illness in child care centers, but new vaccines seem to be promising preventive agents.

In the seventh chapter, entitled "Diarrheal Disease in Infants and Toddlers," Churchill and Pickering report that proper hand washing and hygiene practices and the exclusion of infected children have proven effective in reducing the incidence of diarrhea. Vaccines being tested now also seem to show promise in preventing diarrhea. Specific studies on the common pathogens causing diarrheal outbreaks through both person-to-person and food-borne transmission are covered in the chapter, along with studies of successful preventive measures that can be practiced in child care settings.

The final chapter in this section, entitled "The Early Intervention System and Out-of-Home Child Care," focuses on programs for children who are particularly vulnerable for a variety of reasons, both social and physical. Because of the separation of disciplines, the literature on early intervention programs for children with identified disabilities is not generally known by early childhood educators. Now that infants and toddlers with disabilities are more frequently included in community child care programs, this body of research has much to offer both the practitioner and the researcher.

The last section of the book deals with the larger ecological context in which infant and toddler programs are embedded. The first of the three chapters in this section, "The Cultural Context of Infant and Toddler Care," deals with the topic that is unarguably the most pressing and emotion-laden issue in the book. In this chapter, Bernhard and Gonzalez-Mena express the perspective that "culture defines what constitutes development." They argue for a pluralistic approach to understanding development and urge the field of child care to implement this pluralistic approach by increasing collaboration with families and communities, demonstrating a deeper understanding of cultural issues, and including more bilingual and bicultural staff.

In the second chapter in this section, "Supporting Infants and Toddlers: The Nascent Policy Agenda," Kagan and Taaffe McLearn draw examples from the fields of health, child care, family support, and home visiting to describe the current state of our public policies and to explain the underlying reasons for their fragmentation. They recommend policy action needed to implement our present understanding of the crucial role of the first 3 years in cognitive and social development. The third chapter in this section deals with the role of the workplace in supporting families. Galinsky and Bond in "Supporting Families as Primary Caregivers: The Role of the Workplace" delineate the relationship between studies of child development, the effects of parental employment, and workplace support of families.

Of course, one book cannot cover all the possible topics of concern about infants and toddlers. However, by bringing together information based on research from various fields, we hope to enrich understanding and motivate improvement in practice. We start with the amazing development of infants and toddlers during the first 3 years; then go on to what programs need to do to provide the high quality of care and education that promote healthy development; and finally consider the larger ecological perspective from the viewpoint of culture, public policy, and the workplace.

Although many of the chapters in this book end with specific recommendations for research and practice, we include a final chapter, "The Whole Child: Transdisciplinary Implications for Infant and Toddler Care," in order to interrelate the recommendations of the various disciplines included in this book. In this final chapter of the book, overall recommendations are presented for practice, personnel preparation, and policy, as well as for further research.

Section I

♦❖♦

Current Knowledge
on Early Development

♦❖♦

2

Cognitive Development in Infants

Looking, Listening, and Learning

◆❖◆

Judy S. DeLoache

From relatively humble cognitive beginnings, infants manage within 2 years to develop a remarkable amount of knowledge about the physical world, the social world, and the interactions between the two. By the end of this period, they have also begun to use a variety of symbols—a distinctively human cognitive achievement. In reviewing this development, we address the following five questions: 1) What do infants know? 2) When do they know it? 3) How do they know it? 4) How do we know what they know? and 5) What are the implications of our knowledge for infant and toddler care?

The most hotly debated of these questions is what role do innate factors play in cognitive development in the first 2 years of life. Innate factors could include inborn biases or predispositions for paying attention to some classes of stimuli more than others, constraints that make it easy or difficult to learn certain things, innate knowledge in ecologically significant domains, and specific learning mechanisms. This issue is alluded to throughout the chapter.

The primary focus is on the development of knowledge about the physical world. Infants are active participants in their own development. Infants are not just seeing, they're looking; infants are not just hearing, they're listening. This highly selective review of early cognitive development includes brief accounts of some aspects of what

developmental neuroscientists are   about brain development
in infancy.

NEUROLOGICAL FOUNDATIONS
FOR EARLY LEARNING AND DEVELOPMENT

The early development of the central nervous system involves two opposing processes—the production of massive numbers of synapses and the subsequent elimination of a large proportion of them. Synapses are the connections among neurons, which are the basic units of the nervous system. Synaptogenesis, the formation of these connections, begins before birth in the cortex, and it is especially pronounced in the first year after birth, with bursts of activity at different times in different regions. Trillions of synapses are formed as each neuron connects almost randomly with thousands of others.

This exuberant growth of synapses creates an excess of neural connections that must then be pruned back. A 6-month-old infant has almost twice as many synapses as an adult, and his or her brain functions much less efficiently. The elimination of excess synapses begins even before birth and is not fully complete until adolescence (Huttenlocher, 1994). During peak pruning periods, as many as 100,000 synapses may be eliminated per second.

How does the brain decide what to prune and what to spare? The rule seems to be "use it or lose it." Synapses that receive frequent stimulation are selectively preserved, and inactive ones disappear. Thus, synaptic pruning and preservation are regulated by experience. The sculpting of the brain via experience is the normal and necessary developmental path. It is crucial for the efficient functioning of the brain that the excess synapses be eliminated. At the same time, however, new synaptic connections are being established, also as a function of experience.

The partnership between nature and nurture in the creation and elimination of synapses involves what William Greenough has referred to as *experience-expectant processes* (Greenough, Black, & Wallace, 1987). Sources of stimulation that are present in the environment of every child selectively activate and stabilize some synapses, leading to their preservation. Thus, the normal development of the visual and auditory systems depends on the presence of patterned light and sound stimulation. In the absence of such stimulation, the brain will be wired differently than it would normally be.

The brain is also sculpted by idiosyncratic experience through what Greenough calls *experience-dependent processes*. New neural connections are formed as a function of experience unique to the individual, that is, through learning. As a result, a stimulating environment that provides the opportunity for exploration and learning is important for early development. Brain development differs for animals that are reared in restricted, unstimulating environments versus those that grow up in rich, complex environments full of objects to explore. Among other effects, the animals in the enriched environment have more neural connections, and they perform better in a variety of learning tasks.

Leaving the final wiring of the brain up to experience is highly economical—less information has to be encoded in the genes. It is also beneficial in that there is greater potential for recovery from early brain damage than if everything were predetermined. However, adaptability is accompanied by vulnerability. If an infant is deprived of some fundamental source of stimulation that the brain is "expecting" to fine tune its circuits, development may be impaired. In addition, the development of the brain of an infant growing up in an extremely unstimulating environment may be compromised by the lack of opportunity for exploration and learning.

LEARNING THROUGH LOOKING, LISTENING, AND EXPLORING

Infants' impressive neural superstructure makes it possible for them to begin interacting with the environment and learning from their experience, even before birth. Infants' experience gives rise to mental representations; some aspects of their experience are encoded and stored in the nervous system. These representations constitute the basis for further learning, for memory, and for the development of knowledge.

In the last few months of prenatal life, the fetus is listening and learning. As a consequence, newborns display a natural preference for female voices similar to their mother's voice that they heard in the womb, and they also prefer listening to speakers of the language they eavesdropped on before birth. Newborns can even recognize a particular pattern of words they heard prenatally; they prefer to listen to a story that their mother repeatedly read aloud during the last weeks of her pregnancy. The evidence for the existence of these preferences is that newborn infants will learn to suck on a pacifier in the particular pattern that turns on a tape of a woman versus a man speaking, someone speaking their mother's language versus a different language (Mehler et al., 1988; Moon, Cooper, & Fifer, 1993), or a person reading a familiar versus an unfamiliar story (DeCasper & Spence, 1986).

From birth on, infants learn about the world by actively exploring it using whatever means they have available. Very young infants look and listen, smell and taste. They turn their heads toward a sound, thereby getting simultaneous auditory and visual information about events. They are particularly responsive to moving objects and become increasingly skillful at tracking them. Older infants avidly explore objects—feeling, banging, shaking, squeezing, and throwing whatever they can get their hands on. This manipulation provides substantial information about the properties of objects and what the infant can do with them. With the advent of self-produced locomotion, older infants have ever new opportunities for exploration and discovery.

At every point there is an enormous amount of information available to the attentive infant. Imagine 4-month-old Benjamin in an infant seat, watching his parents wash the dinner dishes. While they converse with one another, the two humans manipulate a variety of glass, ceramic, and metal objects of various sizes and shapes. Water, suds, and dishcloths, as well as containers and surfaces, are also involved in the complex set of events that constitute the cultural phenomenon of "doing the dishes." Think for a moment about all that is available for the infant's perusal. The humans produce sounds and move in ways that the other objects never do, and vice versa. Objects pass into the water, but never through one another. Glasses, silverware, and skillets all make different sounds when placed on the counter. Sponges make no noise at all but do absorb and drip water. A distinctly different pattern of stimulation occurs if a fork or a crystal goblet falls to the floor (including distinctly different verbalizations from the humans). The more you think about this homey scene, the more information you will realize is present in it, and it's all readily available to the looking, listening, and learning infant.

What do infants learn from the wealth of objects and events they experience? They come to recognize entities that they have encountered previously, and they build knowledge of the permanent features of the world. They learn about the predictable relations between events and about the efficacy and consequences of their own actions. In addition, infants learn an enormous amount through careful scrutiny of the behavior of other people.

Habituation

Probably the simplest form of learning is recognizing something that has been experienced before. Babies—like everybody else—tend to respond relatively less to stimuli they have previously experienced and relatively more to novel ones. For example, Benjamin may pay attention the first several times he observes his father place a plate on the countertop, but he will gradually pay less attention to that recurrent event. The decrease in responding to repeated stimulation, known as habituation, shows that the infant has formed a mental representation of the stimulus—the object or event—that enables him or her to recognize it when it occurs again. Dishabituation, an increase in responding, occurs to a novel stimulus that the infant can discriminate from the familiar one. Responding less to some part of the world is important: If someone reacted fully to every stimulus as if it had never been encountered before, he or she would make little progress. Habituation to the old enables the infant to pay attention to and learn about what is new. Habituation has become the basis for a powerful tool in the study of infant development.

Neural Underpinnings

Researchers have begun to identify neural activity involved in this simple form of recognition memory. Electrodes placed on the scalp of an infant record electrical activity occurring in various regions of the brain. Evoked response potentials (ERPs) are recordings of the brain's activity in response to specific stimulation. Different ERP patterns occur to familiar and novel stimuli. For example, the ERPs of 6- to 8-month-olds, and even some 3-month-olds, differ when they look at a photograph of a face they have seen repeatedly versus when they see a relatively novel face (Nelson & Collins, 1992; Pascalis, deHaan, Nelson, & deSchonen, 1998). At 6 months of age, infants show different patterns of brain waves in response to photographs of their own mother and a dissimilar woman (deHaan & Nelson, 1997). Although there is as yet no direct evidence, it is assumed that these characteristic patterns may reflect activity in temporal lobe structures, such as the hippocampus, known to be associated with memory in adults (Nelson, 1994).

Relation to Later Cognitive Ability

The rate at which infants habituate to repeated stimuli, as well as the degree to which they prefer novel over familiar stimuli, is considered an index of their general information processing ability. Older infants habituate more rapidly than younger infants, who take longer to study and remember a stimulus (Bornstein, Pecheux, & Lecuyer, 1988). In babies of a given age, there are individual differences in rate of habituation; some babies very quickly stop responding to a new stimulus, whereas others continue attending for much longer (Bornstein & Benasich, 1986; DeLoache, 1976; McCall & Kagan, 1970). Infants who habituate rapidly and infants who exhibit a higher degree of novelty preference tend to have higher IQ scores when tested several years later (Bornstein & Sigman, 1986; McCall & Carriger, 1993; Rose & Feldman, 1995, 1997). Thus, there is a fairly remarkable degree of continuity between rapid and efficient information processing in infancy and later in life.

Perceptual Learning

In addition to recognizing familiar entities, infants learn the meaning or significance of many of them. Take, for example, one of the most meaningful of all entities in the world of the infant: Mom. Mother is a recurrent stimulus to which infants do not habituate; quite the opposite occurs. As infants learn more about this entity, ever greater significance is attached to her. Such learning begins with simply identifying specific perceptual features. For example, at birth, newborns prefer to listen to their own mother's voice over that of a female stranger (DeCasper & Fifer, 1980), and by the end of the first week, breast-fed infants recognize the scent of their mother and prefer it to that of another woman (MacFarlane, 1975). By 3 months of age, infants look longer at a photo of their mother than a photo of a different woman (Barerra & Maurer, 1981). Along with learning these specific maternal attributes, infants detect the relations among them. Thus, 3 1/2-month-old infants have learned to relate the sight of their mother's face with the sound of her voice (Spelke & Owsley, 1979).

Discovering relations among entities—noticing and remembering regularities in which stimuli typically occur together, either at the same time or in predictable temporal succession—is a crucial part of learning about the world. Because objects and events are multifaceted, our experience of them is typically multimodal; that is, we experience simultaneous visual, auditory, and tactile stimulation, and sometimes olfaction and taste as well. In natural events, the stimulation from these various sensory modalities is coherent—Benjamin hears a single sound at the same moment he sees a pot deposited on the counter, a more complex sound as a pile of silverware is dumped in a drawer, and something quite different when a wet sponge is squeezed over the water.

How do Benjamin and other infants perceive such events? Do they, like adults, integrate stimulation from separate senses as a single object or event, or do infants have to learn through experience to associate what they see with what they hear? According to the sensory integration view of Jean Piaget (1954) and other theorists (e.g., Bryant, 1974), stimulation of different senses is initially experienced separately and only gradually does it become integrated. In contrast, Eleanor Gibson (1969, 1988) and proponents of differentiation theories argue for an inborn ability to detect "amodal invariant relations," or information from an object or event that is perceived simultaneously, through different senses. For example, in many events, there is a common pattern to the auditory and visual stimulation. When a fork strikes a plate, the sound of the impact is heard at the same moment that the contact is seen. Vocal sounds are closely related to lip movements. The relation between the information from the different senses does not vary because of the inherent structure of the events.

An innate tendency to detect such invariants would help both to focus infants' attention on meaningful, unitary events and to buffer them from forming associations among less meaningful, arbitrary aspects of events. Thus, learning is not required to detect amodal invariants in natural events, such as the fact that a sound occurs when an object contacts a surface, but learning would be involved in expecting different sounds from a plate versus a fork's being placed on a countertop. Learning is also necessary for more or less arbitrary relations, such as the relation between what an object is made of and whether it is used to drink juice or eat cereal from or between how a food looks, smells, and tastes.

That infants do detect invariant relations has been firmly established, thanks in part to a very clever technique. Two films are simultaneously presented, side by side, while a soundtrack is played that is consistent with one of the films. Greater responding to whichever film is synchronized with the currently heard soundtrack is taken as evidence that the infant detects the relation between them, that is, the infant detects the common structure in the auditory and visual stimulation.

In an early study using this procedure, Elizabeth Spelke (1976) showed 4-month-old infants two videos, one of a person playing Peek-aboo and the other of percussion instruments being played. The infants responded more to the film that matched the sounds they were hearing. Investigators have further found that in the first few months of life, infants are sensitive to common tempo, rhythm, and duration in the auditory and visual aspects of events, whether the synchrony is between real objects and natural sounds or flashing lights and pulsing tones (Allen, Walker, Symonds, & Marcell, 1977; Pickens & Bahrick, 1995).

It has also become clear that quite early on, infants know a great deal about the relation between human faces and sounds. Four-month-olds listening to a videotape of someone talking look longer at the face whose lip movements are synchronized with the speech (Dodd, 1979; Spelke & Cortelyou, 1981). Four-month-olds even detect the relation between specific sounds, such as /a/ and /i/, and the specific lip movements associated with them (Kuhl & Meltzoff, 1984a, 1984b). Between 5 and 7 months of age, infants are capable of detecting common emotional expressions in faces and voices (Walker-Andrews, 1997). When they hear a voice with positive affect, they look preferentially at a smiling face, but an angry face is looked at longer while an angry voice is heard.

Natural sensory relations are generally easier to learn than arbitrary ones (Bahrick, 1994), but purely arbitrary relations among stimulation–indifferent modalities can be learned. For example, 7-month-old infants have successfully been taught an arbitrary association between the color of a cup and the taste of the food inside (Reardon & Bushnell, 1988). (This laboratory demonstration of a color–taste association will come as no surprise to parents whose infants clamp their mouths shut at the sight of a spoon conveying anything green.) Other arbitrary relations are apparently more difficult: Even 11-month-olds failed to learn the relation between the color and temperature of objects (Bushnell, 1986).

Classical Conditioning

From birth, infants also learn relations between environmental events that provide signals for their own behavior. Consider, for example, the following plausible scenario for how babies begin to develop the positive feelings for their mothers that will eventually deepen into love. The feeding situation, which is a crucial occasion in the life of the infant, occurs frequently and has a predictable structure. The hungry infant is picked up by the mother (with her unique constellation of perceptual features) and held in a particular way. A breast or bottle is introduced into the infant's mouth, which causes the infant to begin sucking reflexively. Milk flows through the nipple, and the infant experiences the pleasurable sensations involved in the satiation of hunger.

Learning is revealed when sucking motions, which initially occurred reflexively after stimulation of the infant's mouth, gradually start to be made earlier in the sequence of events—to the sight of the bottle or breast, to being held in the usual position, and so on. The pleasurable feelings that are part of the infant's response to feeding also come to occur earlier, eventually evoked simply by the presence of the mother.

This form of learning, which Pavlov first discovered in dogs, is referred to as *classical conditioning*. The basic components of classical conditioning are the pairing of an initially neutral stimulus (e.g., the sight of breast or bottle) with a stimulus (e.g., insertion of the nipple into the infant's mouth) that reliably elicits a response (i.e., the sucking reflex). Gradually, the response comes to occur to the initially neutral stimulus, which has come to signal the likely occurrence of the response-eliciting stimulus.

It is thought that many emotional responses are initially learned through classical conditioning. One of the first demonstrations was the case of Little Albert, who was conditioned to fear a white rat by John B. Watson, the founder of behaviorism (Watson & Raynor, 1920). Nine-month-old Albert initially had a positive reaction when exposed to a perfectly nice white rat. However, after a loud, fear-eliciting noise was repeatedly paired with the rat, the baby came to be afraid of the rat itself. Infants and young children often show fear at the white coat of a doctor or nurse based on their previous association of painful injections with people wearing white coats. This is one reason modern pediatricians often sport colorful lab coats.

Instrumental Conditioning

Infants also learn about the effects that their behavior has on other people and objects. In everyday life, infants learn that shaking a rattle produces an interesting sound, but exploring the dirt in a potted plant leads to a parental reprimand.

In laboratories, researchers have engineered a great variety of ingenious situations to enable them to observe infants' ability to learn the relation between their own behavior and some outcome that is contingent upon their behavior. For example, 3-week-old infants modified how they sucked on a pacifier when sucking in a particular way resulted in an interesting visual display (Siqueland & DeLucia, 1969), and 5- to 12-week-old infants did the same to keep a movie in focus (Bruner, 1973). Two-month-olds readily learned that turning their head in one direction would cause a mobile above their crib to revolve, a very enjoyable event for a young infant (Watson & Ramey, 1972), and 6-month-olds learned to push a lever to cause a toy train to move around a track (Hartshorn & Rovee-Collier, 1997). In an extensive series of studies, Carolyn Rovee-Collier (1997) and her colleagues used a very simple procedure to study learning and memory; they tied a ribbon around an infant's ankle and connected it to a mobile above the crib. Infants as young as 2 months learn within minutes to kick their foot to cause the enjoyable sight of the jiggling mobile. They also learned that the harder they kick, the more the mobile moves.

In the terms of instrumental conditioning (also referred to as operant conditioning), the interesting mobile movement serves as a reward or reinforcement for the kicking behavior; that is, it causes the behavior to occur more frequently. There is a contingency relation between the infant's behavior and the reward—if the infant makes the response, then he or she receives the reinforcement. In Rovee-Collier's foot-kicking situation, the intensity of the reward—the amount of movement of the mobile—depends on the intensity of the baby's behavior, a procedure known as *conjugate reinforcement*.

Although infants can learn a great variety of contingency relations, there are a number of constraints on the learning process. For example, the younger the infant, the more immediately the reinforcement must follow the infant's response for learning to occur (Millar, 1972). Also, some stimulus–response relations are learned readily, but others are learned only with difficulty. For example, newborns learned to turn their head to one side to obtain a sweet-tasting solution whenever they heard a click sound, but they failed to learn the same contingency with other sounds (Blass, 1990). Because of the numerous limitations on infant learning capacities, Watson (1972) described the first 3 months of life as a "natural deprivation period." The idea is that few natural events in the life of a young infant provide the opportunity for learning contingencies between one's own behavior and consequences of that behavior. Almost all the opportunities for such learning come through other people, either directly in interactions with others or experiences mediated by others. Infants have such opportunities in many classic parent–infant routines, such as Peekaboo, and through objects and events adults provide them with.

Infants' impressive learning capacity seems to stem in part from intense motivation to explore and master their environment. Infants work hard to find out what things are and how they work; they seem to have what John Flavell referred to as a "'let's see what would happen if' sort of attitude" (1985, p. 26). Infants enjoy being able to predict and control their experience, and they do not enjoy losing control of relations they have established. Researchers have described expressions of joy and interest while infants as young as 2 months old were learning a contingency relation and expressions of anger when a learned response no longer produced the expected reward (Lewis, Alessandri, & Sullivan, 1990). When newborns failed to receive the sucrose they had learned would follow a head-turn response, most of them cried (Blass, 1990). Babies don't like to be double-crossed!

Just as infants readily learn many contingencies between their own actions and consequences of those actions, they also learn the crucial life lesson that they have no influence over a variety of objects, events, and situations. Although this is a necessary fact of life to learn, it is possible for an infant to conclude erroneously that he or she has no effect in a given situation. Watson and Ramey (1972) showed this in their study mentioned previously in which 2-month-old infants learned to turn their heads to make a mobile revolve. Another group of infants had experience with the same mobile, but its movement was unrelated to the infants' behavior. When these infants were given a new mobile that they could control, they failed to learn the contingency. Thus, an experience in which they had no control prevented these infants from learning when control was possible.

This research indicates that infants learn more than just the particular contingency relation to which they are exposed. They also learn about the relation between themselves and the world. In some circumstances, they learn that what they do has a substantial impact on what happens next. In other circumstances, they learn that they have little or no impact on events around them.

Observational Learning

Other people serve as a particularly potent source of learning for older infants. Parents, who are often amused and sometimes chagrined by their toddlers' reproduction of their own behavior, are well aware of the extent to which infants and young children are capable of learning through simple observation. Researchers have discovered that infants are capable of such learning quite a bit earlier than usually observed in everyday settings.

In an extensive investigation of imitation in infancy, Andrew Meltzoff has infants watch as an adult performs some specific novel action on an object. For example, in one case the adult pulls apart a dumbbell shaped toy; in another he touches a box with his forehead. In a slightly more complex example, the adult inserts a stick into a hole in a box to push a button that activates a buzzer. Some time later, the infant is given the opportunity to perform the behavior him- or herself. Infants as young as 9 months old imitate these object-specific actions, even after a delay of 24 hours (Meltzoff, 1988a).

Slightly older infants can reproduce more complex events composed of a novel sequence of actions they have been taught (Bauer, 1996). There is a steady increase with age in the number of actions they can reproduce in correct temporal order, from two-step novel events at 11 months of age (Bauer & Mandler, 1992) to events with as many as five steps at 24 months of age (Bauer & Travis, 1993).

Infants and toddlers are discriminating in their imitative behavior. Eighteen-month-olds observed an adult attempting but failing to pull a dumbbell toy apart (Meltzoff, 1995a). The adult pulled on the two ends, but his hand slipped off, and the dumbbell remained in one piece (Figure 1). When the infants were subsequently given the toy, they pulled the

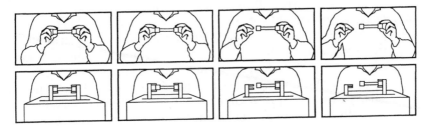

Figure 1.   The top row shows an adult model pulling on the two ends of a dumbbell toy. It appears that he is trying to pull the ends off, but then one of his hands slips off the end. In the bottom row, a mechanical device simulates the human actions shown in the top row. (From Meltzoff, A.N. [1995a]. Understanding the intentions of others: Re-enactment of intended acts by 10-month-old children. *Developmental Psychology, 31,* 844; reprinted by permission.)

two ends apart, imitating what the adult had intended but had, in fact, failed to do. This reveals that infants' imitation is based on some understanding of human action and intention, not just on what they actually see. Further evidence for this point comes from 18-month-olds who watched a mechanical device simulate the same actions: The pincers grasped the two ends of the dumbbell and then slipped off the ends, just as the human hands had done. The infants rarely imitated the mechanical device. Thus, infants consider other people to be appropriate models to imitate, but they do not interpret inanimate objects as appropriate models.

Infants are by no means restricted to learning from the behavior of adult models. Well-trained 14-month-old "expert peers" demonstrated actions for their comrades, either in a laboratory setting or preschool classroom (Hanna & Meltzoff, 1993). A high level of imitation was shown by 14-month-olds who were tested in their own homes 48 hours later. Thus, peers are quite potent models for young children.

MEMORY

Learning requires the storage of information and hence reveals the existence of memory. However, memory in infancy has traditionally been considered to be limited and qualitatively different from memory later in life. *Infantile amnesia* refers to the very well established fact that adults are typically unable to recall much of anything from the first few years of life. The phenomenon of infantile or childhood amnesia suggests either that infants are unable to form coherent memories for events they experience or that, for some reason, their memories become inaccessible.

The view of infant memory as qualitatively distinct is compatible with current neuroscience theories that posit two dissociable memory systems subserved by different neural structures (e.g., Cohen & Squire, 1980; Schacter, 1987). These theories are based in part on observations of amnesic adults who might, for example, learn a new motor skill but cannot remember that they had learned it; these patients have intact implicit or procedural memory. They know how to do something but they are deficient in explicit or declarative memory—they can't remember their own experience of acquiring the skill. It has been proposed that infants are similarly capable of procedural but not declarative memory, possibly because the neural foundation for declarative memory develops relatively late.

There is no question that infants possess procedural memory, as the many demonstrations of infant learning make clear: When babies learn how to do something, they remember it for increasingly long periods of time. For example, 2-month-olds who learned to kick in order to shake a mobile remember how to activate the mobile 2 days later (VanderLinde, Morrongiello, & Rovee-Collier, 1985), 3-month-olds remember it for 1 week (Sullivan, Rovee-Collier, & Tynes, 1979), and 6-month-olds for 2 weeks (Hill, Borovsky, & Rovee-Collier, 1988). When infants have forgotten the contingency, their memory is readily reactivated if they are reminded of the original situation (e.g., by briefly seeing the mobile that was involved in the original learning) (see Rovee-Collier, 1997).

With respect to simple recognition of something that was previously experienced, there is clear evidence of relatively long-term retention even by newborns. For example, newborns who were habituated to specific sounds recognized those sounds 24 hours later (Swain, Zelazo, & Clifton, 1993). Six-month-olds can recognize an abstract pattern after 2 days, and they recognize a picture of a face after 2 weeks (Fagan, 1973).

It has recently become clear that recall memory, a form of declarative memory that was traditionally believed impossible in infancy, is indeed present during the first 2 years of life. The best evidence comes from deferred imitation, imitation of an event some time after it was observed. The earliest and most well-known report of deferred imitation was Piaget's account of his 16-month-old daughter Jacqueline reproducing the temper tantrum she had observed a little friend have the day before.

Contrary to what Piaget believed possible, even 9-month-old infants can reproduce novel object-specific actions they observed 24 hours earlier (Meltzoff, 1988b), and 18-month-olds imitate an event that they observed as many as 4 months earlier (Meltzoff, 1995b). Like Jacqueline, the infants had never before performed the target behaviors, but they nevertheless managed to remember them for several months.

Especially intriguing are reports in which toddlers or young children reveal memory for something they experienced as preverbal infants. For example, infants who were taught to perform novel event sequences at 13, 16, and 21 months of age recalled some of them after a delay of 8 months (Bauer, Hertsgaard, & Dow, 1994). Similarly, 2-year-olds reproduced an unusual event they had observed when they were only 11 months old (McDonough & Mandler, 1994). Toddlers have also been reported to spontaneously verbalize about objects or events they had experienced well before they could have labeled or verbally encoded them (Myers, Clifton, & Clarkson, 1987; Nelson & Ross, 1980; Todd & Perlmutter, 1980).

We are still left with the mystery of infantile amnesia; indeed, it is in some ways even more mysterious now that we know infants are capable of recalling some events they have observed in the first year of life. Two interesting theories propose that the solution lies not in the development of memory itself, but in related developments that make it possible for very young children to form lasting memories for events they have experienced.

One view is that the development of a sense of self is essential to the emergence of autobiographical memory (Howe & Courage, 1997). By 18–24 months of age, infants have a sufficiently well developed sense of self that it can serve as the fulcrum around which personally experienced events can be organized in memory. At about this same time, toddlers begin to recount their memories of events they have experienced. Their earliest accounts tend to be about the immediate past, but with age, increasingly distant events are reported (Miller & Sperry, 1988; Nelson, 1989; Sachs, 1983). These early reports tend to be fragmentary and dependent on considerable prompting from adult listeners to elicit additional information.

An alternative view is that autobiographical memory emerges somewhat later as a result of conversational interactions (Nelson, 1993) in which young children learn to share their memories with other people. Via conversation with significant others, children acquire narrative skills that not only help them recount their memories but also structure how their experiences are organized in memory. Thus, it is language that opens up the possibility for sharing and retaining memories.

KNOWLEDGE OF THE PHYSICAL WORLD

Object Segregation

Consider the array of objects that might litter your desk in the morning after an all-night paper-writing flurry: papers, pens, pencils, books, stapler, paper clips, telephone, coffee cup(s), and potentially many more. When you look at the mess, how do you manage to perceive this scene coherently without being confused about where one objects ends and another begins? In other words, how do you accomplish the process of object segregation?

You do it by exploiting a great variety of available information, and you weigh some sources of information more heavily than others. Infants do the same, and the kind of information they rely on changes with age. Consider the very simple display shown in Figure 2a. Is there a single long rod extending behind the block of wood or two short rods? Adults use their experience with blocks and rods to infer that there is a single rod, but a young infant has limited experience from which to make such an inference. Perceptual information is available to the baby—differences in shape and color—but the perceptual features are consistent with either a single rod or two pieces.

Kellman and Spelke (1983) showed 4-month-old infants this ambiguous display. To find out what the babies thought about it, an approach was used that has become standard in investigations of infant perception and cognition—the habituation of visual attention. Infants are first habituated to a stimulus (meaning they look at it less as it is repeatedly presented), and then they are shown one or more test stimuli. *Dishabituation*, or increased looking at a test stimulus, is taken as evidence that the infant perceives it as novel or unexpected relative to the habituation stimulus. In a related procedure, infants are shown test displays that are either consistent with or that violate the knowledge or expectation being examined. It is assumed that if an infant possesses the knowledge in question, he or she will respond more to the stimulus that is inconsistent with that knowledge.

The infants in Kellman and Spelke's classic study were habituated to the stationary block and rod(s) display. They were then shown the two test displays in Figure 2b—a complete rod and two rod segments. If the infants had assumed there was a single rod behind the block in the habituation display, they would have looked longer at the segments

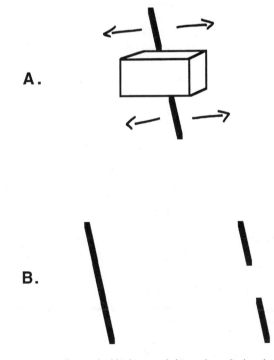

Figure 2.   A. One group of 4-month-old infants was habituated to a display of a stationary rod behind a block, and a second group was habituated to the same rod moving back and forth behind the block. B. They were then shown two test displays of a single long rod or two short rod segments. (From Kellman, P.J., & Spelke, E.S. [1983]. Perception of partly occluded objects in infancy. *Cognitive Psychology, 15,* 489; reprinted by permission.)

because that display would be novel, based on their interpretation of the previous scene. However, the infants looked equally long at the two test displays, suggesting that they were uncertain about the nature of the original display. The same result occurred even when the partially occluded object was more distinctive and complex than the simple rod shown here. Thus, 4-month-old infants do not rely very heavily on perceptual features for interpreting displays such as these.

Four-month-olds do rely quite heavily on a different source of information, as shown by another condition in this study. A second group of 4-month-olds was habituated to the same display except that they saw the rod moving back and forth behind the block. On the test, these infants looked longer at the rod segments than at the whole rod, suggesting that they had perceived the original display as involving a single rod. Thus, these infants apparently relied on common motion of the visible rod segments to decide that they formed a single object. This result indicates that movement is a potent cue.

Amy Needham (1997) has shown that older infants also use perceptual features to figure out object boundaries. She habituated 4 1/2-and 8-month-old infants to the rather peculiar display shown in Figure 3a. The infants then saw a hand reach into the display and pull on the hose-like part: For half the infants, the hose and box moved together as a unit. For the other half, the hose came away from the box. The younger infants looked equally long at these two test events, but the older infants looked longer when the hose and box moved together like a single object. Thus, the older, but not the younger, infants used perceptual features to conclude there were two separate objects (Needham & Baillargeon, 1997).

Other 4 1/2-month-olds were easily made to behave like the older infants by giving them experience with the objects (Needham & Baillargeon, 1998). After exposure to either the box alone or the hose alone, the infants looked longer when the box and hose moved together. Thus, experiential knowledge of the objects influenced the infants' interpretation of the display.

General knowledge about the physical world is another potent source of information for object segregation. Adults are certain there is a single object in Figure 3b because we know objects cannot float in mid-air without some kind of support, so the hose must be attached to the box. By 5 1/2 months, infants share some of our knowledge: They expect that an object that is simply placed against the vertical surface of another object will fall when released (Baillargeon, 1995). Might infants who possess this general physical knowledge about support use it to interpret the display with the elevated hose?

The answer is apparently yes. When 8-month-olds were habituated to this display, they looked longer when the hose moved separately from the box, indicating that they assumed a single unit (Needham & Bail-largeon, 1997). (When the hose is lying on the surface, infants of this age have the opposite reaction.)

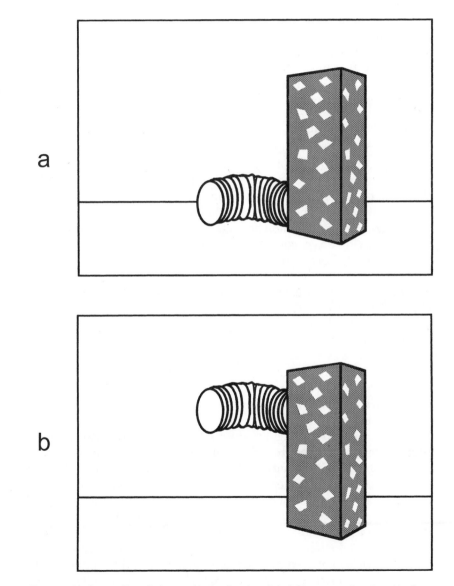

Figure 3.   The hose and box displays used in Needham's studies of object segregation. (From Needham, A., & Baillargeon, R. [1997] Object segregation in 8-month-old infants. *Cognition, 62,* 136; reprinted by permission.)

Notice that knowledge of support took precedence over appearance: When it was physically possible for there to be two separate objects in the display (i.e., when the hose was supported by the table), the infants used the different appearance of box and hose to infer separate entities. However, when knowledge of support dictated that the hose could not be independent of the box, a single entity was inferred. Needham (Needham, 1997; Needham, Baillargeon, & Kaufman, 1997) believes there is a hierarchy in the information used for object segregation: Sources of information that have greater ecological validity, such as support or movement, take precedence over less reliable forms of information, such as perceptual appearance.

Object Permanence

What do infants know about the objects they see around them? Consider just a few examples of adult knowledge about the inanimate physical world. Objects have permanence; they continue to exist even when they aren't visible. Objects are substantial, so one cannot pass through another. Stationary objects remain stationary unless somehow set in motion, and objects in motion have characteristic patterns of movement. When a moving object contacts a stationary one, it may cause the stationary object to begin moving.

Until recently, it was generally assumed that infants share few, if any, of these or other examples of adult's fundamental beliefs about objects. This view was due in large part to Jean Piaget. He believed that young infants lack the capacity for mental representation, so they cannot think about anything not present in the immediate environment. Piaget's view was based in part on his discovery of the phenomenon known as *object permanence.* He found that young infants act as though an object that has disappeared from sight no longer exists. When Piaget hid a desirable toy in his hand or under a cover, none of his three children tried to open his hand or remove the cover until after the age of 8 months. It seemed to Piaget that when the object vanished from the baby's sight, it vanished from the baby's mind as well.

Piaget believed that around 8 months of age, some concept of the permanence of objects emerges, because infants now search for hidden objects. Their concept is not mature, however, because he found that they still make a peculiar mistake, known as the *A/not B error:* Infants who have previously found a toy at location A will often search for it there again, even when they have observed it being hidden at location B. The longer the delay between the second hiding event and the opportunity to search, the more likely infants are to make the error of going back to the original location (Diamond, 1985; Wellman, Cross, & Bartsch, 1987). To Piaget, this was evidence that until after the end of the first year, infants are still unable to mentally represent objects independent of their actions on those objects. These remarkable phenomena that Piaget discovered are extremely reliable. Babies today behave exactly the same as his three children did if an object is hidden while they watch. It is now clear, however, that Piaget's interpretation of this behavior is not correct.

An enormous amount of evidence indicates that young infants are able to mentally represent the existence of invisible objects and can even think about some characteristics of unseen objects and events. The simplest form of support for this is the fact that infants will reach for objects in the dark; if an infant has seen a desirable object and all the lights are extinguished, he or she will reach to the position where the object was last visible (Hood & Willatts, 1986). Furthermore, infants reach differently in the dark depending on what they know about an object. Rachel Clifton and her colleagues (Clifton, Rochat, Litovsky, & Perris, 1991) first showed 6-month-old infants either a small or large object, each of which emitted a different sound. Then the lights were doused, leaving the room in darkness and the objects totally invisible. When the infants now heard the sound of one of the objects, they reached for it, indicating that they assumed its existence even though they could not see it. Most impressive of all, the infants tended to reach in the same way as they had in the light—with both hands toward the sound associated with the larger object, but with only one hand toward the sound of the smaller one. Thus, these babies not only knew that an object was present in the dark, they also knew which particular object it was.

Renee Baillargeon (1994) and her colleagues have provided further evidence that young infants can mentally represent invisible objects, and their research also shows that infants share some of adults' basic beliefs about the physical world. In one series of studies, infants were first habituated to the sight of a screen rotating back and forth through 180 degrees (see Figure 4) (Baillargeon, 1987a; Baillargeon, Spelke, & Wasserman, 1985). Then, a box was placed in the screen's path, and the infants saw two test events. In the possible test event, the screen rotated upward, occluding the box as it did so; the screen stopped when it reached the top edge of the box. In the impossible test event, the screen continued to rotate a full 180 degrees, appearing to pass through the space occupied by the box. Infants as young as 4 1/2-months of age looked longer at the impossible event (even though this was actually the same as the event to which they had been habituated). This result tells us that these infants had a mental representation of the box even after it became invisible. It further indicates that they did not expect one object to be able to pass through the space occupied by a different object.

Baillargeon believes that infants' initial knowledge about the existence and solidity of objects is fairly primitive. At the beginning, they

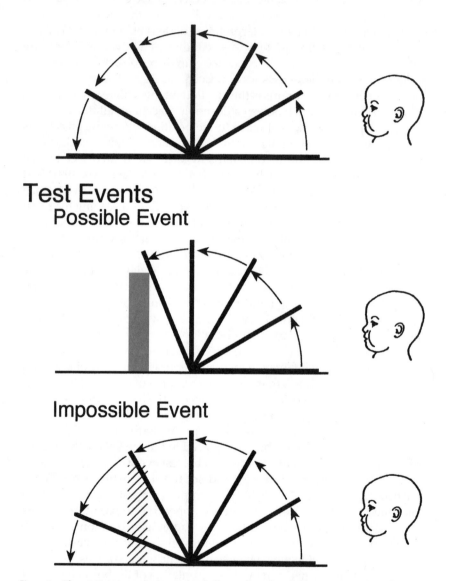

Test Events
Possible Event

Impossible Event

Figure 4.   The rotating screen display used in Baillargeon's studies of object representation. Infants are first habituated to an opaque screen moving back and forth. For the test events, there is an object sitting in the path of the screen. In the possible test event, the screen stops at the point at which it makes contact with the object; in the impossible test event, the screen continues to rotate through the space in which the box appeared. (From Baillargeon, R. [1987a]. Object permanence in 3.5- 4.5-month-old infants. *Developmental Psychology, 23,* 656; reprinted by permission.)

have all-or-none expectations. Initially, infants expect the progress of the screen to be arrested by the presence of the box in its path, but they cannot judge exactly where it should stop. For example, 4 1/2-month-old infants look longer, expressing surprise, if the screen rotates 100% of the way through the space occupied by the box, but they do not react if it passes through only 80% of the box—an equally implausible event to an adult. This core knowledge is gradually elaborated as a result of experience. By 6 1/2 months, infants are surprised by the 80% violation, but not by a smaller one. Even the younger age group can make accurate judgments if an identical box is present on the side of the display to remind them of the height and position of the occluded box (Baillargeon, 1991).

Infants' expectations about where the screen will stop are also influenced by their knowledge about the texture of the occluded object (Baillargeon, 1987b). Groups of 7 1/2-month-olds were allowed to handle a soft, compressible object (e.g., a ball of gauze) or a hard, rigid object (e.g., a wooden box). The infants who saw the screen appear to rotate partially through the solid box looked longer than the infants who saw it appear to compress the soft object.

A subsequent development in infants' representation of invisible objects is the ability to infer the existence and some characteristics of an unseen object (Baillargeon & DeVos, 1991). This was demonstrated with the display shown in Figure 5. Infants first saw two identical soft cloth covers on a table, each showing the same small protuberance or lump (suggesting to an adult the presence of something under the cloth). A screen then rotated up, concealing one of the covers. In the possible event, a hand reached behind the screen twice, first reappearing with the cover and next with a small toy dog of the same size as the lump. The impossible event was exactly the same except that a large dog was retrieved—an object too large to have been under the cloth. The 12 1/2-month-olds, but not the 9 1/2-month-olds, looked longer when the large dog appeared. They apparently expected the object to be the same size as the lump. Thus, the older infants drew an inference about the existence and height of an object they had never seen before.

We, thus, see more sophistication in infants' knowledge about objects than Piaget believed possible. Why, then, do infants fail Piagetian object permanence tasks: If they are capable of representing the existence and other aspects of a hidden object, why don't they try to retrieve it; and when they do begin searching, why do they commit the A/not B search error?

One part of the answer is that infants have difficulty organizing a sequence of goal-directed actions. To retrieve a hidden object, an infant must carry out one action on an object in order to make it possible to perform a second; they have to remove the cover in order to reach for the

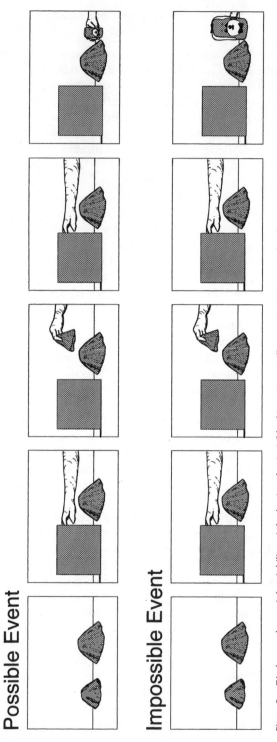

Possible Event

Impossible Event

Figure 5.   Displays used to test infants' ability to infer the size of an invisible object. (From Baillargeon, R. [1994]. How do infants learn about the physical world? *Current Directions in Psychological Science, 3,* 137; reprinted by permission.)

object. Before the age of 8 or 9 months, infants have difficulty organizing means-end sequences, even with respect to fully visible objects. For example, not until around 8 months of age will infants immediately pull on the near end of a cloth to bring within reach a desirable toy resting on the far end of the cloth (Willatts, 1985). Before 12 months of age, infants even have trouble retrieving an object from a transparent box when they cannot reach directly for it. It is hard for them to perform a two-part reach in which they must first move their hand away from the object visible through the front of the box in order to approach it through the open side of the box (Diamond & Gilbert, 1989).

Infants' difficulty with organizing means-end sequences does not appear to stem from failure to understand such sequences. Indeed, infants know something about what actions can and cannot retrieve an object from under an obstacle well before they are capable of performing such a search themselves (Baillargeon, Graber, DeVos, & Black, 1990). Infants as young as 5 1/2 months of age first saw two covers standing side by side with a toy bear visible under one of them—either the inverted transparent cup on the left or the small cage on the right in Figure 6. The test event was the same for the two groups. A screen rotated up in front of the objects, shielding them from view. Next, a hand entered from the right side of the display, disappeared behind the screen, and reappeared holding the cage. The hand then reached behind the screen again and came out holding the bear. This sequence constituted a possible test event for infants for whom the bear was initially under the cage; removing the cage first would make the bear accessible to the hand. The sequence was an impossible test event for the infants who initially saw the bear under the cup; removing the cage would not have made it accessible as it would still be protected by the inverted cup. Looking times were longer for the impossible event, suggesting that infants who do not themselves search for invisible objects can nevertheless identify whether an action is sufficient to recover an object.

Infants' difficulty with both object permanence and means-ends tasks may have to do with inhibiting a response to the desired goal object in order to perform the requisite action on a different object. The child has to direct attention and action away from the desired toy to the cover that is making it inaccessible. Adele Diamond (1991; Diamond & Goldman-Rakic, 1989) has argued that the common denominator here, as well as in the *A/not B error*, is maturation of prefrontal cortex. This region is involved in many higher level cognitive functions and shows the most prolonged period of development of any part of the brain (Huttenlocher, 1994). It has been linked in adults and monkeys to memory, planning and executing action sequences, and the inhibition of dominant responses. Support for Diamond's claim comes from infants and young

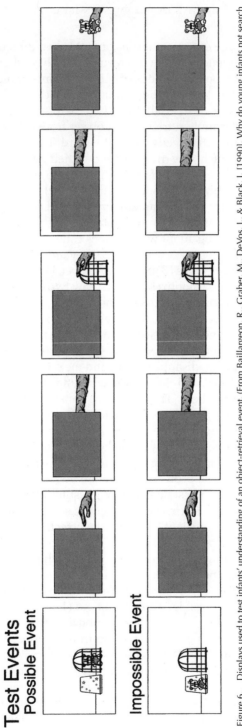

Test Events
Possible Event

Impossible Event

Figure 6.   Displays used to test infants' understanding of an object-retrieval event. (From Baillargeon, R., Graber, M., DeVos, J., & Black, J. [1990]. Why do young infants not search for hidden objects? *Cognition, 36,* 271; reprinted by permission.

children with phenylketonuria (PKU), which even in treated children causes a reduction in a dopamine, a neurotransmitter, in the prefrontal cortex. These children show impaired performance on object permanence and other tasks thought to involve prefrontal cortex but not on similar tasks not assumed to involve this area of the brain (Diamond, Prevor, Callender, & Druin, 1997; Welsh, Pennington, Ozonoff, Rouse, & McCabe, 1990).

Categories and Concepts

In our consumer-oriented society, parents can now purchase baby bottles in a variety of different shapes, colors, and surface patterns. Imagine two infants: Baby Julia is always fed from identical bottles, whereas Baby Emily gets her meals from a variety of different ones. Both babies will be well fed and happy and will learn from their experience so that they will both get excited to see a bottle signaling the beginning of a feeding session. But which will know more about bottles?

The ability to detect similarities and regularities in their experience enables infants to form categories and concepts—summary representations of the relation among a variety of different entities. Baby Julia will simply know a lot about one particular kind of bottle, but Baby Emily will abstract from her varied experience a representation of baby bottles in general. The recognition that disparate entities are similar in the same way or are the same kind of thing is fundamental to all cognitive development.

Most of the research on categorization and conceptual development has followed a basic format in which infants are exposed to multiple instances or exemplars, either pictures or replica objects, of a given category. They are then tested with novel members of the category versus novel noncategory members. If the infant responds to a novel category member in the same way as those previously experienced but treats nonmembers of the category differently, it is inferred that he or she already possessed or has just formed the relevant category. It is fairly remarkable how easily infants can be induced to respond categorically in this situation.

The earliest evidence of categorization comes from studies in which 3- to 4-month-olds were shown color photographs of various animals. After seeing a series of cats, for example, the infants looked less at pictures of cats they had not seen before, indicating generalization, but they looked longer at pictures of other animals, including birds, dogs, horses, and lions (Eimas & Quinn, 1994; Eimas, Quinn, & Cowan, 1994; Quinn & Eimas, 1996; Quinn, Eimas, & Rosenkrantz, 1993).

This same age group can also form perceptual categories for objects such as chairs and couches (Behl-Chadha, 1996), and they can also form higher or more global level categories. Infants who were familiarized with instances of different mammals (e.g., cats, dogs, zebras, elephants) generalized to novel mammals (e.g., deer), but not to nonmammals (e.g., birds, fish, furniture).

These and other categories that young infants can form are purely perceptual, that is, based on similarities in surface appearance. Most infants who dishabituate to cats or fish after seeing pictures of horses know nothing about real horses. Later, as they acquire knowledge about the world, infants form conceptual categories. Some of their perceptual categories become elaborated into concepts, although the process by which this occurs is a matter of debate (Mandler, 1997; Quinn & Eimas, 1996).

Consider, for example, rattles, a type of object with which most infants have considerable experience. From visually inspecting the array of objects in her or his room, an infant might form a perceptual category including things of similar size and overall shape that have a handle. Once the infant begins manipulating these objects, she or he discovers their common invisible property: They make noise when shaken or banged. The infant's category now includes not just the perceptual features common to the set of objects—their common form—but also what can be done with them—their common function.

At some point we would credit the child with a concept of rattles as a kind of thing that produces a noise when shaken. This invisible property is the core meaning of the concept of rattles. Note, however, that perceptual factors remain important in the formation and extension of concepts, in part, because form and function tend to be correlated in the real world.

Concepts provide cognitive power. For instance, they offer a basis for deciding which things are and are not conceptually equivalent. This facilitates the accumulation and further organization of knowledge. Thus, objects that look like known rattles, but fail to make noise when manipulated, are rejected as category members; whereas objects that bear little perceptual similarity to category members, but do possess the potential for producing sound, are included. Further conceptual knowledge provides a basis for making inductive inferences and generalizations, that is, for predicting that a novel entity will share various hidden properties with other category members.

Inductive generalization appears to be present before the end of the first year (Baldwin, Markman, & Melartin, 1993). Nine- to sixteen-month-olds first learned that a novel toy produced an interesting sound or movement. When subsequently presented with a similar toy, the infants actively tried to reproduce the interesting effect. Thus, infants as young as 9 months of age use their experience with an object to draw an inference that a similar novel object should possess the same hidden property.

What evidence do we have of the early development of real-world concepts as opposed to demonstrations of the remarkable ability of infants to abstract perceptual categories from carefully controlled displays presented to them? Mandler and McDonough (1993) presented 7- to 11-month-olds with small replica animals and vehicles and then observed the order in which the infants touched the objects. The infants differentiated between the two categories in the sense that they tended to touch members of one category sequentially. They also responded differently to objects within the vehicle category, distinguishing cars, motorcycles, and airplanes; but within the set of animals they did not differentiate dogs from fish or rabbits. The researchers tried to rule out perceptual similarity as a basis for responding in this study, but the infants' categorical responding may have been in part based on perceptual differences among the replica objects themselves (e.g., toy motorcycles, cars, and planes have very different shapes), perceptual differences among the real entities represented by the replicas (e.g., eyes and fur versus metal and wheels), or conceptual knowledge about the real entities (e.g., animates versus inanimates). Better evidence of conceptual knowledge (distinct from perceptual information) comes from a study of 14-month-olds' differentiation of kitchen and bathroom things. In this case, there was a considerably lower degree of perceptual similarity among category items, but the infants responded differently to the two categories (Mandler, Fivush, & Resnick, 1987).

Probably the best evidence that infants possess some real concepts and can generalize from them comes from recent studies in which 14- month-olds saw a familiar action demonstrated with a set of toys and were then given different toys to re-enact the event (Mandler & McDonough, 1996). For example, after watching the experimenter pretend to give a toy dog a drink from a cup, the children were given the cup, a bird, and an airplane. In this case, they chose the bird over the airplane to enact drinking. The children tended to select animal toys to enact animate activities such as drinking and sleeping, whereas they selected vehicles for target actions such as opening with a key or giving a ride.

Categories enable us to draw inferences about novel entities. One basis on which very young children rely heavily for drawing inferences is physical similarity; they expect that entities that look alike will share other characteristics as well. For example, Gelman and Coley (1990) showed 2 1/2-year-olds a picture of a generic-looking target bird that was said to "live in a nest." The children inferred that another bird that looked virtually identical to the target would also live in a nest. They were unsure about the domicile of highly dissimilar birds (a dodo or pterodactyl) and inferred that a nonbird would not live in a nest.

Young children's categorical inferences are highly influenced by context. For example, the simple act of naming a novel item leads toddlers to assume that the item's shape is critical. When a meaningless object is labeled with a nonsense word ("This is a dax"), 2- and 3-year-old children think that the word also applies to other objects with the same shape but of different size, color, and texture (Landau, Smith, & Jones, 1988). This shape bias seems to indicate that toddlers assume that objects with the same name typically belong to the same category (Waxman & Hall, 1993). This should not be surprising, because overall shape is, in general, highly diagnostic of category membership, especially for natural categories. Thus, a shape bias would generally help toddlers infer which of the large number of possible alternatives is denoted by a novel word they hear.

The shape bias can be influenced by other changes in context. For example, labeling a nonsense shape that has eyes leads 3-year-olds to think that texture is also relevant (Jones, Smith, & Landau, 1991). If the novel entity is not an object but a nonsolid substance (e.g., a pile of sawdust or a blob of Playdoh), 2- and 2 1/2-year-olds ignore overall shape (Soja, Carey, & Spelke, 1991). Instead, they generalize the novel label to stimuli of the same substance.

Toddlers are in the process of forming large numbers of categories and concepts based on their experience. They are aided in doing so by certain biases that lead them to attend more to certain features than others, depending on the context. The ever-increasing number of categories and the richness of those categories provide a powerful springboard for further learning about the world.

Number

Some theorists have proposed that there are "core domains" of knowledge in which innate structures and mechanisms support and guide learning. Gelman (1991) has argued that number, specifically counting, constitutes such a domain. There is no question that infants can distinguish between collections of one to three elements in the first few months of life (e.g., Antell & Keating, 1983; Cooper, 1984; Starkey & Cooper, 1980; Strauss & Curtis, 1981). For example, after habituating to a display of two units (e.g., dots, shapes, objects), infants dishabituate to a new display with either one or three units. (They do not, however, distinguish between larger sets such as 3 versus 4.) In addition, 2- and 3-month-olds can keep track of the number of very simple events. They quickly learn to anticipate the location of the next picture in a repeating sequence such

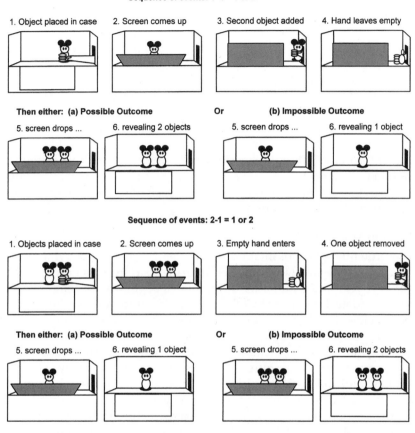

Figure 7. Displays used by Wynn to test infants' understanding of the outcome of simple addition and subtraction events. (From Wynn, K. [1992]. Addition and subtraction by human infants. *Nature, 358,* 749; reprinted by permission.)

as "left, left, right" (Canfield & Haith, 1992). To anticipate where the next picture will be, the infant has to somehow keep track of how many have occurred at the previous location.

According to Karen Wynn (1992), 5-month-old infants are also able to solve the simple addition and subtraction problems shown in Figure 7. In a test of addition, infants saw a hand deposit one mouse toy, and then a screen rotated up, hiding it from view. The hand returned and deposited a second mouse behind the screen. Infants in a test of subtraction saw two toys initially, and then observed one being removed from behind the screen. In both conditions, the screen rotated down, revealing either two toys or only one.

Both groups of babies looked longer at the display with the incorrect number of objects; that is, the addition group looked longer at the single toy, whereas the subtraction group was more interested in the two-object display. A subsequent group of 5-month-olds who saw the 1 + 1 sequence also looked longer when the result was three toys. Thus, these infants knew that the result of adding one object to one other object should not only be more than one—it should be two. Simon, Hespos, and Rochat (1995) have replicated Wynn's results.

Different accounts are offered for infants' quantitative abilities. Some attribute their discrimination of different numerosities to *subitizing*, or the immediate apprehension of small numbers without counting or other numerical knowledge. Others think more is involved: Wynn believes that infants possess an innate capacity for performing simple arithmetic calculation upon which later arithmetic competence is built.

Symbolization

The crowning glory of infant development is the onset of symbolization, the achievement that most sets humans apart from other species. In the first year and a half after birth, infants begin first to comprehend words and gestures made by others, then to produce some of these symbols themselves, and even to combine them into novel utterances.

In Western literate societies, infants are routinely exposed to a variety of symbolic things, including pictures, books, video, models, replica toys, and so forth. Their introduction to symbolic media vastly expands infants' and toddlers' cognitive horizons as they encounter entities, events, and ideas never experienced in everyday life. Infants clearly learn vocabulary and concepts from picturebook interactions (Whitehurst et al., 1988), and they also learn new words from at least some of the television they watch (Rice, Huston, Truglio, & Wright, 1990; Rice & Woodsmall, 1988). Babies who have never been to Africa or even to a zoo can recognize pictures or films of elephants or lions, and 21st century toddlers know a remarkable amount about dinosaurs.

Probably the most common media experienced by infants and toddlers are pictures: television and video. To appropriately interpret and use a symbol such as a picture, one must understand both how a picture is like what it depicts and how it is different. The first comes naturally to infants, but the second must be learned through experience. Infants, even newborns, detect the similarity between objects and their pictures (e.g., Barerra & Maurer, 1981; Dirks & Gibson, 1977; Slater, Rose, & Morrison, 1984). In one study (DeLoache, Strauss, & Maynard, 1979), for example, 5-month-olds who were familiarized with a real doll subsequently looked less at a picture of that doll than at a picture of a novel doll. The infants could also tell the difference between the two. Thus,

Figure 8.   The top row shows manual exploration of pictured objects by two 9-month-old American infants, and the second row shows similar behavior by Beng infants from the Cote d'Ivoire (West Africa). To an observer, the infants' grasping motions appear to be efforts to pick up the depicted objects. (From DeLoache, J.S., Pierroutsakos, S.L., Uttal, D.H., Rosengren, K.S., & Gottlieb, A. [1998]. Grasping the nature of pictures. *Psychological Science, 9,* 206, 208; reprinted by permission.)

these infants in some ways treated the picture as though it were the object itself, just as a mature symbol user would do.

In spite of this seemingly sophisticated behavior, infants do not understand what pictures are or how they differ from what they depict (DeLoache, Pierroutsakos, Uttal, Rosengren, & Gottlieb, 1998). Nine-month-old infants were presented with books containing highly realistic color photographs of individual objects, and the researchers observed what the infants did with them. The babies manually explored the depicted objects—feeling, rubbing, and even trying to grasp and pick the images up off the page (see Figure 8). This behavior was common both in middle-class American infants and in infants from a rural village in Africa where pictures are uncommon.

These babies do not confuse objects and pictures; given a choice, they almost always reach for a real object instead of its picture. However, they do not know what kind of thing a picture is, and their manual exploration is an effort to find out. By 15 months of age, American infants do very little of this kind of investigation of pictures; instead, they point at the pictures and often label them. These infants have presumably learned about the nature of pictures through the extensive experience that most middle-class American infants have with picturebooks. They have learned what kind of thing pictures are and the culturally appropriate way to behave toward them (DeLoache, Pierroutsakos, & Troseth, 1997).

Western infants also have substantial exposure to another pictorial medium: video. On average, American preschoolers watch 2–3 hours of television and videotapes a day (Huston, Wright, Rice, Kerkman, & St. Peters, 1990; National Center for Education Statistics, 1992). In addition, a growing number of families make home videos, so many children have even seen themselves on television. Given that toddlers can learn some things from television (Rice et al., 1990) and video demonstrations (Meltzoff, 1988b), it would be interesting to know to what extent they are able to use television and video as a source of information.

To find out, Georgene Troseth (Troseth & DeLoache, 1998) showed 24-month-old children a live video event. The toddlers watched on a video monitor as an adult walked into the room next door and hid an attractive toy somewhere in the room (e.g., under a table, behind a couch). The adult returned and encouraged the child to find the toy. A different group of 2-year-olds directly watched the same event through a small window (the same size as the monitor) between the two rooms.

Although the children in both groups had watched attentively, those who had seen the hiding event on television usually failed to find the hidden toy, whereas those who had watched directly always found it. Thus, 2-year-old children tend not to take information provided to them on a video screen as relevant to a current situation; they behave as though a televised event, while meaningful in its own right, has nothing to do with current reality. This discounting of what they observe on TV occurred in spite of explicit instructions and demonstrations regarding the relation between the live video and the events in the room.

This account of the children's poor performance with the video event was tested by misleading another group of 2-year-olds. They were led to believe that they were directly watching a hiding event taking place in the room, when in fact they were watching the event on video. To effect this mild deception, the children were told that they could watch through the window while the adult went into the room to hide the toy. When they looked through the window between the rooms, the children were actually seeing the screen of the monitor, which was positioned immediately behind the window so all the rest of it was concealed. Thus, there was no information, other than the two-dimensional nature of the image on the screen, to tell the children that they were not watching the hiding event directly. This somewhat unusual manipulation did help the 2-year-olds—they were more successful at finding the toy in this condition than were children who knew they were looking at a TV screen.

For both pictures and video, infants and toddlers can correctly perceive and interpret the information in an image; they recognize a familiar depicted object, and televised actions are meaningful to them. Children must learn, however, how those images are related to what they represent.

The development of the ability to respond flexibly to symbols continues over time. In another object-retrieval task, 2 1/2- and 3-year-old children observed a miniature toy ("Little Snoopy") being hidden in a scale model of a room (DeLoache, 1987, 1995a, 1995b). They were then asked to find a similar but larger toy ("Big Snoopy") that was hidden in the corresponding location in the room. The 3-year-olds readily used what they knew about the location of the toy in the model to infer where to find the larger toy in the room, but 2 1/2-year-olds seemed to have little or no idea about the relation between the two spaces. Thus, very young children have great difficulty interpreting a scale model as a symbol for a larger space, even if the model looks very much like the room and the relation between them is explicitly explained and demonstrated.

Children of the same age can, however, reason between a room and a model of it if they think the two spaces are actually the same. This was shown in a study (DeLoache, Miller, & Rosengren, 1997) in which 2 1/2-year-old children were led to believe that a machine could shrink a room (that is, it could transform a room into the model of the room). The children watched as the larger toy was hidden in a tent-like room and then the machine supposedly shrank the room. Believing that the model actually was the room after having been shrunk, the children successfully retrieved the miniature toy. The shrinking machine scenario worked because it removed the symbolic or "stands for" relation between the room and model. Forming a mental representation of the relation between a symbol and what it stands for is clearly a substantial challenge for very young children.

RECOMMENDATIONS

This brief and selective review of research on infant cognitive development suggests a number of recommendations with respect to child care practice and the training of child care providers. One should, however, keep in mind that the majority of the research on early cognitive development has been conducted with white middle-class residents of North America or Europe. There has been relatively little cross-cultural research on basic perceptual and cognitive processes. For most topics, there is no reason to expect different developmental processes, but the timing of development might differ. Therefore, one should not assume that the ages reported for various cognitive achievements would be applicable to all groups of infants or toddlers.

The first recommendation is that infants and toddlers need to be provided with a stimulating environment, both in terms of physical and social sources of stimulation. These cannot be separated, because adults constitute and mediate so much of infants' experience—experience that is the fuel for cognitive development. With respect to the physical environment, infants need the opportunity to explore and learn from a range of materials, including a mix of familiar and novel items. These do not necessarily need to be fancy, expensive "educational" toys; there is a great deal to learn from manipulating everyday objects. With respect to the social environment, infants need substantial experience with other people in basic interactions, social routines, interactional games, and so on. Through social interactions, an infant learns about the nature of people, how their behavior affects the infant, and how the infant's own behavior can affect others.

The environmental stimulation that infants experience should have some coherence, and some part of it should be predictable. Infants need repetition and regularity to learn, and they also need novelty to provide the impetus for new learning. They particularly need the opportunity for contingency learning, for discovering the relation between their own behavior and an outcome. Many investigators think that experiences in which the infant causes things to happen either to objects or to other people help him or her to develop a sense of efficacy or a belief in one's ability to control some part of the world.

For very young infants, the main source of contingency relations is other people. Other people provide infants with objects to manipulate and events to observe. They also involve infants in interactions involving contingencies between the infant's and the adult's behavior. With very young infants' limited motor abilities and limited memory, few other ways exist for them to experience contingencies in everyday life. In a child care program, adults can provide optimal levels of contingent stimulation only if they have the opportunity to interact directly with individual infants and toddlers, in other words, only if there is an adequate caregiver–child ratio. There are many reasons why good caregiver–child ratios are crucial, but one of them is for fostering basic cognitive development.

Training of child care practitioners should emphasize two important points with respect to the role that caregivers play in the cognitive development of infants and toddlers. First, they should be made aware of the need to provide the kind of stimulation that fosters the very early growth of cognition. Second, prospective child care workers should appreciate the extent to which the relevant stimulation occurs naturally in reciprocal social interactions between adults and the young children they care for. Finally, the training of child care practitioners should include basic information about the remarkable cognitive abilities that researchers have been uncovering in the first few years of life. Knowing the degree to which infants are actively looking, listening, and learning may inspire caregivers to take an active part in that process.

REFERENCES

Allen, T.W., Walker, K., Symonds, L., & Marcell, M. (1977). Intrasensory and intersensory perception of temporal sequences during infancy. *Developmental Psychology, 13,* 225–229.

Antell, S.E., & Keating, D.P. (1983). Perception of numerical invariance in neonates. *Child Development, 54,* 695–701.

Bahrick, L.E. (1994). The development of infants' sensitivity to arbitrary intermodal relations. *Ecological Psychology, 6,* 111–123.

Baillargeon, R. (1987a). Object permanence in 3.5- and 4.5-month-old infants. *Developmental Psychology, 23,* 655–664.

Baillargeon, R. (1987b). Representing the existence and the location of hidden objects: Object permanence in 6- and 8-month old infants. *Cognition, 23,* 21–41.

Baillargeon, R. (1991). Reasoning about the height and location of a hidden object in 4.5- and 6.5-month-old infants. *Cognition, 38,* 13–42.

Baillargeon, R. (1994). How do infants learn about the physical world? *Current Directions in Psychological Science, 3,* 133–140.

Baillargeon, R. (1995). Physical reasoning in infancy. In M.S. Gazzaniga (Ed.), *The cognitive neurosciences* (pp. 181–204). Cambridge: The MIT Press.

Baillargeon, R., & DeVos, J. (1991). Object permanence in 3.5- and 4.5-month-old infants: Further evidence. *Child Development, 62,* 1227–1246.

Baillargeon, R. Graber, M., DeVos, J., & Black, J. (1990). Why do young infants not search for hidden objects? *Cognition, 36,* 225–284.

Baillargeon, R., Spelke, E.S., & Wasserman, S. (1985). Object permanence in 5-month-old infants. *Cognition, 20,* 191–208.

Baldwin, D.A., Markman, E.M., & Melartin, R.L. (1993). Infants' ability to draw inferences about nonobvious objects properties: Evidence from exploratory play. *Child Development, 64,* 711–728.

Barerra, M.A., & Maurer, D. (1981). Recognition of mother's photographed face by the 3-month-old. *Child Development, 52,* 714–716.

Bauer, P.J. (1996). What do infants recall of their lives? *American Psychologist, 51,* 29–41.

Bauer, P.J., Hertsgaard, L.A., & Dow, G.A. (1994). After 8 months have passed: Long-term recall of events by 1- to 2-year-old children. *Memory, 2,* 317–338.

Bauer, P.J., & Mandler, J.M. (1992). Putting the horse before the cart: The use of temporal order in recall of events by 1-year-old children. *Developmental Psychology, 28,* 441–452.

Bauer, P.J., & Travis, L.L. (1993). The fabric of an event: Different sources of temporal invariance differentially affect 24-month-olds' recall. *Cognitive Development, 8,* 319–341.

Behl-Chadha, G. (1996). Basic-level and superordinate-like categorical representations in early infancy. *Cognition, 60,* 105–141.

Blass, E.M. (1990). Suckling: Determinants, changes, mechanisms, and lasting impressions. *Developmental Psychology, 2,* 520–533.

Bornstein, M.H., & Benasich, A.A. (1986). Infant habituation: Assessments of short-term reliability and individual differences at 5 months. *Child Development, 57,* 87–99.

Bornstein, M.H., & Sigman, M.D. (1986). Continuity in mental development from infancy. *Child Development, 57,* 251–274.

Bornstein, M.H., Pecheux, M.G., & Lecuyer, R. (1988). Visual habituation in human infants: Development and rearing circumstances. *Psychological Research, 50,* 130–133.

Bruner, J.S. (1973). Organization of early skilled action. *Child Development, 44,* 1–11.

Bryant, P. (1974). *Perception and understanding in young children: An experimental approach.* London: Methuen.

Bushnell, E.W. (1986). The basis of infant visual–tactual function: Amodal dimensions or multimodal compounds? In L.P. Lipsit & C.K. Rovee-Collier (Eds.), *Advances in infancy research* (Vol. 4, pp. 182–194). Norwood, NJ: Ablex.

Canfield, R.L., & Haith, M.M. (1992). Young infants' visual expectations for symmetric and asymmetric stimulus sequences. *Developmental Psychology, 27,* 198–208.

Clifton, R.K., Rochat, P., Litovsky, R.Y., & Perris, E.E. (1991). Object representation guides infants' reaching in the dark. *Journal of Experimental Psychology: Human Perception and Performance, 17,* 323–329.

Cohen, N.J., & Squire, L.R. (1980). Preserved learning and retention of pattern analyzing skill in amnesia: Dissociation of knowing how and knowing that. *Science, 210,* 207–209.

Cooper, R.G., Jr. (1984). Early number development: Discovering number space with addition and subtraction. In C. Sophian (Ed.), *The origins of cognitive skills* (pp. 157–192). Mahwah, NJ: Lawrence Erlbaum Associates.

DeCasper, A.J., & Fifer, W.P. (1980). Of human bonding: Newborns prefer their mothers' voices. *Science, 208,* 1174–1176.

DeCasper, A.J., & Spence, M.J. (1986). Prenatal maternal speech influences newborns' perception of speech sounds. *Infant Behavior and Development, 9,* 133–150.

deHaan, M., & Nelson, C.A. (1997). Recognition of the mother's face by 6-month-old infants: A neurobehavioral study. *Child Development, 68,* 187–210.

DeLoache, J.S. (1976). Rate of habituation and visual memory in infants. *Child Development, 47,* 145–154.

DeLoache, J.S. (1987). Rapid change in the symbolic functioning of very young children. *Science, 238,* 1556–1557.

DeLoache, J.S. (1995a). Early symbol understanding and use. In D. Medin (Ed.), *The psychology of learning and motivation* (Vol. 33, pp. 65–114). New York: Academic Press.

DeLoache, J.S. (1995b). Early understanding and use of symbols: The model model. *Current Directions in Psychological Science, 4,* 109–113.

DeLoache, J.S., Miller, K.F., & Rosengren, K.S. (1997). The credible shrinking room: Very young children's performance with symbolic and nonsymbolic relations. *Psychological Science, 4,* 308–313.

DeLoache, J.S., Pierroutsakos, S.L., & Troseth, G.L. (1997). The three Rs of pictoral competence. *Annals of Child Development* (Vol. 12, pp. 1–48). Bristol, PA: Kingsley.

DeLoache, J.S., Pierroutsakos, S.L., Uttal, D.H., Rosengren, K.S., & Gottlieb, A. (1998). Grasping the nature of pictures. *Psychological Science, 9,* 205–210.

Diamond, A. (1985). The development of the ability to use recall to guide action, as indicated by infants' performance on AB. *Child Development, 56,* 868–883.

Diamond, A. (1991). Neuropsychological insights into the meaning of object concept development. In S. Carey & R. Gelman (Eds.), *The epigenesis of mind: Essays on biology and knowledge* (pp. 67–110). Mahwah, NJ: Lawrence Erlbaum Associates.

Diamond, A., & Gilbert, J. (1989). Development as progressive inhibitory control of action: Retrieval of a contiguous object. *Cognitive Development, 4,* 223–249.

Diamond, A., & Goldman-Rakic, P.S. (1989). Comparison of human infants and rhesus monkeys on Piaget's AB task: Evidence for dependence on dorsolateral prefrontal cortex. *Experimental Brain Research, 74,* 24–40.

Diamond, A., Prevor, M.B., Callender, G., & Druin, D.P. (1997). Prefrontal cortex cognitive deficits in children treated early and continuously for PKU. *Monographs of the Society for Research in Child Development, 62*(4).

Dirks, J., & Gibson, E. (1977). Infants' perceptions of similarity between live people and their photographs. *Child Development, 48,* 124–130.

Dodd, B. (1979). Lip reading in infants: Attention to speech presented in and out of synchrony. *Child Psychology, 11,* 478–484.

Eimas, P.D., & Quinn, P.C. (1994). Studies on the formation of perceptually based basic-level categories in young infants. *Child Development, 65,* 903–917.

Eimas, P.D., Quinn, P.C., & Cowan, P. (1994). Development of exclusivity in perceptually based categories of young infants. *Journal of Experimental Child Psychology, 58,* 418–431.

Fagan, J.F. (1973). Infants' delayed recognition memory and forgetting. *Journal of Experimental Child Psychology, 16,* 424–450.

Flavell, J.H. (1985). *Cognitive development* (2nd ed.). Englewood Cliffs, NJ: Prentice-Hall.

Gelman, R. (1991). Epigenetic foundations of knowledge structures: Initial and transcendent constructions. In S. Carey & R. Gelman (Eds.), *The epigenesis of mind: Essays on biology and knowledge* (pp. 293–322). Mahwah, NJ: Lawrence Erlbaum Associates.

Gelman, S.A., & Coley, J.D. (1990). The importance of knowing a dodo is a bird: Categories and inferences in 2-year-old children. *Developmental Psychology, 26,* 796–804.

Gibson, E.J. (1969). *Principles of perceptual learning and development.* New York: Appleton-Century-Crofts.

Gibson, E.J. (1988). Exploratory behavior in the development of perceiving, acting, and the acquiring of knowledge. *Annual Review of Psychology, 39,* 1–41.

Greenough, W.T., Black, J.E., & Wallace, C.S. (1987). Experience and brain development. *Child Development, 58,* 539–559.

Hanna, E., & Meltzoff, A.N. (1993). Peer imitation by toddlers in laboratory, home, and day-care contexts: Implications for social learning and memory. *Developmental Psychology, 4,* 701–710.

Hartshorn, K., & Rovee-Collier, C. (1997). Infant learning and long-term memory at 6 months: A confirming analysis. *Developmental Psychology, 30,* 71–85.

Hill, W.L., Borovsky, D., & Rovee-Collier, C. (1988). Continuities in infant memory development. *Developmental Psychobiology, 21,* 43–62.

Hood, B., & Willatts, P. (1986). Reaching in the dark to an objects' remembered position: Evidence for object permanence in 5-month-old infants. *British Journal of Developmental Psychology, 4,* 57–65.

Huston, A.C., Wright, J.C., Rice, M.L., Kerkman, D., & St. Peters, M. (1990). Development of television viewing patterns in early childhood: A longitudinal investigation. *Developmental Psychology, 26,* 409–420.

Howe, M.L., & Courage, M.L. (1997). The emergence and early development of autobiographical memory. *Psychological Review, 3,* 499–523.

Huttenlocher, P.R. (1994). Synaptogenesis in human cerebral cortex. In G. Dawson and K.W. Fischer (Eds.), *Human behavior and the developing brain* (pp. 137–152). New York: Guilford Press.

Jones, S.S., Smith, L.B., & Landau, B. (1991). Object properties and knowledge in early lexical learning. *Child Development, 16,* 499–516.

Kellman, P.J., & Spelke, E.S. (1983). Perception of partly occluded objects in infancy. *Cognitive Psychology, 15,* 483–524.

Kuhl, P.K., & Meltzoff, A.N. (1984a). The bimodal perception of speech in infancy. *Science, 218,* 1138–1141.

Kuhl, P.K., & Meltzoff, A.N. (1984b). The intermodal representation of speech in infants. *Infant Behavior and Development, 7,* 361–381.

Landau, B., Smith, L.B., & Jones, S.S. (1988). The importance of shape in early lexical learning. *Cognitive Development, 3,* 299–321.

Lewis, M., Alessandri, S.M., & Sullivan, M.W. (1990). Violation of expectancy, loss of control, and anger expressions in young infants. *Developmental Psychology, 26,* 745–751.

MacFarlane, A. (1975). Olfaction in the development of social preferences in the human neonate. *Parent–infant interaction (CIBA Foundation symposium 33).* New York: Elsevier/North Holland.

Mandler, J.M. (1997). Representation. In D. Kuhn & R. Siegler (Eds.), *Handbook of child psychology: Cognition, perception, and language* (5th ed., Vol. 2, pp. 255–308). New York: Wiley.

Mandler, J.M., Fivush, R., & Resnick, J.S. (1987). The development of contextual categories. *Cognitive Development, 2,* 339–354.

Mandler, J.M., & McDonough, L. (1993). Concept formation in infancy. *Cognitive Development, 8,* 291–318.

Mandler, J.M., & McDonough, L. (1996). Drinking and driving don't mix: Inductive generalization in infancy. *Cognition, 59,* 307–335.

McCall, R.B., & Carriger, M.S. (1993). A meta-analysis of infant habituation and recognition memory performance as predictors of later IQ. *Child Development, 64,* 57–79.

McCall, R.B., & Kagan, J. (1970). Individual differences in the infant's distribution of attention to stimulus discrepancy. *Developmental Psychology, 2,* 90–98.

McDonough, L., & Mandler, J.M. (1994). Very long-term memory in infancy: Infantile amnesia reconsidered. *Memory, 2,* 339–352.

Mehler, J., Jusczyk, P., Lambertz, G., Halsted, N., Bertoncini, J., & Amiel-Tison, C. (1988). A precursor of language acquisition in young infants. *Cognition, 29,* 143–178.

Meltzoff, A.N. (1988a). Imitation of televised models by infants. *Child Development, 59,* 1221–1229.

Meltzoff, A.N. (1988b). Infant imitation and memory: Nine-month-olds in immediate and deferred tests. *Child Development, 59,* 217–225.

Meltzoff, A.N. (1995a). Apprehending the intentions of others: Re-enactment of intended acts by 10-month-old children. *Developmental Psychology, 31,* 838–850.

Meltzoff, A.N. (1995b). What infant memory tells us about infantile amnesia: Long-term recall and deferred imitation. *Journal of Experimental Child Psychology, 59,* 497–515.

Millar, W.S. (1972). A study of operant conditioning under delayed reinforcement in early infancy. *Monographs of the Society for Research in Child Development, 31*(2, Serial No. 147).

Miller, P.J., & Sperry, L.L. (1988). Early talk about the past: The origins of conversational stories about personal experiences. *Journal of Child Language, 15,* 293–315.

Moon, C., Cooper, R.P., & Fifer, W.P. (1993). Two-day-olds prefer their native language. *Infant Behavior and Development, 16*(4), 495–500.

Myers, N.A., Clifton, R.K., & Clarkson, M.G. (1987) When they were very young: Almost-threes remember 2 years ago. *Infant Behavior and Development, 10,* 123–132.

National Center for Education Statistics (1992). *Home activities of 3- to 8-year-olds.* (NCES Publication No. 92-004). Washington, DC: U.S. Department of Education Office of Educational Research and Improvement.

Needham, A. (1997). Factors affecting infants' use of featural information in object segregation. *Current Directions in Psychological Science, 6,* 26–33.

Needham, A., & Baillargeon, R. (1998). Effects of prior experience on 4.5-month-old infants' object segregation. *Infant Behavior and Development, 21,* 1–24.

Needham A., & Baillargeon, R. (1997). Object segregation in 8-month-old infants. *Cognition, 62,* 121–149.

Needham, A., Baillargeon, R., & Kaufman, L. (1997). Object segregation in infancy. In C. Rovee-Collier & L. Lipsitt (Eds.), *Advances in infancy research,* (Vol. 11, pp. 1–44). Norwood, NJ: Ablex.

Nelson, C.A. (1994). Neural correlates of recognition memory in the first postnatal year. In G. Dawson & K.W. Fischer. (Eds.), *Human behavior and the developing brain.* (pp. 269–313). New York: Guilford Press.

Nelson, C.A., & Collins, P.F. (1992). Neural and behavioral correlates of visual recognition memory in 4- and 8-month old infants. *Brain and Cognition, 19,* 105–121.

Nelson, K. (Ed.). (1989). *Narratives from the crib.* Cambridge, MA: Harvard University Press.

Nelson, K. (1993). The psychological and social origins of autobiographical memory. *Psychological Science, 4,* 7–14.

Nelson, K., & Ross, G. (1980). The generalities and specifics of long-term memory in infants and young children. In M. Perlmuter (Ed.), *New directions for child development: Children's memory* (pp. 87–101). San Francisco: Jossey-Bass.

Pascalis, O., deHaan, M., Nelson, C.A., & deSchonen (1998). Long term recognition memory for faces assessed by visual paired comparison in 3- and 6-month old infants. *Journal of Experimental Psychology: Learning, Memory & Cognition, 24,* 249–260.

Piaget, J. (1954). *The construction of reality in the child.* New York: Basic Books.

Pickens, J., & Bahrick, L.E. (1995). Infants' discrimination of bimodal events on the basis of rhythm and tempo. *British Journal of Developmental Psychology, 13,* 223–236.

Quinn, P.C., & Eimas, P.E. (1996). Perceptual organization and categorization in young infants. In C. Rovee-Collier & L.P. Lipsitt (Eds.), *Advances in infancy research* (Vol. 10, pp. 1–36). Norwood, NJ: Ablex.

Quinn, P.C., Eimas, P.D., & Rosenkrantz, S.L. (1993). Evidence for representations of perceptually similar natural categories by 3-month-old and 4-month-old infants. *Perception, 22,* 463–475.

Reardon, P., & Bushnell, E.W. (1988). Infants' sensitivity to arbitrary pairings of color and taste. *Infant Behavior and Development, 11,* 245–250.

Rice, M.L., Huston, A.C., Truglio, R. & Wright, J. (1990). Words from Sesame Street: Learning vocabulary while viewing. *Developmental Psychology, 26,* 421–428.

Rice, M.L., & Woodsmall, L. (1988). Lessons from television: Children's word learning when viewing. *Child Development, 59,* 420–429.

Rose, S.A., & Feldman, J.F. (1995). Prediction of IQ and specific cognitive abilities at 11 years from infancy measures. *Developmental Psychology, 31,* 531–539.

Rose, S.A., & Feldman, J.F. (1997). Memory and speed: Their role in the relation of infant information processing to later IQ. *Child Development, 68,* 630–641.

Rovee-Collier, C. (1997). Dissociations in infant memory: Rethinking the development of implicit and explicit memory. *Psychological Review, 104,* 467–498.

Sachs, J. (1983). Talking about the there and then: The emergence of displaced reference in parent–child discourse. In K. Nelson (Ed.), *Children's language* (Vol. 4, pp. 1–28). New York: Gardner Press.

Schacter, D.L. (1987). Implicit memory: History and current status. *Journal of Experimental Psychology: Learning, Memory, and Cognition, 13,* 501–518.

Simon, T.J., Hespos, S.J., & Rochat, P. (1995). Do infants understand simple arithmetic? A replication of Wynn. *Cognitive Development, 10,* 253–269.

Siqueland, E.R, & DeLucia, C.A. (1969). Visual reinforcement of non-nutritive sucking in human infants. *Science, 165,* 1144–1146.

Slater, A., Rose, D. & Morrison, V. (1984). Newborn infants' perception of similarities and differences between two- and three-dimensional stimuli. *British Journal of Developmental Psychology, 2,* 287–294.

Soja, N.N., Carey, S., & Spelke, E.S. (1991). Ontological categories guide young children's inductions of word meaning: Object terms and substance terms. *Cognition, 38,* 179–211.

Spelke, E.S. (1976). Infants' intermodal perception of events. *Cognitive Psychology, 8,* 533–560.

Spelke, E.S., & Cortelyou, A. (1981). Perceptual aspects of social knowing: Looking and listening in infancy. In M.E. Lamb & L.R. Sherrod (Eds.), *Infant social cognition* (pp. 61–84). Mahwah, NJ: Lawrence Erlbaum Associates.

Spelke, E.S., & Owsley, C. (1979). Intermodal exploration and knowledge in infancy. *Infant Behavior and Development, 2,* 13–17.

Starkey, P., & Cooper, R.G. (1980). Perception of number by human infants. *Science, 200,* 1033–1035.

Strauss, M.S., & Curtis, L.E. (1981). Infant perception of numerosity. *Child Development, 52,* 1146–1152.

Sullivan, M.W., Rovee-Collier, C., & Tynes, D.M. (1979). A conditioning analysis of infant long-term memory. *Child Development, 21,* 142–162.

Swain, I., Zelazo, P., & Clifton, R. (1993). Newborn infants' memory for speech sounds retained over 24 hours. *Developmental Psychology, 29,* 312–323.

Todd, C.M., & Perlmutter, M. (1980). Reality recalled by preschool children. In M. Perlmutter (Ed.), *Children's memory: New directions for child development* (pp. 69–85). San Francisco: Jossey-Bass.

Troseth, G., & DeLoache, J.S. (1998). The medium can obscure the message: Young children's understanding of video. *Child Development, 69,* 950–965.

VanderLinde, E., Morrongiello, B.A., & Rovee-Collier, C. (1985). Determinants of retention in 8-week-old infants. *Developmental Psychology, 21,* 601–613.

Walker-Andrews, A.S. (1997). Infants' perception of expressive behaviors: Differentiation of multimodal information. *Psychological Bulletin, 121,* 437–456.

Watson, J.B., & Raynor, R. (1920). Conditioned emotional reactions. *Journal of Experimental Psychology, 3,* 1–14.

Watson, J.S. (1972). Smiling, cooing, and "the game." *Merrill-Palmer Quarterly, 18,* 323–340.

Watson, J.S., & Ramey, C.T. (1972). Reactions to response-contingency stimulation in early infancy. *Merrill-Palmer Quarterly, 18,* 219–227.

Waxman, S.R., & Hall, D.G. (1993). The development of a linkage between count nouns and object categories: Evidence from 15- to 21-month-old infants. *Child Development, 64,* 1224–1241.

Wellman, H.M., Cross, D., & Bartsch, K. (1987). Infant search and object permanence: A meta-analysis of the A/not B error. *Monographs of the Society for Research in Child Development, 51*(Serial No. 214).

Welsh, M.C., Pennington, B.F., Ozonoff, S., Rouse, B., & McCabe, E.R.B. (1990). Neuropsychology of early treated phenylketonuria: Specific executive function deficits. *Child Development, 61,* 1697–1713.

Whitehurst, G.J., Falco, F.L., Lonigan, C.J., Fischel, J.W., DeBaryshe, B.D., Valdex-Menchaca, M.C., & Caulfield, M. (1988). Accelerating language development through picture book reading. *Developmental Psychology, 24,* 552–559.

Willatts, P. (1985). Adjustment of means–ends coordination and the representation of spatial relations in the production of search errors by infants. *British Journal of Developmental Psychology, 3,* 259–272.

Wynn, K. (1992). Addition and subtraction by human infants. *Nature, 358,* 749–750.

3

Language Development in Early Childhood

The Role of Social Interaction

◆❖◆

Jane R. Katz and Catherine E. Snow

This chapter presents an overview of research on early language development with a focus on environmental, and particularly social, factors that influence it. We present this research with two goals. First, we wish to highlight how environmental factors that influence young children's language development may vary as a function of conditions of early child care. As parents try to piece together necessary and affordable child care arrangements, very young children may experience an array of caregivers and caregiving environments. Children may, for example, be in full-time, center-based care outside the home, spending days with several caregivers in a consistent cohort of peers; in part-time care with a relative; or in a home child care situation with a changing group of children, a play group, and care from a young baby sitter. It is important to think about how these different care environments might relate to aspects of the child's language environment. Second, we wish to provide information on language development that might inform caregivers' practice. We assume an interactionist model, which maintains that language is acquired for purposes of communication in the context of meaningful social relationships. We hope, though, to refine and expand this model, which is largely based on research describing mother–child interaction, to incorporate an understanding of language development in the many and varied settings and relationships that young children are likely to have. We emphasize also the bidirectionality of this model.

Young children are not simply acted upon, but exert their own influence on situations and caregivers that in turn alters the quality of the language environment (Snow, 1994).

Most of the research on social support for language development is based on monolingual English-speaking, mainstream Anglo-American children interacting in pairs; information about how these findings might differ for children of different cultural or linguistic groups is severely limited. Furthermore, although the primary concern here is language, a division between linguistic and social development is somewhat artificial. Optimal support for language development is only possible within the context of ongoing, mutual relationships between caregivers and young children. Accordingly, we begin by briefly discussing these three topics—cultural differences, children who speak languages other than English, and the centrality of relationships—as a prelude to our review of work on language development.

CROSS-CUTTING THEMES

There can be no dissociation of language and culture: language shapes and articulates thought, social experiences, relationships, personal identity, and salient world knowledge—all of which are, to some degree, socially constructed (see Chapter 9). Language is also a major medium for transmitting culture across generations. Through language socialization, adult caregivers convey to children, from infancy onward, culturally valued beliefs, behaviors, and processes (Heath, 1983; Rogoff, Mistry, Goncü, & Mosier, 1993; Schieffelin & Ochs, 1986). In this process, it is not only the content of talk that carries important cultural information, but also the paralinguistic and extra-linguistic features of talk: When is talk appropriate? Whom can one address, and what are the appropriate ways of addressing people of different status or age? What is the acceptable volume or tone of voice for speech? When should talk be brief, discreet, or dispassionate? When can it be unguarded or emotional, and how does this vary by situation? What constitutes a "good" story? Who can tell it?

An important part of the current research agenda is to study language development and the factors that support it in a wider variety of linguistic and cultural communities than those studied so far. Understanding how support for language development occurs across a wider array of cultures will improve our understanding of the process of language acquisition and will inform early childhood practitioners dealing with increasingly diverse populations. This chapter presents findings from the available research, recognizing that large, crucial pieces of the story on language development are just beginning to emerge.

Bilingual and Language Minority Children

Ideally, work on the language development of bilingual children and of young second language learners would be presented in a fashion integrated with information about language development in general. Unfortunately, many of the topics that are well researched for monolingual learners of English are completely unresearched for bilingual children. A brief look at some basic information about children's simultaneous acquisition of two languages is in order here.

Children who acquire a second language before the age of 3 are generally referred to as *simultaneous bilinguals*. Although simultaneous bilingualism can result when two languages are present in the child's home, it often results instead from exposure to a second language in an out-of-home care setting. Questions naturally arise whether such exposure is desirable, producing native-like competence in both languages, or whether it involves some danger to the child's ultimate language competence. The answer is, unsurprisingly, "it depends": the myriad factors related to the different contexts of a child's life can affect individual children in different ways. Many children in the world are true bilinguals, passing as natives in more than one language, but many others who have had preschool exposure to two languages end up speaking one poorly or not at all (De Houwer, 1995).

Similarly, questions arise about the optimal age and type of exposure to a second language for young children; here again, evidence suggests that exposure at any age and in a variety of settings can lead to good language learning but that real proficiency in a language requires its use in a variety of interactive settings and over many years. Although research has suggested the potential value of exposure to more than one language in infancy in supporting the maintenance of a wide array of phonemic distinctions, high-level second language competence is clearly quite feasible even for those who start much later than infancy (Kuhl et al., 1997).

It is clear also that young children can be fully bilingual, using two languages well and showing typical, monolingual-like development in both. Simultaneous bilinguals typically have smaller vocabularies in either language than monolinguals but larger total vocabularies than monolingual age-mates (Pearson, Fernandez, Lewedey, & Oller, 1997). Typically developing bilingual children tend to show some amount of language mixing—using the "wrong" language sometimes, in particular when the weaker language would be appropriate—but this does not imply that they cannot distinguish their two languages nor that they are confused. Bilingual children tend to address monolingual speakers in the appropriate language, even when their own proficiency in that language is quite limited; this reflects their full understanding that the two languages are distinct communication systems (Lanza, 1997; Nicoladis & Genesee, 1996).

There is considerable, and not unjustified, concern that young language-minority children exposed to English in child care settings might lose their home language (Wong Fillmore, 1991). Young children are surprisingly sensitive to the larger sociolinguistic forces at work and tend to concentrate on learning languages that are of higher status and greater utility for wider communication. However, when parents are consistent in the use of the home language, children are unlikely to stop acquiring that language just because of exposure to another one (Pearson & Fernandez, 1994). In general, for children growing up in bilingual environments, the level of proficiency in each language directly reflects the amount of exposure to that language (Pearson, Fernandez, Lewedey, & Oller, 1997)—but "exposure" here means use in interaction, not simply overhearing a language or watching people speak it on television. Even being addressed in a language may not be sufficient to ensure its acquisition unless the child has an ongoing relationship with the adult speaking it. The context of language use is extremely important for young bilingual children, and as Lanza pointed out, "Context is not a static variable. Talk continually creates a context for more talk" (1997, p. 253). Moreover, parents and other significant adults can metalinguistically define a situation as monolingual or bilingual by their interactional style and their response to a child's language mixing.

Fundamental to quality out-of-home care is the ability of the caregiver and the child to establish effective communication; although quality care can happen when the caregiver and the child don't speak the same language, children who are already somewhat advanced in language learning will probably function better in a child care setting in which someone understands them. However, quality of care reflects many factors, and sensitive caregivers can use many forms of communication in addition to conventional language. Thus, any unconditional recommendations that infants and toddlers should or should not be placed in out-of-home care where particular languages are used are overzealous. We feel strongly that infants and young children should not be placed in environments in which the quality of communication is poor but the quality of communication is somewhat independent of the language in which communication occurs.

Importance of Relationships

A central aspect of determining the quality of care in out-of-home settings is the nature of the relationships children can develop with caregivers and with each other. Such relationships matter, of course, in all aspects of children's development; they are crucial to language development (Raikes, 1993). Relationships are the context in which language-based communication develops, while, at the same time, language is the primary means of establishing the shared meaning that gives relationships depth and complexity (Bloom, 1993; Stern, 1985). Unfortunately, when caregiving facilities are taxed by too many children, too little space, and too few resources, and when caregivers are stressed by high ratios, limited play resources, little emotional support, inadequate preparation, and low pay, relationships in the child care setting suffer. Significant relationships among children and among caregivers and children have different characteristics and parameters in different cultural systems. Recognizing and respecting this variation, we do not promote a single kind of relationship. We maintain that, just as the quality of children's relationships with caregivers is a factor in children's language learning in the home, the quality and consistency of relationships affect children's language learning in out-of-home care situations.

DOMAINS OF LANGUAGE DEVELOPMENT

Of the many aspects of language development, we focus here on a few developing capacities: conversational competence, vocabulary, and extended discourse skills. We focus on these three distinct but related domains because:

1. Performance in all three areas carries high social value.
2. These domains are sensitive to environmental influences and are furthermore likely to reflect cultural differences and the effects of bilingualism.
3. Performance in each domain can serve as an indicator of developmental delay or disorder or dissonance with the environment.
4. Each of these three domains is related to school success in some form.

We offer an overview of the process of developing competence in each domain and examine how this process may be supported or hindered by features of the child's social environment in out-of-home care.

Conversational Competence

The different facets of conversational competence should be examined in some detail first because the complexity of conversation skill is often underestimated. In fact, being a competent conversationalist within any language community requires familiarity with a wide array of specific rule systems and capacities. Second, conversation is the context for the acquisition of language: Children engage in conversation with adults and with each other before they have acquired their first conventional word. We discuss in the following sections how certain kinds of conversational interactions provide opportunities for vocabulary learning and how the production of extended discourse grows out of conversation as well. The reader will see that children who are effective conversationalists are also in a position to learn grammar, vocabulary, and extended discourse skills more efficiently.

The Nature of Conversational Exchange   Our focus on conversation as an accomplishment on the part of the child and as a context for language acquisition rests on certain fundamental assumptions. The first of these, the refutation of egocentrism in early childhood, has several corollaries. Counter to Piaget's (1926) thesis, very young pre–school-age children are capable of meaningful conversational exchange. Their speech is not primarily egocentric (i.e., produced for the self alone and so not adapted to an interlocutor); young children are capable of the decentering necessary for taking account of other minds and realities. Further, even very young children have communicative intents and can respond to the communicative intent of their partner (Garvey & Hogan, 1973; Snow, Pan, Imbens-Bailey & Herman, 1996).

A second and related idea maintains that it is not exclusively mastery of the adults' communicative and conversational system that is driving children's conversational development, but the drive for both "human attunement" and "interpersonal relatedness" (Stern, 1985) and the communication of mental meanings. Such meanings may include 1) the desire to express and interpret the intentional states of beliefs, desires, and feelings (Bloom, 1993); and 2) the desire "to get things done" in a particular cultural context (Bruner, 1983). This intentionality of communication seems to require a basic theory of mind, that is, an awareness of mental states, mental processes, and the similarity between one's own mental states and those of another (Tomasello, 1995). It rests also on the development of intersubjectivity (i.e., having a shared focus of attention and shared understanding within this shared attention) (Trevarthen & Hubley, 1978). Intersubjectivity is typically a developmental achievement of the first year of life. However, a caregiver's role in this development is crucial and involves establishing with an infant a shared focus of gaze and attention in early interactions, being attentive to the child's vocalizations, and responding to them in a meaningful way by interpreting vocalizations within a communicative system. By treating children's early gestural and vocal, but mostly preverbal, communication as meaningful, caregivers foster the sense of mutual understanding necessary for the development of more sophisticated intentional communication; they also encourage children to develop ways of communicating their intentions interpersonally (Bloom, 1993; Meltzoff, 1995; Moore & Dunham, 1995; Stern, 1985). Bruner maintained that sharing attention is the basis for patterns of interactive communication: "Mother and child are not simply sharing common foci of attention, but are also constructing them, extending them over time by embedding them in task structures, and conventionalizing them in terms of canonical forms in the culture" (1995, p. 6).

Tomasello and Farrar (1986) highlighted the importance of joint attention in early language development in a study of interaction between 15- and 21-month-old children and their mothers. They observed that, during periods of joint attention, mother–child pairs had longer conversations with more talk from both mothers and children and shorter sentences and more comments from both mothers and children than outside episodes of joint attention. Noting that causality is difficult to determine in these findings, Tomasello and Farrar adopted a "transactive" interpretation: Joint attention supports the use of language, thus facilitating further establishment of joint attention, which fosters further language use. Conversation, itself based on joint attention, functions as a way for creating and sharing joint attention through the representational system of language.

The Complexity of Conversational Skill   In addition to being an external representation of intersubjectivity, conversation is a deeply cultural accomplishment, and the rules for engagement in conversation differ enormously in different contexts and language communities. Conversational competence entails broad linguistic, interpersonal, and cultural knowledge that work together. Conventional linguistic knowledge, such as the development of a varied lexicon of both abstract and concrete terms and the development of correct syntax, is fundamental. But conversational skill has many other components. For example, turn taking is a challenging aspect of conversational skill because the rules governing it are language specific. Speakers of different languages vary enormously in their definitions of how long to pause between speakers, how many people can speak at once, and how much the listener is expected to indicate understanding. Infants must and do learn these microlevel aspects of conversational engagement from quotidian, routine interactions.

However, conversation requires more than just turn taking. More sophisticated and elusive linguistic knowledge is also required to combine turn-taking skills with the skills of semantic continuity, topic selection and maintenance, and topic elaboration and relevance. In addition, being an effective conversationalist requires having learned the rules of interpersonal space and distance, gesture, and gaze orientation, as well as rules for interpersonal politeness and awareness of communicative breakdowns and the ability to make repairs (Ninio & Snow, 1996; Schley & Snow, 1992). High levels of accomplishment in these domains rest on social and interpersonal skills (e.g., self–other distinction, social perspective-taking, partner monitoring, and responsiveness), on cultural knowledge of appropriate and effective communication, and on knowledge of the conventional linguistic system.

We look now at some of the literature addressing the social influences on conversational competence, focusing on children's accomplishments in three areas that have received considerable attention from researchers: turn taking, topic maintenance, and procedures for effective expression of communicative intents. Although research in these three areas does not exhaust the possibilities for thinking about social influences on conversational skill, it does serve to summarize the major research efforts carried out so far in this field.

Turn Taking Stern (1985) maintained that the infant's subjective world is fundamentally social from birth. One reflection of this basic sociability is the coordination of vocalization between an infant and an attentive caregiver: turn taking is an aspect of conversational skill that emerges early, at least with a responsive adult partner (Ninio & Snow 1996), with infants as young as 3 months able to alternate vocalization with an adult (Kaye & Fogel, 1980). Stern (1985; Stern, Jaffe, Beebe, & Bennett, 1975) reported that infant vocalizations at 3–4 months tend to be co-actional with their caregivers, rather than sequential; however, within their first 19–20 months, infants learn sequential turn taking. Bloom, Rocissano, and Hood (1976, reporting Stern et al., 1975) noted children's early learning of interactive rules: By the time they are producing one-word speech, children know that only one person speaks at a time and that contributions are made sequentially. By the age of 3 years, children know how to hold a reciprocal conversation within the rules of turn taking in which utterances are both contingent and adjacent (i.e., the topic is maintained and additional utterances add new information to the topic).

These remarkable accomplishments depend to a large extent on having experienced interactions with a responsive adult. "Vocalization with a socially responsive adult, whether contingent or random, elicits social responding from an infant.... Infants who experience contingent responses are more likely to pause after the response, so that their interaction assumes a basic property of turn taking" (Bloom, 1993, p. 73). Social cues and aspects of social context affect amount and quality of infant vocalizing. For example, infants vocalize differently depending on whether they are on the floor or seated on a lap and on whether they are held vertically or horizontally. They vocalize more in interaction with their mothers than when alone and more with silent toys than with noisy toys (Bloom, 1993). Furthermore, infants' vocalizations become more word-like if responded to by adults' vocalizations (Bloom, Russell, & Wassenberg, 1987). The phonetic and prosodic features of speech to infants are also well designed for ensuring optimal attention, as well as supplying information about the language. Experimental studies show that infants prefer high-pitched voices and lively intonation contours, such as those typical of "baby talk" or child-directed speech. The slower and more high-pitched speech directed to infants is also more informative about phonetic targets in the adult's language than is the faster, sloppier, lower pitched speech typical among adults (Bernstein Ratner, 1993; Kuhl et al., 1997).

Despite infants' conversational immaturity, mothers in Anglo-American and northern European cultures treat very young children as conversational partners, crediting children with meaningful conversational turns even if the child's contribution is less than meaningful. Through this style of interaction, mothers structure interaction with their infants with pauses for turns and so maintain interactional engagement. For example, a British mother observed by Snow (1977) structured the following interaction with her 3-month-old daughter, treating burps and minor movements as turns in conversation:

Ann:	(smiles)
Mother:	Oh, what a nice little smile! Yes, isn't that nice? There. There's a nice little smile.
Ann:	(burps)
Mother:	What a nice wind as well! Yes, that's better isn't it? Yes. Yes. Yes!
Ann:	(vocalizes)
Mother:	There's a nice noise. (p. 12)

The degree to which this kind of interaction is culturally specific becomes clear when it is compared with interactions in other cultural groups. For example, among the Kaluli of New Guinea (Schieffelin, 1990), mothers often talk for their infants, giving them appropriate lines in simulated interactions with others but do not talk to them in conversation-eliciting ways until they demonstrate the capacity to produce some comprehensible speech. Among the Samoans, children are also not legitimately full-fledged partners in discussions but are frequent recipients of directives (Ochs, 1988; see also Schieffelin & Ochs, 1986). Heath (1983) reported that in a working-class black community of the Carolina Piedmont, adults do not attribute meaning to infants' vocalizations or use child-directed speech to engage them, although LeVine et al. (1994) reported that mothers of the Gusii in Kenya prefer to keep their infants peaceful and contented, rather than stimulated through reciprocal interaction.

Caregivers other than mothers are no less effective or successful in engaging infants in turn-taking interactions of this type. However, such interactions do require attentiveness to an infant's state and signals and the ability to focus extended attention on a single infant at unpredictable times. In child care settings involving infants, opportunities for such focused, attentive interaction can be rare. Furthermore, the caregiver, who might be responsible for providing primary care for several infants, has the burden of engaging individually with children whose interactive rhythms and signals may be vastly different.

As children acquire their first words and growing control over grammar, their turn-taking skills continue to develop. By about 18 months of age, children respond reliably (although not unfailingly) to adult conversational turns that require a response, such as questions (Bloom, Rocissano, & Hood, 1976; McDonald & Pien, 1982). It is striking that young children demonstrate an understanding of the obligation to respond well in advance of knowing how to respond semantically. For example, young children often acquire either "yes" or "no" and use whichever form they have mastered to respond indifferently to all yes–no questions.

One mechanism for raising children's level of participation in conversational turn taking during the one-word speech period is to rely on well practiced formats or routines that reduce the child's burden to provide content for the interactions, while providing the child with models for interpersonal engagement. Within the context of home-based parent–child interaction, parents typically enact routines (e.g., rituals for greetings and departures, verbal games, telephone conversations, joint book reading) with young children well in advance of the child's ability to understand the content of the interaction or to participate equally (e.g., Ninio & Bruner, 1978; Ratner & Bruner, 1978). Within the context of child care, caregivers also enact and model routines that scaffold children's interactional and linguistic skills. Although some of these routines may duplicate those familiar from home, others may be particular to the interpersonal and educational features of child care (e.g., negotiating use of toys, singing games, group book reading and talk, mealtimes, birthdays).

Observations of young children in peer interaction reveal their motivation to engage in turn-taking interactions and their capacity to do so if the obligation to provide informative content is removed. Thus, young children often engage in "nonsense" conversations, using repetition and word play to provide the material for the turns they take (Eckerman & Didow, 1996; Keenan, 1977; Mueller, Blair, Krakow, Hegedus, & Cournoyer, 1977). These interactions show that the role of the adult is more crucial in providing substance for interactive turn taking than in regulating the exchange of turns, once children are a year old.

During this period of early language acquisition, different maternal styles have been identified along a continuum of effectiveness in establishing and maintaining conversational turn taking and overall engagement. In particular, two clusters of maternal conversational behaviors have been identified (McDonald & Pien, 1982). *Conversation-eliciting style* is characterized in part by frequent questions, brief conversational turns, maintenance of a mutually interesting topic, and infrequent use of directives and monologues; a *directive style* is characterized by frequent directives and monologues, infrequent questions, rapid topic changes by the mother, and a low level of topic maintenance within the pair. This distinction in conversational styles is an important one for caregivers in out-of-home care situations: Despite intentions to support children's verbal skills, caregivers frequently find themselves in a consistently directive mode of talk. This study also indicates a point of contact between children's acquisition of turn-taking skills and another crucial aspect of conversational capacity—the ability to maintain and extend a topic.

Topic Maintenance Topic maintenance is a more complex area of conversational skill. Piaget (1926) believed that young children were not capable of engaging in coherent conversational exchanges, sharing topics, and extending shared meaning, until cognitive decentering allowed them to take account of their conversational partner's concerns. Subsequent research has effectively disproved this thesis (Donaldson, 1979; Dunn, 1988, 1993). Starting at 16 months of age, toddlers have been shown to make thematically related (although nonverbal) responses to a play partner (Eckerman & Didow, 1989). Much of the toddlers' first interactional coordination consists of nonverbal and then verbal imitation, but their increasing use of verbal directives to regulate and direct shared activity is an early form of topic continuity (Eckerman & Didow, 1989, 1996). Mueller et al. (1977) found a substantial increase in the percentage of related utterances produced by 2-year-old boys, indicating growth in both speakers' and listeners' ability to sustain interaction and joint attention through talk. Here again, routines and scripts used by an adult interacting with a child provided the structure of semantic continuity in advance of the child's ability to create that continuity in his talk, and so scaffolded the child's developing ability to sustain a topic (Ninio & Bruner, 1978; Snow & Goldfield, 1982). Snow and Goldfield, for example, show how recurrent, shared book reading between a mother and her toddler provides the context and the structure for the child to sustain a topic over conversational turns and over separate book reading episodes.

Children's ability to maintain topic coherence and their sophistication in doing so shows development with age (Dorval & Eckerman, 1984; Howes, 1988; Wanska & Bedrosian, 1985). However, topic coherence also demonstrates the effects of a child's social environment on language development and the mutual influence of a child and the people with whom he or she interacts. In a longitudinal study of older toddlers' (19–36 months) developing adjacent and contingent talk, children's linguistic contingency occurred more often after adults' questions than after nonquestions, and the adults asked proportionately more questions as the children's responses became increasingly more contingent (Bloom, Rocissano, & Hood, 1976). Similarly, reciprocating engagement (i.e., talk that repeats and briefly expands on the children's previous utterance) produced more topic maintaining replies in 2-year-old children than nonreciprocating talk (Dunham & Dunham, 1996). Hoff-Ginsberg (1987) highlights the bi-directional influence in the conversations of a caregiver and a child and the role that a child can play in his or her own language-learning experience. Studying topic continuity in mother–toddler pairs, she observed that the frequency of mothers' topic continuity increased as the frequency of child-initiated topics increased. Furthermore, the toddlers' responsiveness to their mothers was greatest when the mothers continued the topic of the children's previous utterance, as compared with initiating a new topic or continuing a topic of their own.

Setting and activity also affect the development of topic maintenance. Different play contexts (Haden & Fivush, 1996) and different styles of motor play (Morris, McCabe, & Roberts, 1991) appear to affect mothers' conversational styles with their children, including topic maintenance features, and to show some effect on the children's topic maintenance. For instance, children showed more continuous discourse and maintained topic for a greater number of turns when playing with Legos instead of with a toy hospital or hospital props (Wanska, Pohlman, & Bedrosian, 1989). Three-and-a-half-year-olds also displayed notably more noninteractive pretend play when using high-structure toys (e.g., replica toys and dolls) than when using low-structure toys (e.g., pipe cleaners, blocks, paper cups) (McLoyd, 1983). This suggests that toys with inherent play scripts may reduce connected interaction for some groups of young children. Although these studies focus on preschoolers, their applicability to infants and toddlers is worth considering. Certain kinds of interactions develop around certain activities: play activity, play props (Howes & Rubenstein, 1978), and forms of caregiver talk that may be associated with particular settings or activities are part of the ecology that affects young children's development of topic maintenance skills.

An important analytic unit here is the *turnabout,* a turn that is both contingent and projective (i.e., that both refers to the previous utterance and establishes a direction for the next turn). French and Pak (1991), for example, found that older toddler girls produced equivalent amounts of turnabouts talking with a peer and with their mothers. With peers, however, they were more likely to produce unlinked turns or projective turns that were noncontingent than with their mothers; with their mothers they were more likely to produce contingent turns that were nonprojective. This result points to the tendency of mothers, more than peers, to scaffold young children's topic continuity through the use of questions. It also demonstrates the differing supports and challenges that more skilled and equally skilled conversational partners present: Although the adult's conversational skill enables greater contingency, the autonomy and persistence required to maintain joint attention with a peer pushed young children to find ways of extending topics. Thus, adult–child conversation may contribute more directly to the development of cohesion in extended discourse but peer–peer interaction may contribute more directly to the acquisition of repair techniques and interpersonal sensitivity, and to the development of conversational self-reliance.

It is worth noting that conversations between adults and young children do not require much verbal participation on the part of the child. Nonverbal gestures, actions, or even gaze direction can serve as topic nominating moves for the sensitive, attentive adult. But the conversational gesture must be directed to the child: Hoff-Ginsberg (1987) suggested that although caregivers' responses *to* children's nonverbal behavior support conversation, caregivers' utterances *about* children's nonverbal behavior are ineffective at creating conversation. Particularly in group care settings where two or more caregivers are present, caregivers should note that conversation among adults, even if it is about the children, does not support children's communicative growth.

Procedures for Expressing Communicative Intents Effectively   So far, we have talked about turn taking and topic maintenance as aspects of social participation—and indeed it is clear that social participation is a primary goal of much early communicative activity. However, it is also the case that children, from at least the age of 10–12 months, have specific communicative goals or intents and seek ways to express these intents comprehensibly. Children's earliest communications typically consist of showing an object, giving an object, or engaging in attention-attracting behavior while monitoring audience response. In other words, children are communicating complex messages gesturally before they have any words (Bates, Camaioni, & Volterra, 1975).

Children's developing capacity to express their own intents is characterized by an increasing frequency of communicative attempts as well as by increasingly conventional expressions (Snow et al., 1996). For example, 14-month-old children observed interacting with their mothers in a laboratory setting expressed an average of 4.37 communicative attempts per minute; at 20 months their communicative attempts increased to an average of 7.91 per minute; and at 32 months, 11.2 per minute. This difference emerged despite the fact that coders credited the children's gestural and vocal expressions, as well as verbal expressions, with communicative intent. Thus, although children do clearly express communicative intents before they have conventional language, the acquisition of conventional linguistic forms occurs together with a striking increase in attempts at communication.

Further analysis of this same corpus shows that any mother–child pair engaged in relatively few types of communicative exchanges; there was also considerable convergence across the entire group on a limited set of communicative activities (Pan, Imbens-Bailey, Winner, & Snow, 1996). When the children were 14 months old, for example, almost all the mother–child pairs engaged in episodes in which one partner directed the other's attention to a focal object, typically followed by episodes of shared attention to the object. Most pairs also engaged in some negotiation of activity (e.g., rolling a ball back and forth, scribbling on paper, playing Peekaboo) with talk designed to tell the partner what to do. Furthermore, most pairs displayed mutual knowledge of well established marking routines (e.g., saying "uh-oh" if something fell, "thank you" if the possession of an object was transferred). Because the types of communicative intents were limited, mothers could better interpret their children's often primitive expressions, and the children could better understand their mothers' intended communicative activity. Relatively rich interactions and seamless transitions could occur precisely because of the history of such interactions within specific mother–child pairs.

Varying Participant Structures   Of course, extended interaction with a single, highly responsive caregiver is infrequent in the lives of most children and may not even be optimal. Having a variety of conversational partners nudges children to express their intents more fully, less ambiguously, and in a way that takes the other person into account. In Western-style nuclear families, fathers and siblings, who may be less responsive or sensitive than mothers to young children's communicative intents, have been described as the "bridge" between highly attuned conversational partners and total strangers (Barton & Tomasello, 1994; Mannle, Barton, & Tomasello, 1992). In cultural contexts in which young children experience multiple caregivers, older siblings, child relatives, older peers, adult friends, and adult relatives may play this role (see, e.g., on rural Mexican families, LeVine, 1992; on African American families, Jackson, 1993; on the Efe of Zaire, Tronick, Morelli, & Ivey, 1992; on families in a North Indian village, Sharma & LeVine, 1998). In child care settings, adult caregivers and other children may serve a similar "bridging" function. Although particular forms of adult–child interaction, rather than peer interaction, provide the greatest support for children's language development in both home (Hart & Risley, 1995) and child care settings (McCartney, 1984), talk with adults and children of various ages may support different features of conversational competence (e.g., persistence, reformulations, topic initiation).

Children also respond differently to different kinds of conversational partners. Although interactions with adults may tend to be based on substantive content, interactions with peers may involve prelinguistic activity and, subsequently, language to define "being together." For example, Eckerman and Didow (1996) described 2-year-olds imitating each other's actions with objects as a step toward coordinating their activities, and Garvey and Hogan (1973) described lengthy "conversations" between pairs of previously acquainted 3¹/₂- to 5-year-olds that include a high proportion of vocal play and contentless imitation and elaboration. Peer conversational partners seem to impose a different set of communicative intents and open up different possibilities for communicative effectiveness. At the same time, the lack of conversational scaffolding from child partners may encourage a child's conversational initiative and sensitivity to cues (French & Pak, 1991; Hoff-Ginsberg & Krueger, 1991).

Consistent with our assumption that children's communicative behavior is not restricted by egocentricity, considerable evidence suggests that preschool-age children are capable of adjusting their talk for different audiences. Young children adjust their talk for younger children (e.g., Garvey & Hogan, 1973; Shatz & Gelman, 1973) and for peers with developmental delays (Guralnick & Paul-Brown, 1989). They reformulate their requests differently in answer to different maternal responses (Marcos & Chanu, 1992) and supply additional information when describing a peer or a new toy to an unfamiliar adult (Sachs, Donnelly, Smith, & Bookbinder, 1991). Children as young as 3 years old also take considerable responsibility in simplifying their own speech and teaching English to non-English speakers in group environments (Tabors, 1996) and can be easily trained to be even more effective in checking comprehension and initiating conversation with English-language learners (Hirschler, 1991). Thus, even very young children are clearly aware of the different needs of different audiences and can adjust their speech based on those differences. Again, it seems likely that experience with a wide variety of different interactive partners may help children acquire facility in both gauging and adjusting to audience needs. We would, therefore, expect children who have had high-quality group care experiences, in which there are frequent opportunities for effective communication with peers and with the adult caregivers, to display greater skill in communicative sensitivity and flexibility.

Vocabulary Development

Vocabulary development is of central interest in part because of its relation to later outcomes: It is strongly related to readiness for school entry

(Anderson & Freebody, 1981; Stahl & Fairbanks, 1986); it eases entry into reading; and it is the most reliable single predictor of such important school outcomes as reading scores. Vocabulary is also of interest because it is the aspect of language development where learning is evident across the entire age span. Because vocabulary acquisition is a cumulative process, children with large vocabularies when they begin school have typically started learning words early and learned as many as 900 by 30 months of age (Fenson et al., 1994). Vocabulary knowledge also encompasses not just developing a broad knowledge of words but also depth of knowledge about the nature of word forms and word meanings. This kind of word knowledge develops continuously during childhood. Furthermore, vocabulary knowledge both reflects a child's breadth of knowledge about the world and enhances opportunities to learn more about the world. It is impossible to separate vocabulary development from those aspects of cognitive development that relate to knowing things. This example indicates that, even with very young children, use of unusual vocabulary goes along with exposure to interesting and challenging bits of world knowledge:

> Mother: Who are you?
> Child: Fireman.
> Mother: Hello, fire chief. (dials telephone) Special *emergency* for the fire chief.
> Child: [Unintelligible words] *emergency.*
> Mother: You have a fire down 4th and Maple.
> Child: Oh.
> Mother: We need the fire engine right away.
> Child: OK. (Beals & Tabors, 1995, p. 67–68)

Young children have remarkable capacities to acquire new vocabulary rapidly and efficiently; the 15,000-word vocabulary of the middle-class first grader implies the child has acquired 12–15 new words a day from the age of 3 years old to the time of school entry. Bilingual children, of course, acquire even more words (though perhaps not quite twice as many) as monolinguals (Pearson, Fernandez, & Oller, 1993). Vocabulary development is, however, exquisitely sensitive to the amount and conditions of input. As such, understanding the social influences on vocabulary development at home and in child care settings is tremendously important. However, as in the other domains of language development we are examining, more is known about the social influences in home than in child care, preschool, or family child care environments.

Social Influences on Vocabulary Development The range of reported child vocabulary sizes reflects enormous individual and social class differences (Hart & Risley, 1995). Smaller vocabularies are typically found among children from families with a lower socioeconomic status (Arriaga, Fenson, Cronan, & Pethick, 1998), in which parents have less education, less engagement in high-level literacy activities, and fewer economic resources; and in which there is less talk overall and less child-directed talk in particular (Hart & Risley, 1995; Hoff-Ginsberg & Tardif, 1995).

The best single predictor of a young child's vocabulary, during the period of early language acquisition when total vocabulary ranges up to 600 words, is density of maternal speech—simply, how many words the child hears during a typical hour (Huttenlocher, Haight, Bryk, Seltzer, & Lyons, 1991). The amount of talk addressed to infants and toddlers shows wide variation across families of different educational, professional, and economic attainment. Children in two-parent, middle-class families may hear up to three times as much talk as that heard by children in relatively isolated, welfare-dependent, single-parent families (Hart & Risley, 1995; Hoff-Ginsberg & Tardiff, 1995); the children's own vocabulary scores reflect this disparity (Hart & Risley, 1995). This difference in talk encompasses not only the total amount of talk experienced by the young child but also the kinds of talk experienced. Children from families of higher socioeconomic status experience greater diversity and richness in word use, in sentence structure, in discourse functions, and in the informational content of talk than children from families of low socioeconomic status.

Conversational Contexts for Vocabulary Acquisition In addition to sheer quantity of talk, adults' contingent responses to the child's focus of attention support early vocabulary acquisition for children up to about age 3. For example, caregivers can foster infants' early lexical learning by following, rather than leading or diverting, the children's focus of attention (Dunham, Dunham, & Curwin, 1993). Nouns are most easily learned if mothers name objects that children are looking at or manipulating (Tomasello & Todd, 1983), and verbs are best learned if mothers name the action that is about to happen (Tomasello & Kruger, 1992). The child whose parents consistently change the topic of talk away from the child's focus, issue directives, or fail to respond to the child's topics in general will tend to talk later and less complexly than the child whose parents follow up on the child's utterances with topic-related responses, extend the child's topics over several conversational turns, and avoid initiating new topics when the child is focused on something of interest (see Snow, 1989, for a review). Such careful tuning of input implies monitoring the child's attention and activity, and willingness to be responsive to the child's interest.

Although the focus of vocabulary development during the infant/toddler period is primarily on a few thousand highly frequent words, vocabulary development beyond those basic words builds on earlier accomplishments. Relatively sophisticated vocabulary is likely to be introduced through books; thus, families who use book reading as a context for interaction with their children may well be promoting sophisticated vocabulary acquisition selectively. Families who use sophisticated vocabulary during storytelling or discussions of how things work, when children are 3 and 4 years of age, have children with higher vocabulary scores (Beals & Tabors, 1995); similar mechanisms are probably at work with younger children as well, as in the following example of Adam looking at a book with his mother:

> Adam: What is dat one?
> Mother: That's a lizard.
> Adam: What's a lizard?
> Mother: He's a little animal who lives outside. (Bodin & Snow, 1994, p. 89)

The type of talk in which a family engages may be critical in generating contexts in which more sophisticated vocabulary can be encountered and in which enough contextual support is available to help the child learn the meaning of the unfamiliar word. Similarly, routine aspects of play and care in a child care environment can be contexts of vocabulary development. This research highlights the fact that caregivers' use of interesting vocabulary in both casual conversation and in more routinized activities like book reading can provide both exposure to interesting words and ideas and contextual support for learning them.

Extended Discourse

Extended discourse refers to stretches of talk in which organization extends over utterance or sentence boundaries—narratives, explanations, arguments, sermons, and other such socially recognized genres of talk. A discussion of extended discourse skills in the context of infant/toddler language development would seem to presume enormous and unrealistic precocity on the part of the children. However, even young toddlers begin to construct discourse structures that extend over a few utterances or turns at talk, and these emerge overwhelmingly from conversation (e.g., Ninio & Snow 1996; Ochs & Schieffelin, 1983). The quality and characteristics of the conversational environment that young children are part of and participate in is crucial to their growing ability to sustain and expand meaning in more, and more sophisticated, linguistic structures. Furthermore, this ability to create oral extended discourse is associated with a child's developing ability to comprehend and to manipulate decontextualized language—that is, language that refers to events, objects, mental states, or narratives for which little or no support is available in the immediate context and for which the speaker must create or provide contextualizing information, as required, to communicate effectively with a partner.

Like vocabulary, extended discourse skills relate to children's school achievement. In fact, mother–child co-construction of past event narratives in conversation is a stronger predictor of preschoolers' later print and semantic skills than book-reading activity (Reese, 1995). The foundation of these skills in early childhood therefore deserves attention. Findings from the Home-School Study of Language and Literacy Development (Dickinson & Tabors, 1999; Snow, 1991) suggest several aspects of language interaction during the preschool period that support young children's extended discourse skills. Such interactions included talk during book reading that includes reaction, prediction, and inference; the use of narratives and explanations during mealtimes; the use of sophisticated vocabulary; and the talk of pretend play.

Adult Support of the Development of Extended Discourse
We know less about the factors influencing the development of extended discourse skills than about the sources of vocabulary knowledge; however, it seems likely that experience hearing and participating in the production of extended discourse is a major determinant of skill in this area. Among the research supporting this conclusion, we note that Beals and De Temple (1993) found that exposure to narrative and explanation at the dinner table is related to children's narrative production; similarly, Aukrust and Snow (1998) found that Norwegian children, exposed at the dinner table to more stories and fewer explanations than American children, both requested and told more stories, while American children reflected their parents' preferences in both giving and requesting more explanations. Further, adult scaffolding of storytelling through questions and prompts shapes older toddlers' developing skill in telling past-event narratives (Peterson & McCabe, 1994).

Although young children experience and participate in the various forms of extended discourse mentioned above, research in this area has focused largely on narrative genres. One body of research seeks the effects of differences within social groups on children's narrative skills, examining both children's solo performances and dialogic co-construction of narrative between a child and an adult. In this area, as in other areas of language development that we have surveyed, the child's social environment is a prime influence on the child's developing skills. McCabe and Peterson (1991), studying parents' past-event conversation with their toddlers, noted that none of the children were "natural storytellers"; rather, the children's varying skill was associated with parents' different styles of interacting with them and eliciting stories from them. Topic-extending utterances supported the children's construction of narrative, while an increase in parents' clarifying questions was associated with increased evaluation, orientation, and added narrative material from the children (see Fivush, 1991). Reese and Fivush (1993) noted that parents with daughters talked more and provided more elaboration through questions, statements, and evaluative comments when reminiscing about past events than parents of sons. Both sons and daughters displayed comparable language skills; however, the daughters participated in the past-event talk more than the sons and seemed to contribute more reminiscences.

The effect of social influences and context is evident also in young children's monologic and co-constructed narratives about identity and self. Miller, Mintz, Hoogstra, Fung, and Potts's (1992) and Mintz's (1995) studies of the social comparisons embedded in 2.6- and 5-year-olds' conversational narratives of past experience, and Snow's (1990) discussion of young children's narratives about memories both point to children's active participation in the construction of extended discourse and to the importance that such discourse holds for the understanding of self and other. This excerpt of a conversation between a mother and her almost 2.6-year-old child shows how the adult's questions structure the child's recounting and understanding of the event:

Mother:	We put your ice skates on.
Child:	Ice skates on.
Mother:	And we went ice-skating.
Child:	Ice-skating.
Mother:	'Member ice-skating?
Child:	'Member ice-skating?
Mother:	Was it fun to go ice-skating?
Child:	Fun...slip.
Mother:	You slipped, yes.
Child:	Fell down.
Mother:	You fell down and bumped your head.
Child:	Head hurt.
Mother:	It hurt, didn't it? But you were very brave.
Child:	Brave.
Mother:	You didn't cry very long.
Child:	Cry very long.
Mother:	Nooo.
Child:	Noo.

Mother: Didn't cry very long. And then we came home in
          the car. (Snow, 1990, p. 229–230)

In out-of-home care settings, the opportunities to engage in such inter-actions may be few. However, such joint constructions of events and sto-ries help to extend children's control of both the language and structures of extended discourse.

Pretend Play as a Context for Practicing Extended Dis-course   Pretend play offers particularly fertile ground for the devel-opment of extended discourse forms. Both in order to, and as a result of, sustaining meaning over many utterances, the language of pretend play tends to be more complex and sophisticated than the language of non-pretend (Garvey & Kramer, 1989). Young children's pretend-play talk also seems to be related to later school performance. Metacognitive and symbolizing features of preschoolers' pretend-play talk appear to be predictive of emergent reading and writing skills (Pellegrini & Galda, 1993), and 3-year-olds' opportunities for pretend play in preschool class-rooms are related to their language and preliteracy skills at 5 years of age (Dickinson & Smith, 1991). Studies on mothers' pretend interactions with their young children have findings similar to those we have seen in other domains: Reciprocal interaction with young children, following the child's lead, as well as contingent responses including prompts and elab-orations, support the development of pretend play and the growth of extended discourse within pretend-play talk (Fiese, 1990; Haight & Miller, 1993). Because pretend play is often random and spontaneous, and may be shared primarily with peers, caregivers may not be aware of its potential as a context for language development nor of how they can support it effectively. Here, a preschool teacher promotes extended discourse skills by discussing the pretend play of two boys; the boys are pretending that they have put fierce sharks in a cage where "they get no spinach, no drink, no nothing":

Teacher: Do you think sharks miss eating spinach?
First child: Sharks think they could get out with spinach.
Teacher: You must be very brave and daring men to go
           down there and take all these sharks back to
           this special place.
First child: We're protecting them.
Teacher: Do you have to wear special suits? What kind
           of suits do you wear in the water?
Second child: I wear climbing.
Teacher: Climbing suit?
Second child: Yeah.

> Teacher: What do you wear?
> First child: A shark suit.
> Teacher: Those things on your back, are those oxygen
>   tanks? To help you breathe under water?
> Second child: They can breathe under water.
> Teacher: Wow. That's a special trick to learn how to do.
>   (Snow, 1991)

Cultural Differences in Extended Discourse   Discourse genres can vary in subtle but significant ways across different ethnolinguistic groups in their internal organization, in the rules defining what information to present and which aspects to elaborate, and in the social meaning and purpose of narration as a discourse activity. Caregivers working with culturally diverse groups of children must be informed about these differences. Cultural differences in styles of extended discourse are evident as soon as children produce extended discourse—at the age of 2 or 3 (Heath, 1983). Minami and McCabe (1995), for instance, show that the narrative styles of Japanese and North American preschoolers develop in culturally approved styles, shaped by mothers' conversational elicitations. Michaels' (1981, 1991) work on sharing time in first grade provides a detailed description of the conflict resulting when young African American children, socialized to an elaborated, episodic, topic-linked style of narrative, confront the mainstream factual, topic-centered style of discourse preferred by European American teachers. Sperry and Sperry's (1995, 1996) discussion of African American toddlers' production of fictional versus past-event narratives points to a cultural value for fictionalizing experience and to culturally approved ways of defining the self. We note, too, that the heavy focus on narrative in the research on young children's extended discourse may obscure young children's talents, tendencies, and accomplishments in other discourse forms. Some children prefer nonnarrative genres such as explanation or the exposition of information; although this preference has so far been documented primarily for older children (Caswell & Duke, 1998; Hicks, 1996; Pappas, 1993), it clearly exists for very young children also. Social, cultural, familial, and individual differences in style of extended discourse production are enormous; children may be judged as showing inadequate extended discourse skill because the rules they follow differ from those of the caregiver or the dominant culture.

Impact of Early Childhood Education and Care Settings

In addition to characteristics of the child care settings, various background features of the children themselves are associated with infant and toddler language development in out-of-home care; a child's age when entering care, attachment to the caregivers, and family character-istics are a few of the many variables. Here, however, the focus is on the effects of child care settings. Reviewing some of the literature on the effects of these settings, we found a *de facto* distinction between care and education. We challenge that dichotomy: For young children, sensitive care and stimulating cognitive environments should both be features of any environment in which they find themselves. Because care and cog-nitive stimulation for young children involve opportunities for play, for stimulating and nurturing social interaction, for effective communica-tion, and for establishing meaningful relationships rather than formal, explicit instruction, there is no principled basis for distinguishing care from education. We do not suggest that an excellent care setting for an 18-month-old is indistinguishable from a setting for a 4-year-old. Yet, both of these children need settings in which age-appropriate forms of nurturing, stimulation, play, relationships, and rich talk are available. Therefore, in the following section, we draw upon literature and research regarding infants, toddlers, and preschoolers in a variety of settings to establish that the overall quality of the care environment, including the language environment, matters crucially to children's developing lan-guage competence.

The support given to children's developing language in different child care settings varies considerably. For instance, Melhuish, Money, Martin, and Lloyd (1990) found notable differences in British 18-month-olds' interactional experiences both within and across four child care settings: at home, in the care of relatives, with "childminders" (i.e., fam-ily child care homes), and in child care centers. For this group of children, home interactions showed, on average, the greatest amount of respon-siveness, joint attention, communication from adult to child, and joint play. Center-based care showed, on average, the lowest frequencies of verbal interaction and responsiveness, with relative care and family child care located between the two. Although the children in all four settings showed no significant differences in cognitive development or in single word production, the children in the center-based care group were less likely to have a high number of different word combinations; this out-come was directly attributable to the caregivers' responsiveness to the child and to total language addressed to the child (Melhuish et al., 1990).

Early Childhood Classrooms as Language Environments

Studies that examine the quality of preschools use broad gauge tools that include language and literacy as only one small portion of the assess-ment. Such studies have found that it is precisely on measures of the language environment that care settings are likely to be most inadequate. When assessing the quality of early childhood care environments, research has consistently found that structural determinants of quality—in particular, small group size, low child–adult ratio, and higher levels of teacher education—influence the language environment of the setting by affecting the social and interactional environment (Cost, Quality, and Child Outcomes Study Team, 1995; Hayes, Palmer, & Zaslow, 1990). However, it is also crucial to assess the interactional and language-use environment—aspects of process quality—to understand how these caregiving environments affect young children's early language development. Variables of process quality, for example, point to the importance in child care of kinds of talk that have been identified as affecting young children's language development in the home: a sufficient quantity of language that is directed to the child and in which the child participates; conversational partners who are responsive and using contingent questions that elicit and foster further talk; and talk that engages the child through exchange of information, descriptive and increasingly decontextualized language, and exposure to challenging vocabulary. Overwhelmingly, research findings show that overall high-quality care and engaged, responsive interactions with caregivers for infants and toddlers lead to better language performance (Whitebook, Howes, & Phillips, 1989; NICHD, 1997, 1999). That such language can be available in child care settings is confirmed by Clarke-Stewart's (1984) study of child care in Chicago. Measuring the social and cognitive skills of 2- to 3-year-old children across six different child care settings, she found that the children in center-based care were more advanced in verbal ability than those in home-based care, including care from parents and family child care.

Although the body of research on the quality of infant/toddler care settings as language environments is growing quickly, considerably more research has focused on the quality of preschools. Some of the findings concerning preschool classrooms are instructive here on a couple of dimensions. First, care settings for younger children have been found to be generally poorer quality than those for children older than 3 years of age (Cost, Quality, and Child Outcomes Study Team, 1995), so knowing what is going on in preschools may set an upper limit on the quality likely to be encountered in infant/toddler care settings. Second, the difficulty of establishing a rich and stimulating language environment for infants and toddlers seems to be greater than that for older children; again, the quality observed in preschool may suggest the likelihood of finding quality language environments in infant/toddler care settings.

Preschool programs, particularly those serving poor children, have shown low ratings on aspects of quality related to the language environment. A study of North Carolina Public Preschools (Bryant, Peisner-Feinberg, & Clifford, 1993), for example, found lower ratings on the

Language and Reasoning Subscale of the Early Childhood Environment Rating Scale (ECERS; Harms & Clifford 1986) than for other scales. Particularly low scored items on the nonlanguage scales included dramatic play (a context for rich language use), and cultural awareness. Moreover, the Language and Reasoning Subscale showed the lowest score across 32 Head Start classrooms studied (Bryant, Lau, Burchinal, & Sparling, 1994). Studies have shown that children's exposure to cognitively challenging talk, for example, is associated with the amount of time they interact with teachers (McCartney, 1984; Smith & Dickinson, 1994). Given the importance of adult–child interaction to children's developing language skills, it is disturbing that in some centers and preschools any individual child typically interacts rather little with a teacher and receives little or no individualized attention (Kontos & Wilcox-Herzog, 1997; Layzer, Goodson, & Moss, 1993; Wilcox-Herzog & Kontos, 1996).

Studies reporting on the quality of programs that serve infants and toddlers show similarly somber results. The National Child Care Staffing Study (Whitebook et al., 1989), for example, found two thirds of the centers studied to be just above "minimally adequate," with infant/toddler rooms receiving the lowest ratings. Characteristics of the low scoring centers were big groups, too many children per teacher, and a low rating on caregiver–child interactions. The Cost, Quality, and Child Outcomes Study Team (1995) similarly found that only one of twelve infant/toddler rooms studied provided high-quality care. Both studies further confirmed the impact of low-quality care on young children's language. Young children attending low-quality centers with more staff turnover had lower scores on tests of vocabulary (Whitebook et al., 1989), and children in lower quality centers, with fewer and less warm relationships with teachers, had less advanced language (Cost, Quality, and Child Outcomes Study Team, 1995). Conversely, a higher quality care environment showed a positive effect on young children's language (NICHD, 1997, 1999). Teacher training and group size had an effect on adults' social and verbal interactions with children, while teachers' stability affected the quality of classroom interactions and relationships (studies cited in Hayes, Palmer, & Zaslow, 1990; Howes & Hamilton, 1993). Lower child–adult ratios were associated with more gestural and vocal imitations, and more vocalizations from infants overall, and more responsive teacher interactions are associated with more advanced language performance from children (Whitebook et al.,1989; NICHD, 1997, 1999).

Although center-based care is becoming more common for infants and toddlers, family child care seems to be chosen more frequently for this age group (Galinsky, Howes, Kontos, & Shinn, 1994; Howes & Hamilton, 1993); the language environment in these settings is therefore of particular interest. However, the weight of research suggests that family child care is at least more variable in quality than center-based care (Goelman & Pence, 1987) and may be overall of lower quality (studies cited in Howes & Hamilton, 1993), with an attendant effect on the language environment. For instance, both licensed and unlicensed family child cares have shown lower mean ratings on every subscale of the ECERS and the Day Care Home Environmental Ratings Scale (Harms, Clifford, & Padan, 1983) than child care centers; characteristics of these care settings are low frequencies of verbal exchanges (indicated by the frequency of solitary play and television watching) and of information based interactions between caregivers and children, with unlicensed homes showing the lowest frequencies (Clarke-Stuart, 1987; Goelman & Pence, 1987). Furthermore, large groups in home care have been associated with fewer positive interactions (Howes, 1983) and less advanced development (Clarke-Stewart, 1991). Interestingly, quality in home-based care appears to be a stronger predictor of child language development than quality in centers (Goelman & Pence, 1987). And, not surprisingly, overall quality as measured by the Family Day Care Ratings Scale (Harms & Clifford, 1989) was associated with better receptive language in older toddlers and preschoolers, while a greater amount of high-level teacher interaction with children was associated with more language-based interactions (Kontos, 1994; see also NICHD, 1997, 1999). The occurrence of responsive, reciprocating, contingent verbal interactions between caregivers and children in these settings varies widely; the different social ecologies in these settings also clearly affect the communicative environment. For example, Goelman (1986) found a significantly greater amount of caregiver–child talk in mixed-age child care homes than in same-age homes, and a greater amount of child–child talk in same-age homes than in mixed-age homes.

Lessons from Infant/Toddler Intervention Programs

Studies have also addressed the language environments needed by children who are likely to develop inadequate language skills because of social or medical risk. These programs offer lessons about what excellent early childhood environments may look like. For very young children in demographically identified risk groups, such intervention programs have in general consisted simply of providing excellent care environments, rather than targeted instruction or specific "therapies." Thus, successful intervention programs for infants and toddlers offer useful lessons about practices in early child care environments that enhance language and literacy development.

The Abecedarian Project (Campbell & Ramey, 1994, 1995; Ramey, Bryant & Suarez, 1985) served children from low-income, single-parent families, starting in early infancy, in a group care setting. It combined high-intensity, high-quality care with a wide range of additional services to families and found positive effects that extended into the school years. Randomized trial assessments of the effect of the center care component in programs like CARE (Roberts et al., 1989; Wasik, Ramey, Bryant, & Sparling, 1990), the Infant Health and Development Program (IHDP, 1990; Brooks-Gunn, McCormick, Shapiro, Bernasich, & Black, 1994), the Comprehensive Child Development Program (St. Pierre & Lopez, 1994), and Even Start (St. Pierre, Swartz, Murray, Deck, & Nicke, 1993) have isolated the enhanced value of high-quality classroom-based experiences to children of poverty, with bigger effects from more intensive and better quality programs and evidence for positive effects on language development in particular. In a study of infants primarily from low-income families, Burchinal, Roberts, Nabors, and Bryant (1996) found that higher quality infant care has an effect on children's cognitive and communicative skills, even in the children's first year. This study found that infants in rooms with better educated teachers showed more advanced expressive language, and infants in rooms with better adult–child ratios showed higher levels of receptive language and communicative skill. More modest enhancements of the quality of classroom experiences also show positive effects on children's language development and preliteracy skills (Whitehurst, Epstein, Angell, Crone, & Fischel, 1994). A comprehensive review of early childhood programs by Barnett (1995) concluded that early childhood programs can produce large effects on IQ scores during the early childhood years and sizable persistent effects on achievement, grade retention, special education, high school graduation, and socialization.

CONCLUSION

We have reviewed research on language development in three specific domains, focusing on aspects of social interaction, and with some attention to the effect that different care environments might have on very young children's language learning. This research highlights the role of adult caregivers in children's language development. Although incomplete on many important points, it offers considerable information to caregivers in out-of-home care settings about how they may strengthen the language aspects of their caregiving environments. For example, caregivers must first know that encouraging children's developing conversational skill is important because most other aspects of language development are based in shared talk. They must also be aware that children's conversational abilities emerge early. Children acquire skills of coordinated action by the time they are toddlers, are responsive to each other, and can fine-tune speech to listeners. Even very young children can develop substantive relationships through talk. It is critical that care-givers understand that conversational skill can be fostered by engaging with children in talk during play and routine aspects of caregiving, by fol-lowing the children's focus of attention and interest, and by making con-tingent responses to children's utterances.

Another strategy for strengthening language use is to make use of formats and schemas in both play and ritualized classroom interactions with young children: Formats and schemas give a structure to young chil-dren's knowledge and support their ability to participate in various kinds of language-based interactions in advance of their ability to contribute meaningful content. Caregivers may follow up on schemas introduced by parents (e.g., social routines or book reading) and introduce some that are not familiar from home, such as schemas that are related to group care and that anticipate later school routines (e.g., group participation in activities, sharing a caregiver's attention, getting a caregiver's attention in a useful way, and making a request or need known in a group).

Caregivers must also be aware that a language-rich environment means both talking about things that are grounded in the immediate context and providing models for decontextualized talk, such as fan-tasy, speculations, explorations, explanations, definitions, and talk about feelings, beliefs, and other mental states.

It is important for caregivers to recognize the importance of early vocabulary development to children's later literacy and to be aware that differences in children's vocabulary emerge early and persist in child-hood if no intervention is available. Caregivers should thus be aware of factors in young children's vocabulary development: the amount of lan-guage input children receive, their own adult responsiveness to a child's language, and children's exposure to sophisticated vocabulary in socially supported settings.

Sensitivity to differences in children's developing extended-discourse skills is also important. There are early emerging and persist-ent differences in children's extended discourse capacities. These differences can be observed in the ease of production of extended dis-course, coherence of extended discourse, and flexibility in genre selec-tion as well as in culturally specific rules for the organization of extended discourse. These differences can typically be traced back to differences in participation in extended discourse within multiparty conversations.

It is important to provide contexts for the emergence of extended discourse in the care setting, including book reading, pretend play, extended discussions about personal experiences, storytelling, discus-sions involving inference about causes, motives, feelings, and outcomes of events. Through their engagement with adult speakers, young chil-dren learn to control and expand on larger discourse forms.

Finally, concerning young children's bilingualism or multilingualism, caregivers should be aware that knowledge of more than one language is, for many young children, a fact of life; it is also a cognitive strength. If caregivers do not speak the same language as the children in their care, they should encourage young children's maintenance of their home language while helping them to develop the linguistic skills needed for negotiating the caregiving environment comfortably.

Caregivers must also become more educated about cultural differences in the style, the form, and the content of talk. This kind of information will help caregivers to appreciate the way language is used in the children's homes, to understand the patterns of language development shown by the children they teach, and to determine better how they might extend individual children's language skills.

We conclude with a word about language in developmentally appropriate practice. We believe strongly that very young children's language development should be promoted in child care settings because of its inherent importance. In their joint statement *Learning to Read and Write: Developmentally Appropriate Practice for Young Children* (1998), the National Association for the Education of Young Children (NAEYC) and the International Reading Association set forth their position that language development is important in its own right, that literacy development is rooted in young children's experience with oral and written language, and that interactions with interested, engaged caregivers are crucial to children's language growth. We heartily support this statement because it points to creating child care environments that combine nurturing, responsive, child-centered caregiving with explicit attention to linguistic enrichment and cognitive challenge. A caregiving environment with such an intentional approach to language is of particular importance for children from homes where low parental education and low literacy levels are associated with little preparation for school entry. It is, however, vitally important for all children in out-of-home care.

REFERENCES

Anderson, R., & Freebody, P. (1981). Vocabulary knowledge. In J. Guthrie (Ed.), *Comprehension and teaching: Research reviews* (pp. 77–117). Newark, DE: International Reading Association.

Arriaga, R.I., Fenson, L., Cronan, T., & Pethick, S.J. (1998). Scores on the MacArthur Communicative Development Inventory of children from low and middle income families. *Applied Psycholinguistics, 19,* 209–223.

Aukrust, V.G., & Snow, C.E. (1998). Narratives and explanations in Norwegian and American mealtime conversations. *Language and Society, 27,* 221–246.

Barnett, W.S. (1995). Long-term effects of early childhood programs on cognitive and school outcomes. *The Future of Children, 5,* 29–50.

Barton, M., & Tomasello, M. (1994). The rest of the family: The role of fathers and siblings. In C. Halloway & B. Richards (Eds.), *Input and interaction in language acquisition* (pp. 109–134). New York: Cambridge University Press.

Bates, E., Camaioni, L., & Volterra, V. (1975). The acquisition of performatives prior to speech. *Merrill-Palmer Quarterly, 21*, 205–226.

Beals, D.E., & De Temple, J. (1993). Home contributions to early language and literacy development. In D. Leu & C. Kinzer (Eds.), *Examining central issues in literacy research, theory and practice* (pp. 207–215). National Reading Conference.

Beals, D.E., & Tabors, P.O. (1995). Arboretum, bureaucratic, and carbohydrates: Preschoolers' exposure to rare vocabulary at home. *First Language, 15*(1) 57–76.

Bernstein Ratner, N. (1993). Interactive influence on phonological behavior: A case study. *Journal of Child Language, 20*(1), 191–197.

Bloom, K., Russell, A., & Wassenberg, K. (1987). Turn-taking affects the quality of infant vocalizations. *Journal of Child Language, 14*(2), 211–227

Bloom, L. (1993). *The transition from infancy to language.* New York: Cambridge University Press.

Bloom, L., Rocissano, L., & Hood, L. (1976). Adult–child discourse: Developmental interaction between information processing and linguistic knowledge. *Cognitive Psychology, 8*, 521–552.

Bodin, L. & Snow, C.E. (1994). What kind of birdie is this? Learning to use subordinates. In J.L. Soklov & C.E. Snow (Eds.), *Handbook of research in language development using CHILDES* (p. 89). Mahwah, NJ: Lawrence Erlbaum Associates.

Brooks-Gunn, J., McCormick, M.C., Shapiro, S., Bernasich, A., & Black, G.W. (1994). The effects of early education intervention on maternal employment, public assistance, and health insurance: The Infant Health and Development Program. *American Journal of Public Health, 84*, 924–930.

Bruner, J.S. (1983). *Child's talk: Learning to use language.* New York: Norton.

Bruner, J.S. (1995). Introduction. In C. Moore & P. Dunham (Eds.), *Joint attentions: Its origins and role in development* (pp. 1–14). Mahwah, NJ: Lawrence Erlbaum Associates.

Bryant, D.M., Lau, M., Burchinal, L.B., & Sparling, J.J. (1994). Family and classroom correlates of Head Start children's developmental outcomes. *Early Childhood Research Quarterly, 9*, 289–309.

Bryant, D.M., Peisner-Feinberg, E.S., & Clifford, R.M. (1993). *Evaluation of public preschool programs in North Carolina: Executive summary.* Chapel Hill, NC: Frank Porter Graham Child Development Center.

Burchinal, M.R., Roberts, J.E., Nabors, L.A., & Bryant, D.M. (1996). Quality of center child care and infant cognitive and language development. *Child Development, 67*, 606–620.

Campbell, F.A., & Ramey, C.T. (1994). Effects of early intervention on intellectual and academic achievement: A follow-up study from low-income families. *Child Development, 65*, 684–698.

Campbell, F.A., & Ramey, C.T. (1995). Cognitive and school outcomes for high-risk African-American students at middle adolescence: Positive effects of early intervention. *American Educational Research Journal, 32*, 743–772.

Caswell, L., & Duke, N. (1998). Non-narrative as a catalyst for literacy development. *Language Arts, 75* (2), 108–117.

Clarke-Stewart, K.A. (1984). Day care: A new context for research and development. In M. Perlmutter (Ed.), *The Minnesota symposium on child psychology, 17* (pp. 61–100). Mahwah, NJ: Lawrence Erlbaum Associates.

Clarke-Stewart, K.A. (1991). A home is not a school: The effects of child care on children's development. *Journal of Social Issues, 47*(2), 105–123.

Clarke-Stewart, K.A. (1987). In search of consistencies in child care research. In D. Phillips (Ed.), *Quality in child care: What does research tell us? Research Monograph of the National Association for the Education of Young Children* (Vol. 1, pp. 21–41). Washington, DC: National Association for the Education of Young Children.

Cost, Quality, and Child Outcomes Study Team (1995). *Cost, quality and child outcomes in child care centers: Technical report, public report and executive summary.* [ERIC Document No. 386 297]. Denver: University of Colorado at Denver, Economics Department.

De Houwer, A. (1995). Bilingual language acquisition. In B.P. Fletcher & B. MacWhinney (Eds.), *The handbook of child language* (pp. 219–250). Oxford, England: Blackwell Scientific Publishers.

Dickinson, D.K., & Smith, M.W. (1991). Preschool talk: Patterns of teacher–child interaction in early childhood classrooms. *Journal of Research in Childhood Education, 6,* 20–29.

Dickinson, D.K., & Tabors, P.O. (Eds.). (2001). *Preparing for literacy at home and school: The critical role of language development in the preschool years.* Manuscript submitted for publication. Baltimore: Paul H. Brookes Publishing Co.

Donaldson, M. (1979). *Children's minds.* New York: Norton.

Dorval, B., & Eckerman, C. (1984). Development trends in the quality of conversation achieved by small groups of acquainted peers. *Monograph of the Society for Research in Child Development, 49*(2).

Dunham, P., & Dunham, F. (1996). The semantically reciprocating robot: Adult influence on children's early conversational skills. *Social Development, 5,* 261–274.

Dunham P., Dunham F., & Curwin A. (1993). Joint attentional state and lexical acquisition at 18 months. *Developmental Psychology, 29*(5), 827–831.

Dunn, J. (1988). *The beginnings of social understanding.* Newbury Park: Sage Publications.

Dunn, J. (1993). *Young children's close relationships: Beyond attachment.* Individual Differences and Development Series (Vol. 4.). Newbury Park: Sage Publications.

Eckerman, C., & Didow, S. (1989). Toddlers' social coordinations: Changing responses to another's invitation to play. *Developmental Psychology, 25,* 794–804.

Eckerman, C., & Didow, S. (1996). Non-verbal imitation and toddler's mastery of verbal means of achieving coordinated action. *Developmental Psychology, 32,* 141–152.

Fenson, L., Dale, P.S., Reznick, J.S., Bates, E., Thal, D., & Pethick, S.J. (1994). Variability in early communicative development. *Monographs of the Society for Research in Child Development, 59*(5).

Fiese, B. (1990). Playful relationships: A contextual analysis of mother–toddler interaction and symbolic play. *Child Development, 61,* 1648–1656.

Fivush, R. (1991). The social construction of personal narratives. *Merrill-Palmer Quarterly, 37*(1), 59–81.

French, L., & Pak, M.K. (1991, April). *Mothers and peers as conversational partners: Quality and quantity of talk.* [ERIC Document #337 296]. Paper presented at the biennial meeting of the Society for Research in Child Development, Seattle, WA.

Galinsky, E., Howes, C., Kontos, S., & Shinn, M. (1994). *The study of children in family child care and relative care.* New York: Families and Work Institute.

Garvey, C., & Hogan, R. (1973). Social speech and social interaction: Egocentrism revisited. *Child Development, 44,* 562–568.

Garvey, C., & Kramer, T. (1989). The language of social pretend play. *Developmental Review, 9,* 364–382.

Goelman, H. (1986). The language environments of family day care. *Advances in Early Education and Day Care, 4,* 153–179.

Goelman, H., & Pence, A. (1987). Effects of child care, family, and individual characteristics on children's language development: The Victoria Day Care research project. In D. Phillips (Ed.), *Quality in child care: What does research tell us? Research Monograph of the National Association for the Education of Young Children* (Vol. 1., pp. 89–104). Washington, DC: National Association for the Education of Young Children.

Guralnick, M., & Paul-Brown, D. (1989). Peer related communicative competence. *Journal of Speech and Hearing Research, 32,* 930–943.

Haden, C.A., & Fivush, R. (1996). Contextual variation in maternal conversational styles. *Merrill-Palmer Quarterly, 42*(2), 200–227.

Haight, W., & Miller, P. (1993). *Pretending at home: Development in sociocultural context.* Albany: State University of New York Press.

Harms, T., & Clifford, R.M. (1986). *Early childhood environmental rating scale.* New York: Teacher's College Press.

Harms, T., & Clifford, R.M. (1989). *The family day care rating scale.* New York: Teachers College Press.

Harms, T., Clifford, R., & Padan, E. (1983). *The day care home environmental rating scale.* Chapel Hill, NC: Frank Porter Graham Child Development Center.

Hart, B., & Risley, T.R. (1995). *Meaningful differences in the everyday experience of young American children.* Baltimore: Paul H. Brookes Publishing Co.

Hayes, C.D., Palmer, J., & Zaslow, M.J. (1990). *Who cares for America's children? Child care policy for the 1990's.* Washington, DC: National Academy Press.

Heath, S.B. (1983). *Ways with words: Language, life, and work in communities and classrooms.* New York: Cambridge University Press.

Hicks, D. (1996). *Discourse, learning and schooling.* New York: Cambridge University Press.

Hirschler, J. (1991). *Preschool children's help to second language learners.* Unpublished doctoral dissertation, Harvard University Graduate School of Education, Cambridge, MA.

Hoff-Ginsberg, E. (1987). Topic relations in mother–child conversations. *First Language, 7,* 45–158.

Hoff-Ginsberg, E., & Krueger, W. (1991). Older siblings as conversational partners. *Merrill-Palmer Quarterly, 37*(3), 465–482.

Hoff-Ginsberg, E., & Tardiff, T. (1995). Socioeconomic status and parenting. In M. Bornstein (Ed.), *Handbook of parenting* (Vol. 2, pp. 161–188). Mahwah, NJ: Lawrence Erlbaum Associates.

Howes, C. (1983). Caregiver behavior in center and family day care. *Journal of Applied Developmental Psychology, 4,* 99–107.

Howes, C. (1988). Peer interaction of young children. *Monograph of the Society for Research in Child Development, 53*(1).

Howes, C., & Hamilton, C. (1993). Child care for young children. In B. Spodek (Ed.), *Handbook of research on the education of young children* (pp. 322–336). New York: Macmillan.

Howes, C., & Rubenstein, J.L. (1978, March/April). *Peer play and the effect of the inanimate environment.* Paper presented at the Annual Conference of the Eastern Psychological Association.

Huttenlocher, J., Haight, W., Bryk, A., Seltzer, M., & Lyons, T. (1991). Early vocabulary growth: Relation to language input and gender. *Developmental Psychology, 27,* 236–248.

Infant Health and Development Program. (1990). Enhancing the outcomes of low-birth-weight premature infants. *Journal of the American Medical Association 263*, 3035–3042.

Jackson, J.F. (1993). Multiple caregiving among African Americans and infant attachment. *Human Development, 36*, 87–102.

Kaye, K., & Fogel, A. (1980). The temporal structure of face-to-face communication between mothers and infants. *Developmental Psychology, 16*, 454–464.

Keenan, E. (1977). Making it last: Repetition in children's discourse. In S. Ervin-Tripp & C. Mitchell-Kernan (Eds.), *Child discourse* (pp. 125–138). New York: Academic Press.

Kontos, S. (1994). The ecology of family daycare. *Early Childhood Research Quarterly, 9*, 87–110.

Kontos, S., & Wilcox-Herzog, A. (1997). Teachers' interactions with children: Why are they so important? Research in review. *Young Children, 52*(2), 4–12.

Kuhl, P., Andrusti J., Chistovich, I., Chistovich, L.A., Kozhevnikova, E., Ryskina, V., Stolyarova, E., Sundberg, U., & Lacerda, F. (1997). Cross-language analysis of phonetic units in language addressed to infants. *Science, 277*(5326), 684–686.

Lanza, E. (1997). *Language mixing in infant bilingualism: A sociolinguistic perspective.* New York: Oxford University Press.

Layzer, J., Goodson, B., & Moss, M. (1993). *Observational study of early childhood programs, Final report: Vol. 1. Life in preschool.* Washington, DC: U.S. Department of Education.

LeVine, S. (1992). *Mothers and toddlers in three cultures.* [Film] (Available from S. LeVine, c/o Harvard Graduate School of Education, Larsen Hall, Appian Way, Cambridge, MA 02138).

LeVine, R., Dixon, S., LeVine, S., Richman, A., Leiderman, P.H., Keefer, C.H., & Brazelton, T.B. (1994). *Childcare and culture: Lessons from Africa.* New York: Cambridge University Press.

Mannle, S., Barton, M., & Tomasello, M. (1992). Two-year-olds' conversations with their mothers and preschool-aged siblings. *First Language, 12*(34), Pt. 1, 57–71.

Marcos, H., & Chanu, K. (1992). Learning how to insist and clarify in the second year: Reformulations and requests in different contexts. *International Journal of Behavioral Development, 15*(3), 359–376.

McCabe, A., & Peterson, C. (1991). Getting the story: A longitudinal study of parental styles in eliciting narratives and developing narrative style. In A. McCabe & C. Peterson (Eds.), *Developing narrative structure* (pp. 217–253). Mahwah, NJ: Lawrence Erlbaum Associates.

McCartney, K. (1984). Effects of quality of day care environment on children's language development. *Developmental Psychology, 20*(2), 244–260.

McDonald, L., & Pien, D. (1982). Mother conversational behavior as a function of interactional intent. *Child Language, 9*, 337–358.

McLoyd, V. (1983). The effects of the structure of play objects on pretend play of low-income preschool children. *Child Development, 54*, 626–635.

Melhuish, E.C., Money, A., Martin, S., & Lloyd, E. (1990a). Type of childcare at 18 months: I. Differences in interactional experience. *Journal of Child Psychology and Psychiatry, 31*(6), 849–859.

Melhuish, E.C., Money, A., Martin, S., & Lloyd, E. (1990b). Type of childcare at 18 months: II. Relations with cognitive and language development. *Journal of Child Psychology and Psychiatry, 31*(6), 861–870.

Meltzoff, A. (1995). Understanding the intentions of others: Reenactment of intended acts by 18-month-old children. *Developmental Psychology, 31*(5), 838–850.

Michaels, S. (1981). Sharing time. *Language in Society, 10*, 423–447.

Michaels, S. (1991). The dismantling of narrative. In A. McCabe & C. Peterson (Eds.), *Developing narrative structure* (pp. 303–351). Mahwah, NJ: Lawrence Erlbaum Associates.

Miller, P., Mintz, J., Hoogstra, L., Fung, H., & Potts, R. (1992). The narrated self: Young children's construction of self in relation to others in conversational stories of personal experience. *Merrill-Palmer Quarterly, 38*(1), 45–67.

Minami, M., & McCabe, A. (1995). Rice balls and bear hunts: Japanese and North American family narrative patterns. *Journal of Child Language, 22*, 423–445.

Mintz, J. (1995). Self in relation to other: Preschoolers' verbal social comparisons within narrative discourse. In L. Sperry & P. Smiley (Eds.), Exploring young children's concepts of self and other through conversation. *New Directions for Child Development, 69*, 61–73.

Moore, C., & Dunham, P. (1995). *Joint attention: Its origins and role in development.* Mahwah, NJ: Lawrence Erlbaum Associates.

Morris, T., McCabe, A., & Roberts, B. (1991, April). *Contextual influences in mother–child conversation: Gross versus fine motor play.* [ERIC Document No. 342 495]. Paper presented at the biennial meeting of the Society for Research in Child Development, Seattle, WA.

Mueller, E., Blair, M., Krakow, J., Hegedus, K., & Cournoyer, P. (1977). The development of peer verbal interaction among 2-year-old boys. *Child Development, 48*, 284–287.

National Association for the Education of Young Children and International Reading Association (1998). Learning to read and write: Developmentally appropriate practices for young children. A joint statement. [ERIC Document No. 420052]. *Young Children, 53*(4), 30–46.

National Institute for Child Health and Human Development (NICHD)(1997, April). Preliminary findings of NICHD study of early child care, reported at biennial meeting of the Society for Research in Child Development, Washington, DC.

National Institute for Child Health and Human Development (1999, April). Effect sizes from the NICHD study of early child care. In K.A. McCartney & A. Clarke-Stewart (Chairs), *Does child care quality matter?* Symposium conducted at biennial meeting of the Society for Research in Child Development, Albuquerque, NM.

Nicoladis, E., & Genesee, F. (1996). A longitudinal study of pragmatic differentiations in young bilingual children, *Language Learning, 46*(3), 439–464.

Ninio, A., & Bruner, J. (1978). The achievement and antecedents of labeling. *Child Language, 5*, 1–15.

Ninio, A., & Snow, C.E. (1996). *Pragmatic development: Essays in developmental science.* Boulder, CO: Westview Books.

Ochs, E. (1988). *Culture and language development: Language acquisition and language socialization in a Samoan village.* Cambridge, England: Cambridge University Press.

Ochs, E., & Schieffelin, B. (1983). *Acquiring conversational competence.* London: Routledge and Kegan Paul.

Pan, B.A., Imbens-Bailey, A., Winner, K., & Snow, C. (1996). Communicative intents expressed by parents in interaction with young children. *Merrill-Palmer Quarterly, 42*, 248–266.

Pappas, C.C. (1993). Is narrative primary? Some insights from kindergarteners' pretend readings of stories and information books. *Journal of Reading Behavior: A Journal of Literacy, 25,* 97–129.

Pearson, B.Z., & Fernandez, S.C. (1994). Patterns of interaction in the lexical growth in two languages of bilingual infants and toddlers. *Language Learning, 44,* 617–653.

Pearson, B.Z., Fernandez, S.C., Lewedey, V., & Oller, D.K. (1997). The relation of input factors to lexical learning by bilingual infants. *Applied Psycholinguistics, 18,* 41–58.

Pearson, B.Z., Fernandez, S.C., & Oller D.K. (1993). Lexical development in bilingual infants and toddlers: Comparison to monolingual norms. *Language Learning, 43*(1), 93–120.

Pellegrini, A., & Galda, L. (1993). Ten years after: A reexamination of symbolic play and literacy research. *Reading Research Quarterly, 28*(2), 162–175.

Peterson, C., & McCabe, A. (1994). A social interactionist account of developing decontextualized narrative skill. *Developmental Psychology, 30*(6), 937–948.

Piaget, J. (1926). *The language and thought of the child.* New York: Harcourt Brace.

Raikes, H. (1993). Relationship duration in infant care: Time with a high-ability teacher and infant–teacher attachment. *Early Childhood Research Quarterly, 8*(3), 309–325.

Ramey, C.T., Bryant, D.M., & Suarez, T.M. (1985). Preschool compensatory education and the modifiability of intelligence: A critical review. In D. Detterman (Ed.), *Current topics in human intelligence* (pp. 247-296). Norwood, NJ: Ablex.

Ratner, N., & Bruner, J.S. (1978). Games, social class, and the acquisition of language. *Journal of Child Language, 5,* 391–401.

Reese, E. (1995). Predicting children's literacy from mother–child conversations. *Cognitive Development, 10,* 381–405.

Reese, E., & Fivush, R. (1993). Parental styles of talking about the past. *Developmental Psychology, 29*(3), 596–606.

Roberts, J., Rabinowitch, S., Bryant, D.M., Burchinal, M., Koch, M., & Ramey, C.T. (1989). Language skills of children with different preschool experiences. *Journal of Speech and Hearing Research, 32,* 773–786.

Rogoff, B., Mistry, J., Goncü, A., & Mosier, C. (1993). Guided participation in cultural activity by toddlers and caregivers. *Monographs of the Society for Research in Child Development, 58*(8).

Sachs, J., Donnelly, J., Smith, C., & Bookbinder, J. (1991). Preschool children's conversational intrusions: Behavior and metapragmatics. *Discourse Processes, 4*(3), 357–372.

Schieffelin, B. (1990). *The give and take of everyday life.* New York: Cambridge University Press.

Schieffelin, B., & Ochs, E. (1986). *Language socialization across cultures.* New York: Cambridge University Press.

Schley, S., & Snow, C.E. (1992). The conversational skills of school-aged children. *Social Development, 1,* 18–35.

Sharma, D., & LeVine, R. (1998). Child care in India: A comparative developmental view of infant social environments. In D. Sharma & K. Fischer (Eds.), *Socioemotional development across cultures* (pp. 45–67). San Francisco: Jossey-Bass.

Shatz, M., & Gelman, R. (1973). The development of communication skills: Modifications in the speech of young children as a function of listener. *Monographs of the Society for Research in Child Development, 38*(5).

Smith, M., & Dickinson, D.K. (1994). Describing oral language opportunities and environments in Head Start and other preschool classrooms. *Early Childhood Research Quarterly, 9*(3-4), 345–366.

Snow, C.E. (1977). The development of conversation between mothers and babies. *Journal of Child Language, 4,* 1–22.

Snow, C.E. (1989). Understanding social interaction and language acquisition: Sentences are not enough. In M. Bornstein & J.Bruner (Eds.), *Interaction in human development* (pp. 83–103). Mahwah, NJ: Lawrence Erlbaum Associates.

Snow, C.E. (1990). Building memories: The ontogeny of autobiography. In D. Cicchetti & M. Beeghly (Eds.), *The self in transition* (pp. 213–242). Chicago: The University of Chicago Press.

Snow, C.E. (1994). Introduction. In C. Galloway & B. Richards (Eds.), *Input and interaction in language acquisition* (pp. 3–12). Cambridge, England: Cambridge University Press.

Snow, C.E. (1991a). The theoretical basis for relationships between language and literacy development. *Journal of Research in Childhood Education, 6*(1), 5–10.

Snow, C.E. (1991b). [Transcription of preschool interaction from data collected for the Home/School Study of Language and Literary Development]. Unpublished raw data.

Snow, C.E., & Goldfield, B. (1982). Building stories: The emergence of information structures from conversation and narrative. In D. Tannen (Ed.), *Georgetown University roundtable and language and linguistics 1981, analyzing discourse: Text and talk* (pp. 127–141). Washington, DC: Georgetown University Press.

Snow, C.E., Pan, B.A., Imbens-Bailey, A., & Herman, J. (1996). Learning to say what one means: A longitudinal study of children's speech act use. *Social Development, 5,* 56–84.

Sperry, L., & Sperry, D. (1995). Young children's presentation of self in conversational narration. In L. Sperry & P. Smiley (Eds.), Exploring young children's concepts of self and other through conversation. *New Directions for Child Development, 69,* 47–60.

Sperry, L., & Sperry, D. (1996). Early development of narrative skills. *Cognitive Development, 11,* 443–465.

St. Pierre, R., & Lopez, M. (1994, December). *The comprehensive child development program.* Paper presented to the National Research Council, Board on Children and Families, Washington, DC.

St. Pierre, R., Swartz, J., Murray, S., Deck, D., & Nicke, P. (1993). *National evaluation of the Even Start family literacy program, report on effectiveness.* Washington, DC: U.S. Department of Education, Office of Policy and Planning.

Stahl, S.A., & Fairbanks, M.M. (1986). The effects of vocabulary instruction: A model-based meta-analysis. *Review of Educational Research, 56,* 72–110.

Stern, D. (1985). *The interpersonal world of the infant: A view from psychoanalysis and developmental psychology.* New York: Basic Books.

Stern, D., Jaffee, J., Beebe, B., & Bennett, S. (1975). Vocalizing in unison and in alternation: Two modes of communication within the mother–child dyad. *Developmental Psycholinguistic and Communication Disorders, 263,* 89–100.

Tabors, P. (1996). *One child, two languages: A guide for preschool education of children learning English as a second language.* Baltimore: Paul H. Brookes Publishing Co.

Tomasello, M. (1995). Joint attention as social cognition. In C. Moore & P. Dunham (Eds.), *Joint attention: Its origins and role in development* (pp. 103–130). Mahwah, NJ: Lawrence Erlbaum Associates.

Tomasello, M., & Farrar, M. (1986). Joint attention and early language. *Child Development, 57,* 1454–1463.

Tomasello, M., & Todd, J. (1983). Joint attention and early lexical acquisition style. *First Language, 4,* 197–212.

Tomasello, M., & Kruger, A.C. (1992). Joint attention on actions: Acquiring verbs in ostensive and non-ostensive contexts. *Journal of Child Language, 19,* 311–333.

Trevarthen, C., & Hubley, P. (1978). Secondary intersubjectivity: Confidence, confiding, and acts of meaning in the first year. In A. Lock (Ed.), *Action, gesture and symbol: The emergence of language* (pp. 183–229). London: Academic Press.

Tronick, E., Morelli, G., & Ivey, P. (1992). The Efe forager and toddler's pattern of social relationships: Multiple and simultaneous. *Developmental Psychology, 28*(4), 568–577.

Wanska, S., & Bedrosian, J. (1985). Conversational structure and topic performance in mother–child interaction. *Journal of Speech and Hearing Research, 28,* 579–584.

Wanska, S., Pohlman, J.C., & Bedrosian, J.L. (1989). Topic maintenance in preschoolers' conversation in three play situations. *Early Childhood Research Quarterly, 4,* 393–402.

Wasik, B.H., Ramey, C.T., Bryant, D.M., & Sparling, J.J. (1990). A longitudinal study of two early intervention strategies: Project CARE. *Child Development, 61,* 1682–1696.

Whitebook, M., Howes, C., & Phillips, D.A. (1989). *Who cares: Final report of the National Child Care Staffing Study.* [ERIC Document No. 323 032]. Oakland, CA: Child Care Employee Project.

Whitehurst, G.J., Epstein, J., Angell, A., Crone, D., & Fischel, J. (1994). Outcomes of an emergent literacy intervention in Head Start. *Journal of Educational Psychology, 80,* 542–555.

Wilcox-Herzog, A., & Kontos, S. (1996). *The nature of teacher talk in early childhood classrooms and its relationship to children's competence with objects and peers.* Manuscript under review. West Lafayette, IN: Department of Child Development and Family Studies.

Wong Fillmore, L. (1991). When learning a second language means losing the first. *Early Childhood Research Quarterly, 6*(3), 323–347.

4

Social Development, Family, and Attachment Relationships of Infants and Toddlers

Research into Practice

◆ ❖ ◆

Carollee Howes

In a period of 3 years, young children construct the fundamentals of social interaction and relationship formation. With optimal or even adequate life circumstances, infants and toddlers make the transition to preschool as experts in complex social interaction. They can conduct complex social interactions and play action reversal games with peers as well as adults. They engage in social pretend play, sharing symbolic meaning as well as social content. They are well on their way toward internalized self-regulation of emotions and aggressive behavior. Again, provided with adequate adult caregiving, infants and toddlers poised to make the transition to preschool have co-constructed social relationships that permit them to use adults as resources and sources of social support.

This chapter examines the research and theoretical underpinnings of social development during the first 3 years and explores the implications of this research for practice. The basic assumption underlying this chapter is that children's social development cannot be considered separately from the contexts of development. Important contexts of social development for infants and toddlers are illustrated in Figure 1. This figure draws from the important work of Bronfenbrenner's theory

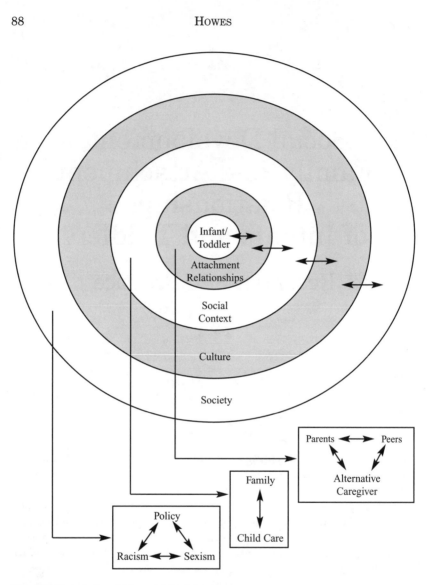

Figure 1.   Theoretical model for social development.

of human ecology (1979) and from more recent work that interprets the development of all children within a cultural context (Garcia Coll et al., 1996). However, an important distinction between these sociocultural theories and this chapter is the centrality of relationships in the understanding of development. Children's social development does not occur outside of relationships. Instead, development is embedded within relationships.

CONCEPTUAL MODEL

Although the best explanatory model for understanding relationship formation and development is Bowlby's (1969/1982) theory of attachment formation, this model considers other types of relationships (e.g., adult playmates, peer playmates, friends), as well as attachment relationships, to be important in the social development of infants and toddlers. This thinking is consistent with Emde's (1989) and Hinde's (1976) conceptual work on relationship function, formation, and development.

Infant/Toddler

At the middle of Figure 1 is the infant/toddler. The infant, from the moment of birth, is engaged with others. The parents or other caregivers interpret the infant's physiological behaviors through their own relationship history and cultural beliefs about the sociability of infants. Is the upward turn of the infant's lips a smile? Can the infant look at me and see me as her or his mother? Do the baby's cries have social meaning, and what is the social meaning? Is she or he tormenting me on purpose with these demands? Does she or he need comforting? Are those babbles and coos language to be answered, or is she or he just making noise? Adult caregivers answer these questions based on their own experiences of being cared for and their understanding about themselves and others. They also base their answers on cultures—the culture of their family and community of origin, the culture of formal education, and the interplay of their culture of origin and their experiences with the dominant culture, including formal education. Infants respond to the behavior of caregivers based on their temperaments, their developmental capacities, and, over time, their history of social interaction. The behavioral sequences that are repeated endlessly as adults care for infants become the content of social interaction skills and the foundation of relationships.

Attachment Relationships

The second circle in Figure 1 contains those people with whom infants and toddlers form relationships. Those who are part of the other–infant/toddler relationships include parents and extended family members, alternative caregivers, and peers. These others play roles that include attachment figures, playmates, and teachers. Dominant American culture has long drawn this diagram another way, with a circle enclosing the infant designated either as the mother or the family and then the outer circle designated as, perhaps, child care and school or peers. This model deliberately describes a network of primary relationships instead of a model that nests the family within child care and peers. Families outside of the dominant culture (particularly people of color, immigrant families, and families living in or close to poverty) historically have used a variety of child-rearing configurations involving networks of caregiving adults rather than a single caregiver (Jackson, 1993). In order to understand children's social development, it is important to consider a network of relationships, rather than focus only on the mother–child relationship. With the changing roles of women and men in family life and with the growing economic necessity of two-income families, most children, even in the dominant culture of the United States, are regularly cared for by more than one adult.

While examining the figure, it is important to notice the arrows. The characteristics that each partner brings to the other–infant/toddler relationship influence the quality and form of the relationship that is constructed. Research in many areas of social development supports Hinde's (1976) notion that the nature of the relationship and of the resulting child behavioral profile is more than a bi-directional effect of the influences of both partners, but instead a new formation only understood by examining not only the behaviors of both partners but also the general pattern of social interaction between the pair (Crockenberg, 1981; Howes, Hamilton, & Phillipsen, 1998; Kochanska, 1997). This phenomena is illustrated by the double-headed arrow between the first and second circles. There are double-headed arrows, as well, among the others included in the second circle. One of the fastest growing areas of research in developmental psychology concerns the transmission of caregiving patterns based on relationship history both within relationships (Steele, Steele, & Fonagy, 1995) and in intergenerational relationships (George, Kaplan, & Main, 1985; George & Solomon, 1996). A caregiver's state of mind about being cared for influences her or his patterns of caring for others. Thus, the grandmother–mother relationship influences the mother–child relationship. The relationship between caregivers influences caregiving as well. The mother–father relationship influences the mother–child and the father–child relationship, the mother–alternative caregiver relationship influences the mother–child and the alternative caregiver–child relationships, and so on. Not all these influences are equally powerful, adding to the complexity of both real life and of research in this area.

Social Context

The third circle indicates the particular social contexts of the infant/toddler. The two most important social contexts in this developmental period are the family and the child care arrangement used by the family. Variations that appear to be important in the family social context include income and educational level of the parent, the degree to which the family is embedded in a positive and supportive social network, and the emotional climate of the family. Variations that appear to be important in the child care social context include dimensions of quality.

Social Class and Poverty Status   Social class, defined by the income and educational level of the parents, serves as an organizer of American society. Access to resources is defined by class status. Because formal education and social class are confounded, beliefs about appropriate childrearing strategies are embedded within social class (Rubin, Mills, & Rose-Krasnor, 1989). For example, parents and child care providers who have lower social status and less access to formal education have less experience with the abstract and formal thinking inherent in childrearing strategies that involve explaining what will happen next or clarifying an emotional state to an infant or toddler who cannot yet talk or engage in conversation. The stress associated with poverty also influences caregiver–child social interaction patterns and the ability of caregiving adults to be responsive. McLloyd, Jayarante, Ceballo, and Borquez's (1994) work on families in poverty demonstrates links between the emotional distress associated with poverty and adult–child interactions that are harsher than intended.

Social Networks and Support   The degree to which a family is embedded within a social network also influences patterns of social interaction. In most cases, adults who are more socially supported are expected to be better able to engage in a positive and warm manner with their infants and toddlers (Cochran & Brassard, 1979; Crockenberg, 1981). However, in other cases, social networks can drain the emotional resources of caregivers, leading them to be distant or harsh with their infants and toddlers, or they can distract caregivers from engaging with their infants and toddlers (McLloyd et al., 1994).

Emotional Background or Climate of the Family   Within the family, the emotional background or climate of childrearing, particularly domestic conflict or violence, can influence infant/toddler social development. This influence can be both direct and indirect. Domestic conflict or violence will interfere with the primary caregiver's capacity for warm and responsive interactions with her or his infant/toddler. Furthermore, work by Cummings and Davies (1994) suggests that infant/toddler social and emotional development is directly influenced by background anger and violence. Children who experience high levels of background anger and violence are unable to be confident about the emotional security available in caregiver–child relationships.

Child Care Quality   The child care environment is another important social context for an infant/toddler. Using this conceptual model, it becomes clear how crucial quality child care is to the social development of a child. A rich literature on child care quality (see Howes & Hamilton, 1993b, for a review of this literature) suggests that child care environments are heterogeneous in their ability to enhance child development. Child care quality is usually defined as including both structural and process quality. Structural quality refers to aspects of care that can be regulated, including adult–child ratio, group sizes, and caregiver characteristics such as education and training in early childhood education. Process quality refers to the children's experiences in care, particularly whether their social interactions with the teacher are positive or harsh. Research linking quality of child care to later childhood outcomes suggests that structural quality tends to influence process quality, which in turn influences children's development, particularly social development (Howes, Phillips, & Whitebook, 1992; Phillipsen, Burchinal, Howes, & Cryer, 1997). Child care environments with low structural quality often interfere with responsive and sensitive adult care of infants and toddlers by placing too many infants and toddlers in the care of each adult. More than three or four infants and toddlers per adult caregiver means that the adult is overwhelmed by the children's demands and becomes unresponsive. The caregiver becomes so busy keeping the children clean and safe that she or he cannot provide individual attention or play, and she or he may instead focus on a harsh and restrictive management style rather than individualized care. This association between child care quality and social development may be particularly salient for infants and toddlers because several representative studies of child care report that child care structural quality and process quality may be worse for toddlers and infants than it is for preschool-age children (Helburn, 1995; Kontos, Howes, Shinn, & Galinsky, 1995; Ruopp, Travers, Glantz, & Coelen, 1979; Whitebook, Howes, & Phillips, 1990).

Family and child care influences on children's social development are not independent. More affluent and better educated families tend to use higher quality child care arrangements for their children (Howes & Hamilton, 1993b). This correlation holds true even when associations are examined between family income, education level, and child care quality in nonformal care arrangements, such as relative care or unregulated family child care homes (Kontos et al., 1995). This lack of independence makes it difficult to compare the differential influences of family and child care on child development. However, researchers who have used regression analysis to control statistically for family influences report that child care quality continues to influence children's social development independent of family characteristics (Helburn, 1995; NICHD Early Child Care Research Network, 1997).

Culture

The fourth circle in Figure 1 represents culture as understood and enacted by the child's primary caregivers. A basic assumption in this chapter is that individual primary developmental processes (e.g., the formation of attachment relationships or the construction of social pretend-play sequences) operate similarly for minority children as for children in the dominant culture. That is, warm, sensitive, and positive reciprocal interactions are expected to be associated with social competence in children of color as well as in Caucasian children. However, further concepts justify the inclusion of culture as a circle of influence. First, there are cultural differences in social interaction style. Therefore, the particular patterning of individual behaviors in a responsive and reciprocal interaction may be different in adult–child pairs from different cultural backgrounds. Second, the pervasive influence of racism, prejudice, and discrimination in American society means that families of color have developed an adaptive culture (Garcia Coll et al., 1996). Adaptive culture is a group of goals, values, attitudes, and behaviors that set families and children of color apart from the dominant culture. Both the adaptive culture and the dominant culture influence the social context of infant/toddler development. Furthermore, aspects of an adaptive culture may serve to protect families from the more detrimental effects of their individual social context. For example, kinship or extended social networks help families living in poverty to cope with the demands of employment and child care. The bicultural experiences of increasing numbers of immigrant families living in the United States represent another aspect of adaptive culture. Several studies report that mothers who are more acculturated (i.e., understand more of the beliefs and behaviors of the dominant culture as well as their culture of origin) are better able to understand and differentiate multiple influences on children's development and thus are better able to provide individualized and sensitive care (Garcia Coll, Meyer, & Brillon, 1995; Gutierrez & Sameroff, 1990).

Given the increasing cultural complexity of many urban areas and the families who live there, it is more likely than not that infants and toddlers will experience primary adult caregivers and peer partners from several cultures. There are increasing numbers of children whose parents are each from a different culture. Child care providers, as well, are more and more likely to be of a different culture than the infant/toddler. Under optimal conditions, these experiences will help infants and toddlers to learn codes or styles that are appropriate in more than one culture. There is some evidence that older children with bicultural skills are less likely to experience school and family conflicts or to become involved in illicit activities (Garcia Coll et al., 1996). In order to accomplish this optimal goal, one culture cannot be given a favored or privileged status within the social context. Therefore, Caucasian infants or toddlers in Los Angeles with Latina nannies are as likely to learn social status differentials as they are to learn Spanish, but infants and toddlers in a child care center that respects home languages and multicultural issues have a better chance of becoming bicultural, as well as proficient in Spanish.

Society

The fifth and final circle in Figure 1 is society. Three aspects of the larger society that indirectly influence infant/toddler social development are illustrative. The first is social policy. Social policies (including the lack of a national child care policy or child care regulations; the new welfare policy, which requires mothers on welfare to work; or parental leave policies) influence the social context of development. For example, if mothers on welfare must work, then they must arrange child care. With limited resources for child care, they are less likely than more affluent women to find high quality child care. Poor child care is unlikely to provide the infant/toddler with experiences that facilitate optimal social development.

A second aspect of society is racism. Both institutional racism and symbolic racism (i.e., "a set of moral abstractions and attitudinal predispositions about how minorities ought to act, whether or not they are treated equitably, and what they deserve"; Garcia Coll et al., 1996, p. 1899) influence access to societal resources, treatment of different people, and beliefs about the self and other. These factors affect the social context of development for infants and toddlers primarily by influencing the capacity of significant caregiving adults to respond positively and sensitively to infants and toddlers.

The final illustrative aspects of society are sexism and beliefs about gender roles. Like racism, sexism can control access to societal resources. If women have less economic value in society, then single mothers have more difficulty providing a financial foundation for their family, and child care workers, who are primarily female, are not paid a living wage. When child care providers live in poverty, they are in danger of suffering the same emotional distress and subsequent interference with sensitive caregiving as mothers who live in poverty. Sexism, as well as racism, influences behavior. Therefore, infants and toddlers who are judged by a racist or sexist society to have less value are in danger of receiving less appropriate care.

DEVELOPMENT OF RELATIONSHIPS

Because infant/toddler social development occurs within relationships, the following section of this chapter focuses on relationship development. The processes of relationship formation described by attachment theory (Bowlby, 1969/1982; Bretherton, 1985; Thompson, 1998) will be used as the explanatory theory. Two types of relationships are of fundamental importance for infants' and toddlers' social development: attachment relationships and playmate relationships. Infants and toddlers develop attachment relationships with the adults who provide them with physical and emotional care. From attachment relationships infants and toddlers derive emotional security, a sense of trust (or distrust) that they will be cared for. Infants and toddlers develop playmate relationships with the adults and peers who play with them. It is unlikely but not impossible for an infant or toddler to have an attachment relationship that is not also a playmate relationship, but it is likely that infants and toddlers have adult–child playmate relationships that are not attachment relationships. For example, infants and toddlers in child care centers most often have one attachment relationship with a primary caregiver and a number of playmate relationships with secondary caregivers (Howes & Oldham, in press). By the toddler developmental period, some playmate relationships with peers become friend relationships, which have some, but not all, of the attributes of attachment relationships (Howes, 1996). From playmate relationships with both adults and peers, infants and toddlers derive the social skills needed for smooth and coordinated social interaction.

Relationships, whether attachment or playmate relationships, develop through multiple and recursive interactive experiences. Recursive interactions are well scripted social exchanges (Bretherton, 1985), for example, the infant's and caregiver's interactions around bedtime or the toddler's and peers' run-and-chase games. These social exchanges are nearly identical in script and are repeated with only slight variations many times. From these interaction experiences, the infant internalizes a set of fundamental social expectations about the behavioral dispositions of the partner in these interactions (Bowlby, 1969/1982). These expectations form the basis for an internal working model of the relationship. Thompson (1998) suggested that, during the toddler period, internal working models are revised and updated according to two new developmental phenomenon. Increased brain development during the toddler period permits general and specific memories of experiences to be retained in long-term memory. Furthermore, significant adults begin a shared discourse with the toddler about daily and past events (e.g.,

"Remember the last time we went to this park and you had such fun playing with Sonia?"). This shared discourse shapes and guides the toddler's representations of personal experience, self, and relationships. Internalized expectations of caregivers' and peers' accessibility and responsiveness, as well as concurrent beliefs about one's deservedness of such interaction, then guide children's future relational expectations, self-appraisals, and behavior towards others.

In summary, children construct relationships with a small number of significant adults and peers when they are infants and toddlers. The nature of their interactional experiences with these partners shapes the nature of the relationships constructed. Furthermore, the child develops internalized expectations and beliefs about the self and the other from these relationships. This internalized model serves to influence the child's future interactions with others.

Attachment Relationships

Traditional research derived from attachment theory usually positions mothers and fathers as attachment figures. When caregivers who are not the child's parents are included as attachment figures, standard criteria become necessary for their identification. Two groups of researchers have provided guidelines for identifying alternative attachment figures. First, van IJzendoorn, Sagi, and Lambermon (1992) identified two categories of alternative attachment figures, child care providers and metapelets (i.e., caregivers on kibbutzim), on the basis of existing empirical research. In contrast, Howes, Hamilton, and Althusen (in press) expect a specific set of attachment figures to be identified for each child. The three criteria for the identification of attachment figures proposed by Howes et al. (in press) are that the person must 1) provide physical and emotional care, 2) contribute to continuity or consistency in the child's life, and 3) have an emotional investment in the child.

Father–infant attachment relationships have been studied since the 1970s (cf. Lamb, 1977). Father–infant attachments appear to be formed and develop in a similar fashion to mother–infant attachments (Howes, 1999). Child care provider–child attachments were first described in the 1980s (Anderson, Nagel, Roberts, & Smith, 1981) and now are well established in the literature (cf. Goossen & van IJzendoorn, 1990; Howes & Hamilton, 1992a, 1992b). Child care provider–child attachment relationships may be formed at different developmental periods than mother–child attachment relationships and may be sequentially developed as opposed to concurrently developed. That is, very young infants can form attachments to their mothers and to their child care providers in the same time period. These differences appear to lead to some differences in the development of child care provider–child attachments

(Howes, 1999). For example, child care provider–child attachment relationships between alternative adults and children with previous difficult relationships may require extra sensitivity on the part of the alternative adult (Howes & Ritchie, 1998, 1999a, 1999b). Extant research on alternative attachment figures has rarely examined more than two or possibly three attachment figures for each child. Further work is needed to examine attachment relationships and their inter-relationships, using the child's entire network of attachment figures. This kind of work is particularly important for understanding the development of attachment relationships in infants and toddlers of color who are living in poverty, especially within immigrant families.

Concordance and Nonconcordance of Attachment Relationships Two superficially incompatible theoretical propositions inform the concordance and nonconcordance of attachment relationships. Concordance and nonconcordance refer to similarity and dissimilarity in the nature or quality of each attachment relationship. First, because each attachment relationship is constructed from recursive interactions between the infant/toddler and a particular adult, each attachment relationship should be independent of other attachment relationships. However, the internalized working model of relationships tends to operate in such a way that expectations and beliefs about the "loveableness" of self are derived from prior relationships and tend to be acted on in the context of new relationships. The infant who expects to be loved and cared for in a positive manner greets a new caregiver as if she or he will respond sensitively and positively; an infant with a very different set of expectations about relationships is dependent and clingy or rejects the new caregiver's overtures. If the behavior of the new caregiver contradicts the expectations the infant/toddler brings to the relationship, then the resulting interactions lead to a different relationship (Howes & Ritchie, 1998, 1999b). If the new caregiver is "entrapped" by the child into behaving in a harsh, rejecting, or ignoring manner, then the previous maladaptive attachment relationship is more likely to be replicated (Howes & Ritchie, 1999b; Sroufe, 1983). If alternative caregivers believe that all subsequent attachment relationships are predetermined by the mother–infant attachment relationship quality, then they may tend to give up and fail to contradict the child's prior troubled relationship expectations.

The literature on concordance between mother–infant attachment and alternative caregiver–infant attachment suggests that these relationships tend to be nonconcordant or independent in quality (Goossen & van IJzendoorn, 1990; Howes & Hamilton, 1992a, 1992b; Oppenheimer, Sagi, & Lamb, 1988). The data reported in these studies tended to be based on typical children in better-than-average child care centers. Most of the attachment relationships in both environments tended to be secure attachments. One study of atypical preschool children in a therapeutic setting (Howes & Ritchie, 1998) also reported nonconcordance of mother–child and teacher–child attachments. In this case, attachments at school tended to be more secure than attachments at home. As the literature on nonconcordant home and child care attachment relationships and on the differential developmental influences of maternal and child care attachments (Howes, 1999) suggests, in some cases child care relationships compensate for poor home relationships or are more influential for children's social development than home relationships (Howes, 1999; Thompson, 1998). These findings may necessitate a modification of the traditional belief that the family's influence is the most important for social development. The implication of this research is that the child care system must receive more social and societal support in order to promote the positive social development of infants and toddlers. In the future, researchers should examine concordance and nonconcordance of attachment relationship quality in samples of infants and toddlers experiencing difficult relationships at home or in child care. As the number of children facing difficult life circumstances continues to increase, the potential for alternative attachment relationships to perform a compensatory function grows.

Interaction Patterns Associated with Secure Attachment
Beginning with the classic Ainsworth Baltimore study of behaviors in the home that secure the mother–infant attachment (Ainsworth, Blehar, Waters, & Wall, 1978), it has been well established that a secure mother–infant attachment occurs when the recursive social interactions of the pair are characterized by warmth and sensitivity rather than hostility and anger, detachment, or inconsistent responsivity. Inadequate responsiveness is linked to insecure and disorganized attachment relationships (Cassidy & Berlin, 1994; Del Carmen, Pedersen, Huffman, & Bryan, 1993; Lyons-Ruth, Connell, Grunebaum, & Botein, 1990). Concurrent studies of caregiver–child attachment in child care also found that caregivers who are rated as more sensitive and who are observed in more positive interaction with children are associated with children with greater attachment security (Goossen & van IJzendoorn, 1990; Howes & Hamilton, 1992a; Howes & Smith, 1995; Kontos et al., 1995). The implications of these findings are fairly clear: Enhancing adult sensitivity and responsiveness to infant/toddler social overtures and needs for comfort and reassurance will improve children's social development. However, considerably more research is needed to identify which types of interventions with which caregivers will enhance sensitivity. This issue will be further examined in a subsequent section of this chapter.

Infant/Toddler Attachment Relationship History and Later Behaviors   Infants' and toddlers' secure attachment relationships are associated with a number of positive outcomes. Theoretically, two developmental outcomes are of particular interest for infant/toddler social development. These are later trust and confidence in the adult and better relationships with peers.

The outcome of trust and confidence in the adult attachment figure is particularly salient for the toddler period. Optimal developmental outcomes for toddlers include appropriate resolution of autonomy issues and the emergence of self-regulation (e.g., the beginnings of emotional and aggressive self-control, the emergence of compliance with adults). All of the research on this topic has been focused on mother–infant attachment. Because alternative caregiver–infant attachment relationships appear to function similarly to mother–infant attachments (Howes, 1999), a similar pattern of results should be found for alternative caregiver–infant attachment relationships.

Early researchers examining links between attachment security and self-regulation found that infants who were classified as secure were more compliant and showed less frustration and aggression than toddlers (Londerville & Main, 1981; Matas, Arend, & Sroufe, 1978). More recently, Kochanska (1997) used Maccoby's (1984) concept of a mutually reciprocal relationship to examine the processes linking secure attachment and self-regulation. If toddlers trust their caregiver, then they are more willing and eager to be socialized.

Furthermore, the experience of a mutually reciprocated relationship means both partners, the toddler and the adult, "feel invested in and responsible for each other's welfare; one feels concern for and acts responsively to the other's needs, and, at the same time, one comes to expect the other to be responsive to one's needs and to be concerned about one's welfare" (Kochanska, 1997, p. 94). This kind of relationship is very different from the adversarial relationship sometimes implied in the socialization literature. In terms of behavioral interaction, a mutually responsive relationship means that there is a diminished need for adult use of power or coercion strategies. Instead, because the toddler is eager to cooperate with the adult, socialization strategies do not need to be harsh or restrictive. The existence of a mutually reciprocal relationship means that toddler socialization can extend beyond task compliance toward building a foundation for rules of conduct and morality.

There are implications in these associations between attachment security and self-regulation for classroom management in center-based child care. If teachers can construct secure attachments with the children in their care, then they will have less need for discipline strategies, such as time out or behavior consequences, that are outside of a cooperative relationship. Particularly with difficult children, the same teacher behaviors that lead to a harmoniously functioning classroom also promote positive teacher–child relationships (Howes & Ritchie, 1999b). Clear and consistent enforcement of reasonable rules in a context of warmth and responsiveness is necessary for the construction of positive teacher–child attachment relationships.

Attachment and Peer Relationships   A large and rich body of empirical literature supports the theoretical assumptions that secure maternal attachments will be linked to more positive peer interactions in early childhood (e.g., Elicker, England, & Sroufe, 1992; Jacobson & Wille, 1986; LaFreniere & Sroufe, 1985; Sroufe, 1983; Turner, 1991). Children with a history of secure mother–child attachment relationships are more competent in their social interactions with peers, more sought after by others as partners, and are more likely to construct friendships with others than children with insecure attachment relationship histories.

Many children, however, construct their social relationships with peers in a way that seems to be independent of their attachment relationship history with their mothers. In this situation, children's relationships with peers appear to be better predicted by the attachment relationships the children form with their adult caregivers within the social context than with their maternal attachment relationship. In two different child care samples, Howes and colleagues found that peer interaction and play were predicted by earlier and concurrent attachment relationships with their child care providers rather than with their mothers (Howes, Hamilton, & Matheson, 1994; Howes, Matheson, & Hamilton, 1994). Likewise, the peer interaction of children from a kibbutz was predicted by their infant–metapelet attachment relationship rather than by their maternal or paternal attachment relationship.

Playmate Relationships

Infants and toddlers have playmate relationships with adults as well as children.

Adult–Infant/Toddler   Many of the early adult–infant interaction sequences that form infants' emerging internal models of relationships can be considered play. The caregiver may be changing a diaper but when she blows on the infant's tummy and says, "look at that cute little nose, I'm going to give it a kiss" as she does it, the interaction is also playful. These face-to-face interactions and social games provide opportunities for children to engage in the construction of socially appropriate modes of interaction and communication (Hay, 1985; Stern, 1977). But these social interactions are an activity with no other goal than to have fun. In the optimal interaction, the affect is positive, and the partners adjust and readjust to one another to establish and maintain the interaction.

As children develop better motor skills, adults and toddlers often engage each other in social games with differentiated roles such as Peek-aboo, "I'm gonna get you," and Pat-a-cake. As toddlers acquire the capacity to manipulate symbols, adult–child pretend games become more common. In the beginning, the adults are the experts at these games; they structure the children's actions and may correct them to fit the game. As the toddlers master the game, particularly more sophisticated pretend sequences, the adult becomes an interested spectator who creates a context for the play and then supports the child's enactment (Howes, 1996). By the time toddlers move to the next phase of development, pretend play is usually firmly situated in the social world of peers. Adults still play a role, but it is as a facilitator rather than as a full participant.

Peer–Infant/Toddler   Although caregiver–infant/toddler attachment relationships can provide infants and toddlers with a positive or negative orientation to peer social interaction, and caregiver–infant/ toddler playmate relationships provide infants and toddlers with positive or negative experiences in social interaction, the construction of play sequences with a peer teaches different skills. Peers, unlike adults, are not particularly more knowledgeable or skillful in social interaction than the infant/toddler. But, to their advantage, the peers of infants/toddlers share interests in activities that adults generally do not. Most adults quickly tire of games like chase or jumping off a step. Howes (1987, 1988) outlined a sequence of competent social interactions that serve as markers of social competence with peers and has designed the Peer Play Scale, an assessment of increasing complexity in peer social interaction (Howes, 1980, 1988; Howes & Matheson, 1992). Infants (i.e., children from birth to 12 months of age) are socially competent when they can recognize the peer as a social partner. The behavior that defines recognition of the peer as a social partner is distinctive social behavior accompanied by a visual gaze (Hay, 1985). Most often, socially directed behaviors occur in the context of shared activity. Shared activities can be using the same toy (e.g., trucks) or being in the same activity (e.g., both playing in the water table). The first two scale points of the Peer Play Scale recognize that common activity with mutual awareness. Mutual awareness is defined as visual gaze without social behaviors. If an infant directs a social behavior to a peer and the peer responds with a social behavior, then a turn-taking interaction is begun. Simple social play (point three of the Peer Play Scale) captures this type of interaction. Although both parallel play and simple social play re-occur as transitional play forms throughout early childhood, the mastery of this social interaction is a major accomplishment in infancy. Once a peer is recognized as a partner and simple interaction has begun, the infant is well on her or his way toward constructing more complex play with a peer partner.

In the early toddler period (13–24 months), the marker behavior for competent peer social interaction is the capacity to engage in social interaction with a complementary and reciprocal game structure (Eckerman, Davis, & Didow, 1989). In complementary and reciprocal interaction, partners exchange both turns and roles in action; that is, the children engage in different but complementary actions, such as run-and-chase, offer-and-receive, and hide-and-seek. These games are sometimes considered action scripts because the toddlers know how to play the game.

These games do not depend on common language or culture; take, for example, the spontaneous run-and-chase games observed at airports between toddlers whose parents may not even speak the same language. However, there is considerable evidence that peer social skill interaction is rooted within particular friendship relationships. In longitudinal studies of peer social skill development, pairs of friends are observed to be more skilled at every point in time than pairs of acquaintances (Howes, 1983). This suggests that reciprocal interactions between toddler peers may be dependent on the particular combination of children. If only one toddler is interested in the social exchange or understands continent relations between social actions, the more complex interaction cannot occur. Friendships may dispose children toward engaging in interaction. Children who remain in the same peer group over the span of their infant/toddler developmental period are more likely to maintain their friendships and to increase in their social skills (Howes, 1988).

By the later toddler period (25–36 months), toddlers who are socially competent with peers are able to communicate meaning as well as construct play that is structurally complex (Howes, 1985, 1987). The communication of meaning is most strikingly found in pretend play, but it is a part of all games with innovations. As younger toddlers, a pair could play run-and-chase—now they can construct a different, more complex game that includes a common signal or invitation to begin the game (e.g., eye gaze plus run to the wagons together), a signal to switch roles (e.g., "my turn" plus a tug), and a way to communicate that they share this knowledge (e.g., "I pulled you").

The Peer Play Scale uses cooperative pretend play as the marker behavior for socially competent peer interaction in the late toddler period. This is a period in which children first attempt to integrate nonliteral meanings and role exchanges without a more expert partner. The resulting play consists of enacted role exchanges without metacommunication about pretend play. That is, the toddlers act out a script without saying, "Let's pretend. I'll be the mommy and you be the baby." The toddlers do have a script for their pretend that can be readily inferred from their actions (e.g., one child holds out a toy cup and the other child fills it from a toy pitcher).

By this period, there are individual differences in complexity of peer play, in aggression, and in withdrawal from peers (Howes & Matheson, 1992). Within the toddler and preschool developmental periods, children who engage in more complex play are less aggressive and less withdrawn (Howes & Matheson, 1992). Children who engage in complex play have opportunities to develop and perfect social skills. Children who are more socially skilled are less likely to be aggressive because they will be more likely to resolve rather than escalate conflicts. Furthermore, children who have successfully engaged peers in earlier developmental periods are unlikely to withdraw from peers in subsequent periods.

Longitudinal studies suggest that between the toddler and preschool developmental periods, children demonstrate stability in individual differences in their socially complex play with peers (Howes, 1988). By middle childhood, individual differences in aggression with and withdrawal from peers are more important markers of social competence than structural complexity of play with peers (Rubin, Bukowski, & Parker, in press). A longitudinal study that spans the toddler to middle childhood (age 9) developmental periods suggests that children who engaged in more complex play with peers as toddlers were more prosocial, engaged in more complex play and were less withdrawn from peers as preschoolers, and were less aggressive and withdrawn as 9-year-olds (Howes & Phillipsen, 1998). Children who were more aggressive and withdrawn as preschoolers were more aggressive as 9-year-olds. These findings highlight the importance of providing social contexts that facilitate positive peer interaction.

Peer Friendships   Infants and toddlers form internal representations of their relationships with particular peer partners in much the same way that they form internal representations of their relationships with caregiving adults (Howes, 1996). The relationship is considered a friendship when these conditions are met: 1) toddlers have opportunities in their daily lives for regular play interactions with a particular partner; 2) the toddler partners are sufficiently well acquainted to have constructed scripted social interactions; and 3) companionship, intimacy, and affection can be inferred from these interactions. Behaviorally defined, friendships appear some time after children's first birthdays (Howes, 1983). Within the young toddler period, friendship appears to be a context for the development of social interaction skills. As toddlers approach the preschool developmental period and become adept at pretend play, friendships become a context for intimacy and the exploration of trust (Howes, 1992).

If there is stability in the peer group, toddler friendships are stable over several years (Howes, 1988). Stable friendships provide children with emotional support. When children move between classrooms or child care centers accompanied by well-acquainted peers, they fare better than those who move alone (Howes, 1988).

CONTRIBUTIONS TO RELATIONSHIPS

Relationships are constructed by two people, and the individual characteristics that each partner brings to the relationship help shape the initial form of the relationship. This section reviews research on the influence of individual differences. For infants and toddlers, the origins of individual differences are primarily biological. In order to understand the antecedents of individual differences in the adult caregiver, it is necessary to return to the multiple level of influence depicted in Figure 1.

Infant/Toddler Contribution

Infants bring to relationships a biological contribution (e.g., cuddly little body with big eyes) and a unique style or temperament (Kagan, 1997). They also bring a developmental timetable of physical development, particularly brain development (Kotulak, Andrews, & McMeel, 1996). These essential biological attributes are very difficult to examine separately from their interpretation within the social context because "the phenomena of human existence and experience are always simultaneously biological and social, and an adequate explanation must involve both" (Rose, 1995, p. 380). For example, an infant's cry may be a physiological event, but, from the beginning, caregivers interpret infant's cries based on social cues rather than the sound of the cry (Thompson, 1993). The social cues—and the decision on which cues to act—influence the caregiver's responsiveness, which in turn converts the infant's cries into socially expressive behavior.

Temperament has become a volatile construct within the early childhood field. At one extreme, temperament is seen as a biological style. The infant is born highly reactive, difficult, or easy, and caregivers must simply adjust. At the other extreme, temperament is seen as "in the eye of the beholder," and in this case the beholder is the adult caregiver who is interpreting temperament from her or his interactions with the infant/toddler. A key difficulty is the measurement issue—is temperament measured by independent observers, by physiological correlates, or by caregiver reports? As the ability to use physiological measures in developmental research increases, the picture becomes more complex rather than less complex because temperament does not fit neatly with variability in biological functioning (Gunnar, 1994; Gunnar, Marvinney,

Isensee, & Fisch, 1992). Whatever the relation between physiology and caregiver perception, most caregivers can readily classify the infants and toddlers in their care as more or less reactive, or as easy, difficult, or restrained (Kagan, 1997; Lieberman, 1993). For about 20% of extreme cases, these temperamental styles tend to persist over time (Kagan, 1997). The task for caregivers is to recognize temperament styles and adjust their behavior rather than to simply classify the infant/toddler's temperament. Infants and toddlers who are difficult or restrained will require adaptive and sensitive caregiving from their caregivers if the caregiver–infant/toddler relationship is to become a mutually reciprocal and positive one. A classic study illustrates this point: Infants classified as fussy and irritable at birth constructed insecure attachment relationships with their mothers when their mothers consistently ignored their crying and experienced little social support themselves (Crockenberg, 1981). Other difficult infants in this study were able to construct secure mother–infant attachment relationships. The mothers of these infants were responsive to their crying and had supportive social systems.

Adult Contributions

As this review of the development of relationships and the positive influences of good relationships on infant/toddler social development has demonstrated, adults who are able to engage with infants and toddlers in a socially skilled, sensitive, and responsive manner are most likely to be able to enhance development. This section of the chapter returns to Figure 1 to examine internal and external influences on adult caregivers that influence their capacity to construct relationships with infant and toddlers.

Early childhood and clinical psychology practices have a long history of acknowledging that an adult's style of caregiving and social interaction echo that adult's own experiences of being cared for (Fraiberg, 1959). Two strands of literature are derived from attachment theory that examine adult caregiving relationships. One strand asks adults to characterize their interpersonal style on the basis of major attachment categories used with children (Hazen & Shaver, 1987). Adults who describe themselves as secure are generally more positive in their interactions with others. A second strand is the Adult Attachment Interview (George, Kaplan, & Main, 1985; George & Solomon, 1996). A clinical interview taps into the adult's state of mind regarding attachment. Although childhood memories consistent with secure attachment relationships often lead to secure attachment representations, some adults have transformed their representations from insecure to secure. The adults who have "earned" their secure representations have as an older person changed their state

of mind about early experiences of insecurity. The children of adults classified as secure with the Adult Attachment Interview tend to have secure
mother–infant attachment relationships (George & Solomon, 1996).

Mothers who are depressed tend to construct insecure attachment
relationships with their children (Lyons-Ruth et al., 1990; Teti, Gelfand,
Messinger, & Isabella, 1995). Depressed mothers also have difficulty in
constructing playmate relationships because of the effect of their illness
on their patterns of social interaction. Maternal depression interferes
with both responsiveness and with joyful interaction with infants and
toddlers. A depressed mother, whatever her intentions, cannot move
past her own feelings of despair to engage with the infant/toddler. Furthermore, irritability or simple bids for attention by the infant/toddler
may be misperceived as hostile by the mother and further contribute to
her depression.

This relation between the internal psychological state of the adult
caregiver and that caregiver's ability to construct secure adult–infant/
toddler attachment relationships has implications for practice. An extensive review and meta-analysis of attachment intervention programs
aimed at mothers (van IJzendoorn, Juffer, & Duyvesteyn, 1995) suggest
that, with relatively modest intervention, adults can be helped to become
more sensitive and responsive to their infants and toddlers and, as a
result, the relationships that they construct with children are more secure.
Another recent study of family child care and center-based providers
(Howes, Galinsky, & Kontos, 1998) also suggested that again, with a short-
term intervention, child care providers can increase their sensitivity and
children's security. It is important to note that these interventions appear
to be successful only with caregivers who were initially capable of being
sensitive to children in their care. These interventions appear to be unable
to change the behaviors of caregivers who, for whatever reason (e.g.,
depression, stress, state of mind regarding attachment), would be resistant to major changes in their caregiving strategies. For caregivers who
are resistant to changing their behaviors, more therapeutic interventions
designed to change representations of attachment in these caregivers may
be necessary.

For parents and for adults already working in the child care field,
interventions to increase sensitivity may be indicated. However, it also
may be more beneficial to prescreen caregivers (e.g., Raikes, 1993) in
order to assure that severely depressed adults or adults with maladaptive concepts of attachment and caregiving relationships do not enter
the field, given the resistance to change in these individuals. Prescreen-
ing does not have to involve such intensive methods as the Adult Attachment Interview. One study found that a short social perspective-taking
task distinguished mothers who could and could not adopt the psy-

chological perspective of the other (Kochanska, 1997). Mothers in this study who could adopt the psychological perspective of the other person were better able to co-construct a mutually reciprocal relationship.

Another more easily measured indicator of the capacity to be sensitive and responsive to infants and toddlers as a child care provider is formal education in child development. Caregivers who have completed formal degree programs at the bachelor's level or beyond are more sensitive and responsive to the children in their care than caregivers with less formal education (Howes, 1997). Although caregivers who have completed an associate's degree or child development associative program engage children in more developmentally appropriate activities than caregivers with only college courses or no formal education in child development, they are not as sensitive or responsive as caregivers with even more advanced training. These findings suggest that with advanced education caregivers can 1) re-work their own personal experiences of being cared for or of being a caregiver, 2) understand the importance of responsiveness and sensitivity for children's development, and 3) incorporate these behaviors into their own caring for children. Formal education also may serve as a screening function because many potential caregivers whose own life circumstances interfere with sensitive caregiving are unable to meet the demands of formal schooling.

IMPORTANT CONSIDERATIONS

There are three areas that need further consideration in the future: the relationship between family culture and the culture of the child care environment, shifting language environments in child care, and the effects of rapid employee turnover on children's social development.

It is sometimes argued, particularly in the case of infants/toddlers from a different cultural background than the parents, that the child care arrangement should incorporate caregiving routines from home (Wong Fillmore, 1991). Research on these topics lags far behind the belief system of early childhood education. Several strands of research inform the belief system and should be used to modify it. First, some literature (Garcia Coll et al., 1996) cited in the introduction suggests beneficial influences from bicultural socialization. A primary issue in bicultural socialization is whether both cultures are respected. If one culture is considered better than the other, then there is danger that the other culture will be considered shameful and that children will lose their connection to it (Wong Fillmore, 1991). Second, it is important to distinguish between respect for a culture and being in the culture, and between culture and language. One study completed in the culturally diverse and complex community of Hawaii found that child care teachers were more sensitive and responsive and teacher–child attachment relationships were more secure when the child care center was more sensitive to ethnic issues and when the child's home language was represented in the center, but not when there was an ethnic match between the child and the teacher or when the mother and teacher perceived themselves as having a better relationship (Howes & Rosenbatt, 1997). As this study indicates, further research is needed to elucidate the relationship between family and child care.

A second issue for both research and practice in the cultural context of infant/toddler social development is to increase understanding of the role of caregiving in the child's home language when the child is in alternative care (Wong Fillmore, 1991). The 1990 census data suggested that 1 of every 25 children in this country was living in a family in which all members speak a language other than English, and no adult reported being able to speak English well (Center for the Study of Social Policy, 1992). This is an issue that will only continue to grow and must be addressed.

A final issue that must be addressed has clear links to social policy: the issue of turnover in child care providers. The turnover rates of child care providers in all parts of the child care system, from informal care to the most formal of publicly supported child care centers, continue to remain around 40%–45% annually. A large body of research indicates that when good child care providers are adequately compensated for their work, they remain in the field. However, compensation rates are so very low that few providers can afford to stay, particularly the providers who are have advanced formal education and are the most sensitive and responsive to the infants and toddlers in their care. There is mounting evidence that caregiver turnover is detrimental to infant/toddler social development. Following a series of changes in caregivers, toddlers no longer are as likely to construct their relationship with the newest caregiver on the basis of her or his behavior but are more likely to replicate the quality of the previous relationship (Howes & Hamilton, 1992a). This means that if a toddler encounters a more sensitive and responsive caregiver than previous caregivers, the establishment of a positive adult–toddler relationship will require extra sensitivity on the part of the new caregiver. Furthermore, the more caregiver losses that preschoolers experience, the more likely they are to be aggressive with their peers (Howes & Hamilton, 1993a).

Infant and toddler social development is embedded within relationships with others—relationships with parents, alternative caregivers, and peers. These relationships and social interaction skills are primarily developed within the social contexts of the family and child care. This period of development is critical for the establishment of social interaction skills and the construction of positive relationships. Positive relationships provide a context for the development of social skills, and the experience of positive relationships leads to positive relationships with others. Adult sensitivity and responsiveness are essential for infants and toddlers to construct positive and secure relationships.

REFERENCES

Ainsworth, M.D.S., Blehar, M.C., Waters, E., & Wall, S. (1978). *Patterns of attachment: A study of the strange situation.* Mahwah, NJ: Lawrence Erlbaum Associates.

Anderson, C. W., Nagel, P., Roberts, M., & Smith, K. (1981). Attachment in substitute caregivers as a function of center quality and caregiver involvement. *Child Development, 52,* 53–51.

Bowlby, J. (1969/1982). *Attachment and loss: Loss, sadness and depression.* New York: Basic Books.

Bretherton, I. (1985). Attachment theory: Retrospect and prospect. In I. Bretherton & E. Waters (Eds.), *Growing points of attachment: Theory and research* (pp. 3–38). *Monographs of the Society for Research in Child Development, 50*(1-2, Serial no. 209).

Bronfenbrenner, U. (1979). *The ecology of human development.* Cambridge, MA: Harvard University Press.

Cassidy, J., & Berlin, L. (1994). The insecure/ambivalent pattern of attachment: Theory and research. *Child Development, 65,* 971–991.

Center for the Study of Social Policy. (1992). *The challenge of change: What the 1990 census tells us about children.* Washington, DC: Author.

Cochran, M.M., & Brassard, J.A. (1979). Child development and personal social networks. *Child Development, 50,* 601–616.

Crockenberg, S. (1981). Infant irritability, mother responsiveness, and social influences on the security of the infant–mother attachment. *Child Development, 52,* 857–865.

Cummings, E.M., & Davies, P. (1994). *Children and marital conflict.* New York: Guilford Press.

Del Carmen, R., Pedersen, F.A., Huffman, L.C., & Bryan, Y.E. (1993). Dyadic distress management predicts subsequent security of attachment. *Infant Behavior and Development, 16,* 131–147.

Eckerman, C.O., Davis, C.C., & Didow, S.M. (1989). Toddlers' emerging ways of achieving social coordination with a peer. *Child Development, 60,* 440–453.

Elicker, J., England, M., & Sroufe, L.A. (1992). Predicting peer competence and peer relationships in childhood from early parent–child relationships. In R.D. Parke & G.W. Ladd (Eds.), *Family–peer relationships: Modes of linkage* (pp. 77–106). Mahwah, NJ: Lawrence Erlbaum Associates.

Emde, R.N. (1989). The infant's relationship experience: Developmental and affective aspects. In A.J. Sameroff & R.N. Emde (Eds.), *Relationship disturbances in early childhood* (pp. 33–51). New York: Basic Books.

Fraiberg, S. (1959). *The magic years.* New York: Scribner.

Garcia Coll, C.T., Lamberty, G., Jenkins, R., McAdoo, H.P., Cunic, K., Wasik, B., & Garcia, H.V. (1996). An integrative model for the study of developmental competencies in minority children. *Child Development, 67,* 1891–1914.

Garcia Coll, C.T., Meyer, E.C., & Brillon, L. (1995). Ethnic and minority parenting. In M. Bornstein (Ed.), *Handbook of parenting: Vol 2. Biology and ecology of parenting* (pp. 189–209). Mahwah, NJ: Lawrence Erlbaum Associates.

George, C., Kaplan, N., & Main, M. (1985). *Adult attachment interview.* Unpublished interview, University of California, Berkeley.

George, C., & Solomon, J. (1996). Representational models of relationship: Links between caregiving and representation. *Infant Mental Health Journal, 17,* 198–216.

Goossen, F.A., & van IJzendoorn, M.H. (1990). Quality of infant's attachment to professional caregivers: Relation to infant–parent attachment and daycare characteristics. *Child Development, 51,* 832–837.

Gunnar, M. (1994). Psychoendocrine studies of temperament and stress in early childhood: Expanding current models. In J. Bates & T.D. Wachs (Eds.), *Temperament: Individual differences at the interface of biology and behavior* (pp. 213–253). Washington, DC: American Psychological Association.

Gunnar, M.R., Marvinney, D., Isensee, J., & Fisch, R.O. (1992). Coping with uncertainty: New models of the relations between hormonal, behavioral, and cognitive processes. In D. Palermo (Ed.), *Coping with uncertainty* (pp. 101–130). Mahwah, NJ.: Lawrence Erlbaum Associates.

Gutierrez, J., & Sameroff, A. (1990). Determinants of complexity in Mexican-American conceptions of child development. *Child Development, 61,* 384–394.

Hay, D. (1985). Learning to form relationships in infancy: Parallel attainments with parents and peers. *Developmental Review, 5,* 122–161.

Hazen, C., & Shaver, P. (1987). Romantic love conceptualized as an attachment process. *Journal of Personality and Social Psychology, 52,* 511–524.

Helburn, S. (Ed.). (1995). *Cost, quality and child outcomes in child care centers.* Denver: University of Colorado.

Hinde, R. (1976). On describing relationships. *Journal of Child Psychology and Psychiatry, 17,* 1–19.

Howes, C. (1980). Peer play scale as an index of complexity of peer interaction. *Developmental Psychology, 16,* 371–372.

Howes, C. (1983). Patterns of friendship. *Child Development, 54,* 1041–1053.

Howes, C. (1985). Sharing fantasy: Social pretend in toddlers. *Child Development, 56,* 1253–1258.

Howes, C. (1987). Social competence with peers in young children: Developmental sequences. *Developmental Review, 7,* 252–272.

Howes, C. (1988). Peer interaction of young children. *Monographs of the Society for Research in Child Development, 53*(1, Serial no. 217).

Howes, C. (1996). The earliest friendships. In W.M. Bukowski, W.F. Newcomb, & W.W. Hartup (Eds.), *The company they keep: Friendships in childhood and adolescence.* (pp. 66–86). New York: Cambridge.

Howes, C. (1997). Children's experiences in center based child care as a function of teacher background and adult–child ratio. *Merrill Palmer Quarterly, 43,* 404–426.

Howes, C. (1999). Attachment relationships in the context of multiple caregivers. In J. Cassidy & P.R. Shaver (Eds.), *Handbook of attachment theory and research* (pp. 671–687). New York: Guilford Press.

Howes, C., Galinsky, E., & Kontos, S. (1998). Caregiver sensitivity and child care attachment. *Social Development, 7,* 25–36.

Howes, C., & Hamilton, C.E. (1992a). Children's relationships with caregivers: Mothers and child care teachers. *Child Development, 53,* 859–878.

Howes, C., & Hamilton, C.E. (1992b). Children's relationships with child care teachers: Stability and concordance with maternal attachment. *Child Development, 53,* 879–892.

Howes, C., & Hamilton, C.E. (1993a). The changing experience of child care: Changes in teachers and in teacher–child relationships and children's social competence with peers. *Early Childhood Research Quarterly, 8,* 15–32.

Howes, C., & Hamilton, C. E. (1993b). Child care for young children. In B. Spodek (Ed.), *Handbook of research on the education of young children,* (pp. 322–336). New York: Macmillan.

Howes, C., Hamilton, C.E., & Althusen, V. (in press). Using the attachment Q-Set to describe non-familial attachments. In B. Vaughn & E. Waters (Eds.), *Attachment.* Mahwah, NJ: Lawrence Erlbaum Associates.

Howes, C., Hamilton, C.E., & Matheson, C.C. (1994). Children's relationships with peers: Differential associations with aspects of the teacher–child relationship. *Child Development, 65,* 253–263.

Howes, C., Hamilton, C.E., & Phillipsen, L.C. (1998). Stability and continuity of child–caregiver and child–peer relationships. *Child Development, 69,* 418–426.

Howes, C., & Matheson, C.C. (1992). Sequences in the development of competent play with peers: Social and social pretend play. *Developmental Psychology, 28,* 961–974.

Howes, C., Matheson, C.C., & Hamilton, C. (1994). Maternal, teacher, and child care history correlates of children's relationships with peers. *Child Development, 65,* 264–273.

Howes, C., & Oldham, E. (in press). Processes in the formation of attachment relationships with alternative caregivers. In A. Goncü & E. Klein (Eds.), *Essays in honor of Greta Fein.*

Howes, C., Phillips, D., & Whitebook, M., (1992). Thresholds of quality: Implications for the social development of children in center-based childcare. *Child Development, 63,* 449–460.

Howes, C., & Phillipsen, L.C. (1998). Continuity in children's relations with peers. *Social Development, 7,* 340–349.

Howes, C., & Ritchie, S. (1998). Changes in child–teacher relationships in a therapeutic preschool program. *Early Education and Development, 9,* 411–422.

Howes, C., & Ritchie, S. (1999a). Teachers and attachment in children with difficult life circumstances. *Development and Psychopathology, 11,* 254–268.

Howes, C., & Ritchie, S. (1999b). Teachers and attachment. In preparation.

Howes, C., & Rosenblatt, S. (1997). *Relations among relationships: Child care and home.* Paper presented at the biannual meeting of the Society for Research in Child Development, Washington, DC.

Howes, C., & Smith, E. (1995). Child care quality, teacher behavior, children's play activities, emotional security and cognitive activity in child. *Early Childhood Research Quarterly, 10,* 381–404.

Jackson, J.F. (1993). Multiple caregiving among African Americans and infant attachment: The need for an emic approach. *Human Development, 35,* 87–102.

Jacobson, J.L., & Wille, D.E. (1986). The influences of attachment behavior on developmental changes in peer interaction from the toddler to preschool period. *Child Development, 57,* 338–347.

Kagan, J. (1997). Temperament and the reactions to the unfamiliar. *Child Development, 68,* 139–143.

Kochanska, G. (1997). Mutually responsive orientation between mothers and their young children: Implications for early socialization. *Child Development, 68,* 94–112.

Kontos, S., Howes, C., Shinn, M., & Galinsky, E. (1995). *Quality in Family Child Care and Relative Care.* New York: Teachers College Press.

Kotulak, R., Andrews, W., & McMeel, P. (1996). *Inside the brain: Revolutionary discoveries of how the mind works.* New York: John Wiley & Sons.

LaFreniere, P.J., & Sroufe, L.A. (1985). Profiles of peer competence in the preschool: Interrelations among measures, influence of social ecology and peer competence. *Developmental Psychology, 21,* 56–69.

Lamb, M. (1977). Father–infant and mother–infant interaction in the first year of life. *Child Development, 48,* 167–181.

Lieberman, A.F. (1993). *The emotional life of the toddler.* New York: Free Press.

Londerville, S., & Main, M. (1981). Security of attachment, compliance, and maternal training methods in the second year of life. *Developmental Psychology, 17,* 289–299.

Lyons-Ruth, K., Connell, D.B., Grunebaum, H., & Botein, S. (1990). Infants at social risk; Maternal depression and family support services as mediators of infant development and security of attachment. *Child Development, 61,* 85–98.

Maccoby, E.E. (1984). Socialization and developmental change. *Child Development, 55,* 317–328.

Matas, L., Arend, R.A., & Sroufe, L.A. (1978). Continuity of adaptation in the second year: The relationship between quality of attachment and later competence. *Child Development, 49,* 547–556.

McLloyd, V., Jayarate, T., Ceballo, R., & Borquez, J. (1994). Unemployment and work interruption among African-American single mothers. *Child Development, 65,* 562–589.

NICHD Early Child Care Research Network. (1997). The effects of infant child care on infant–mother attachment security. *Child Development, 68,* 860–879.

Oppenheimer, D., Sagi, A., & Lamb, M.E. (1988). Infant–adult attachments on the Kibbutz and their relation to socio-emotional development 4 years later. *Developmental Psychology, 27,* 727–733.

Phillipsen, L.C., Burchinal, M.R., Howes, C., & Cryer, D. (1997). The prediction of process quality from structural features of child care. *Early Childhood Research Quarterly, 12,* 281–303.

Raikes, H. (1993). Relationship duration in infant care: Time with a high ability teacher and infant–teacher attachment. *Early Childhood Research Quarterly, 8,* 309–325.

Rose, R.J. (1995). Genes and human behavior. In J.T. Spence, J.M. Darley, & D.P. Foss (Eds.), *Annual Review of Psychology* (pp. 803–814). Palto Alto, CA: Annual Reviews.

Rubin, K., Mills, R.S.L., & Rose-Krasnor, L. (1989). Maternal beliefs and children's competence. In B.H. Schneider, G. Attili, J. Nadel, & R.P. Weissberg (Eds.), *Social competence in developmental perspective* (pp. 313–331). Norwell, MA: Kluwer Academic Publishers.

Rubin, K.H., Bukowski, W., & Parker, J.G. (1998). Peer interaction, relationships, and groups. In N. Eisenberg (Ed.). *Handbook of Child Psychology.* New York: Wiley.

Ruopp, R., Travers, J., Glantz, F., & Coelen, C. (1979). *Children at the center: Final results of the national day care study.* Cambridge, MA: Abt Associates.

Sroufe, L.A. (1983). Infant caregiving attachment and patterns of maladaption in preschool: The roots of maladaption and competence. In M. Permutter (Ed.), *Minnesota symposium on child psychology,* (Vol. 16, pp. 41–81). Mahwah, NJ: Lawrence Erlbaum Associates.

Steele, H., Steele, M., & Fonagy, P. (1995). Associations among attachment classifications of mothers, fathers, and their infants. *Child Development, 57*, 571–555.

Stern, D. (1977). *The first relationship.* Cambridge MA: Harvard University Press.

Teti, D.M., Gelfand, D.M., Messinger, D.S., & Isabella, R. (1995). Maternal depression and the quality of early attachment: An examination of infants, preschoolers, and their mothers. *Developmental Psychology, 31*, 364–376.

Thompson, R. (1993). Socioemotional development: Enduring issues and new challenges. *Developmental Review, 13*, 372–402.

Thompson, R. (1998). Early sociopersonality development. In W. Damon (Series Ed.) & N. Eisenberg (Vol. Ed.) *Handbook of child psychology: Vol 3. Social, emotional, and personality development* (5th ed., pp. 483–561). New York: John Wiley & Sons.

Turner, P.J. (1991). Relations between attachment, gender, and behavior with peers in preschool. *Child Development, 62*, 1475–1488.

van IJzendoorn, M.H., Juffer, F., & Duyvesteyn, M. (1995). Breaking the intergenerational cycle of insecure attachments: A review of attachment-based interventions on maternal sensitivity and infant security. *Journal of Child Psychology and Psychiatry, 36*, 225–248.

van IJzendoorn, M.H., Sagi, A., & Lambermon, M. (1992). The multiple caregiver paradox: Data from Holland and Israel. In R.C. Pianta (Ed.), Beyond the parent: The role of other adults in children's lives. *New Directions for Child Development, 57*, 5–27.

Whitebook, M., Howes, C., & Phillips, D. (1990). *Who cares? Child care teachers and the quality of care in America: Final report of the National Child Care Staffing Study.* Oakland, CA: Child Care Employee Project.

Wong Fillmore, L. (1991). When learning a second language means losing the first. *Early Childhood Research Quarterly, 6*, 323–346.

Section II

◆❖◆

Child Care and Intervention Programs

◆❖◆

5

New Directions
for Studying Quality
in Programs for
Infants and Toddlers

◆❖◆

John M. Love, Helen Raikes,
Diane Paulsell, and Ellen Eliason Kisker

High-quality child care programs can positively influence the development of infants and toddlers. However, children do not benefit when
placed in low-quality child care settings, and, in fact, their development
may be impeded. Because the primary concern is the well-being of
infants and toddlers in searching for the most meaningful definition of
quality, this chapter focuses on those program features that research has
found to be most strongly associated with infants' and toddlers' positive development and well-being.

In this chapter, we examine five central questions: 1) What types of
programs for infants and toddlers exist? 2) How prevalent are they?
3) What features of these programs have been shown to influence
infant/toddler development? 4) What is missing in the way quality has
been defined and measured in the program and research literature? and
5) How might a definition of quality more completely encompass programmatic features that are positively associated with enhanced
infant/toddler development?

This chapter draws themes, issues, and evidence from two bodies
of literature—research on child care quality and the research literature

on comprehensive intervention programs. These two bodies of knowledge have emerged in a parallel manner, with somewhat overlapping approaches and focusing on many of the same outcomes for children but with different emphases and attention to different process variables. This is a critical time for understanding the potential benefits of programs for infants and toddlers, and these two bodies of literature provide an opportunity to advance understanding. Taken together, they lead to an expanded concept of quality with an increased potential for informing policy and practice for programs serving infants and toddlers.

NEED FOR INFANT/TODDLER PROGRAMS

The Carnegie Corporation of New York, in its widely noted volume *Starting Points*, identified the vulnerability of American infants. According to the National Center for Children in Poverty, the poverty rate for children younger than age 6 increased from 17% in 1972 to 26% a decade later, with the number of children living in poverty almost doubling to 6 million. One infant in two in the country is vulnerable to compromised development by virtue of one or more of five factors: substandard child care, inadequate prenatal care, isolated parents, poverty, or insufficient stimulation (Carnegie Corporation of New York, 1994). In 1990, 60% of infants and toddlers in low-income families lived in single-parent families. In contrast, only 8% of infants and toddlers who did not live in poverty were in single-parent families (U.S. General Accounting Office, 1994). In 1996, 55% of mothers of children younger than the age of 3 were in the labor force, including 50% of mothers of infants younger than 1 year of age (U.S. Department of Labor Statistics and U.S. Bureau of Census, 1999). The National Center for Education Statistics' National Household Education Survey (West, Wright, & Hausken, 1995) reported for 1994 that 45% of all infants less than 1 year of age, 50% of 1-year-olds, and 54% of 2-year-olds were enrolled in nonparental child care and early education programs on a regular basis.[1]

In 1998, one infant in four lived in poverty (U.S. Bureau of Labor Statistics and U.S. Bureau of the Census, 1999). As is widely known, infants born into poverty are less likely to have received prenatal care, more likely to be born prematurely, and more likely to be born of low or very low birth weight than infants in middle- and higher-income families. Inadequate health care and having only one, or a very young, par-

---

[1]In the NHES, no attempt is made to distinguish settings in which children receive "care" from settings in which they receive "education" as, "any such distinction would be largely artificial" (West, Wright, & Hausken, 1995, p. 2). We endorse this approach to defining early care and education programs.

ent are known to compromise chances for optimal development as well. For example, in 1993, 41% of children between 19 and 35 months of age living in poverty were not adequately immunized (Children's Defense Fund, 1995).

The Carnegie report has provided a wake-up call for the nation to examine the environments of very young children and enhance their support for children's development. *Starting Points* emphasized the need for programs that promote responsible parenthood, guarantee quality child care, ensure good health and safety, and mobilize communities to support young children. The report recommended expanding Head Start and using it as a model to meet the needs of more low-income families with infants and toddlers. To enhance the development of children in poverty, there is an increased need to provide environments that mitigate the effects of poverty; provide the child with a safety net for basic health, nutrition, and stimulation needs; and support parenting.

Since that report, the U.S. Department of Health and Human Services (U.S. DHHS) has established a program for infants and toddlers, Early Head Start (EHS), funded through the Head Start Bureau in the Administration on Children, Youth and Families (ACYF).[2] The Personal Responsibility and Work Opportunity Reconciliation Act (PL 105-93) enacted in 1996 requires increasing numbers of low-income parents of infants to enter the labor force. Therefore, increases in the number of infants in out-of-home care are expected. The need for quality programs for infants and toddlers has never been greater.

The first part of this chapter describes types of programs, reviews what is known about how many exist, and concludes by summarizing existing definitions of quality in child care. The second part of this chapter summarizes what is known about the levels of quality in child care and how the children who participate in child care and comprehensive intervention programs fare. The third part raises issues in the study of quality, beginning with an examination of what is missing in current definitions and then discussing how research on comprehensive intervention programs contributes to an expanded definition. Finally, the last part presents a broadened concept of quality that emerges at the juncture of the child care and comprehensive intervention program literature and suggests some directions for future research.

Research suggests that only under conditions of high quality do child care and comprehensive intervention programs have the potential to enhance the development of the infants and support their eventual success in school. It is therefore critical that program administrators,

---

[2] As of spring 1999, Early Head Start programs exist in more than 500 communities throughout the United States, and more will be funded in the future.

policy makers, and researchers alike closely examine how quality in a variety of infant and toddler programs can be defined, measured, and fostered. Whether infants and toddlers enter programs through child care, through a comprehensive intervention program designed to mitigate the effects of poverty, through state health care, or through parenting programs serving many or even all infants in a state, these programs will influence the lives of millions of children.

TYPES OF PROGRAMS FOR INFANTS AND TODDLERS

Comprehensive intervention programs for infants and toddlers fall along a continuum, ranging from custodial child care to comprehensive two-generation programs that provide a large array of services for both children and parents. Some child care programs offer ancillary services. Some comprehensive programs provide child care, and others provide child development services in other ways, such as in-home visits or parent–child group activities and parenting education.

Child Care Programs for Infants and Toddlers

Child care programs for infants and toddlers are diverse. Broadly speaking, child care includes all regular care for infants and toddlers while parents work, attend school or training, or do other things. Thus, it includes formal center-based child care programs; formal, regulated family child care programs; and informal, unregulated family child care provided by relatives or nonrelatives. Regulated care refers to care that requires a government-issued license or registration designed to ensure minimal health and safety in environments serving children. State regulations vary enormously in coverage and strictness. Unregulated care is of two types—legal and illegal. Legal unregulated care is provided in homes for small numbers (varying by states) of family and nonfamily children. This care is sometimes called "licensed exempt" care. Illegal unregulated care typically refers to care provided to more children than the limit set by the state for exemption from license or registration.

Comprehensive Intervention Programs that Promote Healthy Infant/Toddler Development

Programs that promote healthy infant and toddler development include child-focused programs that provide services to meet multiple needs of infants and toddlers and two-generation programs that provide services to both infants/toddlers and their parents, with the goal of improving parental self-sufficiency and children's development. Two-generation programs typically include such services as case management, early childhood education, parenting instruction, and adult education. Many also offer other ancillary services, such as transportation, health care assistance, meals, family advocacy assistance, nutrition services, referrals for employment services, counseling, child care, mental health services, referrals for child protective services, referrals for services for battered women, treatment for substance abuse, and translators. Comprehensive intervention programs may provide services directly or through a combination of direct services and referrals to other community services.

AVAILABILITY OF PROGRAMS

Reliable up-to-date information on the number of programs providing child care for infants and toddlers does not exist. Licensing lists are not comprehensive because not all programs and child care providers are required to be licensed. Some programs providing child care, such as church-sponsored or part-time programs, are exempt from licensing in some states. Many family child care providers are also not required to be regulated. Thus, counting the number of programs on state licensing lists may significantly understate the number of child care programs and providers. However, programs that have stopped providing care are not immediately purged from licensing lists, so counting the number of programs on state licensing lists may overstate the number of programs or providers caring for children at a particular point in time. Surveys provide more reliable information about the supply of child care programs, but none of the available data are very recent.

Comprehensive intervention programs that do not provide child care are not required to be licensed and are not included on any licensing lists. Moreover, there are no national professional associations to which all comprehensive programs belong. Thus, the available information on comprehensive programs that do not provide child care is incomplete.

Availability of Child Care for Infants and Toddlers

Reliable information about the national supply of centers and family child care providers is now somewhat dated as well. At the beginning of 1990, approximately 80,000 center-based early education and care programs with the potential to serve more than 5 million children and 118,000 regulated family child care providers with the capacity to serve 860,000 children were operating in the United States (Kisker, Hofferth, Phillips, & Farquhar, 1991). According to licensing data collected and analyzed by the Children's Foundation, the number of centers appears to have increased slowly during the early 1990s to about 97,000 centers in 1997 (about a 21% increase), and the number of regulated family child care homes grew more dramatically, by about 140%, to about 283,000 in 1997 (Children's Foundation, 1997a; 1997b).

Only rough estimates of the number of unregulated family child care providers have been made. Depending on the estimation method used, Hofferth and Kisker (1991) estimated that between 550,000 and 1.1 million unregulated family child care providers with the capacity to care for 3.3 million children were caring for children at the beginning of 1990. Raikes (1998) estimated that unregulated care has been a fast-growing segment of the market in this current era of welfare reform.

Although nearly all regulated family child care providers and most unregulated family child care providers in 1990 reported that they accepted infants and toddlers, only slightly more than one half (55%) of centers did so. Approximately 16% of children enrolled in centers, 45% of children enrolled in regulated family child care settings, and 33% of children cared for by unregulated family child care providers in 1990 were infants or toddlers younger than 3 years old. This translates into about 799,000 infants and toddlers in center-based care, about 746,000 infants and toddlers in regulated family child care homes, and 1.1 million infants and toddlers in unregulated family child care homes (Hofferth & Kisker, 1991; Kisker et al., 1991).

Center-based child care for infants and toddlers is in short supply relative to demand. In the majority of centers, all slots for infants and at least 98% of all slots for toddlers were reported to be filled in early 1990. These high utilization rates suggest that, as parents and policymakers have perceived, a shortage of center-based care for infants and toddlers exists in many local areas. For example, the U.S. General Accounting Office (1995) reported shortages of infant care in all of the seven communities serving JOBS participants in which it conducted surveys. The need for more infant and toddler care was echoed in the report of child care workshops by the National Academy of Sciences (Phillips, 1995).

States are attempting to meet the need for infant and toddler care for mothers leaving public assistance in order to work by providing subsidies and assistance in finding care. They face a challenge in ensuring adequate quality of care at the same time: Pavetti and Duke (1995) reported that in states with welfare reform demonstrations, the greatest growth in the child care supply was in the unregulated sectors. Shortages also may have exerted downward pressure on the quality of the care provided for infants and toddlers in centers. Even in 1990, infants and toddlers in the average center were being cared for in relatively large groups with staff–child ratios exceeding professional recommendations (Kisker et al., 1991). With the welfare changes, this situation may be worsening.

Availability of Comprehensive
Intervention Programs for Infants and Toddlers

Information about the number of programs and numbers of infants and toddlers served is sketchy at best. The most complete information pertains to programs that provide home-based services to children and parents. A national survey of programs offering prenatal services and home-based services to children from birth through age 18 was conducted in 1987–1988. Because there was no national association of home visiting programs from which to obtain a complete list of programs for survey sampling, survey staff listed programs by contacting health, welfare, and social services agencies in all 50 states. Through this process, they identified 4,162 programs offering home-based services to children. Among the 1,904 programs that responded to the survey, an estimated one third focused on children from birth to 3 years of age (Gomby, Larson, Lewitt, & Behrman, 1993; Wasik, Bryant, & Lyons, 1990). These programs identified the primary purpose of the home visits for children as promotion of their development in one or more domains (e.g., physical, cognitive, social-emotional) and the primary purpose for parents as providing general support or enhancing parenting skills.

Comprehensive early intervention services for families of infants and toddlers with disabilities or who are at risk of having substantial developmental delays are provided by states with funds from multiple federal and state sources in accordance with the requirements of Part C (formerly Part H) of the Individuals with Disabilities Education Act (IDEA) Amendments of 1997 (PL 105-17). Under these requirements, states are responsible for ensuring that services are provided to all children with disabilities between birth and age 2. During the 1995–1996 school year, approximately 172,000 infants and toddlers and their families were expected to receive Part H services (Office of Special Education Programs, 1997). In 1998, 197,376 children received IDEA services under Part C, a 5.6% increase from 1997 (National Early Childhood Technical Assistance System, 1999).

TRADITIONAL DEFINITIONS OF QUALITY

Quality has been defined in a variety of ways. In an ideal world, researchers would know how variations in children's environments influence the children's learning, development, and well-being. Evidence is mounting that particular features of child care settings are empirically associated with certain outcomes in the children. The empirical relationships are less clear in the case of comprehensive intervention programs. Furthermore, research and practice in these programs have not focused on defining quality or identifying specific program features that influence development.

Early studies of child care did not distinguish variations in quality of care, perhaps because of an assumption that infant child care was detrimental to the mother–infant bond (Barton & Williams, 1993). In fact, the studies focused on the broad question "Is child care harmful?" often without even acknowledging differences among family, relative, or center-based care (Zaslow, 1991). In the 1980s and 1990s, however, the situation changed dramatically, with professional organizations, practitioners, and researchers all devoting considerable energies to defining and measuring quality in child care.

Definitions of quality in infant/toddler child care have generally centered on characteristics of the children's immediate environment—their classroom or family child care home. Two common features appear in most definitions: the dynamics of caregiver–child interactions, and structural or more static features, such as caregiver–child ratios, group size, safety features of the room, and qualifications of the caregivers. Layzer, Goodson, and Moss (1993) defined quality at the preschool level in terms of three sets of classroom dynamics or process variables: 1) the pattern and content of activities and groups across the day, 2) behavior and interactions of teaching staff, and 3) behavior and interactions of the children. Howes (1992) distinguished two major sets of program variables: administration and children's program functions. Children's program functions include both structural variables (e.g., space, materials, people, recurring patterns) and the dynamic processes or interactions between staff and children.

QUALITY AND HOW CHILDREN FARE

We are interested in learning more about quality in programs for infants and toddlers, whether the programs are child care or comprehensive intervention programs. Increasing the knowledge base about child care quality while examining salient features in comprehensive programs will enable program planners to improve environments for infants and toddlers. This section takes stock: What is the quality of child care serving infants and toddlers? What happens to children when child care quality varies? What are the consequences when programmatic features vary in comprehensive intervention programs?

Levels of Quality in Center-Based and Family Child Care

The quality of center-based child care for infants and toddlers in this country often does not meet professional standards for good quality care. On average, group sizes and staff–child ratios for infants and toddlers younger than age 3 in early 1990 were at or slightly above the state-regulated maximum levels for those ages; however, average group sizes and staff–child ratios for infants and toddlers were well above the maximum levels recommended by the National Association for the Education of Young Children (NAEYC). In most infant and toddler age groups, one third to two thirds of all centers did not meet NAEYC standards in 1990. Centers were least likely to meet the NAEYC standards for groups of toddlers (Kisker et al., 1991).

Average group sizes and staff–child ratios for infants and toddlers did not differ significantly among centers according to the proportion of children enrolled whose families were living in poverty or the extent to which centers cared for children whose fees were paid by a public agency. However, centers serving higher proportions of low-income children were more likely than other centers to provide supplemental services, such as health screening and developmental testing (Kisker et al., 1991).

Observational data on the quality of center-based care collected in five states in 1993 confirm that the quality of center-based care for infants and toddlers is often less than minimal. Only 8% of infant and toddler classrooms were rated as providing good or excellent care, and 40% were rated as providing poor quality care. In poor quality classrooms, basic sanitary conditions for diapering and feeding were not met; warm, supportive relationships with adults were missing; and books and toys required for children's physical and intellectual growth were lacking (Cost, Quality, and Outcomes Study Team, 1995). Observational data from the National Child Care Staffing Study also showed that a significant proportion of centers provided poor-quality infant and toddler care. Although teacher characteristics and global indices of child care quality did not differ significantly between centers predominantly serving children in low-income families and those serving children in higher income families, teacher sensitivity was significantly lower and detachment significantly more common in low-income than in middle- or upper-income centers (Phillips, Voran, Kisker, Howes, & Whitebook, 1994). Some evidence also exists that very young infants (6 months of age), whose nonmaternal caregivers included fathers during the early months of maternal employment, may experience higher levels of process quality than has been found in mixed samples of infants and toddlers (National Institute of Child Health and Human Development [NICHD] Early Child Care Research Network, 1996a).

Although structural indicators of quality in family child care homes suggest that the quality of family child care may be higher than that of center-based child care, observational data suggest that family child care providers often provide poor quality care. Only a minority of family

child care providers in 1990 did not meet the benchmarks for good quality care established in the 1980 Health, Education, and Welfare Day Care
Requirements (HEWDCR). However, family child care providers had
less formal education than teachers in center-based settings, and they
were less likely to have had any child-related training (Hofferth & Kisker,
1991). Moreover, the Study of Children in Family Child Care and Relative Care conducted in three communities in the early 1990s found that
only 9% of family child care providers were rated as providing high-
quality care, and 35% were rated as providing poor-quality care. In contrast to studies of centers, the Study of Children in Family Child Care and
Relative Care found that children from lower income families were in
lower quality family child care than their higher income counterparts
(Galinsky, Howes, Kontos, & Shinn, 1994).

How Children Fare in Infant/Toddler Programs

Research that has examined the effectiveness of programs in terms of
the well-being of infants and toddlers is highly varied. Clear conclusions about how children fare are difficult to reach because of the great
variability across studies. Studies vary not only in the nature of the programs and the services they provide (even among those labeled as "child
care" programs, which might be thought to be more similar as a group
than the more comprehensive programs), but vary along such dimensions as age at which children enter the program, program duration,
families' socioeconomic status, participants' race and ethnicity, and
designs and measures used in the research. Nevertheless, the chances
that infants and toddlers will benefit from participating in child care and
other programs appear to be less than they could be.

Findings from Infant/Toddler Child Care Studies   In the
1950s and 1960s, researchers were concerned about maternal separation
and focused their studies on the potential negative effects of "child care"
on the child's attachment to his or her mother. More recently, studies
have recognized the importance of other relationships and have included
measures of children's relationships with their caregivers and with each
other. Lamb and Sternberg (1990) summarized a number of studies, concluding that children in out-of-home care could remain attached to their
parents. At the same time, the children might be more sociable with
peers and other adults. Belsky (1988) argued that nonmaternal care in the
first year of life both increased the risk for insecure mother–infant attachment and was likely to lead to elevated aggressiveness, noncompliance,
and withdrawal as the infants got older. Unfortunately, the wave of
attachment research that followed Belsky's conclusions failed to take
into account variations in quality of care.

In the 1980s and 1990s, a growing body of research showed that quality in infant/toddler child care, as defined and measured in various ways, is positively associated with multiple dimensions of children's development. The potential benefits for infants and toddlers are seen in their attachment with their caregivers, their language and cognitive development, and their social behavior and development. Although child care for preschoolers has been studied more extensively than care for infants and toddlers (Love, Schochet, & Meckstroth, 1996), a substantial body of literature includes infants/toddlers in center and family child care. Of the 28 studies of center-based child care reviewed by Love and colleagues (1996), 11 included infants and toddlers (although the infants were usually a small portion of the total sample). Infants and toddlers are more likely to be cared for in family child care settings, and this is reflected in the research. Although fewer studies of family child care settings have been done, more than half of them have included infants and toddlers, and several have focused exclusively on this age group.

Attachment and Interactions with Adults   Preliminary findings from the Study of Early Child Care (NICHD Early Child Care Research Network, 1996b) indicated that at 15 months of age, neither center care, family child care, nor father care diminishes the mother–infant attachment so long as the child does not simultaneously experience inattentive mothering while in poor-quality child care. Howes, Phillips, and Whitebook (1992) reported that in the National Child Care Staffing Study, infants and toddlers in higher quality classes were more securely attached to their caregivers than children in poor or minimally adequate care. Galinsky, Howes, Kontos, and Shinn (1994) and Kontos, Howes, Shinn, and Galinsky (1995) also found greater security of attachment when caregivers were rated as sensitive and responsive. Galinsky, Howes, and Kontos (1995) found children to be more securely attached after their caregivers received a special training course.

The NICHD study showed that quality of child care contributed significantly (though not as much as maternal factors) to positive mother–child interactions across the first 3 years. Quality in child care predicted mother–child interaction for low-income children. When the babies were 6 months of age, low-income mothers using quality child care had higher positive involvement with their children than low-income mothers not using care or those using lower-quality full-time care. Alternatively, mothers were less engaged when children were 24 months of age if they used low-quality care, in contrast with those not using care. High-quality child care enhanced interactions between mother and child when the children were young infants, and poor quality diminished those interactions when children were 2 years of age (NICHD Early Child Care Research Network, 1997).

Howes, Phillips, and Whitebook (1992) included 68 infants and 175 toddlers in their study. In classrooms rated higher in "appropriate caregiving," children were more likely to be seen as secure, and less avoidant or ambivalent. In classrooms rated higher on "developmentally appropriate activities," children were more likely to be both adult- and peer-oriented. Similarly, Howes, Smith, and Galinsky (1995), in their national study of 880 children in 150 centers, found that more favorable adult–infant ratios were associated with more secure attachment to caregivers. In a study of the effects of caregiver training with 130 family providers and their children, Galinsky, Howes, and Kontos (1995) found that children ages 1–5 years were more securely attached following the caregivers' 16-hour training course.

Cognitive and Language Development   The preceding studies have shown that security of the infants' attachment to their caregivers was positively associated with quality variables. Howes and Smith (1995) furthered understanding of this relationship when they reported that quality (as measured by the Infant/Toddler Environment Rating Scale [ITERS]) and security of attachment with the caregiver were mediated by positive child-focused social interactions with caregivers (as measured by the Adult Involvement Scale). Moreover, both positive social interaction and attachment security predicted cognitive activity for most groups of children they studied. (An exception was African American infants and toddlers in nonsubsidized centers, for whom positive caregiver social interaction was more highly associated with cognitive activities than was security in attachment.) In general, these researchers regarded classroom quality as a critical context for the cognitive stimulation that occurs between caregivers and children. Good caregivers can have positive interactions that support children's cognitive development, directly and indirectly, even under adverse conditions, but it is more likely they will be "constrained in constructing relationships and activities in poorly equipped, understaffed, or crowded classrooms" (Howes & Smith, 1995, p. 403).

A more direct link between quality and cognitive/language development was reported by Burchinal, Roberts, Nabors, and Bryant (1996). These researchers examined the relationships between the quality of center-based child care and measures of development in 79 African American infants. They found that ratios were positively and significantly related to communication skills of 12-month-olds; process quality was associated with Bayley Mental Development Index (BMDI) scores, but not language scores. The NICHD Early Child Care Research Network (1997) reported that positive caregiving and language stimulation were related to children's better performance on both language and cognitive assessments at 15, 24, and 36 months of age. Melhuish, Mooney, Martin, and Lloyd (1990a, 1990b), who assessed children at 5 and 18 months of age, found that children who were in center settings that provided less verbal communication with and less responsiveness to children scored lower in language development.

Social Behavior and Development   Howes and Olenick (1986), studying children between 1 and 3 years of age, found that boys (but not girls) in higher quality centers showed less resistant behavior and greater self-regulation. Center quality predicted social behaviors when the children were in kindergarten (Howes, 1990): Higher quality infant care was associated with children being less distractible, more task-oriented, and more considerate in kindergarten. Howes (1990) also found that among children enrolled as infants, child care quality was a better predictor of child outcomes than family socialization practices. (The opposite was true for the children who enrolled in child care as toddlers or preschoolers.)

Howes and Rubenstein (1981) looked at both center and family settings with children from 18 to 24 months of age. In family child care homes, smaller group sizes and the presence of older children in the group positively influenced children's vocalizations to peers. Children in centers of higher quality showed more positive levels of interactive play.

Howes, Smith, and Galinsky (1995) studied 880 children ranging from 10 months to 5 years in age in 150 centers. In addition to the attachment findings referred to previously, improving ratios for infants and toddlers led to more complex child play with both peers and objects, greater adaptive language proficiency, and fewer behavior problems (e.g., aggression, anxiety, hyperactivity).

Ruopp, Travers, Glantz, and Coelen (1979) summarized findings of the infant/toddler observation substudy of the National Day Care Study conducted with 74 caregivers in 38 centers. Although child outcomes were not measured, the study found that group composition (i.e., ratio and group size) was associated with the quality of children's experiences. Infants in centers with better ratios exhibited less overt distress and less apathetic behavior, and were exposed to fewer potentially dangerous situations; infants cared for by better educated (but less experienced) staff showed less apathy and were exposed to fewer potentially dangerous situations; and toddlers in centers with better ratios showed less overt distress. Larger infant groups were associated with greater distress and more apathetic children.

Studying children 11–30 months of age in family child care homes, Howes and Stewart (1987) found that more provider changes adversely affected level of play with objects and peers. For boys, earlier entry into care and fewer provider changes were also associated with higher level play with objects. Overall quality of care related to higher levels of competent play with adults and with objects. For girls, the relationship was also significant for higher level play with peers. In the family child care homes included in the Howes and Rubenstein (1981) study, smaller group sizes and the presence of older children in the group positively influenced children's vocalizations to peers.

Galinsky, Howes, and Kontos (1995), in the study cited previously, followed 130 children and family providers with children ages 1–5 years. When caregivers had a special training course of 15–25 hours of class time and supervised home visits, children were more engaged in activities and showed less aimless wandering compared to children whose caregivers did not receive the training. Training included such topics as health, safety, and nutrition; child development and age-appropriate activities; environments to promote learning; guidance and discipline; parent–caregiver relationships; and diversity issues (Kontos, Howes, & Galinsky, 1996).

Studies with Longitudinal Follow-Up   Field (1991) followed up children who began center care when they were younger than 2 years old and were in care an average of 2.7 years. Follow-up at 11.5 years of age found that children who spent more time in high-quality settings showed greater physical affection during peer interactions, were more likely to be assigned to a gifted academic program, and received higher math grades.

Howes and Hamilton (1992) followed up children at ages 4–5 who had been in center and family child care when they were 1–2 years old. They found important evidence of the value of continuity of care. When more changes in teachers occurred, children were less gregarious and more socially withdrawn and aggressive. More secure teacher–child relationships (or those that became more so) were associated with more positive, gregarious, and prosocial interactions with peers and less withdrawn and aggressive behaviors. Increasing the number of changes in centers or settings, however, had no demonstrable effect on social competence with peers.

Lamb, Hwang, Broberg, and Bookstein (1988) studied 1- and 2-year-olds in centers, family child care, and maternal home care. Children's sociability and personal maturity when followed up at 2–4 years of age were not related to the type of child care they had earlier. Quality of care (regardless of type) and family social support were both important for later personal maturity and social skills with familiar peers and unfamiliar adults.

Findings from Studies of Comprehensive Intervention Programs   Comprehensive intervention programs that have evolved since the 1970s include programs known by such labels as two-generation, family support, home visitation (with varying degrees of support services), and comprehensive interventions. At the risk of oversimplifying, this review is limited to those most clearly known as two-generation and family support programs. However, the classification of particular interventions into these groups is often somewhat arbitrary. Nevertheless, this review addresses the purpose in attempting to identify program features and strategies that are most likely to have beneficial effects on infant and toddler development.

Two-Generation Programs   True two-generation programs tackle problems on two fronts, aiming to foster both children's development and parents' self-sufficiency (Smith, 1995). These programs have adopted a great diversity of program models, with some delivering services through home visiting, and others offering center-based child care or adult service referral through case management. Services to both generations have been mixed in a variety of ways and intensities. One review of these programs (St. Pierre, Layzer, & Barnes, 1994) proposed that two-generation programs share three features (or foci): 1) a developmentally appropriate early childhood program or the child focus; 2) parenting education or the family focus; and 3) adult education, literacy, or job skills training or the adult focus. Blank (1997) described two-generation programs as providing two mutually reinforcing sets of services: employment-related services for parents (e.g., education, training, job placement, and pre- and postemployment services), and child and family services (e.g., high-quality child care and early childhood education, preventive health care, parenting education, and family support).

Findings are reviewed from a variety of two-generation comprehensive intervention programs. Some of the programs have emphasized services to the infants and toddlers to a greater extent than services to parents or have emphasized parenting education but not adult education as the adult component. Others have stressed self-sufficiency and adult education with minimal child development services. However, all have included both a child and parent component at some level. Programs included in this review are the Parent and Child Centers (PCCs), Parent and Child Development Centers (PCDCs), the Child and Family Resource Program (CFRP), the Abecedarian Project, the Family Development Research Program (FDRP), Project CARE, the Infant Health and Development Program (IHDP), the Comprehensive Child Development Program (CCDP), the Prenatal/Early Infancy Project (PEIP), and other programs with a home-visit focus.

The Center for Community Research (1973b) conducted parent and child impact studies at selected PCC sites. Outcomes were examined in the areas of parenting skills and attitudes; self-esteem and feelings of control; knowledge and use of community resources; use of health facilities; and nutrition practices. Few treatment-control differences appeared. Evidence of impact on children was similarly weak (Center for Community Research, 1973a). A descriptive study of 36 PCCs in the early 1980s assessed program practices along a number of quality indicators. The activities designed to promote infants' and toddlers' cognitive, socioemotional, and physical development were frequently not developmentally appropriate. Programs were plagued by poor facilities, high staff–child ratios, insufficient space, inadequate amounts of language interaction between teachers and children, and limited health services. On the positive side, PCCs implemented high quality home-based services, established a positive affective environment for participating families, and provided comprehensive approaches to parent education and guiding parents in the use of community resources (Hubbell & Barrett, 1984).

Three PCDCs developed out of PCCs and implemented randomized experiments. Considerable diversity existed across sites in children's age at entry, ethnic groups, program intensity, and whether services were primarily center- or home-based. The evaluation focused on mother–child interactions and infant/toddler cognitive development. Two sites found positive impact on measures of positive maternal behavior; another two found significantly higher Stanford-Binet IQ scores favoring the PCDC children (Dokecki, Hargrave, & Sandler, 1983).

The CFRP was a program effort by the ACYF that also received an intensive process and impact evaluation. Analysis of the impact of program participation, which included parent–child group socializations and home-based services, yielded mixed findings (Nauta & Travers, 1982). No CFRP-control group differences on assessments of children's cognitive and social development were significant, but after 3 years, CFRP mothers were more likely than control group mothers to be employed or in job training (even in sites hardest hit by the recession of the late 1970s and early 1980s). Program participation enhanced parents' coping skills and increased parents' sense of control of events in their lives, and CFRP parents increased their parent–child teaching skills. CFRP participation was only moderately linked to use of preventive health care services.

Yet, the Abecedarian study (Ramey & Campbell, 1991), which featured full-time child care together with pediatric care and family support services, was very successful in affecting children's cognitive development. In this classic study, beginning in 1972, 109 low-income families were randomly assigned to experimental and control groups. Those in the experimental group received child care and support services beginning in infancy and continuing until the children were 5 years old. Assessments of children's intellectual competence at 12, 16, 24, 36, 48, 60, 78, 84, and 96 months of age showed consistent differences favoring the experimental group at every testing interval.

The Syracuse University Family Development Research Program (FDRP) served low-income high school dropout mothers from the second trimester of pregnancy until children were 5 years old (Lally, Mangione, & Honig, 1987). Children attended the Children's Center half days from 6 to 18 months of age and full days from 18 months to 5 years of age. Families also received weekly home visits from trained paraprofessionals who provided parent education and family support. A follow-up study conducted when the children were 15 years old revealed that there were only 4 of 65 FDRP children who had juvenile delinquency records compared with 12 of 54 control group youths. Program youths were also less likely to be truant and more likely to have passing grades (Lally et al., 1987).

Project CARE (Wasik, Ramey, Bryant, & Sparling, 1990) was designed to test the effectiveness of home-based parent education and social services, with and without full-time, center-based child care as part of the program model. This study randomly assigned parents to one of three groups—child care combined with family education, family education only, or a control group. When children were 2 years old, group differences in language and cognitive outcomes significantly favored the group who had received child care combined with family education. By the time the children were 4 years old, differences were smaller, though still significant and in the same direction as the 2-year findings. The authors attributed the narrowing difference among the groups to effects of community child care that was used by a large number of control group and home-based parent education group families.

The Infant Health and Development Program (IHDP) provided a combination of home visiting, center-based education, and family services to low birth-weight premature infants and their families during the first 3 years of life. At age 3, intervention group children attained significantly higher Stanford-Binet IQ scores and lower behavior problem scores. The heavier low birthweight infants benefited more at ages 2 and 3, both in IQ and behavior problems scores, with these effects somewhat sustained 2 years after the intervention ended (Brooks-Gunn, Klebanov, Liaw, & Spiker, 1993; IHDP, 1990). This may have been because the lower weight infants required ongoing medical and educational support that rendered them less able to benefit from the typical home- and center-based education and support services that the program provided for all families (Brooks-Gunn et al., 1993; Brooks-Gunn et al., 1994). The IHDP intervention was more beneficial for the children whose families had few or a moderate number of risk factors and for families who had center-based early childhood programs or medical services to augment the IHDP home visiting or both (Liaw & Brooks-Gunn, 1994). A follow-up analysis of the service data from this project (Liaw, Meisels, & Brooks-Gunn, 1995) demonstrated that the greatest benefits were realized when both parents and children were highly involved in project activities and that benefits were sustained 5 and 8 years later for the heavier low birth weight groups (Brooks-Gunn et al., 1994; McCarton et al., 1997).

The Comprehensive Child Development Program (CCDP) featured intensive social services and parent education, although direct child development services and program-sponsored child care were far less intensive than in the IHDP and Abecedarian programs. The final evaluation report demonstrated that, overall, the CCDP did not yield the cognitive and language effects for children found in programs featuring more intense child development services; however, at one site, the program had significant and moderately large positive effects on children's cognitive development, parenting skills, and several outcomes related to self-sufficiency (St. Pierre, Layzer, Goodson, & Bernstein, 1997).

The Prenatal/Early Infancy Project (PEIP), which began in 1977 in the Appalachian region of New York, was designed to meet low-income parents' needs for information, emotional support, and relief of life stress. Four hundred pregnant adolescents were randomly assigned to several treatment groups or a control group. Nurse home visitors worked with the women assigned to the treatment groups during pregnancy and the children's infancy. Two clear findings related to parenting emerged: 1) 2 years after giving birth, the women at high risk who received visits from nurse home visitors had one fifth the number of verified child abuse or neglect reports as those in the control group; and 2) PEIP mothers punished and restricted their children less and provided more appropriate toys (Olds, Henderson, Tatelbaum, & Chamberlin, 1986a). Furthermore, women who received home visits had greater increases in their knowledge of community services and use of social supports (Olds, Henderson, Tatelbaum, & Chamberlin, 1986b). A 15-year follow-up found that mothers who received services over a longer time period had lower levels of child maltreatment, subsequent birth rates, welfare enrollment, substance abuse, and encounters with the criminal justice system (Olds et al., 1997).

Home visiting programs can be considered to be a subset of two-generation programs. Olds and Kitzman (1993), after reviewing 31 home visiting programs and focusing on families with low birth weight and preterm infants or families at risk for maltreatment, concluded that home-visiting programs are most successful when 1) families are initially at greater risk for poor outcomes, 2) programs are comprehensively designed, 3) services are delivered by well-trained professionals, and 4) visitors meet frequently enough to establish a working relationship and address their needs. In general, in two-generation programs, attribution of effects to specific program features has been difficult to establish. Although St. Pierre and colleagues (1994) proposed that the findings indicate that two-generation programs may be at risk of taking a broad approach that does not provide enough of any single type of service to be effective, Gomby and colleagues (1993) suggested that home-visiting programs achieve larger gains when center-based early childhood programs and/or medical services augment home visiting. Weiss (1993) noted that many of the evaluated home-visiting programs provide other services in addition to home visiting, making it difficult to attribute positive outcomes to home visiting.

Although some home visiting programs have reported program effects on infants and toddlers, center-based services appear to be more likely to affect children directly, especially in terms of cognitive and language development. Benasich, Brooks-Gunn, and Clewell (1992) reviewed 27 early intervention programs and found that 90% of the center-based programs (compared with 64% of the home-based programs) resulted in immediate effects on cognitive outcomes; 67% of the center-based programs (versus 44% of home-based programs) sustained these effects 1 year after the program had ended.

As even this small sample of studies demonstrates, two-generation programs vary on a number of key dimensions: ages of children served, duration of services, intensity of services, timing of services, whether services are offered through a center-based or home-based approach (or both), duration and intensity of the parenting component, extent of reliance on case management, and the nature of the adult education or job training component. Parker, Piotrkowski, Horn, and Greene (1995) concluded that several aspects of two-generation program strategies were inadequately developed in some programs. This helps explain why it is difficult to obtain a clear picture of relationships between program features and positive infant/toddler outcomes. They found, for example, inadequate guidelines for establishing parent self-sufficiency goals and caseloads too large for establishing effective staff–parent relationships. Other important program elements—such as full-day child care, services extending beyond a single year, and training for social services staff—were missing altogether.

Family Support Programs   Kagan and Neville identified family support programs as "among the most notable of the efforts to integrate services at the local level" (1993, p. 61). These are programs committed to serving the entire family, preventing social problems, and encouraging broad-based community engagement. These programs are included in this review because the efforts at local levels often include infants and toddlers within their wide net of targeted recipients. Family support programs encompass at least as much diversity as do two-generation programs; in fact, there is considerable overlap. Policymakers and program operators have created various typologies, all of which are multifaceted. They include such diverse program goals and elements as preventing child abuse and neglect, enhancing prenatal and infant wellness, creating home–school linkages, providing parent education and support, providing early childhood education, implementing family-oriented child care, and being neighborhood-based (Kagan & Shelley, 1987).

With such diversity in programmatic approaches, one might expect great diversity in evaluation findings. Weiss's (1988) review of evaluations of family support and education program effectiveness concluded that some evidence of program effectiveness exists, but not much has been learned about how programs work: "Knowledge about family support and education program effectiveness is not only narrow, due to restricted outcomes, but is also shallow due to few efforts to unpack the black box of treatment" (p. 8). Barnett (1995) considered family support programs to include early care and education programs, home visiting programs, and two-generation models, as long as they deliver services that address the needs of both children and parents. He concluded that considerable knowledge has accumulated. For example, his review suggests first that high-quality, center-based early care and education can produce "substantial and persistent" effects on many dimensions of children's development. Second, timing and duration of programs matter— beginning in the first year of life and continuing until children start school may produce larger and more persistent gains in cognitive development and school success than beginning later or lasting a shorter period of time. Third, impact varies directly with the difference between center and home in quality and quantity of human capital and other resources. Fourth, home visits may be most effective for children when they seek to improve child rearing. Finally, efforts to produce larger effects for children and parents by providing more comprehensive services has been "more costly and less effective than hoped."

A difficulty in summarizing lessons from studies of family support programs is that the programs encompass a wide variety of approaches. They can include comprehensive service delivery strategies with family and community goals, and they can include part-day preschool programs with occasional home visits. Barnes, Goodson, and Layzer (1995) grouped family support programs into universal access programs, programs targeted at children considered at risk because of environmental factors, and programs targeting children at risk because of biological factors. They conclude that a variety of family-focused interventions has "improved the immediate developmental status of infants and young children." Some of the factors that influence variations in program effectiveness include the risk status of the child, the timing of the intervention in the child's life, and the intervention methods. Programs for children environmentally at risk have greater positive effects for children with more risk factors.

Conclusions About How Children Fare   Many reviewers have offered general principles derived from the body of research that has been only briefly summarized here. At the national policy level, the report of the Advisory Committee on Services for Families with Infants and Toddlers (US DHHS, 1994) identified a number of critical ingredients for successful infant/toddler programs. These provide a useful summary at this stage of our research knowledge. The committee concluded that successful ingredients include

- Early prenatal services
- Two-generation focus
- Family-centered services that address self-sufficiency through social services and parent education
- Quality child development services coupled with family services
- Continuity of service delivery for children and their families that ensures availability of support over a number of years, with smooth transitions to other service delivery systems
- Continuity of caregivers
- Intensive service delivery—availability, accessibility, and usage
- Consolidation or integration of service delivery systems

These can be succinctly summarized with the conclusion that comprehensive intervention programs and services are most effective when they begin early, are intense, have a two-generational focus, provide direct child development services, provide for continuity of service, and coordinate with other services and programs. In designing its new Early Head Start program, the Administration on Children, Youth, and Families made every effort to incorporate as many of these ingredients as possible into the program guidelines and principles.

ISSUES IN THE STUDY OF QUALITY

A study of quality in relation to child care and comprehensive intervention programs identifies missing elements related to quality and illustrates that both literatures contribute to a broader conception of quality. Each supplies some of what is missing in the other. On the one hand, the child care literature has made an enormous contribution to the study of quality, whereas the literature on comprehensive intervention programs has not explicitly examined quality in child care or other features of program quality. On the other hand, standard definitions of child care quality omit elements that can be found through examination of the focus of comprehensive programs.

What Is Missing in Definitions of Quality in Infant/Toddler Child Care

We see four critical features of child care and comprehensive intervention programs that have been relatively neglected in definitions and research on quality: relationships, continuity, culture, and context. For each, we propose that indicators can be identified at both the program and individual child levels. Traditional definitions emphasize program-level variables; there is a need for research to focus on indicators defined at the level of the individual child.

Relationships   Because the developmental needs of infants and toddlers differ from those of their older peers, it is important to identify program features that have particular salience for the developmental levels of the children enrolled. One of children's major developmental "tasks" in the first 2 years of life is to establish secure relationships with their primary caregivers. Given infants' heavy reliance on their relationships with caregivers, definitions of quality should take into account the nature of that relationship. Infants and toddlers require much from relationships: contact comfort, appropriate and predictable responses from a familiar caregiver, reassurance in times of stress, and a secure base for exploration (Ainsworth, Blehar, Waters, & Wall, 1978; Bowlby, 1969). Because of these considerations, security-promoting relationships within the infant care setting should be included on the list of standard indicators of quality for infant/toddler programs, and not be treated simply as an outcome variable. This feature of quality is different from the often reported process quality that examines the stream of interaction that the infant receives at a single point or even multiple points in time. Typical measures of interactions do not embed these interactions within relationships. This proposed feature of quality also goes beyond staff stability as a structural variable, positing the staff–child relationship to be at the very heart of the infant's child care experience and at the heart of the infant's development while in child care.

Continuity   For infants to form quality relationships, it is important for them to be in consistent caregiving environments. Repeatedly entering new child care arrangements is likely to be detrimental to infants' developing relationships. Multiple changes in child care arrangements have been associated with higher rates of insecure attachment to the mother (Suwalsky, Zaslow, Klein, & Rabinovich, 1986; Vaughn, Gove, & Egeland, 1980) and lower levels of complexity in play among children (Howes & Stewart, 1987). Greater continuity with teachers has been associated with secure teacher–child attachment (Raikes, 1993, 1996). Instability, or lack of continuity, may occur at the level of the teacher or the child. Teacher instability is caused by staff turnover, which is particularly high in child care, or by internal changes within programs due to "graduations" of children from rooms for younger children to those for older children. Instability at the child level occurs with changes in child care arrangements, which are notably high among infants at all income levels (NICHD Early Child Care Research Network, 1996c) but especially so among low-income working families (Siegel & Loman, 1991). Although turnover is often included as a structural indicator of quality, a propensity for consistent relationships within a program and continuity over time across programs (i.e., stability from the child's point of view) have not often been employed as indicators of quality.

Culture   There is little research on the role of cultural congruence between program staff and infants/toddlers and their families; however, few would dispute the need to understand the role of cultural congruence among programmatic features that are likely to have an impact on child development. It is reasonable to assume children's development would be enhanced by staff who speak the same language; who share values, traditions, and emphases with parents; and who look and interact in ways that are familiar to the children. Aspects of the cultural climate that are likely to be included in measures include parent–professional partnerships; language issues, including bilingualism; anti-bias curriculum; materials; and staff training (Chang, Muckelroy, & Pulido-Tobiassen, 1996).

Context   Many researchers have begun to recognize the importance of context and build into their definitions program characteristics that influence the classroom structure and dynamics. Phillips and Howes (1987), for example, considered the contribution of such contextual features as the type of setting and staff stability, in addition to structural features of the program such as group composition, staff qualifications, and dynamic aspects of the children's experience. Love, Ryer, and Faddis (1992) considered staff qualifications, child turnover, program auspices, and parent involvement as potentially important contextual features.

In some of the most recent and more comprehensive analyses of child care quality, Ferrar (1996) and Ferrar, Harms, and Cryer (1996) described quality in terms of goals—that is, objectives that providers can work toward and against which they can measure their progress. Drawing upon experience in the Expanded Child Care Options project (funded by the Rockefeller Foundation), these authors describe detailed quality characteristics in four domains that apply to both center-based settings (Ferrar, 1996) and family child care homes (Ferrar, Harms, & Cryer, 1996): the classroom or home environment and daily program, supportive services, administration, and safety. The following example gives a flavor of the detailed analysis of quality provided. For classroom goals, Ferrar described specific quality goals in seven areas: daily routines, physical environment, materials and equipment, daily schedule, developmentally appropriate learning activities, staff–child interactions, and staff collaboration and support. The administrative component of quality in family child care included adult–child ratios, provider qualifications, planning and evaluation, business management, and continuity of care.

Especially relevant to the discussion is the supportive services domain that Ferrar (1996) and Ferrar and colleagues (1996) described in both center and family settings. Supportive service goals in five areas apply to both types of settings: health services, nutrition, mental health services, social services, and parent involvement. According to the definitions of Ferrar and her colleagues, a high-quality child care program begins to have features in common with more comprehensive infant/toddler programs.

Quality on an Individual Level   Also missing in current definitions is a way of knowing the specific features of quality as they are experienced by individual children. Although it is presumed that global program quality increases the probability of individual children having quality experiences within child care, child-specific observations would increase understanding of the variability of quality actually received by different children in terms of relationships, interactions, and stimulation. Evidence of within-program variability on quality dimensions confirms the importance of considering individual experience. For example, Fein (1995) showed that caregivers responded more to expressive than detached infants, and Liaw and colleagues (1995) reported that the lowest-income, most disadvantaged children were the least likely to become engaged in the program's child development activities designed for them. Both such experiences would be possible within settings that are generally of good quality according to global measures. Relationships, continuity, culture, and context, as well as more traditionally measured indicators of quality, each have relevance to the individual child's experiences within a program. Recommendations for measuring the individual child level of quality are explicated in the final section of the chapter.

Comprehensive Intervention Programs and the Study of Quality: A Missing Variable

The question of quality in comprehensive intervention programs presents itself in several ways: What is known about the quality of child care in comprehensive intervention programs, whether directly provided by the program or brokered through the community? What is known about the quality of the other services the children and families in comprehensive programs receive? Are there variant or holistic features of comprehensive programming that should be considered indexes of quality for programs for infants and toddlers because they have been shown to bring about positive effects?

Quality of Child Care in Comprehensive Intervention Programs   Most comprehensive intervention programs include a child care component as a means for enhancing child development or as a service to meet family goals of self-sufficiency and/or education. As more of the families eligible for comprehensive programs are also involved in welfare-to-work programs, the child care aspect of comprehensive programs for low-income families can be expected to grow in importance. Although it is generally assumed that the child care that comprehensive programs offer on site is of good quality, studies have rarely assessed program quality directly. The issue of quality of child care in comprehensive programs may be viewed in two ways, depending on whether the program provides child care directly or families use of community-based child care.[3]

When child care is an integral part of the comprehensive intervention program or is offered on site, there are typically procedures in place for quality control. Examples are seen in the Abecedarian, IHDP, and EHS programs. Infants who began attending center-based care (mean age of entry, 8.8 weeks) in the Abecedarian project were in a nursery of 14 infants, staffed by four caregivers. Abecedarian staff worked to provide a "safe and healthful environment staffed by sensitive and resourceful early childhood educators who would offer high quality education and emotional support" (Ramey & Campbell, 1991, p. 195). This program followed an infant curriculum created by Sparling and Lewis (1979) especially for this program. Children received primary medical care on site, and parents were involved in the center-based program. IHDP child care, which children attended for at least 20 hours per week when they reached 12 months of age, had the following controls on quality: ratios of 1:3 in groups of six infants and 1:4 in groups of eight toddlers. In

---

[3] We must keep in mind that there are very few strong studies that can inform our understanding of child care effects on infants and toddlers in the context of comprehensive intervention programs.

142   LOVE, RAIKES, PAULSELL, AND KISKER

addition, supervisors and head teachers had degrees in early childhood education and followed a specific early childhood curriculum. In EHS, programs are required either to provide high-quality child care to their families or to ensure that the community child care families receive meets the Head Start Program Performance Standards (U.S. DHHS, 1996).

Community-based child care in comprehensive intervention programs is another matter. The program may provide this care through referrals, by brokering it with other agencies, or by simply letting families find their own. There are two points to make about community child care. First, findings from studies of comprehensive intervention programs may be confounded by community child care, and second, we know little about the quality of this care. The CCDP study illustrates both points.

In the CCDP study, center-based care was singled out for analysis. Although center-based care was used by more program families than by control group families when children were 2 and 3 years of age, both groups used very small amounts of center-based child care per month. For example, during the infant/toddler years, the average child using center-based care received about 7 hours a week of that kind of care (8 hours for CCDP children and 5 for control group children). From birth to age 5, the average child using center-based care received about 8 1/2 hours of that form of care (about 11 hours a week for CCDP children and 7 hours a week for control-group children, a small amount when contrasted to the 35 or 40 hours a week that many children spend in full-time child care). Still, the evaluation found a modest and significant effect for center-based care on the Kaufman Assessment Battery for Children (K-ABC) when children were 5 years of age, such that children in both the CCDP and control groups who had participated in center-based care had higher K-ABC scores than those who had not been involved in center-based care (St. Pierre et al., 1997).[4]

This finding is similar to the 1991 CARE program finding discussed previously and also demonstrates the difficulty of measuring impacts when control group children receive center-based care. In this study, program impacts appear to have been diluted by effects of community child care (Ramey & Campbell, 1991). In the CARE study, program impacts were significant over several years, showing better outcomes for the group that received a center-based program plus family education services than for the group using family education only and the control groups, although the difference became slightly smaller as children in the latter two groups received more community child care.

---

[4] Complicating the research, sometimes program and control group children attended the same community child care programs.

Child care appears to be a potent influence on children's early development, regardless of whether this care is delivered within or outside of an intervention program. As noted previously, studies of child care quality suggest that quality and quantity of care intersect, and both must be taken into account in assessing impacts of comprehensive intervention programs. Those knowledgeable about comprehensive intervention programs will argue that program effects are a function of many program features taken together. We do not disagree with this assumption but argue that child care's contribution to the effects must be quantified in its own right.

Quality of Comprehensive Intervention Programs' Other Components   Studies of quality in child care lead us to ask about the other features of quality in comprehensive intervention programs designed to have a positive impact on the development of infants and toddlers. That is, if child care quality makes a difference in the development of children, wouldn't one expect quality of other aspects of intervention programs to be important also? The science of quality as it relates to multiple program features in comprehensive programs is poorly developed. What is known about assessment of quality of the components of comprehensive programs? Quality in home visit programs? In case management? Or in the other service areas of comprehensive programs?

Home Visiting Programs   Home visitation is a common service delivery mechanism in comprehensive intervention programs focused on infant and toddler development. During the visit, a home visitor generally works with a parent to enhance parenting skills and/or provide case management for the parents' social services.

Home visitation programs have been found to be more effective in influencing children's development when a health professional, rather than a paraprofessional, carries out the home visit (Olds & Kitzman, 1993), although there is not universal agreement on the importance of professional staff (Weiss, 1993). Olds and colleagues (1998) conducted one of the few experimental studies of any aspect of quality by contrasting effects of paraprofessionals with those of health professionals.

Another indicator of quality of a home visiting program has to do with how often the visits are carried out. Olds and Kitzman (1993) reported that program effects were more likely to be achieved when the visits were conducted frequently enough to establish a working relationship and address the family's needs. The CCDP program carried out home visits for early childhood education on an average of 1.1 times a month during the first year of infancy. By most accounts, this would be considered a low frequency of services during the critical first year of life and very likely contributed to the weak program impacts found in the CCDP evaluation (St. Pierre et al., 1997). Although the recommendation is not without controversy, frequency of home visitation could become a regulated feature of home visitation programs; it is currently included in the revised Head Start Program Performance Standards (U.S. DHHS, 1996).

In the child care literature, caregiver education and training are often seen as quality indicators. In the field of home visiting, researchers have not reached a consensus about whether professional or paraprofessional home visitors are most effective. For example, Olds and Kitzman (1993) found in some studies that programs using professional home visitors have produced better results than those using paraprofessionals. However, Gomby and colleagues (1993) suggested that the evidence about whether professional or paraprofessional home visitors are more effective is based on studies of programs that differ significantly in scope and content. Wasik (1993) wrote that paraprofessionals recruited from the community served by the home visiting program can be effective because of their knowledge of the community. Furthermore, the values and beliefs they share with families facilitate the development of trust and rapport (Aaronson, 1989). Because the results of research on this question are inconclusive, Wasik, Bryant, and Lyons (1990) recommended that decisions about whether to recruit professional or paraprofessional home visitors be made in relation to each program's goals and structure. In particular, programs should consider their specific goals, the complexity of families' needs, and the roles and responsibilities of home visitors.

Case Management   Case management has become a major service delivery strategy in many human services fields. It refers to the planning and integration of services carried out by a social services professional and a client through mutually determined goals and activities in the context of a relationship over time. In some programs, it may be a subset of a home-visiting delivery system. Case management is a prominent feature of many mental health, child welfare programs, welfare-to-work initiatives, and service integration projects (Doolittle & Riccio, 1990; Marks, 1995; Ooms, Hara, & Owen, 1992), and it increasingly plays a role in comprehensive intervention programs designed to enhance the development of infants and toddlers. In these programs, the quality of case management would be expected to affect parents, who in turn would be expected to influence their children's development.

Marks (1995) noted that a broad acceptance of case management in human services has taken place without adequate information about its effectiveness as a service delivery strategy. Rothman (1991) concurred that little high-quality research about case management has been conducted. Based on evaluation studies and recommended practices, the following are 13 potential indicators of case management quality in comprehensive intervention programs: 1) caseload size (American Public Welfare Association, 1992); 2) location of the case management service (Ooms et al., 1992); 3) authority given to case managers to negotiate on behalf of families (Hagen, 1994; Rubin, 1987); 4) supportive supervision (Rubin, 1987); 5) case conferencing (Ooms et al., 1992); 6) preservice and in-service training (Ooms et al., 1992); 7) staff skills in communication and empathy (Berkowitz, Halfon, & Klee, 1992); 8) organization (Berkowitz et al., 1992); 9) time management (Weil & Karls, 1985); 10) problem solving (Doolittle & Riccio, 1990); 11) effective and ongoing assessments of family needs (Ooms et al., 1992; Morley, 1989); 12) effective tailoring of plans to individual strengths, needs, and goals of families, while involving the family (Morley, 1989; National Association of Social Workers, 1992; Ooms et al., 1992; Weil & Karls, 1985); and 13) in some cases, advocacy on behalf of families (National Association of Social Workers, 1992; Rubin, 1987). Further development of quality indicators for case management would examine the relation of these factors to client outcomes and study client outcomes as they relate to infant and toddler development.

Comprehensive Features   Research on comprehensive intervention programs generally lacks variables that correspond to the process quality and structural quality features studied in child care, and functional definitions of quality are needed. The comprehensive and cumulative nature of comprehensive services, as well as a "goodness-of-fit" with family needs, may be what accounts for the degree of success they have had. Unfortunately, these features (or configurations of features) have not been quantified for research purposes. It appears that the quest for quality in comprehensive programs is converging with recommended directions for child care quality. In other words, both require comprehensiveness, as Ferrar (1996) and Ferrar and colleagues (1996) have shown in the area of child care.

RECOMMENDATIONS
FOR PROGRAMS AND FUTURE RESEARCH

We have reviewed concepts of quality in programs for infants and toddlers from two vantage points: the child care literature and the literature on comprehensive intervention programs. There are many lessons to be learned from each regarding future programmatic and policy planning for defining, measuring, and implementing high-quality programs for infants and toddlers.

This approach uses concepts and findings about quality from these two literatures to inform each other. Mixing brings out three implications for programs, policy, and research. It expands the notion of what

quality in child care is; it demonstrates the necessity of more fully incorporating the study of quality into evaluations of comprehensive programs; and it provides an expanded conception of quality for all
programs that is more than the sum of the parts.

From the child care literature, we described definitions of quality
and associated research that focused on programmatic level variables
that often can be regulated (e.g., ratio, group size, staff background, staff
training), as well as process or dynamic variables. There has not been the
same explicit study of quality in the comprehensive intervention program literature. There, the purpose of research has been to identify
whether particular program practices lead to improved child outcomes,
especially for vulnerable children. In many cases, there has been a search
to learn about the programs as a whole and the services children and
families receive, but the literature has come to increasingly differentiate
specific program features in order to understand how they contribute to
various child outcomes. By reviewing these features, a glimpse of the
elements of an expanded definition of quality is revealed.

Now, the tasks are to identify the parameters of a proposed
expanded definition of quality, to propose a model to undergird an
expanded definition of quality, and to recommend several directions for
future research on program quality.

An Expanded Definition of Program Quality

The implicit definition of quality adopted as the theme of this chapter has
been a very general one—quality is equated with those features of child
care and comprehensive intervention programs that are most clearly
associated with positive outcomes for infants and toddlers. A large net
is cast in order to address the challenge, presented by the Carnegie Corporation and implicit in the April 1997 White House Conference on
Infants and Toddlers, to develop programs that promote the early development of infants and toddlers.

An expanded approach to the study of quality can be created by
weaving together lessons from research and practice in child care and
comprehensive intervention programs. This results in seven key features
of quality:

- Structural features of environments for infants and toddlers, including adult–child ratios; group size; staff education and training; staff
  wages; staff turnover; and programmatic licensing and certifications
- Process features of environments for infants and toddlers, including
  the sensitivity, responsiveness, and lack of harshness of caregivers.
  Process quality has been well measured in child care environments
  using the Infant/Toddler Environment Rating Scale (ITERS; Harms,

Cryer, & Clifford, 1990), as well as scales such as the Arnett Scale of Caregiver Behavior (Arnett, 1989) that identify the quality of interactions within the program.

- Relationships, including secure attachments between infants and caregivers and the opportunity to form and maintain primary caregiver relationships, as well as relationships between staff and parents
- Continuity in relationships and services for children over time. The child care literature includes some evidence that stability of relationships and continuity of programming over time benefits children's well-being.
- Cultural relevance, or the extent to which a program embodies principles relating to combating racism, promoting cross-cultural understanding, preserving family languages, working with parents to incorporate these principles in the program, and providing time and resources for staff and parents to reflect on cultural issues (Chang, Muckelroy, & Pulido-Tobiassen, 1996)
- Comprehensive services, including health services, parenting education, home visitation, and social or employment services, depending upon the clientele. A major contribution of the comprehensive program literature has been to show that the addition of these elements has the potential to enhance program effects on children's development.
- Contextual elements of quality, including administrative structure and mission. The evidence for the importance of these elements is less abundant, but findings from comprehensive intervention programs with these features suggest their importance for children's well-being.

In each of these areas, our expanded approach to quality also takes a child-oriented view of quality. Global quality fails to capture the experiences of individual children, which could be of high or low quality even within the same program. This expanded definition, therefore, penetrates more deeply into the critical elements within the environments that children directly experience. For two-generation programs, it is possible to develop the principles to assess quality of adult services as well. At this stage of research, it is not known whether "quality" in the adult portion of two-generation programs will significantly affect child outcomes over and above the benefits of quality in child care and child development services.

Previous sections of this chapter discuss the prevalence of quality as defined in traditional assessments of child care process features and structural features of programs. Although not as much is known about the additional features under an expanded definition, a few key studies begin to show how prevalent these quality features are. For example, what is known about the prevalence of secure relationships in programs for infants and toddlers comes from a small number of studies of caregiver–infant attachment. Howes, Rodning, Galluzzo, and Myers (1988) reported that 66% of infants had secure attachments with their caregivers. Goossens and van IJzendoorn (1990) found that 56% of the babies they studied had secure relationships with caregivers. Raikes (1993) reported only 50% of infants had secure relationships after 6 months with a caregiver. Over time, the majority of infants experience many changes in their child care arrangements: The Study of Early Child Care found that by age 3 the average infant had experienced more than six new caregiving arrangements ("starts"), and this was true for children of all income levels (NICHD, 1996c). Siegel and Loman (1991) also found that frequent change characterized the child care that low-income families used. Thus, as low-income parents move into the workforce, their children's development becomes increasingly vulnerable to low levels of this dimension of quality. Finally, little is known about the prevalence of health and other comprehensive services offered through child care programs. National data indicate that such services are more likely in centers in which they serve higher proportions of low-income families. Kisker and Love (1996) examined child care services in relation to the income levels of the neighborhoods served and found that 20% of centers in the poorest neighborhoods provided physical examinations, compared with only 8% of centers serving the highest-income neighborhoods.

Proposed Model For an Expanded Concept of Quality

The proposed model for guiding future research in child care and comprehensive intervention programs incorporates the concepts of quality found in the two bodies of literature reviewed here—child care research and research on comprehensive intervention programs. This broader framework takes into account multiple levels of input and output in relation to infant/toddler program quality as shown in Figure 1. This emerges from the expanded features of quality, as described in the beginning of this chapter, by organizing quality features according to the levels at which they may be applied. These levels are the program, the teachers and staff, the children, and the community/policy context.

Program-Level Quality Variables This cluster of variables includes the most frequently studied child care quality variables, including program structural variables (e.g., ratio, group size, wages), context variables (e.g., program administration), comprehensive services (i.e., health and other services for families that need them), cultural variables (including whether the program promotes cultural

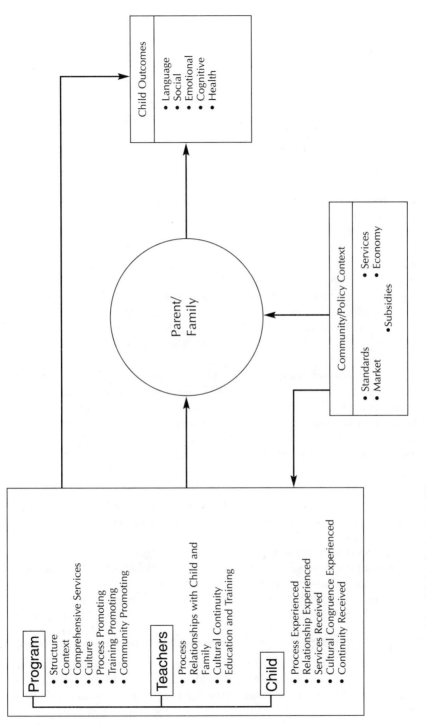

Program
- Structure
- Context
- Comprehensive Services
- Culture
- Process Promoting
- Training Promoting
- Community Promoting

Teachers
- Process
- Relationships with Child and Family
- Cultural Continuity
- Education and Training

Child
- Process Experienced
- Relationship Experienced
- Services Received
- Cultural Congruence Experienced
- Continuity Received

Parent/Family

Community/Policy Context
- Standards
- Market
- Subsidies
- Services
- Economy

Child Outcomes
- Language
- Social
- Emotional
- Cognitive
- Health

Figure 1.   An expanded model of quality in infant/toddler programs.

149

continuity between children/families and program practices), continuity-promoting variables (whether the program fosters long-term relationships between children and caregivers), process-promoting quality variables (systems that support positive interactions between staff and children), and training (whether the program supports staff development through child development training). As shown in Figure 1, the program-level quality variables are expected to contribute to child developmental outcomes, parenting skills, and teacher/caregiver effectiveness with children.

Teacher/Caregiver-Level Quality Variables The teacher or caregiver has primary responsibility for transmitting the program to the child. Infants in particular experience the world in the context of relationships. This cluster of quality variables would target teachers within a program. Variables include teacher-level process (whether the teacher is warm, reciprocal, and not harsh), teachers' relationships with children (whether the teacher promotes secure attachments), cultural continuity with children and families, and teacher-specific attitudes and professional development. As seen in Figure 1, these quality indicators are expected to influence child development and parenting skills over and above the effects of program-level quality.

Child-Level Quality Variables For program- and teacher-level variables to have their influence, children must engage in the program with a teacher/caregiver who exhibits particular quality features. From an individual child's perspective, important variables include child process variables (including whether the child experiences warm and reciprocal interactions that are not harsh), relationship variables (e.g., child engagement in one or more secure relationships), service variables (whether the particular child receives the needed health and other comprehensive services), cultural congruence (e.g., whether a child's teacher shares the child's culture and speaks his or her language), and continuity of care (whether the child is able to maintain a relationship with the same caregiver or a few caregivers over time). Figure 1 shows the expectation that child-level quality variables will influence both child outcomes and parent-child relationships.

Community/Policy-Level Context Variables This cluster of variables includes factors that exert upward or downward forces on the program-, teacher-, and child-level quality. Variables include the stringency of state regulatory standards, the demand for and supply of programs for infants and toddlers, the extent to which families can gain access to government child care subsidies and abide by the regulations associated with them, the extent to which health and other services promote collaboration with child care, and whether there is a healthy economy that supports child care wages or offers competing jobs. These variables have more indirect effects on the child, being more likely to affect program-level factors directly. The next section discusses specific future research directions that build on this conception of variables and the directions of influence as presented in the model.

FURTHER RECOMMENDATIONS

Given that the majority of infants and toddlers in this country experience out-of-home programs, an overarching question for this chapter is whether these programs can have a positive impact on the infants' and toddlers' development and whether programs can compensate for risk factors in the children's lives. When implemented with quality, programs appear to offer hope in response to the "quiet crisis" identified by the Carnegie Corporation (1994). Yet, crowded classrooms, infrequent home visits, unstable child care, harsh and unresponsive caregiving, parents in vital need of support and assistance, inadequate health care, and other features associated with poor quality will not safeguard the development of infants and toddlers. We propose that an appropriate response to the challenge—in terms of programs, policies, and research—requires an expanded notion of quality and of potential influences on children's development and well-being.

Specific Recommendations

Many studies have focused on the direct relationships between child care program quality and child outcomes, and several studies have examined the relative contributions of family and child care environments. The proposed framework recommends research approaches that will identify and measure both direct and indirect pathways by which programs and their contexts influence child outcomes. Here are nine specific recommendations.

Expand the Definitions of Quality   Programs and research should expand their conceptions of quality to consider the elements we have introduced. All variables that have been identified would apply to all programs. For example, it may be that programs serving vulnerable populations are most likely to provide comprehensive services, but programs serving children of all levels of risk should be accountable for documenting health care for children and for providing linkages for families who lack services.

Measure the Dimensions of Quality in Comprehensive Intervention Programs   Comprehensive intervention programs should measure the quality of their program services, especially child care and services that target child development outcomes. Although these programs often include evaluations of program services, few take the quality of services into account. At a minimum, given how much is known about child care quality and its relationship to child development outcomes, future studies should clearly identify the amount and quality of child care, both in program and comparison groups, to understand the effects of their intervention more fully and accurately. To be most useful for shaping new programs and policies, future studies should measure quality in other components as well.

Examine Quality from the Perspective of the Individual Child   Knowledge of the global quality level of a program does not necessarily indicate what specific quality features a particular child will experience. For program regulation and monitoring, global indicators may suffice. For understanding and predicting child outcomes, however, it is essential that researchers begin obtaining data on how the child care or comprehensive program environment is experienced by each child. The dimensions of this experience should include caregiver–child relationships and the degree of continuity in relationships over time.

Measure the Intensity of Program Services   The intensity of program services has not been taken into account as an indicator of quality for child development programs that cut across comprehensive intervention programs and child care. Yet intensity is an important variable, as has been shown in home visitation and child care–related interventions. Given that home visits or child care delivered at low levels of intensity are not likely to have an impact upon child development, it might be reasonable to consider intensity to be an indicator of quality.

Learn More About the Relationships Among Different Measures of the Various Dimensions of Quality   Although the ITERS and Family Day Care Rating Scale (FDCRS) are the measures of choice for global process quality, the NICHD Observational Ratings of the Caregiving Environment (ORCE) has been used as well. The Arnett Scale of Caregiver Behavior (Arnett, 1989) and the Assessment Profile (Abbott-Shim, Sibley, & Neel, 1992) have also been used. Most measures show moderately strong, but not perfect, correlations with each other. Some specify thresholds separating good, mediocre, and poor care, whereas others leave that judgment to the researcher or program personnel. Thresholds are likely to be at different points on different measures. Thus, studies using different measures are likely to report different percentages of quality care, which leads to the conclusion that care varies in the population when in fact it may vary in the eyes of the beholder.

Identify Structural and Process Quality Variables within Comprehensive Intervention Programs   The definition and measurement of these two types of variables have been fruitful in child care research. Standard language would make possible the holistic assessment of quality for both generations of two-generation programs.

The additional features of quality, such as relationships, continuity, context, and comprehensiveness, have importance for the parent as well as the child in comprehensive intervention programs.

Identify the Effects of Programs on Parents   Identify ways that parenting is strengthened through participation in child care and comprehensive programs in order to examine both direct and indirect effects on children participating in infant/toddler programs. It is reasonable to assume there would be effects on parenting as a function of both child care and comprehensive programs, although the effects might be assumed to be different depending on the degree of intentionality and intensity of parent education within the programs.

Learn More About How Home and Program Environments Cumulate to Enhance Child Outcomes   A few studies of early child care, including the NICHD Study (NICHD Early Child Care Research Network, 1997), have identified the variance added by child care over home environments. Howes and Stewart (1987) found that children who had secure attachments with both parents and caregivers fared best. Research focused on the relationship between quality variables and child outcomes has sometimes statistically controlled for the influence of family characteristics. Yet, little is known about the joint contributions of child care quality and family variables, or the value added to family variables by participation in quality child development programs. Nor is it clear whether the relative contribution of home and program variables to children's development is different for children at risk. Researchers need to understand better how much value a quality program adds. The equation might examine the variance contributed by elements as follows:

Parent/home environment + child care/development programs + parent support program = total variance in child development outcomes contributed by environments

Strengthen Research Designs with Carefully Selected Comparison Groups, Controls for Selection Bias, and the Measurement of Outcomes Before and After Quality Assessments   Most of our knowledge about the relationship between child care quality and child outcomes is from studies in which the two sets of variables are measured at the same point in time. This research approach does not control for any pre-existing differences among children who enroll in programs with different levels of quality. Methods to correct for sample selection bias exist and should be used more systematically in our research (Love et al., 1996). The Howes et al. (1995) Florida study exemplifies in which child outcomes can be compared before and after a systematic change in particular quality variables.

Example of the
Early Head Start Research and Evaluation Project

The Early Head Start Research and Evaluation Project (see Love, Kisker, Raikes, & Tarullo, 1998, 1999) illustrates how the design of one comprehensive set of studies, conducted at both national and local levels, has endeavored to incorporate many of these recommendations. Early Head Start, which began in 1995, is a two-generation program that includes intensive services beginning before the child is born and concentrating on enhancing the child's development and supporting the family during the critical first 3 years of the child's life. Programs are designed to produce outcomes in four domains:

- *Child development,* including health, resiliency, social competence, and cognitive and language development
- *Family development,* including parenting and relationships with children, the home environment and family functioning, family health, parent involvement, and economic self-sufficiency
- *Staff development,* including professional development and relationships with parents
- *Community development,* including enhanced child care quality, community collaboration, and integration of services to support families with young children

In 1996, ACYF selected 17 programs from across the country to participate in the Early Head Start National Research and Evaluation Project. The 17 programs include center-based, home-visiting, and mixed-approach programs. The Early Head Start National Research and Evaluation Project, which is being conducted by Mathematica Policy Research, Inc. and Columbia University in collaboration with 15 local research teams and coordinated by the Early Head Start Research Consortium, includes five major components: an implementation study; an impact evaluation, based on an experimental design; local research studies to learn about pathways to desired outcomes; policy studies to respond to information needs in areas of emerging policy-relevant issues; and continuous program improvement. Through these components, the Early Head Start evaluation has endeavored to address issues of quality in a number of ways.

The Early Head Start implementation study includes a broad definition of program quality but with special emphasis on the quality of child development services. Full implementation of planned services in all areas is key to high quality. The evaluation has developed ratings of full implementation that provide a comprehensive assessment of the degree of program implementation. The study is also assessing the quality of child care that children receive using standard instruments (e.g., the ITERS and FDCRS), reviewing what goes on during home visits through home visit documentation procedures for the national study and videotaping and qualitative research in selected local research studies (U.S. DHHS, 1999). When Early Head Start children are in family or center-based child care at the time of the 14-, 24-, and 36-month birthday-related assessments, the researchers measure teacher/caregiver-level quality with the Arnett scale, as well as dimensions of the ITERS and FDCRS and child-level quality using an instrument developed especially for the Early Head Start study. This instrument, the Child–Caregiver Observation System (C-COS; Boller, Sprachman, and the Early Head Start Research Consortium, 1998) was developed for observing interactions between adult caregivers and 2-year-old children. It builds on features from the ORCE (NICHD Early Child Care Research Network, 1997) and the Adult Involvement Scale (Howes & Smith, 1995).

In addition to program-, teacher/caregiver-, and child-level measures of quality, the Early Head Start study obtains data on relationships using measures of parent–caregiver relationships. The study is also assessing other quality-related variables proposed in this chapter: 1) continuity of child care at the level of program, teacher, and child; 2) cultural relevance at those three levels; 3) comprehensive services; 4) intensity of services; and 5) many contextual factors mentioned in this chapter as important additional, often overlooked dimensions of quality.

The evaluation will be able to examine the relationships among the various measures of quality. On-site interviews conducted for the implementation study obtain community/policy-level context data on the service "richness" of the communities served by Early Head Start programs. The amount and quality of child care available in the community is estimated by measuring the child care received by children in the evaluation's control group.

In addition, program effects on multiple dimensions of parents will be assessed. Outcomes such as parenting, parent–child relationships, and the quality of the home environment are being evaluated to examine their effects on children's development. By including measures of both program and home environments, the Early Head Start National Research and Evaluation Project will obtain estimates of the extent to which the two interact in their contributions to children's development. Finally, these analyses are being conducted within the context of an experimental design with longitudinal assessments.

A FINAL WORD

There are no easy answers in the quest for quality in programs and services for infants and toddlers and their families. Both child care research and evaluations of comprehensive program interventions contribute ways of thinking about quality, as well as strategies for measuring and evaluating the dimensions of quality. We hope the ideas presented in this chapter will generate further discussion and lead to new ways of conceptualizing quality that will enable researchers, practitioners, and policymakers to move forward in learning how better to meet the needs of our youngest and most vulnerable citizens.

REFERENCES

Aaronson, M. (1989). The case manager home visitor. *Child Welfare, 68,* 339–346.

Abbott-Shim, M., Sibley, A., & Neel, J. (1992). *Research manual, assessment profile for early childhood programs: Research edition.* Atlanta: Quality Assist, Inc.

Ainsworth, M., Blehar, M., Waters, E., & Wall, S. (1978). *Patterns of attachment.* Mahwah, NJ: Lawrence Erlbaum Associates.

American Public Welfare Association. (1992). *Status report on JOBS case management practices.* Washington, DC: Author.

Arnett, J. (1989). Caregivers in child care centers: Does training matter? *Journal of Applied Developmental Psychology, 10,* 541–552.

Barnes, H.V., Goodson, B.D., & Layzer, J.I. (1995). *National evaluation of family support programs: Research review. Volume I: Summary of findings.* Draft report submitted to U.S. Department of Health and Human Services, Administration on Children, Youth and Families. Cambridge, MA: Abt Associates, Inc.

Barnett, W.S. (1995, March). *Research on family support programs: Current status and future directions.* Paper presented at the meeting of the Society for Research in Child Development, Indianapolis, IN.

Barton, M., & Williams, M. (1993). Infant day care. In C.H. Zeanah, Jr. (Ed.), *Handbook of infant mental health* (pp. 445–461). New York: Guilford Press.

Belsky, J. (1988). The effects of infant day care reconsidered. *Early Childhood Research Quarterly, 3,* 235–272.

Benasich, A.A., Brooks-Gunn, J., & Clewell, B.C. (1992). How do mothers benefit from early intervention programs? *Journal of Applied Developmental Psychology, 13,* 311–362.

Berkowitz, G., Halfon, N., & Klee, L. (1992). Improving access to health care: Case management for vulnerable children. *Social Work in Health Care, 17*(1), 101–123.

Blank, S. (1997). *Theory meets practice: A report on six small-scale two-generation service projects.* New York: Foundation for Child Development.

Boller, K., Sprachman, S., & The Early Head Start Research Consortium (1998). *The Child–Caregiver Observation System instructor's manual.* Princeton, NJ: Mathematica Policy Research, Inc.

Bowlby, J. (1969). *Attachment and loss* (Vol. 1). New York: Basic Books.

Brooks-Gunn, J., Klebanov, P.K., Liaw, F., & Spiker, D. (1993). Enhancing the development of low birth weight, premature infants: Changes in cognition and behavior over the first 3 years. *Child Development, 64,* 736–753.

Brooks-Gunn, J., McCarton, C.M., Casey, P.H., McCormick, M.C., Bauer, C.R., Bernbaum, J.C., Tyson, J., Swanson, M., Bennett, F.C., Scott, D.T., Tonascia, J., & Meinert, C.L. (1994). Early intervention in low birth weight, premature infants: Results through 5 years from the Infant Health and Development Program. *Journal of the American Medical Association, 272,* 1257–1262.

Burchinal, M., Roberts, J.E., Nabors, L.A., & Bryant, D. (1996). Quality of center child care and infant cognitive and language development. *Child Development, 67*, 606–620.

Carnegie Corporation of New York. (1994). *Starting points: Meeting the needs of our youngest children.* New York: Author.

Center for Community Research. (1973a). *The impact of Head Start Parent–Child Centers on children.* Final Report. New York: Author.

Center for Community Research. (1973b). *The impact of the Head Start Parent-Child Centers on parents.* New York: Author.

Chang, H.N., Muckelroy, A., & Pulido-Tobiassen, D. (1996). *Looking in, looking out: Redefining child care and early education in a diverse society.* San Francisco: California Tomorrow.

Children's Defense Fund. (1995). *The state of America's children yearbook 1995.* Washington, DC: Author.

Children's Foundation. (1997a). *1997 child day care center licensing study.* Washington, DC: Author.

Children's Foundation. (1997b). *1997 family day care licensing study.* Washington, DC: Author.

Cost, Quality, and Outcomes Study Team. (1995, May). Cost, quality, and child outcomes in child care centers: Key findings and recommendations. *Young Children 50*(4), 40–44.

Dokecki, P.R., Hargrove, E.C., & Sandler, H.M. (1983). An overview of the parent–child development center social experiment. In R. Haskins & D. Adams (Eds.), *Parent education and public policy* (pp. 80–111). Norwood, NJ: Ablex Publishing.

Doolittle, F., & Riccio, J. (1990). *Case management in welfare employment programs.* Madison: University of Wisconsin, Institute for Research on Poverty.

Fein, G. (1995). Infants in group care: Patterns of despair and detachment. *Early Childhood Research Quarterly, 10*, 261–275.

Ferrar, H.M. (1996). *Places for growing. How to improve your child care center.* Princeton, NJ: Mathematica Policy Research, Inc.

Ferrar, H.M., Harms, T., & Cryer, D. (1996). *Places for growing: How to improve your family child care home.* Princeton, NJ: Mathematica Policy Research, Inc.

Field, T. (1991). Quality infant day care and grade school behavior and performance. *Child Development, 62*, 863–870.

Galinsky, E., Howes, C., & Kontos, S. (1995). *The family child care training study: Highlights of findings.* New York: Families and Work Institute.

Galinsky, E., Howes, C., Kontos, S., & Shinn, M. (1994). *The study of children in family child care and relative care: Highlights of findings.* New York: Families and Work Institute.

Gomby, D., Larson, C.S., Lewitt, E.M., & Behrman, R.E. (1993). Home visiting: Analysis and recommendations. *The Future of Children, 3*(3), 6–22.

Goossens, F., & van IJzendoorn, M. (1990). Quality of infants' attachments to professional caregivers: Relation to infant–parent attachment and day care characteristics. *Child Development, 61*, 832–837.

Hagan, J.L. (1994). JOBS and case management: Developments in 10 states. *Social Work, 39*(2), 197–205.

Harms, T., Cryer, D., & Clifford, R. (1990). *Infant-Toddler Environment Rating Scale.* New York: Teachers College Press.

Hofferth, S.L., & Kisker, E.E. (1991). *Family day care in the United States, 1990.* Washington, DC: Urban Institute.

Howes, C. (1990). Can the age of entry into child care and the quality of child care predict adjustment in kindergarten? *Developmental Psychology, 26*, 292–303.

Howes, C. (1992). *Preschool experiences.* Paper prepared for the National Center for Education Statistics, University of California, Los Angeles.

Howes, C., & Hamilton, C.E. (1992). Children's relationships with caregivers: Mothers and child care teachers. *Child Development, 63*, 859–866.

Howes, C., & Olenick, M. (1986). Family and child care influences on toddlers' compliance. *Child Development, 57*, 202–216.

Howes, C., Phillips, D., & Whitebook, M. (1992). Thresholds of quality: Implications for the social development of children in center-based child care. *Child Development, 63*, 449–460.

Howes, C., Rodning, C., Galluzzo, D., & Myers, L. (1988). Attachment and child care: Relationships with mother and caregiver. *Early Childhood Research Quarterly, 3*, 403–416.

Howes, C., & Rubenstein, J. (1981). Toddler peer behavior in two types of day care. *Infant Behavior and Development, 4*, 387–393.

Howes, C., & Smith, E. (1995). Relations among child care quality, teacher behavior, children's play activities, emotional security, and cognitive activity in child care. *Early Childhood Research Quarterly, 10*, 381–404.

Howes, C., Smith, E., & Galinsky, E. (1995). *The Florida child care quality improvement study: Interim report.* New York: Families and Work Institute.

Howes, C., & Stewart, P. (1987). Child's play with adults, toys, and peers: An examination of family and child care influences. *Developmental Psychology, 23*, 423–430.

Hubbell, R., & Barrett, B. (1984). *Short-term assessment of the parent/child centers.* Washington, DC: Administration on Children, Youth, and Families, U.S. Department of Health and Human Services.

Individuals with Disabilities Education Act (IDEA) Amendments of 1997, PL 105-17, 20 U.S.C. §§ 1400 *et seq.*

Infant Health and Development Program (IHDP). (1990). Enhancing the outcomes of low birth weight, premature infants: A multisite, randomized trial. *Journal of the American Medical Association, 263*, 3035–3042.

Kagan, S.L., & Neville, P.R. (1993). *Integrating services for children and families. Understanding the past to shape the future.* New Haven, CT: Yale University Press.

Kagan, S.L., & Shelley, A. (1987). The promise and problems of family support programs. In S.L. Kagan, D.R. Powell, B. Weissbourd, & E.F. Zigler (Eds.), *America's family support programs: Perspectives and prospects* (pp. 3–18). New Haven, CT: Yale University Press.

Kisker, E.E., & Love, J.M. (1996, March). *What choices do they have? The supply of center-based child care in low-income neighborhoods.* Princeton, NJ: Mathematica Policy Research, Inc.

Kisker, E.E., Hofferth, S.L., Phillips, D.A., & Farquhar, E. (1991). *A profile of child care settings: Early education and care in 1990.* Washington, DC: U.S. Department of Education.

Kontos, S., Howes, C., & Galinsky E. (1996). Does training make a difference to quality in family child care? *Early Childhood Research Quarterly, 11*, 427–445.

Kontos, S., Howes, C., Shinn, M., & Galinsky, E. (1995). *Quality in family child care and relative care.* New York: Teachers College Press.

Lally, J.R., Mangione, P.K., & Honig, A.S. (1987). *The Syracuse University family development research program: Long-range impact of an early intervention with low-income children and their families.* San Francisco: Far West Laboratory for Educational Research and Development.

Lamb, M.E., Hwang, C.P., Broberg, A., & Bookstein, F.L. (1988). The effects of out-of-home care on the development of social competence in Swedish preschoolers: A longitudinal study. *Early Childhood Research Quarterly, 3,* 379–402.

Lamb, M.E., & Sternberg, K.J. (1990). Do we really know how day care affects children? *Journal of Applied Developmental Psychology, 11,* 351–379.

Layzer, J.I., Goodson, B.D., & Moss, M. (1993). *Observational study of early childhood programs.* Washington, DC: U.S. Department of Education, Office of the Under Secretary.

Liaw, F., & Brooks-Gunn, J. (1994). Cumulative familial risks and low birth weight children's cognitive and behavioral development. *Journal of Clinical Child Psychology, 23,* 360–372

Liaw, F., Meisels, S.J., & Brooks-Gunn, J. (1995). The effects of experience of early intervention on low birth weight, premature children: The Infant Health and Development Program. *Early Childhood Research Quarterly, 10,* 405–431.

Love, J.M., Kisker, E.E., Raikes, H.H., & Tarullo, L. (1998). Overview of the Early Head Start Research and Evaluation Project. *National Head Start Association Research Quarterly, 1*(4), 181–192.

Love, J.M., Kisker, E.E., Raikes, H.H., & Tarullo, L. (1999). *Overview of the Early Head Start Research and Evaluation Project.* [On-line] Available: http://www.mathematica-mpr.com

Love, J.M., Ryer, P., & Faddis, B. (1992). *Caring environments: Program quality in California's publicly funded child development programs. Report of the 1990-91 Staff/Child Ratio Study.* Portsmouth, NH: RMC Research Corporation.

Love, J.M., Schochet, P.Z., & Meckstroth, A.L. (1996). Are they in any real danger? What research does—and doesn't—tell us about child care quality and children's well-being. *Child care research and policy papers: Lessons from child care research funded by the Rockefeller Foundation.* Princeton, NJ: Mathematica Policy Research, Inc.

Marks, E. (1995). *Who are case managers and what do they do? Case managers in service integration.* New York: National Center for Children in Poverty.

McCarton, C., Brooks-Gunn, J., Wallace, I., Bauer, C., Bennet, F., Bernbaum, J., Broyles, R., Casey, P., McCormick, M., Scott, D., Tyson, J., Tonascia, J., & Meinert, C. (1997). Results at 8 years of intervention for low birth weight premature infants: The Infant Health and Development program. *Journal of the American Medical Association, 267,* 2204–2208.

Melhuish, E.C., Mooney, A., Martin, S., & Lloyd, E. (1990a). Type of child care at 18 months: I. Differences in interactional experience. *Journal of Child Psychology and Psychiatry, 31,* 849–859.

Melhuish, E.C., Mooney, A., Martin, S., & Lloyd, E. (1990b). Type of child care at 18 months: II. Relations with cognitive and language development. *Journal of Child Psychology and Psychiatry, 31,* 861–870.

Morley, D.P. (1989). *The practice of social work.* Newbury Park, CA: Sage Publications.

National Association of Social Workers. (1992). *NASW standards for social work case management.* Washington, DC: Author.

National Early Childhood Technical Assistance System. (1999). *Part C Update.* Chapel Hill, NC: Author.

Nauta, M.J., & Travers, J. (1982). *The effects of a social program: Executive summary of CFRP's infant-toddler component.* Report submitted to ACYF, OHDS, U.S. Department of Health and Human Services. Cambridge, MA: Abt Associates, Inc.

NICHD Early Child Care Research Network. (1996a). Characteristics of infant care: Factors contributing to positive caregiving. *Early Childhood Research Quarterly, 11,* 269–306.

NICHD Early Child Care Research Network (1996b, April). *Infant child care and attachment security: Results of the NICHD study of early child care.* Symposium presented at the meeting of the International Conference on Infant Studies, Providence, RI.

NICHD Early Child Care Research Network (1996c, June). *Child characteristics of poor and near-poor 3-year-olds: Health, cognitive, and social characteristics of Families of Head Start eligible children.* Paper presented at the Third National Head Start Research Conference, Washington, DC.

NICHD Early Child Care Research Network (1996d, June). *Early child care experiences of prospective Head Start children.* Paper presented at the Third National Head Start Research Conference, Washington, DC.

NICHD Early Child Care Research Network. (1997, April). *Mother–child interaction and outcomes associated with early childhood care: Results of the NICHD study.* Paper presented at the biennial meeting of the Society for Research in Child Development, Washington, DC.

Office of Special Education Programs (1997, August). *Infants and toddlers with disabilities (part H).* [On-line] Available: http://www.ed.gov/offices/OSERS/OSEP/PGMS/itd.html

Olds, D.L., Eckenrode, J., Henderson, C.R., Jr., Kitzman, H., Powers, J., Cole, R., Sidora, K., Morris, P., Pettitt, L.M., & Luckey, D. (1997). Long-term effects of home visitation on maternal life course and child abuse and neglect: 15-year follow-up of a randomized trial. *Journal of the American Medical Association, 278,* 637–643.

Olds, D.L., Henderson, C.R., Jr., Kitzman, H., Eckenrode, J., Cole, R., Tatelbaum, R., Robinson, J., Pettitt, L.M., O'Brien, R., & Hill, P. (1998, March). *Prenatal and infancy home visitation by nurses: Program of research.* Paper presented at the Welfare Reform Academy's Conference on Preventing Second Births to Teenage Mothers: Demonstration Findings, American Enterprise Institute, Washington, DC.

Olds, D., Henderson, C., Tatelbaum, R., & Chamberlin, R. (1986a). Improving the delivery of prenatal care and outcomes of pregnancy: A randomized trial of nurse home visitation. *Pediatrics, 77,* 16–28.

Olds, D., Henderson, C., Tatelbaum, R., & Chamberlin R. (1986b). Prevention of child abuse and neglect: A randomized trial of nurse home visitation. *Pediatrics, 78,* 65–78.

Olds, D., & Kitzman, H. (1993). Review of research on home visiting for pregnant women and parents of young children. *The Future of Children, 3*(3), 53–92.

Ooms, T., Hara, S., & Owen, T. (1992). *Service integration and coordination at the family/client level: Part 3. Is case management the answer? Meeting highlights and background briefing report.* Washington, DC: Family Impact Seminars.

Parker, F.L., Piotrkowski, C.S., Horn, W., & Greene, S. (1995). The challenge for Head Start: Realizing its vision as a two-generation program. In S. Smith (Ed.), *Two generation programs for families in poverty: A new intervention strategy* (pp. 135–159). Norwood, NJ: Ablex Publishing.

Pavetti, L.A., & Duke, A. (1995). *Increasing participation in work and work-related activities: Lessons from five state welfare reform demonstration projects.* Washington, DC: Urban Institute.

Personal Responsibility and Work Opportunity Reconciliation Act of 1996, PL 104-193, 42 U.S.C. §§ 103(a) *et seq.*

Phillips, D.A. (1995). *Child care for low-income families: A summary of two work-shops.* Washington, DC: National Academy Press.

Phillips, D.A., & Howes, C. (1987). Indicators of quality in child care: Review of research. In D.A. Phillips (Ed.), *Quality in child care: what does research tell us?* (pp. 1–19). Washington, DC: National Association for the Education of Young Children.

Phillips, D.A., Voran, M., Kisker, E.E., Howes, C., & Whitebook, M. (1994). Child care for children in poverty: Opportunity or inequity? *Child Development, 65,* 472–492.

Raikes, H. (1993). Relationship duration in infant care: Time with a high-ability teacher and infant-teacher attachment. *Early Childhood Research Quarterly, 8,* 309–325.

Raikes, H. (1996). A secure base for babies: Applying attachment concepts to the infant care setting. *Young Children, 51*(5), 59–67.

Raikes, H. (1998). Investigating child care subsidy: What are we buying? *Social Policy Report, Society for Research in Child Development, 12*(2).

Ramey, C.T., & Campbell, F. (1991). Poverty, early childhood education, and academic competence: The Abecedarian experiment. In A. Huston (Ed.), *Children in poverty: Child development and public policy* (pp. 190–221). New York: Cambridge University Press.

Rothman, J. (1991). A model of case management: Toward empirically based practice. *Social Work, 36,* 520–528.

Rubin, A. (1987). Case management. In A. Minhahan (Ed.), *Encyclopedia of social work* (18th ed., Vol. I, pp. 212–222). Washington, DC: National Association of Social Workers.

Ruopp, R.R., Travers, J., Glantz, F., & Coelen, C. (1979). *Children at the center: Final results of the National Day Care Study.* Cambridge, MA: Abt Associates, Inc.

Siegel, G., & Loman, L.A. (1991). *Child care and AFDC recipients in Illinois.* Report prepared for the Institute of Applied Research, St. Louis, MO.

Smith, S. (1995). Two-generational program models: A new intervention strategy and directions for future research. In P.K. Chase-Lansdale & J. Brooks-Gunn (Eds.), *Escape from poverty: What makes a difference for children?* (pp. 229–314). New York: Cambridge University Press.

Sparling, J., & Lewis, I. (1979). *Learning games for the first 3 years.* New York: Walker Publishing Co.

St. Pierre, R., Layzer, J.I., & Barnes, H. (1994, October). *Variation in the design, cost, and effectiveness of two-generational programs.* Paper prepared for the Eighth Rutgers Invitational Symposium on Education: New Directions for Policy and Research in Early Childhood Care and Education, Princeton, NJ.

St. Pierre, R.G., Layzer, J.I., Goodson, B.D., & Bernstein, L. (1997). *National impact evaluation of the Comprehensive Child Development Program: Final report.* Cambridge, MA: Abt Associates, Inc.

Suwalsky, J.T.D., Zaslow, M., Klein, R., & Rabinovich, B. (1986). *Continuity of substitute care in relation to infant-mother attachment.* Paper presented at the convention of the American Psychological Association, Washington, DC.

U.S. Department of Health and Human Services. (1994, September). *The statement of the Advisory Committee on Services for Families with Infants and Toddlers* (DHHS Publication No. 615-032/03062). Washington, DC: U.S. Government Printing Office.

U.S. Department of Health and Human Services, Administration for Children and Families. (1996, November 5). Head Start Program: Final Rule. *Federal Register, 60*(215), 14548–14578.

U.S. Department of Health and Human Services, Administration for Children and Families. (1999, December). *Leading the way: Characteristics and early experiences of selected Early Head Start Programs. Executive summary (Vols I & II).* Washington, DC: Author.

U.S. Department of Labor Statistics and U.S. Bureau of the Census. (1999, March). *Current population survey: Supplement.* [On-line]. Available: http://www.ferret.bls.census.gov

U.S. General Accounting Office. (1994). *Infants and toddlers: Dramatic increases in numbers living in poverty* (HEHS 94-74). Washington, DC: Author.

U.S. General Accounting Office. (1995). *Welfare to work, measuring outcomes for JOBS participants* (HEHS 95-86). Washington, DC: Author.

Vaughn, B., Gove, F., & Egeland, B. (1980). The relationship between out-of-home care and the quality of infant–mother attachment in an economically disadvantaged population. *Child Development, 51,* 1203–1214.

Wasik, B.H. (1993). Staffing issues for home visiting programs. *The Future of Children, 3*(3), 140–155.

Wasik, B.H., Bryant, D.M., & Lyons, C.M. (1990). *Home visiting: Procedures for helping families.* Newbury Park, CA: Sage Publications.

Wasik, B.H., Ramey, C.T., Bryant, D.M., & Sparling, J.J. (1990). A longitudinal study of two early intervention strategies: Project CARE. *Child Development, 61,* 1682–1696.

Weil, M., & Karls, J.M. (1985). *Case management in human service practice: A systematic approach to mobilizing resources for clients.* San Francisco: Jossey-Bass Publishers.

Weiss, H.B. (1988). Family support and education programs: Working through ecological theories of human development. In H.B. Weiss & F.H. Jacobs (Eds.), *Evaluating family programs* (pp. 3–36). Hawthorne, NY: Aldine de Gruyter.

Weiss, H.B. (1993). Home visits: Necessary but not sufficient. *The Future of Children, 3*(3), 113–128.

West, J., Wright, D., & Hausken, E. (1995). *Child care and early education program participation of infants, toddlers, and preschoolers.* (U.S. Department of Education, Office of Educational Research and Improvement NCES05:825). Washington, DC: National Center for Education Statistics.

Zaslow, M.J. (1991). Variation in child care quality and its implications for children. *Journal of Social Issues, 47,* 125–138.

6

Respiratory Disease in Infants and Toddlers

◆❖◆

Albert M. Collier and Frederick W. Henderson

The most common infectious diseases of early childhood (e.g., the common cold, middle ear infections, pharyngitis, bronchitis, pneumonia) affect primarily the respiratory system. The respiratory system—made up of the nasopharynx, sinuses, Eustachian tubes and middle ears, trachea, conducting airways, and alveoli—has the largest surface area exposed to the environment of any body organ. Each breath of air contains particulates, bacteria, and fungi; however, the surfaces of the sinuses, middle ears, and lower respiratory tract normally are sterile when cultured because of the highly developed immune system and mucociliary clearance system.

The most common infecting agents of the respiratory tract in infants and toddlers are viruses. The peak incidence of viral respiratory tract infections is during the second 6 months of life, between 7 months and 1 year of age. It is during this period of time that antibodies, proteins in the blood that provide protection against infectious agents, are at their lowest level in life. This is due to the decreasing level of antibodies passed across the placenta from the child's mother during pregnancy and the postnatal development of the child's immune system, which requires about 2 years to produce antibody levels approaching that of an adult. Figure 1 shows the development of the immune system over time. The vertical axis is the percentage of immunoglobulin G (IgG),

This work was supported by SCOR Grant No. HL56395 from the National Heart, Lung, and Blood Institute and by Cooperative Agreement No. CR824915 from the U.S. Environmental Protection Agency.

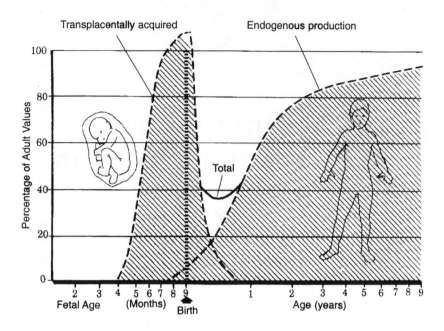

Figure 1.   Plasma IgG concentration at different ages. (From Goldman, A.S., & Goldblum, R.M. [1977]. Primary deficiencies in humoral immunity. *Pediatric Clinics of North America, 24,* 280; reprinted by permission.)

one of the most important classes of immunoglobulins in protecting against infection, in the mother. The horizontal axis is a time line beginning at conception and extending through fetal age in months, birth, and postnatal age in years. At about the fourth month of gestation, the mother starts to pass IgG molecules, which her immune system has manufactured, across the placenta to the fetus. In the last 2 months of gestation the placenta actively pumps IgG across so that when a full-term baby is born, he or she has an IgG immunoglobulin level greater than that of the mother. Some premature babies are born prior to the active pumping of IgG by the placenta and miss this. At birth, with separation from the placenta, IgG contribution from the mother stops, and the IgG immunoglobulin level starts to drop. Almost all of the maternal IgG has disappeared by the time the child reaches 1 year of age.

At 7 months of fetal age, the immune system of the fetus is sufficiently developed to start making its own IgG, but this level goes up slowly and only reaches 80% of the adult level by age 2. It is during the second 6 months of life that infection of the middle ear, otitis media, which is the number one complication of upper respiratory tract infections, has its highest incidence and corresponds to the time when the level of IgG is lowest. Therefore, there is an inverse relationship between the lowest point of IgG levels and the peak of respiratory illness (Goldman & Goldblum, 1977).

This chapter reviews the literature on respiratory diseases in infants and toddlers studied in different forms of child care and summarizes recommendations for future research, practice, policy, and personnel preparation.

RESPIRATORY INFECTIONS AMONG CHILDREN IN CHILD CARE

The first known facility for the care of children outside the home in the United States opened outside of Boston in 1828. The number of care facilities outside of the home has continued to grow in the United States. More than 11 million children younger than the age of 6 years currently spend all or part of their day in care outside of their home. By the year 2000, it is estimated that 80% of our nation's children will have a working mother, and most of these children will require some form of child care (Donowitz, 1991).

The most common types of infant and toddler care in the United States are home care, family child care, and center-based child care. *Home care* has been defined as care of a child or children from a single family in their own home. *Family child care* is care in which a small number of children (usually six or fewer) are cared for in the family child care provider's home. *Center-based child care* has been defined as care in which children (seven or more) from many families are cared for in a child care center for either all or part of a day.

Children younger than 3 years of age who attend center-based child care experience a greater number of respiratory infections than children of the same age who are cared for at home. The severity of these infections in young children is also greater. In center-based child care, the size of the facility is related to the transmission and development of respiratory infectious diseases. The likelihood that a child is exposed to a potential infectious agent is dependent on the frequency with which that infectious agent is introduced into the center-based child care environment by another child. Children who are routinely in contact with only 3 children daily rather than with 30 children have less of a chance of coming into contact with an infectious agent. In addition, center-based child care environments that have age-group mixing increase the likelihood of exposure to an infectious agent.

Several prospective cohort studies have examined the rates, site of infection, severity, and etiology of respiratory infections among children who attend center-based child care. Respiratory infections account for

75%–90% of infections occurring in center-based child care settings. The respiratory pathogens documented to cause disease in center-based child care are listed in Table 1.

The Frank Porter Graham Child Development Center at the University of North Carolina has had a continuous comprehensive study of respiratory infections among children in a center-based child care setting since 1966 (Denny, Collier, & Henderson, 1988). Children enrolled in the center have been followed prospectively from the time of enrollment at 2–4 months of age through entry into kindergarten. All respiratory episodes have been evaluated clinically, with respiratory secretions from the upper respiratory tract cultured for viral, bacterial, and mycoplasmal pathogens, and each time a child contracts an illness, he or she has a physical examination by a nurse practitioner or pediatrician.

In the Frank Porter Graham study, a total of 206 children have been followed for 864 child-years. (Observation of one child for one year equals one child-year). Infants younger than 1 year of age experienced an average of nine respiratory illnesses per year of which 46% were associated with otitis media and 13% with lower respiratory manifestation. Rates of respiratory illness decreased progressively with age. Children between 4 and 5 years of age experienced an average of 3.3 respiratory illnesses per year of which only 9% were complicated by acute otitis media and 9% lower respiratory tract involvement.

We compared data on respiratory illnesses from the Frank Porter Graham Child Development Center children attending center-based

Table 1. Respiratory pathogens transmitted in center-based child care

Common Bacteria	Viruses
Streptococcus pneumoniae	Adenoviruses
Haemophilus influenzae	Cytomegalovirus
Moraxella catarrhalis	Enteroviruses (Coxsackie and ECHO)
Group A streptococcus	Epstein-Barr virus
	HHV6
Less Common Bacteria	Influenza viruses
	Parainfluenza viruses
Bordetella pertussis	Parvovirus B19
Neisseria meningitis	Respiratory syncytial viruses
Mycobacterium tuberculosis	Rhinoviruses
	Viruses–Vaccine Controllable
	Measles
	Mumps
	Rubella
	Varicella

child care with data collected from the Cleveland Family Study children living at home with no siblings in school (Denny et al., 1988; Dingle, Badger, & Jordan, 1964). In the first 2 years of life, the children in the Frank Porter Graham Child Development Center had more respiratory illnesses than the children of the same age in the Cleveland Family Study. The number of respiratory illnesses, during the third year of life, were about the same for both groups. However, the Cleveland Family Study children, living at home with no siblings in school, had more respiratory illnesses at ages 4 and 5 compared with the children in the Frank Porter Graham Child Development Center. When the total number of respiratory illnesses for the first 5 years of life for the children in center-based child care were compared with the children living at home with no siblings in school, the number of respiratory illnesses in each group were the same. These data demonstrate evidence that children in center-based child care have more respiratory illnesses during the first 2 years of life when compared with children in home care. This is the age during which the risk of developing complications are greater due to decreasing passive antibody levels from the mother and maturation of the child's own immune system. In the Frank Porter Graham Child Development Center, 12 children in each class come together for 8 hours a day bringing infectious agents from each of their families to the child care center, with the resulting exposure of the attending children to a larger number of respiratory pathogens than the children who live at home and have no siblings in school. Most of these illnesses are viral, and it is known that throughout the first 6 years of life, children attending center-based child care will be infected with these viruses earlier than children living at home with no siblings in school.

The viral agents cultured from children with symptomatic respiratory illnesses were similar to those recognized as common causes of illnesses in children who did not attend child care. The three viruses isolated most commonly from children in center-based child care during the first 3 years of life were the respiratory syncytial virus (RSV), adenoviruses, and influenza viruses. Respiratory syncytial virus outbreaks occurred during most winters, with the attack rate approaching 90% of infants at risk of primary infection. Outbreaks of adenoviruses were also common, particularly in children younger than 2 years of age. Parainfluenza virus infection, most often without manifestation of croup, and enteroviral infections were the other leading causes of viral respiratory illness. The adenoviruses, RSV, and influenza viruses were associated with the highest prevalence of otitis media; involvement of the lower respiratory tract was most common with infections caused by RSV and parainfluenza viruses.

CHILD CARE ATTENDANCE AND THE OCCURRENCE OF OTITIS MEDIA AND MIDDLE EAR EFFUSION

We have studied the incidence of acute otitis media and the prevalence of middle ear effusion among children attending the Frank Porter Graham Child Development Center since its opening in September, 1966 (Henderson, et al., 1982; Schwartz et al., 1994). More recently, we have studied the prevalence of middle ear effusion (i.e., fluid draining from the middle ear) among children attending eight other center-based child cares in piedmont North Carolina (Zeisel et al., 1995). Acute otitis media, recurrent acute otitis media, and persistent middle ear effusion all occur commonly during the first 3 years of life among young children who begin to attend center-based child care facilities in early infancy. This section describes the findings at the Frank Porter Graham Center and other regional center-based child care programs and puts these data into perspective by briefly reviewing relevant comparison studies from the medical literature.

Since 1966, more than 200 children have participated in respiratory illness surveillance studies at the Frank Porter Graham Center. Most infants are enrolled at the Frank Porter Graham Center before 6 months of age, and they are followed prospectively and longitudinally until graduation from kindergarten. Study children attend center-based child care 8 hours a day, 5 days a week. Children are enrolled annually in groups of 10–12 infants. Except for replacement of drop-outs, older children are not admitted to the center. Between 1966 and 1990, an intensive illness surveillance was conducted on all children attending the center. Since 1990, illness surveillance has been limited to targeted subgroups of the total child care population. The descriptive data presented here are based on the 1966–1990 time period. Illnesses experienced by study children were documented by pediatrician researchers and research pediatric nurse practitioners. Any child with symptoms of respiratory illness was examined and the clinical features of illness characterized. Routine follow-up examinations were made on the fourth day of illness and between Days 10 and 14 to document possible complications of illness and illness resolution. Children with otitis media or middle ear effusion were examined every 2 weeks until effusion stopped. In addition, children were examined once a month, routinely (and independent of illness), to document the presence or absence of otitis media or middle ear effusion. This observation strategy of active surveillance, regardless of illness status, allowed researchers to accurately record the occurrence of both symptomatic and asymptomatic middle ear infections and to estimate the proportion of observation days that study children experienced middle ear effusion.

Table 2 shows the age-specific incidence of acute respiratory illness and acute otitis media during the first 5 years of life. During the first 24 months in center-based child care, infants and toddlers experienced an average of approximately 8–10 respiratory illnesses annually. Otitis media was diagnosed in approximately 35% of children with acute respiratory disease in this age interval. Approximately 50% of children studied experienced more than two episodes of otitis media per year during the first 3 years of life while attending center-based child care. Beyond 3 years of age, the incidence of total respiratory illness and otitis media declined progressively. The fraction of illnesses in which otitis media was observed was less than 10% in children older than 4 years of age.

Examination of the frequency distribution of the Frank Porter Graham study population by the proportion of days with bilateral middle effusion revealed that more than one half of the children studied experienced at least 90 days with bilateral middle ear effusion before age 3 and that 20% of children experienced more than 180 days with bilateral effusion. After age 3, prolonged bilateral middle ear effusion was quite uncommon; only 5% of children between the ages of 3 and 5 experienced more than 90 days with bilateral effusion. Studies at center-based child care programs other than the Frank Porter Graham Center (e.g., Zeisel et al., 1995) revealed a higher burden of bilateral middle ear effusion in the first 2 years of life. However, beyond age 2, most children no longer experienced persistent middle ear effusion.

Most studies in the medical literature concerning the impact of child care attendance on middle ear disease have not included a substantial number of children who began to attend center-based child care facilities before 6 months of age. Furthermore, cohort studies using prospective active surveillance (i.e., frequent routine ear examinations) for middle ear effusion documentation are uncommon. For these reasons, direct comparisons of data from the literature with our findings are

Table 2.   Age-specific incidence* of acute respiratory illness at the Frank Porter Graham Child Development Center, September 1, 1966, to August 31, 1990

Age	Child–years	Total respiratory illness	Acute otitis media	Lower respiratory illness
2 to 12 mos.	158.3	8.9	4.1	1.2
1 to 2 yrs.	200.9	7.8	3.0	0.6
2 to 3 yrs.	185.7	6.0	1.3	0.5
3 to 4 yrs.	167.8	4.4	0.9	0.4
4 to 5 yrs.	150.9	3.3	0.3	0.3

* mean episodes/child/year

frequently difficult. However, the literature provides consistent evidence that the burden of middle ear disease is substantial for children who attend center-based child care in early childhood.

Tos, Poulsen, and Borch (1978) reported one of the first studies to provide convincing evidence of the increased risk of middle ear effusion among children in center-based child care. He conducted a cross-sectional survey in children between 1 and 2 years of age in Copenhagen, in which he measured their ear drums' responses to sound, a procedure known as tympanometry (Tos, Poulsen, & Borch, 1978). A birth cohort of 228 children was examined. Center-based child care attendance was associated with greater than a fourfold increase of odds of having middle ear effusion relative to children in home care. Approximately 24% of children attending center-based child care demonstrated flat tympanograms, indicative of middle ear effusion. Only 5% of children in home care had these findings.

Fleming and colleagues conducted a random telephone survey of 449 families with children younger than 5 years of age living in Atlanta (Fleming, Cochi, Hightower, & Broome, 1987). The odds of having experienced an ear infection in the 2 weeks before the telephone survey was 3.8 times higher among children younger than 3 years of age attending full-time center-based child care. Sixty-six percent of all ear infections occurring in children in this age group who attend center-based child care were attributable to child care attendance. Parental smoking and household crowding also were related to the occurrence of recent middle ear infection.

Wald observed 153 children prospectively from birth for 12–18 months (Wald, Dashefsky, Byers, Guerra, & Taylor, 1988). Thirty-three children were in center-based child care centers (containing seven or more children) from early infancy. Respiratory illness experience was documented by biweekly telephone interviews with the children's parents. Respiratory illness rates were significantly higher among children attending any out-of-home child care. The odds of having tympanostomy tube placement (to drain fluid from the middle ear) for recurrent otitis media (three or more episodes) or persistent middle ear effusion (4 or more months) during the first year of life were seven times higher among children in center-based child care (21%) relative to children in home care (3%).

In a prospective cohort study of 1,013 infants enrolled in a health maintenance organization, Ey and associates demonstrated that recurrent otitis media during the first year of life (four or more episodes in a year or three or more episodes in 6 months) was nearly two times more common in children attending 9 or more hours of out-of-home child care (21%) than in children cared for at home (12.3%) (Ey et al., 1995). The data were not presented for the subset of children in full-time child care, nor was the age of child care entry analyzed; furthermore, the occurrence of otitis media was ascertained by passive surveillance, rather than active surveillance.

In the study most directly comparable to the work conducted at the Frank Porter Graham Center, Owen and colleagues followed 435 children prospectively from early infancy to 2 years of age, performing tympanometry every 2–4 weeks to document the presence or absence of middle ear effusion (Owen et al., 1993). Thirty-one percent of study children began out-of-home child care attendance during the first year of life; an additional 15% entered child care between 1 and 2 years of age. The median age of child care entry was 11 months, and the mean duration of time in child care was 18 hours per week. Early child care entrance was associated with earlier occurrence of first middle ear effusion. In every 6-month interval between birth and 2 years of age, child care attendance was a highly significant predictor of time with middle ear effusion. Between 12 and 18 months of age, full-time child care attendance was associated with a 49% increase in percent of days with middle ear effusion compared to home care.

In summary, consistent evidence has been obtained for an increased risk of otitis media and middle ear effusion among children younger than 3 years of age attending out-of-home child care, particularly for children attending center-based child care. The risk is probably highest for children who begin to attend these facilities during the first 6 months of life, because early child care attendance is associated with an earlier first episode of otitis or middle ear effusion and because early middle ear disease is associated with more frequent subsequent otitis media and more prevalent subsequent effusion.

CHILD CARE AND THE EMERGENCE OF ANTIBIOTIC RESISTANCE IN *STREPTOCOCCUS PNEUMONIAE*

The bacterium *Streptococcus pneumoniae* is the most common cause of bacterial middle ear infections, sinusitis, pneumonia, blood stream infections, and meningitis in preschool children. These bacteria commonly colonize the nasal mucosa of all healthy children. In subsets of children colonized by bacteria, ear infections, sinusitis, and occasionally more severe infections develop, frequently in association with or following common viral respiratory infections. We first reported rates of antibiotic resistance among *S. pneumoniae* recovered from children in center-based child care in 1988 (Henderson, Gilligan, Wait, & Goff, 1988). Isolates of these bacteria obtained from routine biweekly or monthly nasal cultures obtained from children in the Frank Porter Graham respiratory illness surveillance studies were characterized. The initial observations focused on the emergence of resistance to an antibiotic called trimethoprim-sulfamethoxazole. This antibiotic was commonly employed for treatment of ear infections beginning in the early to mid-1980s. After observing ear infections that were resistant to antibiotic treatment and following a case of blood stream infection caused by a trimethoprim-sulfa resistant strain of *S. pneumoniae,* we performed an antibiotic susceptibility survey of nearly 200 isolates of *S. pneumoniae* obtained from children at the Frank Porter Graham Center over a 5-year period (1980 to 1985). Before trimethoprim-sulfa was used for treatment of ear infections, less than 10% of isolates studied were resistant to the antibiotic. However, within 1 year of beginning to employ this drug in clinical practice, resistance rates at the Frank Porter Graham Center were routinely higher than 35%, and in some years were as high as 60%. In our discussion of this finding, we speculated that emergence of antibiotic-resistant bacteria in the center-based child care setting and subsequent spread of these organisms among children in child care facilities might be an important new medical hazard associated with child care attendance.

The significance of this prediction was realized first in 1989 when the spread of a highly penicillin-resistant and multiple antibiotic-resistant strain of *S. pneumoniae* was documented among children attending a center-based child care center in Cleveland, Ohio (Reichler et al., 1992). Subsequently, the spread of a very similar multiple drug-resistant strain of *S. pneumoniae* was observed among children attending the Frank Porter Graham Center in 1990 (Barnes et al., 1995). Fortunately, no child at the Frank Porter Graham Center developed either treatment resistant middle ear infection or more severe disease due to the drug resistant strain. Over the next 4 years, spread of these organisms was demonstrated in communities around the country, and child care attendance was documented as a consistent risk factor for colonization or infection with drug resistant organisms (Hofmann et al., 1995). In central North Carolina, reduced antibiotic susceptibility is now routinely observed in close to 50% of all isolates of *S. pneumoniae* obtained from preschool children. There is little doubt that spread of drug-resistant organisms within the child care environment has contributed substantially to the rapid dissemination of these drug-resistant strains of *S. pneumoniae* in large and small communities throughout the United States.

COMPARISON AMONG
TYPES OF CHILD CARE AND RESPIRATORY ILLNESSES

Wald and colleagues (1988) performed a year-long prospective study on the frequency, nature, and severity of infections that children in three types of child care experienced. The children were enrolled at birth and followed for 12–18 months by a telephone call every 2 weeks. The population consisted of 159 children in home care, 40 in group care, and 45 in child care. Each child had to remain in their prospective group for at least 1 year to be included in the analysis. The study revealed that during the course of a year the children in family child care and center-based child care were more likely than children in home care to have at least six respiratory infections, more than 60 days of illness, and more than four severe illnesses defined as high fever and duration exceeding 10 days or requiring physician visit ($p < 0.01$). This study also found that the children in home care had fewer episodes of infection than did children in child care ($p < 0.01$). No children in this study required hospitalization because of an acute infection, but 21% of the children in child care were hospitalized for middle ear ventilation tubes compared to 3% of children in home care ($p < 0.01$).

In a later study, Wald, Guerra, and Byers (1991) determined the duration and frequency of complications in upper respiratory tract infections in young children from home care, family child care and center-based child care. The children in the individual care groups were enrolled at birth and followed for 3 years. The families were telephoned every 2 weeks to record the data. The mean duration of an upper respiratory tract infection was found to vary between 6.6 days for 1- to 2-year-old children in home care to 8.9 days for children younger than 1 year in center-based child care. Children in center-based child care were more likely than children in home care to have protracted respiratory symptoms. The percentage of simple respiratory tract infections that were found to last more than 15 days ranged from 6.5% for 1- to 3-year-old children in home care to 13.1% for 2- to 3-year-old children in center-based child care. In the first 2 years of life, children in any type of child care were found to have otitis media as a complication of upper respiratory tract infections more than children in home care. In year 3, the risk of otitis media was similar for all types of child care. In 2,741 respiratory tract infections during the 3-year study period, 801 (29.2%) were accompanied by otitis media.

CENTER-BASED CHILD CARE ATTENDANCE AND HOSPITALIZATION FOR LOWER RESPIRATORY TRACT ILLNESS

Anderson and colleagues (1988) examined 102 children younger than 2 years of age hospitalized in Atlanta metropolitan-area hospitals between December 1984 and June 1985 with the diagnosis of lower respiratory tract illness to identify risk factors associated with the hospitalization for acute lower respiratory tract illness. The 102 hospitalized children were compared with 199 age- and sex-matched nonhospitalized children. The results of this study demonstrated that five factors were associated with lower respiratory illness in both a univariant analysis and a multiple logistic regression model ($p < 0.05$). These factors were 1) regular attendance in a center-based child care with seven or more children; 2) the number of people sleeping in the room with the child; 3) a history of prematurity; 4) a history of allergy; and 5) a lack of immunization in the month before the patient was hospitalized. This study found that care received outside the home in family child care (less than or equal to six children in attendance) was not associated with lower respiratory tract illness.

Intervention and Control

Kotch and colleagues (1994) performed a prospective study to evaluate a hygienic intervention in center-based child care. This was a randomized trial of a hygienic intervention in 24 child care centers conducted in Cumberland County, North Carolina. The 24 centers had enrollment of less than 30 children, with at least five children attending in diapers, and were projected to operate for at least 2 years. Centers of similar enrollment were paired and one of the pair randomly assigned as the intervention group. The intervention emphasized 1) hand washing of children and staff; 2) disinfecting of toilet and diapering area; 3) physical separation of diapering areas from food preparation and serving areas; 4) hygienic diaper disposal; 5) availability of soap, running water, and disposable towels; 6) daily washing and disinfecting of toys, sinks, and kitchen and bathroom floors; 7) daily laundering of blankets, sheets, dress-up clothes, and so forth; and 8) hygienic preparation, serving, and clean-up of food. Parental illness reports were blind to the intervention status of their child care center. Respiratory episodes were the most frequent infections reported. No significant difference was found in intervention centers compared to control centers for illness rates of respiratory tract infections.

RECOMMENDATIONS FOR FUTURE RESEARCH, PRACTICE, POLICY, AND PERSONNEL PREPARATION

The increasing use of center-based child care, particularly for children younger than 2, has led to a significant increase in respiratory illness morbidity. These illnesses lead to discomfort, disability, and parental anxiety. There is also increased illness on the part of caregivers (Haskins & Kotch, 1986; Kotch & Bryant, 1990). Haskins (1989) estimated the annual cost of child care illnesses among children to be $1.8 billion.

There is increased risk during the first 18–24 months of life. During this period, the child is infected with respiratory pathogens for the first time and develops protective antibodies that will place him or her in a better position to respond to the next encounter with that particular infecting agent.

The prevention of respiratory infections in center-based child care remains a public health challenge. We have no published data describing a successful intervention to reduce the risk of upper respiratory diseases in center-based child care. There is no evidence that the incidence of acute respiratory disease can be reduced among children attending center-based child care by excluding ill children from the center. Children with viral respiratory infections excrete the infectious virus 4–5 days prior to the time they demonstrate signs and symptoms of the infection.

The strategy we recommend for future research in the control of respiratory tract infections in center-based child care includes the following. Cost-effective control measures for respiratory illnesses that have the highest incidence and morbidity in center-based child care must be identified. It is too expensive to try to control all respiratory tract infections—the most important ones to seek to prevent must be chosen. The most feasible intervention at the present time would seek to increase the individual child's immunity to the most important respiratory infectious agents. First, this should be approached by making sure that the children and child care staff are fully vaccinated on schedule for vaccine-preventable respiratory illnesses. Second, research should be done in the area of maternal immunization during pregnancy to optimize the level of antibodies in the mother to a particular respiratory tract pathogen. These passive antibodies would be at a high level to pass across the placenta to the newborn. The child would then be immunized with new vaccines to develop immunity and memory lymphocytes as the mother's passive antibodies disappear. In the near future, vaccine development will certainly focus on the respiratory syncytial, parainfluenza, and influenza viruses. Adenoviruses could also be an important target for prevention.

Just as the spread of respiratory viral infections is difficult to control by environmental or educational intervention in the child care setting, the spread of respiratory bacteria (including antibiotic-resistant bacterial strains) is also difficult to contain. Ultimately, interventions that reduce the incidence of otitis media will reduce the exposure of children attending child care to antibiotics. This should decrease pressure in selecting for both nasal carriage of and infection with antibiotic-resistant organisms. The interventions with the highest prospects for success at this time are based on development of new vaccines for respiratory pathogens. Protein-conjugated vaccines for *S. pneumoniae* are in development that could reduce the occurrence of otitis media by as much as 20%. Effective vaccines for common viral respiratory infections would also be expected to have an important impact on the occurrence of otitis media and reduce antibiotic utilization (Henderson et al., 1982).

Providing high-quality education to child care personnel on infection control principles and consistent implementation of infection control principles remains the cornerstone of disease control in group child care environments. Research only indicates how difficult control of the spread of respiratory pathogens can be. Immunization is likely to result in the greatest progress in control of respiratory diseases among young children.

REFERENCES

Anderson, L.J., Parker, R.A., Strikas, R.A., Farrar, J.A., Gangarosa, E.J., Keyserling, H.L., & Sikes, R.K. (1988). Day-care center attendance and hospitalization for lower respiratory tract illness. *Pediatrics, 82*(3), 300–308.

Barnes, D.M., Whittier, S., Gilligan, P.H., Soares, S., Tomasz, A., & Henderson, F.W. (1995). Transmission of multidrug-resistant serotype 23F *Streptococcus pneumoniae* in group day care: Evidence suggesting capsular transformation of the resistant strain in vivo. *Journal of Infectious Diseases, 171*, 890–896.

Denny, F.W., Collier, A.M., & Henderson, F.W. (1988). Acute respiratory infections in day care. *Review of Infectious Disease, 8*, 15–29.

Dingle, J.H., Badger, G.F., & Jordan, W.S., Jr. (1964). *Patterns of illness: Illness in the home.* Cleveland, OH: Western Reserve University.

Donowitz L.G. (1991). Preface. In L.G. Donowitz (Ed.) *Infection control in the child care center and preschool* (p. vii). Baltimore: Lippincott Williams and Wilkins.

Ey, J.L., Holberg, C.J., Aldous, M.B., Wright, A.L., Martinez, F.D., & Taussig, L.M. (1995). Passive smoke exposure and otitis media in the first year of life. *Pediatrics, 95*, 670–677.

Fleming, D.W., Cochi, S.L., Hightower, A.W., & Broome, C.V. (1987). Childhood upper respiratory tract infections: To what degree is incidence affected by daycare attendance? *Pediatrics, 79*, 55–60.

Goldman, A.S., & Goldblum, R.M. (1977). Primary deficiencies in humoral immunity. *Pediatric Clinics of North America, 24*, 277–291.

Haskins, R., & Kotch, J. (1986). Day care and illness: Evidence, cost, and public policy. *Pediatrics, 77*(Suppl.), 951–982.

Haskins, R. (1989). Acute illness in day care: How much does it cost? *Bulletin of the New York Academy of Medicine, 65*, 319–343.

Henderson, F.W., Collier, A.M., Sanyal, M.A., Watkins, J.M., Fairclough, D.L., Clyde, W.A., Jr., & Denny, F.W. (1982). A longitudinal study of respiratory viruses and bacteria in the etiology of acute otitis media with effusion. *New England Journal of Medicine, 306*, 1377–1381.

Henderson, F.W., Gilligan, P.H., Wait, K., & Goff, D.A. (1988). Nasopharyngeal carriage of antibiotic resistant pneumococci by children in day care. *Journal of Infectious Diseases, 157*, 256–263.

Hofmann, J., Cetron, M.S., Farley, M.M., Baughman, W.S., Facklam, R.R., Elliot, J.A., Deaver, K.A., & Breiman, R.F. (1995). The prevalence of drug-resistant *Streptococcus pneumoniae* in Atlanta. *New England Journal of Medicine, 333,* 481-486.

Kotch, J.B., & Bryant, D. (1990). Effects of day care on the health and development of children. *Current Opinions in Pediatrics, 2,* 883–894.

Kotch, J.B., Weigle, K.A., Weber, D.J., Clifford, M.R., Harms, T.O., Loda, F.A., Gallagher, P.N., Jr., Edwards, R.W., LaBorde, D., McMurray, M.P., Rolandelli, P.S., & Faircloth, A.H. (1994). Evaluation of hygienic intervention in child daycare centers. *Pediatrics*(Suppl.), 991–994.

Owen, M.J., Baldwin, C.D., Swank, P.R., Pannu, A.K., Johnson, D.L., & Howie, V.M. (1993) Relation of infant feeding practices, cigarette smoke exposure, and group child care to the onset and duration of otitis media with effusion in the first 2 years of life. *Journal of Pediatrics, 123,* 702–711.

Reichler, M.R., Allphin, A.A., Breiman, R.F., Schreiber, J.R., Arnold, J.E., McDougal, L.K., Facklam, R.R., Boxerbaum, B., May, D., Walton, R.O. et al. (1992). The spread of multiply resistant *Streptococcus pneumoniae* at a day care center in Ohio. *Journal of Infectious Diseases, 166,* 1346–1353.

Schwartz, B., Giebink, G.S., Henderson, F.W., Reichler, M.R., Jereb, J., & Collet, J.P. (1994). Respiratory infections in day care. *Pediatrics. 94,* 1018–1020.

Tos, M., Poulsen, G., & Borch, J. (1978). Tympanometry in 2 year old children. *ORL; Journal of Oto-Rhino-Laryngology and Its Related Specialties, 40,* 77–85.

Wald, E.R., Dashefsky, B., Byers, C., Guerra, N., & Taylor, F. (1988). Frequency and severity of infections in day care. *Journal of Pediatrics , 112*(4), 540–546.

Wald, E.R., Guerra, N., & Byers, C. (1991). Upper respiratory tract infections in young children: Duration of and frequency of complications. *Pediatrics, 87*(2), 129–133.

Zeisel, S.A., Roberts, J.E., Gunn, E.B., Riggins, R., Jr., Evans, G.A., Roush, J., & Henderson, F.W. (1995). Prospective surveillance for otitis media with effusion among African American infants in group child care. *Journal of Pediatrics, 127,* 875–880.

7

Diarrheal Disease
in Infants and Toddlers

◆❖◆

Robin B. Churchill and Larry K. Pickering

Out-of-home child care is part of everyday life for millions of children in the United States and other countries worldwide (Collet et al., 1994; Hofferth, 1996; Pickering & Morrow, 1991). Cultural and economic factors, including an increased percentage of women in the work force, a greater proportion of single-parent families, and the desire for preschool educational exposures, are responsible for an increase in demand for out-of-home child care. In 1995, approximately 60% of children younger than 5 years of age in the United States were enrolled in child care or early education programs as compared with 22% in 1965 (Hofferth, 1996; Thacker, Addiss, Goodman, Holloway, & Spencer, 1992). This trend is expected to continue with an estimated 75% of mothers of preschool children working outside the home by the year 2000 (Thacker et al., 1992). This change has and will continue to affect physicians and other health care providers who care for children, because children who attend out-of-home settings are at increased risk of contracting a variety of infectious diseases (Churchill & Pickering, 1997; Haskins & Kotch, 1986; Holmes, Morrow, & Pickering, 1996; Jorm & Capon, 1994; Osterholm, 1994; Thacker et al., 1992). Infectious diseases in child care also are of public health significance because of potential transmission of microorganisms to adult care providers and family members and spread of infections into the community (Fornasini, Shults, Morrow, & Pickering, submitted; Reves & Pickering, 1990, 1992).

Children in out-of-home care are at particular risk for both respiratory tract and gastrointestinal tract diseases (Holmes et al., 1996; Long,

1997; Pickering & Osterholm, 1997). This chapter concentrates on diarrheal disease in infants and toddlers in out-of-home care settings and
includes

- Enteropathogens (organisms that cause diarrhea) associated with
  outbreaks
- Asymptomatic excretion of enteropathogens (excretion of pathogens
  by people without signs or symptoms of illness)
- Diarrheal disease in newly enrolled children
- Contamination of the child care environment by enteropathogens
- Transmission of enteropathogens to adult care providers and family
  members
- Hygienic practices in child care
- Effect of antibiotic use on resistance patterns of enteric organisms
- Financial impact of diarrheal disease
- Strategies for control and prevention of diarrheal disease
- Evaluation of the impact of national standards

TYPES OF CHILD CARE FACILITIES

A variety of out-of-home child care settings exist, ranging from family
child care homes to large child care centers, as well as facilities providing care to ill children and children with special needs (Thacker et al.,
1992). Child care facilities can be classified according to the number
and/or ages of children in attendance, the type of environmental setting of the facility, or the health status of children in care (American
Academy of Pediatrics, 1997; Pickering & Osterholm, 1997; Thacker et al.,
1992). Several studies have related the risk of infection to the type of
care facility, specifically child care homes and child care centers
(Anderson et al., 1988; Bell et al., 1989; Collet et al., 1994; Holmes et al.,
1996; Louhiala, Jaakkola, Ruotsalainen, & Jaakkola, 1995; Strangert, 1976).
Physical structures of child care settings vary from private residences
used in family child care to larger nonresidential buildings that house
centers. However, a large percentage of buildings that house child care
centers were not designed for that purpose. One survey revealed that
50% of child care centers surveyed were located in remodeled buildings
not originally intended for child care (Staes, Balk, Ford, Passantino, &
Torrice, 1994). An inappropriate physical facility can make infection control practices difficult or impossible to implement and maintain. For
example, published recommendations for infection control in child care
environments state that hand-washing sinks should be located near each
diapering and toilet area, and these areas should be separated physically from food preparation areas (American Academy of Pediatrics and

American Public Health Association, 1992). If the number of sinks is inadequate or if their locations are not ideal, hand-washing recommendations will not be followed.

Licensing classification of the different types of child care facilities varies from state to state. However, in many states, the following definitions apply. Family child care homes are private residences in which children receive out-of-home care. In small family child care homes, the caregiver usually provides care for six or fewer unrelated children, and in many states licensing is not required. Large family child care homes serve 7–12 children, may employ qualified adults, and, in some states, may be subject to licensing. Child care centers generally are licensed facilities providing care for more than 13 children in a nonresidential environment. Facilities caring for children who are ill may be free-standing or part of a larger child care facility. Centers for children with special needs offer care and education for children with chronic illnesses or disabilities who require unique interventions (American Academy of Pediatrics, 1997; Pickering & Osterholm, 1997; Thacker et al., 1992).

In organized child care centers, children generally are cared for in groups housed in separate rooms. Groups may vary in size but usually are divided by age into the following: infants (6 weeks to 12 months), toddlers (13–35 months), preschoolers (36–59 months), and school-age children (5–12 years) (Pickering & Osterholm, 1997). How children are grouped, mixing of all ages of children before and after their classroom grouping, and movement of caregivers among groups can influence transmission of infectious agents, including enteric pathogens.

ENTEROPATHOGENS ASSOCIATED WITH OUTBREAKS

Infectious diarrhea is common in children attending out-of-home care facilities, with outbreaks involving varying numbers of children occurring at a rate of approximately one to two outbreaks per year in each room that houses diapered children (Pickering & Osterholm, 1997). The rate of diarrheal disease in children cared for out of the home is two to three times the rate of children cared for at home (Bartlett et al., 1985; Reves et al., 1993). An estimated 20% of clinic visits for acute diarrhea in children younger than 3 years of age have been shown to be associated with child care attendance (Reves et al., 1993).

The majority of viral, bacterial, and parasitic pathogens associated with diarrheal outbreaks in children in out-of-home care are transmitted from person-to-person by the fecal–oral route (oral ingestion of organisms from stool) (O'Ryan & Matson, 1990; Pickering, 1990). Organisms most commonly involved in outbreaks are highly infectious and able to cause diarrhea following ingestion of a low inoculum (i.e., number of organisms needed to cause disease; Matson, 1994; Pickering & Oster-holm, 1997). Pathogens most frequently reported in child care outbreaks are similar to those transmitted by low infective doses as determined in studies of adult human volunteers (Table 1). Organisms most commonly implicated include *Cryptosporidium; Giardia lamblia;* enteric viruses including astrovirus, calicivirsus, enteric adenovirus, rotavirus; and *Shigella* (Morrow, Townsend, & Pickering, 1991; O'Ryan & Matson, 1990). In addition, *Aeromonas, Bacillus cereus, Campylobacter jejuni, C. upsalien-sis, Clostridium difficile, Escherichia coli* 0157:H7, *E. coli* 0114:NM, *E.coli* 0111:K8, and *Salmonella* have been associated with child care center outbreaks (Belongia, Osterholm, & Soler, 1993; Bower et al., 1989; Centers for Disease Control and Prevention, 1994; de la Morena et al., 1993; Goossens et al., 1995; Kim, DuPont, & Pickering, 1983; Lieb, Gunn, & Taylor, 1982; Paulozzi et al., 1986; Riordan, Humphrey, & Fowles, 1993).

Although most diarrheal outbreaks in child care settings are due to person-to-person transmission, foodborne outbreaks have been reported. Salmonellosis usually occurs following ingestion of contaminated food (Hayani & Pickering, 1992; Pickering, 1982), but the majority of the few reported child care outbreaks associated with *Salmonella* appear to have resulted from person-to-person transmission (Chorba, Merriwether, Jenkins, Gunn, & MacCormack, 1987; Lieb et al., 1982; Rosdahl, 1980). Strains of *Campylobacter* including both *jejuni* and *upsaliensis* have been shown to cause both person-to-person and foodborne outbreaks in child care settings (Goossens et al., 1995; Riordan et al., 1993). *Bacillus cereus* was identified as the causative agent of food-associated outbreaks at two child care centers in Virginia in 1993 (Centers for Disease Control and Prevention, 1994). Another report describes an outbreak of gastroenteritis characterized by fever, vomiting, and diarrhea in three children in a Danish private child care facility caused by *Listeria monocytogenes*. The children were ill enough to require hospitalization,

Table 1. Pathogens frequently associated with diarrhea in the child care setting and inoculum size necessary to produce symptoms

Organism	Inoculum size for infection	References
Cryptosporidium	136 oocysts	DuPont et al., 1995
Giardia lamblia	101–102 cysts	Rentdorff, 1954; Rentdorff & Holt, 1954
Rotavirus	101–102 viral particles	Ward et al., 1986
Shigella	101–103 bacteria	Gorden & Small, 1993

and *L. monocytogenes* was isolated from blood from the index case and stools from all three children. Stool cultures from members of the child care family and the children's family were negative as were cultures of food supplied to the facility (Heitmann, Gerner-Smidt, & Heltberg, 1997).

Shigella and *E. coli* 0157:H7 pose specific public health problems in the child care setting due to severe clinical manifestations and side effects associated with the illness, difficulty in treatment, and ease of transmission. *Shigella* can produce severe bloody diarrhea associated with fever and systemic toxicity, as well as extraintestinal manifestations (Ashkenazi & Cleary, 1992). Symptoms documented in one child care outbreak included fever, nausea, vomiting, severe bloody diarrhea, abdominal cramps, and tenesmus, painful, ineffective straining at stool (Weissman, Gangarosa, Schmerler, Marier, & Lewis, 1975). In addition, treatment is problematic because of continued increases in resistance of bacteria to antibiotics (Pickering, 1996). Significant morbidity (illness), as well as mortality (death) has been associated with child care outbreaks due to several *E. coli* strains (Belongia, et al., 1993; Bower et al., 1989; Pickering, 1990; Spika et al., 1986). *E. coli* 0157:H7 infection in the child care setting has been associated with bloody diarrhea as well as hemolytic uremic syndrome, the triad of microangiopathic hemolytic anemia, thrombocytopenia, and acute renal dysfunction (Belongia, et al., 1993; Spika et al., 1986). Child care outbreaks caused by *E. coli* 0111:K58 and 0114:NM resulted in severe prolonged diarrhea causing dehydration requiring hospitalization of 12 infants in two outbreaks (Bower et al., 1989; Los Angeles County Department of Health Services, 1980; Paulozzi et al., 1986).

Attack rates for specific pathogens vary depending on host factors, inoculum size, and organism characteristics. Methods used to identify organisms can affect attack rate, especially in terms of asymptomatic infection (Churchill & Pickering, 1997; Mitchell et al., 1995; Pickering & Osterholm, 1997). Attack rates of both symptomatic and asymptomatic infection (when available) with particular organisms responsible for outbreaks in child care settings are shown in Table 2. The importance of the method of detection in determination of attack rate was well illustrated by Mitchell and colleagues in a study comparing detection of astrovirus associated with a child care center diarrheal outbreak using reverse-transcriptase-polymerase chain reaction (RT-PCR) and enzyme immunoassay (EIA) as detection assays (Mitchell et al., 1995). In this study RT-PCR detected a significantly greater number of infections compared with EIA (32% of specimens and 89% of children versus 10% of specimens and 50% of children, respectively) (Mitchell et al., 1995). Newer assays that have improved sensitivity and specificity can provide additional data that will enhance the understanding of enteric pathogens in the child care setting (Wilde, Van, Pickering, Eiden, & Yolden, 1992).

Table 2.   Attack rates of infection by enteropathogens in child care enrollees by organism and type of study

Organism	Attack rate (%)	Type of study	References
Aeromonas	22	Prospective cohort with outbreak investigation	de la Morena, et al., 1993
Astrovirus	3–89	Prospective cohort; Prospective cohort analyzed retrospectively	Lew et al., 1991; Mitchell et al., 1993; Mitchell et al., 1995
Calicivirus	5–32	Prospective cohort/ longitudinal surveillance; Outbreak investigation	Grohmann et al., 1991; Matson et al., 1990
Campylobacter			
jejuni	3–50	Prospective cohort with longitudinal investigation	Goossens et al., 1995
upsaliensis	34	Outbreak investigation	Bartlett et al.,1985; Lauwers et al., 1978
Clostridium difficile	32	Prospective cohort with outbreak investigation	Kim et al., 1983
Cryptosporidium	3–64	Prospective cohort	Addiss et al., 1991; Brian et al., 1993; Pickering et al., 1986
		Outbreak investigation	Alpert et al., 1984; Combee et al 1986; Ferson & Young, 1992; Mohle-Boetani et al., 1995
Enteric adenovirus	33, 38	Prospective cohort/ longitudinal surveillance	Lew et al., 1991; Van et al., 1992
Escherichia coli			
0157:H7	3–38	Outbreak investigation	Belongia et al.,1993; Shah et al., 1996; Spika et al., 1986
0114:NM	29–67	Outbreak investigation	Bower et al., 1989
0111:K58	56	Outbreak investigation	Paulozzi et al., 1986

Table 2. *(continued)*

Giardia lamblia	17–54	Prospective cohort	Ish-Horowicz et al., 1989; Pickering et al., 1981
		Outbreak investigation	Rauch et al., 1990; Steketee et al., 1977
Listeria monocytogenes	75	Outbreak investigation	Heitmann et al., 1997
Rotavirus	3–100	Outbreak investigation	Bartlett et al., 1985; Pickering et al., 1981
		Prospective cohort with longitudinal surveillance	Bartlett et al., 1985; Ekanem et al., 1983; Fonteyne et al., 1978; Matson et al., 1993; Rodriguez et al.,1979
Salmonella	22–80	Outbreak investigation	Lieb et al., 1982; Chorba et al., 1987
Shigella	33–73	Prospective cohort	Brian et al., 1993; Pickering et al., 1981; Weissman et al., 1975
		Outbreak investigation	Lerman et al.,1994; Tacket & Cohen, 1983

ASYMPTOMATIC EXCRETION OF ENTEROPATHOGENS

Excretion of enteropathogens by people who are asymptomatic (i.e., healthy) can occur before, after, or in the absence of symptomatic illness and has been documented in both children and young adults (Guerrero et al., 1994; Pickering, Bartlett, Reves, & Morrow, 1988; Pickering, DuPont, Evans, Evands, & Olarte, 1977). In a prospective study of students attending a Mexican university, enteric pathogens were isolated from 37% of asymptomatic students. Pathogens were isolated from a greater number of newly arrived students than other student groups, indicating that people placed in a new exposure situation may be more susceptible to colonization with enteropathogens than longer-term residents (Mitchell et al., 1995; Pickering et al., 1988; Pickering et al., 1977; Staat, Morrow, Reves, Bartlett, & Pickering, 1991).

In the child care setting, asymptomatic excretion of several enteropathogens including *Aeromonas*, astrovirus, calicivirus, *Clostridium difficile*, *Cryptosporidium*, enteric adenovirus, *E. coli* 0157:H7, *Giardia lamblia*, and rotavirus has been described during and in the absence of outbreaks of diarrhea (Barron-Romero, Barreda-Gonzalez, Doral-Ugalde, Zermeno-Eguaraliz, & Huerta-Pena, 1985; Belongia et al., 1993; Crawford, Vermund, Ma, & Deckelbaum, 1988; de la Morena et al., 1993; Ish-Horowicz et al., 1989; Kim et al., 1983; Matson, Estes, & Tanaka, 1990; Mitchell et al., 1995;.Van et al., 1992). Table 3 illustrates the likelihood of asymptomatic excretion by enteropathogen.

Table 3.   Enteropathogens associated with asymptomatic excretion in the child care setting

Organism	Frequency of asymptomatic excretion	Type of study	References
Aeromonas	Uncommon	Prospective cohort	de la Morena et al., 1993
Astrovirus	Common	Retrospective analysis of prospective cohort	Mitchell et al., 1993; Mitchell et al., 1995
Calicivirus	Common	Prospective cohort	Matson et al., 1990
Clostridiume difficile	Common	Prospective cohort	Kim et al., 1983
Cryptosporidium	Common	Prospective cohort	Crawford et al., 1988
Enteric adenovirus	Common	Prospective cohort	Van et al., 1992
Escherichia coli			
0157:H7	Uncommon	Outbreak evaluation	Belongia et al., 1993; Spika et al., 1986
0114:NM	Uncommon	Outbreak evalaution	Bower et al., 1989
0111:K58	Uncommon	Outbreak evaluation	Paulozzi et al., 1986
Giardia lamblia	Common	Prospective cohort	Ish-Horowicz et al., 1989; Rauch et al., 1990
Rotavirus	Common	Prospective cohort	Barron-Romero et al., 1985; Pickering et al., 1988
Shigella	Common	Prospective cohort	Guerrero et al., 1994

A study of children enrolled in a child care center evaluated asymptomatic excretion of rotavirus associated with diarrheal episodes. Excretion of rotavirus began up to 13 days before the diarrheal episode and continued for 14 days after the diarrheal episode (Pickering et al., 1988). In another study, rotavirus was detected in 30% of 564 children without diarrhea who were attending child care centers in Mexico (Barron-Romero et al., 1985). Asymptomatic *Shigella* infection has been demonstrated in 55% of a cohort of prospectively followed Mexican children younger than 2 years of age in a community setting (Guerrero et al., 1994); the extent of asymptomatic shedding (i.e., excretion) in the child care setting is unknown. A longitudinal study of *Giardia lamblia* infection in a child care center population revealed 33% of the 82 children to be infected with Giardia during a 15-month period; however, 78% of these infected children were asymptomatic (Rauch et al., 1990). A study of asymptomatic child care attendees in New York revealed a 27% infection rate for *Cryptosporidium* in asymptomatic infants and toddlers (Crawford et al., 1988). During a waterborne outbreak of cryptosporidiosis, 29% of the infected children attending child care centers had no history of diarrhea during the period of the outbreak (Cordell et al., 1977). Asymptomatic excretion of *E. coli* 0157:H7 has been documented during an outbreak in child care facilities in Minnesota (Belongia et al., 1993). Although it is clear that asymptomatic excretion of several enteropathogens is common in children attending out-of-home child care, the role of asymptomatic excretion in the spread of enteric disease is unknown (Pickering & Osterholm, 1997).

DIARRHEAL DISEASE IN NEWLY ENROLLED CHILDREN

An increased rate of diarrheal disease has been shown to occur in children newly enrolled in child care centers. This increased susceptibility is likely to be due to exposure to pathogens not previously encountered in the home, analogous to the situation that occurs in travelers from the United States to developing countries. The incidence of diarrhea and asymptomatic excretion of enteropathogens has been found to be higher in United States university students soon after arrival in Mexico compared with those who had resided in Mexico for more than a year (DuPont et al., 1977; Pickering et al., 1977). In children newly enrolled in child care centers followed prospectively, the diarrhea incidence rate was 4.4 cases per child-year in the first 4 weeks of enrollment compared to 2.7 cases per child-year in 442 children who had attended the child care center for longer periods of time (Staat et al., 1991). Younger children also had a higher incidence than older children. In a case-control study examining risk factors for acute diarrhea, the first month of enrollment in any form of out-of-home care was associated with significantly increased risk for diarrhea requiring a visit to a health maintenance organization clinic (Reves et al., 1993). The susceptibility of newly enrolled children to infection in the child care setting also has been reported for *Haemophilus influenzae* type B (Takala, Eskola, & Palmgren, 1989). Increased susceptibility of children in younger age groups is presumably due to lack of previous exposure and subsequent development of immunity to infectious agents.

CONTAMINATION OF THE CHILD CARE ENVIRONMENT BY ENTEROPATHOGENS

The most important factor reported to be associated with the occurrence of diarrhea among children in out-of-home care is the presence of diaper-age children (Pickering & Osterholm, 1997; Soto, Guy, et al., 1994). Studies have demonstrated that fecal contamination in infant and toddler areas of the child care environments is common and is more frequent during diarrheal outbreaks (Cody, Sottnek, & O'Leary, 1994; Holaday et al., 1990; Laborde, Weigle, Weber, & Kotch, 1993).

In two prospective studies of child care centers in North Carolina, fecal contamination in child care center classrooms was most frequent on hands of children and staff members, classroom sinks, toys, and faucets, and it occurred more often in classrooms housing infants than in classrooms for toddlers. Dry surfaces, diapering areas, and bathroom sinks and faucets were less likely to be contaminated, presumably due to the absence of moisture and possibly more frequent cleaning of those areas (Laborde, Weigle, Weber, Sobsey, & Kotch, 1994). Other studies also have shown a high rate of recovery of fecal coliform organisms from hands of children and caregivers (Holaday et al., 1990; Van, Morrow, Reves, & Pickering, 1991). One study evaluated the effect of fecal contamination on rates of diarrheal illness in 221 children attending child care centers and revealed a two-fold increase in the rate of diarrhea in those classrooms with contamination of children's hands or moist environmental surfaces as compared with those without contamination. Classrooms with high coliform levels on the hands of staff also tended to have high levels on children's hands. Levels of coliform organisms on children's hands were correlated positively with those of toys and tables (Cody et al., 1994).

A study using specifically designed DNA markers as surrogate indicators of transmission of enteric and other pathogens in child care settings conducted in both a child care home and a child care center further validated observations reported in previous studies of environmental contamination. DNA markers were introduced into the child care environment via specified objects, then traced using marker-specific polymerase chain reaction (PCR). After introduction in the child care home, environmental spread of the markers was rapid with hand touching of contaminated areas as the primary factor leading to spread. Hand washing and cleaning of contaminated areas decreased spread. After introduction of the markers in the child care center, spread initially was more rapid in the infant room than the toddler room. Twenty-four hours after introduction of the markers, 62% of the hands of infants and teachers, 70% of the surfaces, and 100% of the toys sampled in the infant room were positive for the DNA marker. In the toddler room, 73% of the hands of toddlers and teachers and 100% of the toys and surfaces tested were positive. Two weeks after introduction, markers were still detected in both the infant and toddler rooms (Jiang et al., 1998).

The effect of diaper type and clothing on environmental fecal contamination also has been studied (Holaday, Waugh, Moukaddem, West, & Harsman, 1995; Kubiak, Kressner, Raynor, Davis, & Syverson, 1994; Van, Morrow et al., 1991; Van, Wun, Morrow, & Pickering, 1991). A randomized crossover study of infant and toddler rooms in child care centers in Houston showed significantly less contamination of inanimate objects in rooms in which disposable paper diapers were worn as compared to double cloth diapers with plastic overpants (Van, Wun et al., 1991). A lower prevalence of fecal coliform contamination of hands, toy balls, and inanimate objects in rooms in which clothes were worn over diapers was demonstrated in another study (Van, Wun et al., 1991). A comparison of stool containment using cloth and single-use diapers in which simulated feces were introduced showed higher rates of complete containment of the simulated feces and lower leakage rates with disposable diapers (Kubiak et al., 1994). Thirty-nine percent of laundered vinyl pants that had been previously used over cloth diapers were found to be positive for fecal coliform organisms (Kubiak et al., 1994).

TRANSMISSION OF ENTEROPATHOGENS
TO ADULT CARE PROVIDERS AND FAMILY MEMBERS

Transmission of several enteropathogens including rotavirus, *Cryptosporidium, E. coli* 0157:H7, *Giardia lamblia*, and *Shigella* from the child-care setting to family members has been examined in various studies (Pickering & Osterholm, 1997; Pickering et al., 1981; Rodriguez, Kim, & Brandt, 1979; Spika et al., 1986; Tacket & Cohen, 1983). Secondary attack rates for family members vary by pathogen and study but range from 0% to 75% depending on the pathogen and study (Alpert et al., 1986; Black, Dykes, & Sinclair, 1977; Pickering, Evans, DuPont, Vollet, & Evans, 1981; Rodriguez et al., 1979; Steketee, Reid, & Cheng, 1989; Tacket & Cohen,

1983; Weissman et al., 1974). Table 4 shows specific secondary attack rates of diarrheal illnesses for family members of child care enrollees infected with enteropathogens. Transmission of microorganisms from children attending child care centers to family members also has been demonstrated in a study documenting transmission of trimethoprim-resistant *E. coli* from children who have been colonized by the bacteria to their family members (Fornisini et al., 1992). Twenty-six percent of 23 household members of children colonized with trimethoprim-resistant *E. coli* also were found to be colonized, representing 52% of the households tested (Fornisini et al., 1992). Significantly more members of households of colonized children were colonized than people in households of children who were not colonized (OR = 13.3, 95%; CI 1.3–176.6; P <.01). Colonization was more frequent among mothers (35%) and siblings (30%) than among fathers (12%). In the previously discussed study using DNA markers as surrogate indicators of enteric pathogens, transmission from the child care center into children's homes also was examined (Jiang et al., 1998). One day after introduction of the markers in the child

Table 4.   Secondary attack rates for diarrheal disease of family members of child care enrollees

Organism	Secondary rate of attack (%)	Type of study	References
Cryptosporidium	3–15	Outbreak investigation	Alpert et al., 1986
E. coli 0157:H7	18	Outbreak investigation	Spika et al., 1986
Giardia lamblia	17	Prospective cohort	Pickering et al., 1981
	5–18	Outbreak investigation	Steketee et al., 1989
	25	Outbreak investigation	Black et al., 1977
Rotavirus	15	Prospective cohort	Pickering et al., 1981
	75	Outbreak investigation	Rodriguez et al., 1979
Shigella	26	Prospective cohort	Pickering et al., 1981
	0–46	Outbreak investigation	Weissman et al., 1974
	46	Outbreak investigation	Tacket & Cohen, 1983

care center, 78% of car seats, 67% of high chairs, and 33% of toys in the children's homes were positive for the DNA markers. Of nine children whose hands were contaminated with the markers, four remained positive 24 hours later. Hands of 3 of the 19 family members of those children also were positive the next day (Jiang et al., 1998). The identification of *Shigella* from or recognition of the clinical manifestations of hepatitis A in family members of children attending out-of-home child care is often indicative of a shigellosis or hepatitis A outbreak in the child care setting (Reves & Pickering, 1992; Shapiro & Hadler, 1990). Transmission of infectious agents from children to family members is the first step for dissemination of these diseases into the community.

HYGIENIC PRACTICES

Appropriate hygiene practices for child care centers have been published (American Academy of Pediatrics and American Public Health Association, 1992), but their implementation is not consistent. As previously discussed, hands of children and staff are one of the most frequently contaminated areas of the child care environment, and several studies have shown that increased environmental contamination is associated with an increased risk of diarrheal illness. A study by Black and colleagues (1981) evaluated the effect of a hand-washing program on the incidence of diarrhea in two child care centers when compared with two control centers. The incidence of diarrhea in the centers with the hand-washing intervention program, which included observation, was approximately half that of the control centers for the study period (Black et al., 1981). Another study evaluating the value of training in hand-washing techniques resulted in continuous improvement in hand-washing scores in both personnel and children participating in the program (Soto, Guy, & Belanger, 1994). Lower diarrhea rates were associated with the groups with the best scores, but these results may be biased by the fact that children older than 4 years of age obtained the best scores. Training in hygienic practices related to child care including hand washing and diapering techniques in one study resulted in a decrease in severe diarrhea in classrooms caring for children younger than 2 years (Kotch et al., 1994).

Practices of child care center staff and adequacy of the physical facilities have been implicated in spread of enteric disease in child care settings. In one study, a center in which staff members prepared meals, served food, and diapered children on a daily basis had a three-fold higher incidence of diarrhea when compared to centers in which staff did not routinely combine these functions (Ekanem et al., 1983).

Policies for excluding ill children also may affect disease spread in child care centers. When diarrhea occurred in a child, 58% of centers studied sent children home or isolated the child with diarrhea in the center (Sullivan, Woodward, Pickering, & DuPont, 1984). In 25% of the centers, children with diarrhea remained in the center, and in the remaining 17% of the centers, children were either sent home or allowed to remain in the center. In 42% of these centers in which children with diarrhea were not isolated or sent home, the potential for disease transmission presumably was enhanced.

DIARRHEA IN ADULTS ASSOCIATED WITH CHILD CARE

Transmission of organisms from children in child care centers to their child care providers and family members has been reported (Fornasini, Reves, Murray, Morrow, & Pickering, 1992; Pickering et al., 1981). This transmission results in various clinical conditions ranging from diarrhea to asymptomatic excretion, including excretion of strains of bacteria resistant to antimicrobial agents (Fornasini et al., 1992). In a prospective study of diarrhea in children enrolled in 20 child care centers, 10% of 331 family contacts of children with diarrhea became ill (Pickering et al., 1981). Secondary attack rates were higher when *Shigella* (26%), *Giardia lamblia* (17%), or rotavirus (15%) were identified in the child. During an outbreak of diarrhea due to *E. coli* 0157:H7 in a child care center, 18% of 56 family members of ill children developed diarrhea, but only 1 of 45 family members of well children younger than 4 years of age developed diarrhea (Spika et al., 1986).

Outbreaks of *Cryptosporidium* in child care centers have resulted in transmission of these organisms to household contacts and child care providers with subsequent development of diarrhea (Cordell et al., 1997). Hepatitis A virus is transmitted by the fecal–oral route (Hadler et al., 1980) and has been linked to outbreaks in child care centers. These outbreaks generally are not recognized until disease becomes manifested in adults (Hadler, Webster, Erben, et al., 1980). Estimates have been made that approximately 15% of the episodes of hepatitis A virus infection in the United States are related to child care. Transmission of trimethoprim-resistant *E. coli* from stool of children in child care centers to family members is described in the antibiotic use and resistance pattern section that follows.

Diarrheal disease in child care providers has been shown to occur following exposure of providers to children with diarrhea. A study was conducted to evaluate the risks of infectious diseases and inadequate health benefits for female child care providers when compared with other employed women. Results showed that child care providers had a significantly higher risk for at least one infectious disease, including gastrointestinal tract disease, and lost significantly more work days due to infectious diseases than controls did (Fornasini et al., submitted).

ANTIBIOTIC USE AND RESISTANCE PATTERNS

The rate of use of antimicrobial agents among children younger than 15 years of age is approximately threefold higher than that observed among older age groups (McCaig & Hughes, 1995), with respiratory tract diseases, including otitis media, being the leading diagnoses associated with antibiotic use. Although children with diarrhea receive antibiotics less often than children with otitis media, one study showed that 40% of children seen for diarrhea in the office setting by pediatricians affiliated with a pediatric teaching hospital were given antibiotics (Avendano et al., 1993).

Children in child care centers receive antimicrobial agents more frequently than children cared for at home or children in child care homes (Reves et al., 1993; Reves & Jones, 1990; Strangert, 1976). A study of 270 children younger than 3 years of age followed for an 8-week period at a health maintenance organization showed that 36% of children in child care centers received antibiotics compared with 7% of children in family child care homes and 8% of children cared for at home (Reves & Jones, 1990). The estimated annual rate of antibiotic use was 3.6 times higher in children in child care. In addition, duration of antibiotic use was longer in children in child care centers (19.5 days) than in children in child care homes (4 days) or children cared for in their own homes (4.6 days) ($p < .001$). Children attending child care centers accounted for 45% of the antibiotic use but only 16% of the clinic population.

During the 1990s, antibiotic-resistant organisms have been identified with increasing frequency in the United States, due in part to widespread use of antimicrobial agents. An increase in the prevalence of antibiotic-resistant organisms among children in child care compared with children cared for at home may be expected, due to the more frequent use of antimicrobial agents and the gathering together of large numbers of susceptible children. Outbreaks of diarrhea due to resistant *Shigella* in child care centers have been reported (Brian et al., 1993; Tackett & Cohen, 1983). In addition, high rates of colonization with antibiotic-resistant *E. coli* have been reported in children in child care (Fornasini et al., 1992; Reves & Jones, 1990; Reves et al., 1987).

In a study of fecal colonization of children with antibiotic-resistant *E. coli* in seven child care centers, 19% of 79 children in diapers were colonized with trimethoprim-resistant *E. coli*. All strains were multidrug-resistant (Reves et al., 1987). A subsequent study compared diapered children in 12 child care centers with diapered children not attending child care and with medical students (Reves et al., 1990). The prevalence of fecal colonization with trimethoprim-resistant *E. coli* among children in the child care centers (31%) was higher than in the comparison group of children (6%) and in the medical students (8%; *p* <.001). Most isolates also were resistant to other antimicrobial agents. In a case-control study, children younger than 2 years of age attending child care centers were at higher risk for colonization than older children (OR = 2.2, 95%; CI 1.1–4.3), and children attending a center with more than 40 diapered children were at higher risk than those attending centers with fewer children in diapers (OR = 3, 95%; CI 1.5–6) (Reves et al., 1990).

In a prospective study of trimethoprim-resistant *E. coli* in children and family members and the association of resistance with child care center attendance and antibiotic use, children in child care received significantly more courses (*p* < .05) of antimicrobial agents than children cared for at home and were colonized more frequently with trimethoprim-resistant *E. coli* (Mitchell et al., 1997).

FINANCIAL IMPACT OF DIARRHEAL DISEASE

Child care is an important factor in the financial burden of infectious diseases in young children. Two studies have evaluated the financial impact of diarrheal disease in children in the child care setting. A study was conducted to determine costs associated with diarrhea in an ambulatory population of children younger than 3 years of age. The mean cost per episode of diarrhea in children seen in an outpatient practice was $289, including office visits, laboratory tests, medication, dietary changes, oral rehydration solutions, travel, missed work, extra diapers, and extra child care (Avendano et al., 1993). The cost of missed work (household income divided by number of working days per year) and extra child care accounted for nearly 52% of the total cost.

Another study evaluated socioeconomic characteristics of families and care strategies used by parents of children in child care when children with diarrhea were too ill to attend (Hardy, Lairson, & Morrow, 1994). Direct medical costs were estimated based on the number of episodes of diarrhea observed during 2 years of monitoring and the probability that any given episode would be seen by a physician. The average total direct and indirect costs of diarrheal illness was $172 per child-year; 74% of this cost was attributable to nonmedical indirect costs associated with the child's absence from child care. Time lost by parents from work to care for ill children accounts for a large portion of the cost associated with childhood diseases.

IMPACT OF NATIONAL STANDARDS

In 1992, the American Academy of Pediatrics and the American Public Health Association jointly published the *National Health and Safety Performance Standards: Guidelines for Out-of-Home Child Care Programs*. This publication addresses health and safety issues in child care under ten major categories, including "prevention and control of infectious diseases." Information on *National Health and Safety Performance Standards* can be obtained from National Resources Center for Health and Safety in Child Care at 1-800-598-5437 or through the World Wide Web at http://nrc.uchsc.edu. The impact of these national standards on disease prevention and control has never been assessed. The second version of this publication is undergoing revision.

PREVENTION AND CONTROL OF INFECTIOUS DIARRHEA IN OUT-OF-HOME CARE

Control and prevention of diarrheal diseases in the child care environment begins with implementation of proper hygienic practices, including cleaning the environment, hand washing, and an appropriate physical environment. The physical structure of a child care center can influence hygiene, crowding, and food preparation, which may affect transmission of microorganisms among children enrolled and between children and care providers. This may be particularly significant for illnesses spread by the fecal–oral route including diarrheal diseases and hepatitis A (Petersen & Bressler, 1986). The structural layout of child care centers should be arranged so that food preparation areas are completely separated from diapering and toilet areas. Diaper-changing areas should never be used for temporary placement of food (American Academy of Pediatrics, 1997). There should be an adequate number of sinks adjacent to toilet and diapering areas and food preparation areas (Churchill & Pickering, 1997; Ferson, 1994; Petersen & Bressler, 1986). Child-size sinks and toilets are optimal; the use of potty chairs should be discouraged. The use of automated faucet-free hand-washing sinks should be considered because they may aid in decreasing fecal contamination (Holmes et al., 1996). Because environmental contamination appears to be decreased by cleaning, surfaces should be designed and constructed for ease of cleaning (Petersen & Bressler, 1986). For example, diaper-changing surfaces should be nonporous to allow adequate sanitization between uses (American Academy of Pediatrics, 1997). Because some studies have shown fecal contamination of surfaces to be inversely related to the age of children associated with them, facilities should allow separation of children by age group, especially of children in diapers from toilet-trained children (Ferson, 1994; Laborde et al., 1994; Petersen & Bressler, 1986). The most important hygienic practice in prevention of enteric diseases is effective hand washing (American Academy of Pediatrics, 1997). Hand washing is important in prevention of diarrheal disease because of the high rate of asymptomatic excretion of many pathogens, the low inoculum necessary to cause disease, and the rapid environmental contamination that occurs during outbreaks of diarrhea in the child care setting.

Written hand-washing procedures and environmental sanitation policies and procedures should be available to all staff, and implementation of these procedures should be enforced. Hygienic practices and environmental sanitation policies that decrease transmission of infectious agents are provided in the *National Health and Safety Performance Standards* (American Academy of Pediatrics and American Public Health Association, 1992) for out-of-home child care programs and the *1997 Red Book Report of the Committee on Infectious Diseases* of the American Academy of Pediatrics (1997; American Academy of Pediatrics and American Public Health Association, 1992). Child care facilities must have adequate staffing to ensure maintenance of appropriate hygienic practices (O'Ryan & Matson, 1990). Interventions involving parents and the community can be a valuable adjunct in the control of enteric diseases involving child care centers. Education on hygienic practices on a community-wide basis was determined to be effective in controlling community outbreaks of shigellosis associated with child care centers (Mohle-Boetani et al., 1995). Other strategies that aid in prevention and control of enteric diseases include exclusion or cohorting of ill children, appropriate use of antimicrobial therapy and immunization as enteric vaccines become available.

Several options are available for management of children with diarrhea and control of diarrheal outbreaks in the child care setting. These include exclusion of children with diarrhea from the center, grouping together of infected children in a separate area with separate staff (cohorting), temporary exclusion of new admissions, alternative care arrangements including referral to a sick care center, and temporary closing of a center (American Academy of Pediatrics and American Public Health Association, 1992; Pickering et al., 1986). The choice of options depends on the facilities and resources available, as well as the cause and severity of an outbreak. For example, some centers may not have room or separate staff to allow cohorting of ill children. In some areas, special centers for the care of ill children are not available.

Specific recommendations for exclusion of children with diarrhea from the child care setting include children who are acutely ill, children with diarrhea not contained by diapers or toilet use, children whose stools contain blood or mucous, and children infected with a known enteropathogen including those in Table 5. These children generally should be excluded until diarrhea resolves. Children infected with *E. coli* 0157:H7 or *Shigella* should not return to their child care facility until diarrhea has resolved and two stool cultures are negative (American Academy of Pediatrics, 1997; Churchill & Pickering, 1997). Some experts believe that all non–toilet-trained children with diarrhea should be excluded until diarrhea ceases (Cordell, Solomon, & Hale, 1996).

The role of antimicrobial therapy in the control of diarrheal outbreaks in child care is limited. Treatment with an appropriate antimicrobial agent is recommended for symptomatic children infected with *Shigella* and *Giardia* because treatment is effective in shortening the duration of diarrhea and eliminating the organism from feces (American Academy of Pediatrics, 1997). Treatment of other enteric pathogens is not specifically recommended and should be confined to individual cases.

Vaccines against only three gastrointestinal tract pathogens currently are approved by the FDA for use in the United States: *Salmonella typhi, Vibrio cholerae,* and rotavirus. The first two vaccines will have no effect on decreasing diarrheal disease in children in out-of-home child care settings because *S. typhi* and *V. cholerae* are not important pathogens in the child care setting. In August 1998, the FDA approved a tetravalent rhesus rotavirus vaccine. This orally administered vaccine is designed to be given to children at 2, 4, and 6 months of age. Studies conducted in the United States, Peru, and Finland demonstrated that the vaccine had an efficacy rate of 50% against all rotavirus diarrhea and more than 80% in preventing moderate-to-severe rotavirus-associated diarrhea (Bernstein, Glass, Rogers, Davidson, & Sack, 1995; Vesikari, 1993). This

Table 5.   Enteric pathogens for which exclusion from child care is indicated

Organism	Length of exclusion
Campylobacter	Until diarrhea resolves
Cryptosporidium	Until diarrhea resolves
Enteric viruses	Until diarrhea resolves
Giardia lamblia	Until diarrhea resolves
Salmonella	Until diarrhea resolves
E. coli 0157:H7 *Shigella*	Until diarrhea resolves and 2 stool cultures are negative for the organism

vaccine was expected to have excellent potential for decreasing diarrheal disease outbreaks due to rotavirus in children in child care centers. Unfortunately, it has since been removed from the market due to possible adverse reactions.

SUMMARY

Diarrheal disease remains an insidious infectious disease problem in the out-of-home child care setting because of host and environmental factors as well as organism characteristics that contribute to transmission of enteric organisms. Age-specific personal hygiene with contamination of the child care environment is an important contributing factor. Education of child care providers and parents in techniques of good hand washing and other hygienic practices and strict adherence to these practices remains the cornerstone of prevention and control of diarrheal disease in the child care setting. Vaccines against enteric pathogens, especially rotavirus and other viral agents, represent a promising means of control in the future.

REFERENCES

Addiss, D.G., Stewart, J.M., Finton, R.J., Nahlquist, S.P., Williams, R.M., Dickerson, J.W., Spencer, H.C., & Juranek, D.D. (1991). *Giardia lamblia* and *Cryptosporidium infection* in child day care centers in Fulton County, Georgia. *Pediatric Infectious Diseases Journal, 10,* 907–911.

Alpert, G., Bell, L.M., Kirkpatrick, C.E., et al. (1984). Cryptosporidiosis in a day care center (Letter). New England Journal of Medicine 311, 860–861.

Alpert, G., Bell, L.M., Kirkpatrick, C.E., Budnick, L.D., Campos, J.M., Friedman, H.M., & Plotkin, S.A. (1986). Outbreak of Cryptosporidiosis in a day–care center. *Pediatrics, 77,* 152–157.

American Academy of Pediatrics. (1997). Children in out-of-home care. In G. Peter (Ed.), *1997 Red Book: Report of the Committee on Infectious Diseases,* (24th ed., pp. 80–90). Elk Grove Village, IL: American Academy of Pediatrics.

American Academy of Pediatrics, Committee on Infectious Diseases. (1998). Prevention of rotavirus disease: Guidelines for use of rotavirus vaccine. *Pediatrics, 102,* 1483–1491.

American Academy of Pediatrics and American Public Health Association. (1992). *National health and safety performance standards: Guidelines for out-of-home child care programs.* Arlington, VA: National Center for Education in Maternal and Child Health.

Anderson, L.J., Parker, R.A., Strikas, R.A., Farrar, J.A., Gangarosa, E.J., Keyserling, H.L., & Sikes, R.K. (1988). Day care attendance and hospitalization for lower respiratory tract illness. *Pediatrics, 82,* 300–308.

Ashkenazi, S., & Cleary, T.G. (1992). *Shigella* infections. In R.D. Feigin & J.D. Cherry (Eds.), *Textbook of Pediatric Infectious Disease* (3rd ed, pp. 640–641). Philadelphia: W.B. Saunders.

Avendano, P., Matson, D.O., Long, J., Whitney, S., Matson, C.C., & Pickering, L.K. (1993). Costs associated with office visits for diarrhea in infants and toddlers. *Pediatric Infectious Diseases Journal, 12,* 897–902.

Barron-Romero, B.L., Barreda-Gonzalez, J., Doval-Ugalde, R., Zermeno-Eguraliz, J., & Huerta-Pena, M. (1985). Asymptomatic rotavirus infections in day care centers. *Journal of Clinical Microbiology, 22,* 116–118.

Bartlett, A.V., Moore, M., Fary, G.W., Starko, K.M., Erben, J.J., & Meredith, B.A. (1985). Diarrheal illness among infants and toddlers in day care centers. II: Comparison with day care homes and households. *Journal of Pediatrics, 107,* 503–509.

Bell, D.M., Gleiber, D.W., Mercer, A.A., Phifer, R., Guinter, R.H., Cohen, A.J., Epstein, E.U., & Narayanan, M. (1989). Illness associated with child day care: A study of incidence and cost. *American Journal of Public Health, 79,* 479–484.

Belongia, E.A., Osterholm, M.T., & Soler, J.T. (1993). Transmission of *Escherichia coli* 0157:H7 infection in Minnesota child day-care facilities. *Journal of American Medical Association, 269,* 883.

Bernstein, D.I., Glass, R.I., Rogers, G., Davidson, B.L., & Sack, D.A. (1995). Evaluation of rhesus rotavirus monovalent and tetravalent reasortant vaccines in U.S. children. *Journal of the American Medical Association, 273,* 1191–1196.

Black, R.E., Dykes, A.C., Anderson, K.E., Wells, J.G., Sinclair, S.P., Gary, G.W., Hatch, M.H., & Gangarosa, E.J. (1981). Handwashing to prevent diarrhea in day-care centers. *American Journal of Epidemiology, 113,* 445–451.

Black, R.E., Dykes, A.C., & Sinclair, S.P. (1977). Giardiasis in day care centres: Evidence of person-to-person transmission. *Pediatrics, 60,* 486–491.

Bower, J.R., Congeni, B.L., Cleary, T.G., Stone, R.T., Wanger, A., Murray, B.E., Mathewson, J.J., & Pickering, L.K. (1989). *Escherichia coli* 0114: Non-motile as a pathogen in an outbreak of severe diarrhea associated with a day care center. *Journal of Infectious Disease, 160,* 243–247.

Brian, M.J., Van, R., Townsend, I., Murray, B.E., Cleary, T.G., & Pickering, L.K. (1993). Evaluation of the molecular epidemiology of an outbreak of multiply resistant *Shigella sonnei* in a day care center using pulsed-field gel electrophoresis and plasmid DNA analysis. *Journal of Clinical Microbiology, 32,* 2152.

Centers for Disease Control and Prevention. (1994). *Bacillus cereus* food poisoning associated with fried rice at two child day care centers—Virginia, 1993. *Morbidity and Mortality Weekly Report, 43,* 177–178.

Chorba, T.L., Merriwether, R.A., Jenkins, B.R., Gunn, R.A., & MacCormack, J.N. (1987). Control of a non-foodborne outbreak of salmonellosis: Day care in isolation. *American Journal of Public Health, 77,* 979–981.

Churchill, R.B., & Pickering, L.K. (1997). Infection control challenges in child-care centers. *Infectious Disease Clinic of North America, 11,* 347–365.

Cody, M.M., Sottnek, H.M., & O'Leary, V.S. (1994). Recovery of *Giardia lamblia* cysts from chairs and tables in child day-care centers. *Pediatrics, 94* (Suppl.), 1006–1008.

Collet, J.P., Burtin, P., Kramer, M.S., Floret, D., Bossard, N., & Ducruet, T. (1994). Type of day-care setting and risk of repeated infections. *Pediatrics, 94,* 997–999.

Combee, C.L., Collinger, M.L., & Britt, E.L. (1986). Cryptosporidiosis in a hospital-associated day care center. *Pediatric Infectious Diseases Journal, 5,* 528–532.

Cordell, R., Thor, P., Addis, D., Theurer, J., Lichterman, R., Ziliak, S.R., Juranek, D.D., & Davis, J.P. (1997). Impact of a massive waterborne cryptosporidiosis outbreak on child care facilities in metropolitan Milwaukee. *Pediatric Infectious Disease Journal, 16,* 639–644.

Cordell, R.L., Solomon, S.L., & Hale, C.M. (1996). Exclusion of mildly ill children from out-of-home child care facilities. *Infections in Medicine, 13*(41), 45–48.

Crawford, F.G., Vermund, S., Ma, J.Y., & Deckelbaum, R.J. (1988). Asymptomatic cryptosporidiosis in a New York day care center. *Pediatric Infectious Disease Journal, 7,* 806–807.

de la Morena, M.L., Van, R., Singh, K., Brian, M., Murray, B.E., & Pickering, L.K. (1993). Diarrhea associated with *Aeromonas* species in children in day care centers. *The Journal of Infectious Diseases, 168,* 215–218.

DuPont, H.L., Chappell, C.L., Sterling, C.R., Okhuysen, P.C., Rose, J.B., & Jakubowski, W. (1995). The infectivity of *Cryptosporidium parvum* in healthy volunteers. *New England Journal of Medicine, 332,* 855–859.

DuPont, H.L., Haynes, G.A., Pickering, L.K., Tjoa, W., Sullivan, P., & Olarte, J. (1977). Diarrhea of travelers to Mexico: Relative susceptibility of United States and Latin American students attending a Mexican university. *American Journal of Epidemiology, 105,* 37–41.

Ekanem, E.E., DuPont, H.L., Pickering, L.K., Selwyn, B.J., & Hawkins, C.M. (1983). Transmission dynamics of enteric bacteria in day-care centers. *American Journal of Epidemiology 118,* 562–572.

Ferson, M.J. (1994). Control of infections in child care. *Medical Journal of Australia, 161,* 615–618.

Ferson, M.J., & Young, L.C. (1992). *Cryptosporidum* and coxsackievirus B5 causing epidemic diarrhoea in a child-care centre (Letter to the editor). *Medical Journal of Australia, 156,* 813.

Fonteyne, J., Zissis, G., & Lambert, J.P. (1978). Recurrent rotavirus gastroenteritis. *Lancet 1,* 983.

Fornasini, M., Reves, R.R., Murray, B.E., Morrow, A.L., & Pickering, L.K. (1992). Trimethoprim-resistant *Escherichia coli* in households of children attending day care centers. *Journal of Infectious Diseases, 166,* 326–330.

Fornasini, M.V., Shults, J.N., Morrow, A.L., & Pickering, L.K. (Submitted). Infectious diseases and health benefits among child care providers. *Maternal Child Health Journal.*

Goossens, H., Giesendorf, B.A.J., Van Damme, P., Vlaes, L., Van den Borre, C., Koeken, A., Quint, W.G.V., Hanicq, P., Koster, D.S., Hofstra, H., Butzler, J.P., & Van der Pens, J. (1995). Investigation of an outbreak of *Campylobacter upsaliensis* in day care centers in Brussels: Analysis of relationships among isolates by phenotypic and genotypic typing methods. *Journal of Infectious Diseases, 172,* 1298–1305.

Gorden, J., & Small, P.L.C. (1993). Acid resistance in enteric bacteria. *Infection and Immunity, 61,* 364–367.

Grohmann, G., Glass, R., & Gold, J. (1991). Outbreak of human calicivirus gastroenteritis in a day-care center in Sydney, Australia. *Journal of Clinical Microbiology, 29,* 544–550.

Guerrero, M.L., Calva, J.J., Morrow, A.L., Tuz-Dzib, F., Lopez-Vidal, Y., Ortega, H., Arroyo, H., Cleary, T.G., Pickering, L.K., & Ruiz-Palacios, G.M. (1994). Asymptomatic *Shigella* infections in a cohort of Mexican children less than 2 years of age. *Pediatric Infectious Diseases Journal, 13,* 597–602.

Hadler, S.C., Webster, H.M., Erben, J.J., Swanson, J.E., & Maynard, J.E., (1980). Hepatitis A in day care centers: A community-wide assessment. *New England Journal of Medicine, 302,* 1222–1227.

Hardy, A.M., Lairson, D.R., & Morrow, A.L. (1994). Costs associated with gastrointestinal tract illness among children attending day care centers in Houston, Texas. *Pediatrics, 94,* 1091–1093.

Haskins, R., & Kotch, J. (1986). Day care and illness: Evidence, costs, and public policy. *Pediatrics, 77,* 951–982.

Hayani, K.C., & Pickering, L.K. (1992). *Salmonella* Infections. In R.D. Feigin & J.D. Cherry (Eds.), *Textbook of Pediatric Infectious Diseases* (3rd ed., p. 622). Philadelphia: W.B. Saunders.

Heijbel, H., Slaine, K., Seigel, B., Wall, P., McNabb, S.J.N., Gibbon, W., & Istre, G.R. (1987). Outbreak of diarrhea in a day care center with spread to household members: The role of *Cryptosporidium. Pediatric Infectious Diseases Journal, 6,* 532–535.

Heitmann, M., Gerner-Smidt, P., & Heltberg, O. (1997). Gastroenteritis caused by *Listeria monocytogenes* in a private day-care facility. *Pediatric Infectious Diseases Journal, 16,* 827–828.

Hofferth, S.L. (1996). Child care in the United States today. In R.E. Behrman (Ed.). *The Future of Children: Financing Child Care* (Vol. 6, No. 2, p. 41). Los Altos, CA: Center for the Future of Children, The David and Lucille Packard Foundation.

Holaday, B., Pantell, R., Lewis, C., & Gilliss, C.L. (1990). Patterns of fecal coliform contamination in day-care centers. *Public Health Nursing, 7,* 224–228.

Holaday, B., Waugh, G., Moukaddem, V.E., West, J., & Harsman, S. (1995). Fecal contamination in child day care centers: Cloth vs. paper diapers. *American Journal of Public Health, 85,* 30–33.

Holmes, S.J., Morrow, A.L., & Pickering, L.K. (1996). Child care practices: Effects of social changes on epidemiology of infectious diseases and antibiotic resistance. *Epidemiology Review, 18,* 10–28.

Ish-Horowicz, M., Korman, S., Shapiro, M., Har-Even, U., Tamir, I., Strauss, N., & Deckelbaum, R.J. (1989). Asymptomatic *giardiasis* in children. *Pediatric Infectious Disease Journal, 8,* 773–779.

Jiang, X., Dai, X., Goldblatt, S., Buescher, C., Cusack, T.M., Matson, D.O., & Pickering, L.K. (1998). *Journal of Infectious Diseases, 177,* 881–888.

Jorm, L.R., & Capon, A.G. (1994). Communicable disease outbreaks in long day care centres in western Sydney: Occurrence and risk factors. *Journal of Pediatric Child Health, 30,* 151–154.

Kim, K., DuPont, H.L., & Pickering, L.K. (1983). Outbreaks of diarrhea associated with *Clostridium difficile* and its toxin in day care centers. Evidence of person-to-person spread. *Journal of Pediatrics, 102,* 376–382.

Kotch, J.B., Weigle, K.A., Weber, D.J., Clifford, R.M., Harms, T.O., Loda, F.A., Gallagher, P.N., Edwards, R.W., Laborde, D., McMurray, M.P., Roansdelli, P.S., & Faircloth, A.H. (1994). Evaluation of an hygienic intervention in child day-care centers. (Suppl.). *Pediatrics, 94,* 991–993.

Kubiak, M., Kressner, B., Raynor, W., Davis, J., & Syverson, R.E. (1994). Comparison of stool containment in cloth and single-use diapers using a simulated infant feces. *Pediatrics, 91,* 632–636.

Laborde, D., Weigle, K.A., Weber, D.J., & Kotch, J.B. (1993). Effect of fecal contamination on diarrheal illness rates in day-care centers. *American Journal of Epidemiology, 138,* 243–255.

Laborde, D.J., Weigle, K.A., Weber, D.J., Sobsey, M.D., & Kotch, J.B. (1994). The frequency, level and distribution of fecal contamination in day-care center classrooms. *Pediatrics, 94* (Suppl.), 1008–1011.

Lauwers, S., DeBoeck, M., & Butzler, J.P. (1978). *Campylobacter enteritis* in Brussels. (Letter to the editor). *Lancet, 1,* 604–605.

Lerman, Y., Yavzori, M., Ambar, R., Sechter, I., Wiener, M., & Cohen, D. (1994). Epidemic spread of *Shigella sonnei* shigellosis and evidence for development of immunity among children attending day-care centers in a communal settlement (Kibbutz). *Journal of Clinical Microbiology, 32,* 1092–1094.

Lew, J.F., Moe, C.L., Monroe, S.S., Allen, J.R., Harrison, B.M., Forrester, B.D., Stine, S.E., Woods, P.A., Blacklow, N.R., Bartlett, A.V., & Glass, R.I. (1991). Astrovirus and adenovirus associated with diarrhea in children in day care settings. *Journal of Infectious Disease, 164,* 673–678.

Lieb, S., Gunn, R.A., & Taylor, D.N. (1982). Salmonellosis in a day care center. (Letter to the editor). *Journal of Pediatrics, 100,* 1004–1005.

Long, S.S. (1997). Respiratory tract symptom complexes. In S.S. Long, C.G. Prober, & L.K. Pickering (Eds.), *Principles and Practices of Pediatric Infectious Diseases* (p. 144). New York: Churchill Livingstone.

Los Angeles County Department of Health Services. (1980). Day care center outbreak of severe gastroenteritis associated with enteropathogenic *Escherichia coli. Public Health Letter, 2,* 34–35.

Louhiala, P.J., Jaakkola, N., Ruotsalainen, R., & Jaakkola, J.J.K. (1995). Form of day care and respiratory infections among Finnish children. *American Journal of Public Health, 85,* 1109–1112.

Matson, D.O. (1994). Viral gastroenteritis in day-care settings: Epidemiology and new developments. *Pediatrics, 94,* 999–1001.

Matson, D.O., Estes, M.K., & Tanaka, T. (1990). Asymptomatic human calicivirus infection in a day care center outbreak. *Pediatric Infectious Disease, 9,* 190–196.

McCaig, L.F., & Hughes, J.M. (1995). Trends in antimicrobial drug prescribing among office-based physicians in the United States. *Journal of American Medical Association, 273,* 214–219.

Mitchell, D.K., Holmes, S.J., Solomon, S.L., McCraw, A., Hossain, T., White, T., & Pickering, L.K. (1997). Risk factors for carriage of trimethoprim-resistant *Escherichia coli* in stool specimens from young children. *37th Annual Meeting of the Infectious Diseases Society of America, 54.*

Mitchell, D.K., Monroe, S.S., Jiang, X., Matson, D.O., Glass, R.I., & Pickering, L.K. (1995). Virologic features of an astrovirus diarrhea outbreak in a day care center revealed by reverse transciptase-polymerase chain reaction. *Journal of Infectious Disease, 172,* 1437–1444.

Mitchell, D.K., Van, R., Morrow, A.L., Monroe, S.S., Glass, R.I., & Pickering, L.K. (1993). Outbreaks of astrovirus gastroenteritis in day care centers. *Journal of Pediatrics, 123,* 725.

Mohle-Boetani, J.C., Stapleton, M., Finger, R., Bean, N.H., Poundstone, J., Blake, P.A., & Griffin, P.M. (1995). Communitywide shigellosis: Control of an outbreak and risk factors in child day-care centers. *American Journal of Public Health, 85,* 812–816.

Morrow, A.L., Townsend, I.T., & Pickering, L.K. (1991). Risk of enteric infection associated with child day care. *Pediatric Annals, 20,* 427–433.

O'Ryan, M.L., & Matson, D.O. (1990). Viral gastroenteritis pathogens in the day care center setting. *Seminars in Pediatric Infectious Diseases, 1,* 252–262.

Osterholm, M.T. (1994). Infectious disease in child day care: An overview. *Pediatrics, 94,* 987.

Paulozzi, L.J., Johnson, K.E., Kamahele, L.M., Clausen, C.R., Riley, L.W., & Helgerson, S.D. (1986). Diarrhea associated with adherent enteropathogenic *Esherichia coli* in an infant and toddler center, Seattle, Washington. *Pediatrics, 77,* 296–300.

Petersen, N.J., & Bressler, G.K. (1986). Design and modification of the day care environment. *Reviews of Infectious Diseases, 8,* 618–621.

Pickering, L.K. (1982). Reply to: Salmonellosis in day care centers. (Letter to the editor). *Journal of Pediatrics, 100,* 1005.

Pickering, L.K. (1990). Bacterial and parasitic enteropathogens in day care. *Seminars in Pediatric Infectious Diseases, 1,* 263–269.

Pickering, L.K. (1996). Emerging antibiotic resistance in enteric bacterial pathogens. *Seminars in Pediatric Infectious Diseases, 7,* 272–280.

Pickering, L.K., Bartlett, A.V., Reves, R.R., & Morrow, A. (1988). Asymptomatic excretion of rotavirus before and after rotavirus diarrhea in children in day care centers. *Journal of Pediatrics, 112,* 361–365.

Pickering, L.K., Bartlett, A.V., & Woodward, W.E. (1986). Acute infectious diarrhea among children in day care: Epidemiology and control. *Reviews of Infectious Diseases, 8,* 539–547.

Pickering, L.K., DuPont, H.L., Evans, D.G., Evands, E.J., & Olarte, J. (1977). Isolation of enteric pathogens from asymptomatic students from the United States and Latin America. *Journal of Infectious Diseases, 135,* 1003–1005.

Pickering, L.K., Evans, D.G., DuPont, H.L., Vollet, J.J., & Evans, D.J. (1981). Diarrhea caused by *Shigella,* rotavirus and *Giardia* in day care centers: Prospective study. *Journal of Pediatrics, 99,* 51–56.

Pickering, L.K., & Morrow, A.L. (1991). Contagious diseases of child day care. *Infection, 19,* 61–63.

Pickering, L.K., & Osterholm, M.T. (1997). Infectious diseases associated with out-of-home child care. In S.S. Long, C.G. Prober, & L.K. Pickering (Eds.), *Principles and Practices of Pediatric Infectious Diseases* (pp. 31–39). New York: Churchill Livingstone.

Rauch, A.M., Van, R., Bartlett, A.V., & Pickering, L.K. (1990). Longitudinal study of *Giardia lamblia* infection in a day care center population. *Pediatric Infectious Diseases Journal, 9,* 186–189.

Rentdorff, R.C. (1954). The experimental transmission of human intestinal protozoan parasites. II. *Giardia lamblia* cysts given in capsules. *American Journal of Hygiene, 59,* 209.

Rentdorff, R.C., & Holt, C.J. (1954). The experimental transmission of human intestinal parasites. IV. Attempt to transmit *Entamoeba coli* and *Giardia lamblia* cysts by water. *American Journal of Hygiene, 60,* 327–328.

Reves, R.R., Fong, M., Pickering, L.K., Bartlett, A.V., Alvarez, M., & Murray, B.E. (1990). Risk factors for fecal colonization with trimethoprim- and multi-resistant *Escherichia coli* among children in day care centers in Houston. *Antimicrobial Agents Chemotheraphy, 34,* 91429–91434.

Reves, R.R., & Jones, J.A. (1990). Antibiotic use and resistance patterns in day care centers. *Seminars in Pediatric Infectious Diseases, 1,* 212–221.

Reves, R.R., Morrow, A.L., Bartlett, A.V., Caruso, C.J., Plumb, R.L., Lu, B.T., & Pickering, L.K. (1993). Child day care increases the risk of clinic visits for acute diarrhea and diarrhea due to rotavirus. *American Journal of Epidemiology, 137,* 97–107.

Reves, R.R., Murray, B.E., Pickering, L.K., Prado, D., Maddock, M., & Bartlett, A.V. (1987). Children with trimethoprim and ampicillin-resistant fecal *Escherichia coli* in day care centers. *Journal of Infectious Diseases, 156,* 758–762.

Reves, R.R., & Pickering, L.K. (1990). Infections in child day care centers as they relate to internal medicine. *Annual Reviews in Medicine, 41,* 383–391.

Reves, R.R., & Pickering, L.K. (1992). Impact of child day care on infectious diseases in adults. *Infectious Disease Clinic of North America, 6,* 239–250.

Riordan, T., Humphrey, T.J., & Fowles, A. (1993). A point source outbreak of *Campylobacter* infection related to bird-pecked milk. *Epidemiology Infection, 110,* 261–265.

Rodriguez, W., Kim, H.W., & Brandt, C.D. (1979). Common exposure outbreak of gastroenteritis due to Type 2 rotavirus with high secondary attack rate with families. *Journal of Infectious Disease, 140,* 353–357.

Rosdahl, N. (1980). *Salmonella* enteridtidis in gastroenteritis in a day nursery. Epidemiological observations in a primary foodborne infection. *Ugeskr-Laeger, 142,* 2795–2799.

Shah, S., Hoffman, R., Shillam, P., & Wilson, B. (1996). Prolonged fecal shedding of *Escherichia coli* 1057:H7 during an outbreak at a day care center. *Clinical Infectious Diseases, 23,* 835–836.

Shapiro, C.N., & Hadler, S.C. (1990). Significance of hepatitis in child care. *Seminars in Pediatric Infectious Diseases, 1,* 270–279.

Soto, J.C., Guy, M., & Belanger, L. (1994). Handwashing and infection control in day care centers. *Pediatrics, 94,* 1030.

Soto, J.C., Guy, M., Deshaies, D., Durand, L., Gratton, J., & Belanger, L. (1994). A community-health approach for infection control in day care centers. *Pediatrics* (Suppl. 94), 1027.

Spika, J.S., Parsons, J.E., Nordernberg, D., Wells, J.G., Gunn, R.A., & Blake, P.A. (1986). Hemolytic uremic syndrome and diarrhea associated with *Escherichia coli* 0157:H7 in a day care center. *Journal of Pediatrics, 109,* 287–291.

Staat, M.A., Morrow, A.L., Reves, R.R., Bartlett, A.V., & Pickering, L.K. (1991). Diarrhea in children newly enrolled in day care centers in Houston. *Pediatric Infectious Diseases Journal, 10,* 282–286.

Staes, C., Balk, S., Ford, K., Passantino, R.J., & Torrice, A. (1994). Environmental factors to consider when designing and maintaining a child's day-care environment. *Pediatrics, 94* (Suppl.), 1048–1050.

Steketee, R.W., Reid, S., & Cheng, T. (1989). Recurrent outbreaks of giardiasis in a child day care center, Wisconsin. *American Journal of Public Health, 79,* 485–490.

Strangert, K. (1976). Respiratory illness in preschool children with different forms of day care. *Pediatrics, 57,* 191–196.

Sullivan, P., Woodward, W.E., Pickering, L.K., & DuPont, H.L. (1984). A longitudinal study of the occurrence of diarrheal disease in day care centers. *American Journal of Public Health 74,* 987–991.

Tacket, C.O., & Cohen, M.I. (1983). Shigellosis in day care centers: use of plasmid analysis to assess control measures. *Pediatric Infectious Diseases Journal, 2,* 127–130.

Takala, A.K., Eskola, J., & Palmgren, J. (1989). Risk factors of invasive *Haemophilus influenzae* type B disease among children in Finland. *Journal of Pediatrics, 114,* 694–701.

Thacker, S.B., Addiss, D.G., Goodman, R.A., Holloway, B.R., & Spencer, H.C. (1992). Infectious diseases and injuries in child day care: Opportunities for healthier children. *Journal of American Medical Association, 268,* 1720–1726.

Van, R., Morrow, A.L., Reves, R.R., & Pickering, L.K. (1991). Environmental contamination in child day-care centers. *American Journal of Public Health, 133,* 460–70.

Van, R., Wun, C.C., Morrow, A.L., & Pickering, L.K. (1991). The effect of diaper type and overclothing on fecal contamination in day-care centers. *Journal of the American Medical Association, 265,* 1840–1844.

Van, R., Wun, C.C., O'Ryan, M.L., Matson, D.O., Jackson, L., & Pickering, L.K. (1992). Outbreaks of human enteric adenovirus types 40 and 41 in Houston day care centers. *Journal of Pediatrics, 120,* 516–521.

Vesikari, T. (1993). Clinical trials of live oral rotavirus vaccines: The Finnish experience. *Vaccine, 11,* 255–261.

Ward, R.L., Bernstein, D.I., Young, E.C., Sherwood, J.R., Knowlton, D.R., & Schiff, G.M. (1986). Human rotavirus studies in volunteers: Determination of infectious dose and serological response to infection. *Journal of Infectious Disease, 154,* 871–880.

Weissman, J.B., Gangarosa, E.J., Schmerler, A., Marier, R.L., & Lewis, J.N. (1975). Shigellosis in day care centres. *Lancet, 1,* 84–90.

Weissman, J.B., Schmerler, A., Weiler, P., Felice, G., Godboy, N., & Hansen, I. (1974). The role of preschool children and day care centers in the spread of shigellosis in communities. *Journal of Pediatrics, 84,* 779–802.

Wilde, J., Van, R., Pickering, L., Eiden, J., & Yolden, R. (1992). Detection of rotaviruses in the day care environment by reverse transcriptase polymerase chain reaction. *Journal of Infectious Diseases, 166,* 507–511.

8

The Early Intervention System and Out-of-Home Child Care

◆ ❖ ◆

Michael J. Guralnick

Unprecedented numbers of vulnerable children face difficulties few imagined even a generation ago. Taken together, the statistics are staggering: Approximately 25% of children younger than age 6 are born into poverty (Children's Defense Fund, 1996; Huston, McLoyd, & Garcia Coll, 1994); young children live in increasingly hostile environments with well over 50% of children in low-income neighborhoods likely to experience violence in some form (Osofsky, 1995; Taylor, Zuckerman, Harik, & Groves, 1994), and, conservatively put, approximately 1 million children are abused or neglected each year, of which nearly 40% are 5 years of age or younger (U.S. Department of Health and Human Services, 1995). Moreover, due to changing societal attitudes, substantial increases are occurring in the number of mothers with intellectual disabilities raising young children (about 120,000 infants annually; Keltner & Tymchuk, 1992), and these parents are experiencing considerable child-rearing difficulties (Feldman, 1997; Kelly, Morisset, Barnard, & Patterson, 1995). The stress on parenting is also evident in that each year approximately 500,000 children are born to adolescents, most of whom are without adequate parenting skills or supports (Osofsky, Hann, & Peebles, 1993), and about twice as many preschool-age children as school-age children will experience a family break-up (Furstenberg, Nord, Peterson, & Zill, 1983) often accompanied by considerable acrimony and stress (Garmezy & Masten, 1994). Additional concerns arise from the fact that as many as 15% of newborns are exposed prenatally to illicit drugs or alcohol (Brooks-Gunn, McCarton, & Hawley, 1994; Chasnoff, Landress, & Barrett, 1990), and, overall, approximately 1.7 million children ages 1–5 years and 20%–40% of children living in substandard conditions are exposed to lead at levels that can compromise their development (Brody et al., 1994; Paulozzi, Shapp, Drawbaugh, & Carney, 1995). These circumstances, as well as others, constitute well known risk factors that can significantly impair young children's health and development (Bendersky & Lewis, 1994; Guralnick, 1997b; Sameroff, Seifer, Barocas, Zax, & Greenspan, 1987).

Of perhaps greatest concern are those children considered to be most vulnerable. This includes a subgroup of children at *extremely high risk* due to environmental circumstances. A cumulative risk index (e.g., jointly considering low maternal education, poor maternal mental health, and inadequate family support, as well as other risk factors) is most useful in identifying children at extreme risk, as the number of risk factors children experience takes a toll on their development (Sameroff et al., 1987). In the absence of early intervention, the differences in intellectual development for young children between extremely high and low risk groups is in the range of 25–30 IQ points. In fact, for children with four or more risk factors, nearly 25% will have IQ scores below 85 by 4 years of age (Sameroff et al., 1987). Other samples or risk indices yield even higher percentages of poor intellectual development (Ramey & Campbell, 1984). No single factor, even socioeconomic status or poverty alone, despite associations with other risk factors, is as predictive of adverse developmental outcomes as is a child's cumulative risk (see Parker, Greer, & Zuckerman, 1988). Extremely low maternal intelligence, however, is perhaps the most powerful single predictor of children's poor intellectual outcome (see Ramey & Ramey, 1992). Similarly, children who are "doubly vulnerable," that is, those who experience both biological and environmental risks, constitute as might be expected an extremely vulnerable population, with very few children escaping without significant adverse consequences to their health and development (Bradley et al., 1994). Correspondingly, increasingly larger numbers of children are now born prematurely at low birth weight in the United States; each year nearly 300,000 newborns weigh less than 2,500 grams. As mortality continues to decrease due to technological advances, more and more children at low birth weight are surviving but often at the cost of increased vulnerability to a range of developmental problems (McCormick, Workman-Daniels, & Brooks-Gunn, 1996). This vulnerability increases with decreasing birth weight, considerably affecting children's cognitive development (Breslau et al., 1994). At the extreme, although children who are born weighing 750 grams or less constitute only .3% of live births, at least 20% of these children who survive to school age can expect to obtain intelligence test scores in the range for mental retardation. An additional 25% will require special educational services for less severe learning, communication, motor, perceptual, and behavior problems (Hack et al., 1994). There exist as well substantial numbers of young children who manifest established developmental disabilities arising from an array of conditions including genetic disorders and congenital infections (Lipkin, 1996). Systematic surveys indicate that approximately 2.2% of all infants and toddlers manifest significant disabilities that are sufficient to meet eligibility criteria to receive services under current federal legislation for early intervention (Education of the Handicapped Act Amendments of 1986 [PL 99-457]; reauthorized as the Individuals with Disabilities Education Act [IDEA] of 1997 [PL 105-17]; see Bowe, 1995). This is certainly a conservative estimate of actual prevalence for children with established disabilities, due to the difficulties that professionals experience in diagnosing developmental delays in young children; systems problems in early identification; lack of developmental knowledge by parents or caregivers or reluctance to apply that knowledge; or problems, particularly for families representing lower sociodemographic status groups, in finding appropriate professionals and services (First & Palfrey, 1994; Palfrey, Singer, Walker, & Butler, 1987). It has been estimated that 35% of families of young children with significant disabilities fall below the Census Bureau's threshold for low income (Bowe, 1995).

In response to the complex needs of families created by these risk and disability conditions, a system of early intervention (EI) supports and services has been established since the early 1970s (Guralnick, 1997b, 1998; Meisels & Shonkoff, 1990; Zeanah, 1993). This system contains many components including social and resource supports for families, home visitation services, individual child-oriented therapies, and direct services to children in specially designed centers. The overall benefits of both preventive and ameliorative types of supports and services for families of children at risk or those with established disabilities has now been well established (Guralnick, 1997a). However, it is still not clear how the components of the EI system can best be adjusted to variations in child and family characteristics and to family interaction patterns so that child developmental outcomes are maximized. Which components of the EI system are essential, at which intensity are they to be applied, and how are they to be sequenced to ensure optimal short- and long-term outcomes remain important, yet unanswered, questions. It is this task of "second-generation" research that is now occupying the interest of investigators in the field of EI (Guralnick, 1993, 1997a, 1998).

OUT-OF-HOME
CHILD CARE FOR VULNERABLE CHILDREN

The challenge to maximize the effectiveness of the EI system is complicated further by the pressing needs of a substantial number of families,
including those with children at risk for developmental problems and
those with established disabilities, to locate some form of alternate child
care. The remarkable demographic changes that have occurred in the
United States have resulted in a large proportion of mothers who participate in the work force outside their home. For many families, this
process begins early, with approximately half of mothers in the general
population in the United States seeking some form of alternate care when
their child is younger than 1 year of age (see Zigler & Gilman, 1993).
Approximately 40% of these families choose out-of-home care, primarily
family child care or center-based care (Lombardi, 1993). Unquestionably,
obtaining high-quality out-of-home child care constitutes a major concern of families of young children.

For children at risk and for those with established disabilities, precise figures for out-of-home placements are lacking (Fewell, 1993).
Despite the fact that children at risk due to biological factors or those
with established disabilities begin out-of-home care later in their lives,
and more vulnerable children than children in the general population
tend to remain in their mothers' care at least during the first 15 months
of life (Booth & Kelly, 1998), nevertheless, a significant need exists for out-
of-home care for these children (Fewell, 1993; Landis, 1992). For children at high risk due to environmental circumstances, the need for
out-of-home care is especially critical given the relatively large proportion of single mothers in the population and pressures from welfare
reform to return to the workplace. For children with established disabilities, although parents use various forms of out-of-home placements,
family child care is one of the most frequent choices (Golbeck & Harlan,
1997; Kontos, 1988). Due to the adjustments required by out-of-home
care staff to the special needs of children with established disabilities
and related issues, this group of children may constitute an unusually
vulnerable one in the context of out-of-home care.

Given these circumstances, one of the most important issues emerging in the general field of early childhood development is the relationship between the EI system for vulnerable children and the need for
out-of-home child care. Questions concern the extent to which the supports and services that characterize the EI system for infants and toddlers, particularly for those at extreme risk and for those with established
disabilities, are compatible with the experiences of those infants and toddlers receiving out-of-home care. Do these systems work together to

complement one another? If not, can aspects of out-of-home care jeopardize gains that can result from EI? What are the circumstances under which child development can be maximized through participation in early intervention programs and out-of-home care settings?

To examine these and related issues, I first present a model suggesting that high-quality programs within the EI system are designed to respond to specific stressors impinging on families that have resulted from risk or disability conditions. This model provides a framework for evaluating the compatibility of the EI system and out-of-home care environments. Although numerous developmental domains are of interest and importance, most research on the effectiveness of EI has emphasized children's cognitive development. Accordingly, outcomes related to cognitive development are emphasized in this chapter as well. Following the presentation of the general model, the effectiveness of aspects of the EI system that contain services provided outside the home, usually in the form of specialized EI centers or intervention-oriented child care (referred to as EI child care), is discussed. Children at environmental risk, biological risk, and those with established disabilities are considered separately, as is the issue of maximizing long-term developmental outcomes. The final section contains suggestions designed to optimize development for vulnerable children in the context of out-of-home care. The central argument presented is that optimal long-term child developmental outcomes, particularly for children at extremely high risk or those with established disabilities, can only occur when out-of-home care in any of its forms is thoroughly integrated into the EI system. The implications of this position for research that can inform practice, policy, and training are discussed briefly.

STRESSORS, CHILD DEVELOPMENTAL OUTCOMES, AND EARLY INTERVENTION

Figure 1 illustrates a general developmental model intended to represent the major experientially based influences on children's developmental outcomes (see Guralnick, 1997a, 1998). Within that model, three well-established *family patterns of interaction* that together substantially influence child developmental outcomes are identified: 1) the quality of parent–child transactions (e.g., providing contingent, reciprocal, nonintrusive interactions and appropriately structuring and scaffolding the environment); 2) family-orchestrated child experiences (e.g., stimulation value of toys and materials provided by parents, social contacts with others arranged through kin and friendship networks, out-of-home care placement selected by parents); and 3) health and safety provided by the family (e.g., immunizations, nutrition). These three patterns of family interaction have well established and direct (proximal) links with child developmental outcomes, and a diverse array of specific family interaction patterns that appear to be optimal can be identified (see Guralnick, 1997a, 1998).

Of importance, these family interaction patterns are themselves governed by more indirect (distal) factors referred to in the model as *family characteristics*. These characteristics include personal features of the parents such as coping styles, mental health status, and intergenerationally transmitted knowledge and skills regarding child rearing, among others. Families' social support networks, the quality of the relationship between the spouses or partners, financial resources, and the child's temperament are also important family characteristics that can

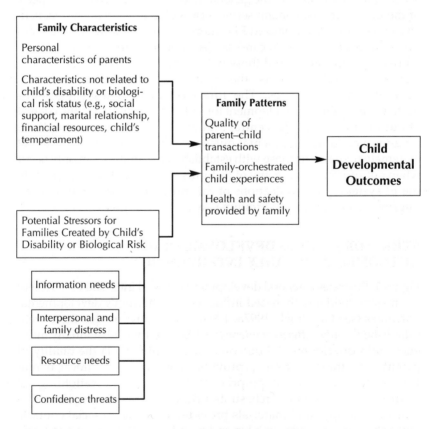

Figure 1. Factors influencing developmental outcomes for children. (From Guralnick, M.J. [1997]. Second-generation research in the field of early intervention. In M.J. Guralnick [Ed.], *The effectiveness of early intervention*, p.7. Baltimore: Paul H. Brookes Publishing Co.; adapted by permission.)

affect child developmental outcomes through their influence on family interaction patterns (Guralnick, 1998).

Stressors typically develop, however, as a consequence of risk or disability circumstances and can reach a magnitude sufficient to produce nonoptimal family interaction patterns. As illustrated in Figure 1, for children at biological risk or for those with established disabilities, four types of potential stressors can be identified: 1) information needs (e.g., health concerns, clarification of diagnostic issues, information regarding the child's expected developmental course, location of qualified professionals, advice in managing child's behavior); 2) interpersonal and family distress (e.g., reassessment of expectations, shared stigma, social isolation); 3) resource needs (e.g., financial needs, respite care); and 4) confidence threats (e.g., challenge to the ability to maintain a sense of mastery and control to fulfill a parenting role). According to the model, these potential sources of stress on families of children at biological risk and those with established disabilities exert their influence on child development by perturbing one or more of the three family interaction patterns. For children at biological risk or for those with established disabilities, a well-established research literature suggests that these four types of stressors arise with considerable frequency during the first 3 years of a child's life, with the potential for creating adverse effects on family interaction patterns (Guralnick, 1997a, 1998).

For children at environmental risk, it is those risk factors associated with family characteristics discussed earlier that serve as the source of potential stressors (see Figure 1). These risk factors include maternal mental illness, inappropriate parental attitudes and beliefs about child rearing, limited financial resources, difficult marital relationships, and intellectual limitations of parents. As noted previously, the cumulative impact of these environmental risk factors appears to create stressors capable of perturbing family interaction patterns (Sameroff et al., 1987). However, evidence does suggest that, in the aggregate, these family characteristics constitute a "buffered" system (Belsky, 1984) in that certain stressors can be mitigated by existing low-risk family characteristics and thereby can protect family interaction patterns from being altered in a nonoptimal fashion. Similarly, stressors from conditions associated with a child's biological risk or disability can be lessened, often to a substantial degree, by favorable family characteristics. In contrast, as discussed previously, when children become "doubly vulnerable," experiencing both high environmental and biological risks, stressors can interact to affect family interaction patterns to such an extent that protective factors have minimal impact, and child developmental outcomes are substantially impaired (Bradley et al., 1994; McGauhey, Starfield, Alexander, & Ensminger, 1991).

When stressors due to risk and disability conditions do exert their influence and produce nonoptimal family interaction patterns, extensive evidence indicates that the net effect is a general decline in children's intellectual development during the first few years of life (Guralnick, 1988). Although these adverse effects can range widely (nearly two standard deviations [SD]), the average order of magnitude of this decline is .50 to .75 SDs and is evident for children at environmental risk (e.g., Ramey & Campbell, 1984), for children at biological risk (e.g., Brooks-Gunn, Klebanov, Liaw, & Spiker, 1993), and for children with established disabilities (e.g., Morgan, 1979; Neser, Molteno, & Knight, 1989).

Mechanisms of Early Intervention

Analyses of high-quality EI programs suggest that they are organized in a systematic manner that is responsive to these stressors (Guralnick, 1997a, 1998). As indicated in Figure 2, comprehensive EI programs con-

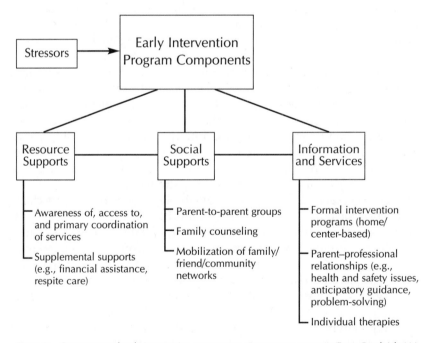

Figure 2. Components of early intervention programs as a response to stressors. (From Guralnick, M.J. [1997]. Second-generation research in the field of early intervention. In M.J. Guralnick [Ed.], *The effectiveness of early intervention*, p. 9. Baltimore: Paul H. Brookes Publishing Co.; reprinted by permission.)

sist of three major components that are capable of addressing the stressors associated with risk and disability conditions. This is accomplished through the process of a well orchestrated series of resource supports, social supports, and information and services. It now appears that these EI components are capable of preventing entirely or at least mitigating substantially the decline in intellectual development that occurs in the absence of early intervention for children at risk (Guralnick, 1997b, 1998). Children with established disabilities still experience significant developmental problems, but further declines related to nonoptimal family interaction patterns can be minimized. The model suggests as well that for EI programs to be successful, they must be comprehensive and capable of adjusting the type and intensity of services and supports in accordance with identified stressors. The intensity issue is especially important where stressors accumulate, as in the case of doubly vulnerable children or when a child's disability is extremely complex or when his or her behavior is difficult to manage. Moreover, threats to optimal family interaction patterns can result from both episodic and chronic stressors. For episodic stressors, effective programs must be sensitive to these circumstances and adjust their content and intensity accordingly. Under some circumstances, interventions recommended by the EI system may suggest that parents engage in interactions with their children that appear on the surface to be unusual but are nevertheless designed in the long-term to promote high quality parent–child transactions. For chronic stressors, EI of long duration may be needed as pressure is continuously exerted that can adversely affect child development through nonoptimal family interaction patterns.

CONTRIBUTIONS OF
CENTER-BASED EARLY INTERVENTION PROGRAMS

Because center-based EI program components for infants and toddlers constitute a form of out-of-home care, it is particularly important to examine how effective these program components are, how they exert their influence, and how compatible they are with other aspects of out-of-home care, as well as the larger EI system. As noted, this analysis will be carried out within the framework of the EI model presented above in an effort to establish those conditions that will maximize a child's developmental outcome. The contributions of center-based EI program components are considered separately for children at environmental risk, for children at biological risk, and for those with established disabilities. For the two at-risk groups, the role of center-based programs for children at *extreme risk* is emphasized.

Environmental Risk

The stressors confronting families at high environmental risk are truly extraordinary and are likely to adversely affect all three family interaction patterns to a substantial degree. As might be expected, interventions designed to alter family characteristics (which in turn would affect family interaction patterns) have met with only limited success (Sameroff et al., 1987). To be sure, some positive impact can result by enhancing social support and by reducing financial burdens, as well as by minimizing similar risk factors. However, altering maternal characteristics such as education, mental health status, or well-established intergenerational patterns of child rearing requires long-term efforts with uncertain outcomes at best. Moreover, illegal drug and alcohol use is often added to this mix of stressors for families at extremely high risk, further limiting the prospects for change (Olsen & Burgess, 1997).

Particularly for these multiple-risk families, even comprehensive home interventions attempting to influence family interaction patterns *directly* (rather than to modify family characteristics) produce few changes in parental behavior and have little impact on child development (Black et al., 1994). Similarly, home visiting programs designed to support families at high risk and to facilitate more optimal family interaction patterns (even cases in which drug use may not be as prevalent) do not yield reliable benefits, especially if the interventions are modest in intensity (less than one visit per week; Scarr & McCartney, 1988; Wasik, Ramey, Bryant, & Sparling, 1990). In contrast, EI programs that have included an intensive EI child care component have been able to prevent important declines in children's intellectual development from occurring for high environmental risk families. The term *EI child care*, as used here, refers to high-quality child care programs, as determined by generally agreed upon criteria, that are explicitly designed to foster the development of children at risk, who are often selected for extreme risk, as well as those children with established disabilities. Risk and disability issues in EI child care are directly addressed through the systematic implementation of a specific and highly individualized child-oriented curriculum. EI child care is sometimes embedded in a more comprehensive intervention and family support program. However, EI child care is characterized by its unusually intensive child-focused component. Of note, many community-based child care programs are of high quality and have characteristics similar to EI child care.

The Abecedarian project in which children from high-risk families were enrolled in full child care (5 days per week, 50 weeks per year) beginning between 6 weeks and 3 months of life (Campbell & Ramey,

1994; Ramey & Campbell, 1984) illustrates the effects of EI child care. A specialized curriculum was designed to be administered by well-trained child care staff addressing a variety of developmental domains (Sparling & Lewis, 1979). Although families were not the focus of this intervention, a variety of social supports and health and individual services were offered. Comparisons between the EI child care group and the control group with respect to children's cognitive development revealed significant differences in favor of the intervention group that were evident by 18 months of age, a difference that remained significant at 24 and 36 months. The effect size even at 36 months was over 1.0 SD.

In essence, children in the control group experienced a relatively steep decline in intellectual development during the course of the first 3 years of life. Although the IQ scores for children receiving EI child care also declined, it was far less severe. Using limited maternal intellectual ability (IQ score less than 70) as an index of extreme environmental risk, the benefits of EI child care were largest for children in this subgroup (Martin, Ramey, & Ramey, 1990). Interestingly, assessments of the quality of the home environment, using scales reflecting many of the family interaction patterns noted in Figure 1 (Caldwell & Bradley, 1979), did not differ between families in the control or intervention groups. By enrolling their child in EI child care, parents may have increased the size of their social support networks (see Burchinal, Follmer, & Bryant, 1996), may have perhaps reduced financial stress because of increased employment possibilities, and may have benefited from interactions with a child whose development was more advanced as a consequence of activities in the EI child care. These and other factors, however, were not sufficient to substantially alter family interaction patterns (Burchinal, Campbell, Bryant, Wasik, & Ramey, 1997). Even quality child care (though not EI child care) has a minimal impact for a general group of families at high risk on those parent–child transaction components of family interaction patterns (NICHD Study of Early Child Care, 1997). Consequently, although some reports of benefits to family characteristics and family interaction patterns can be found (see Benasich, Brooks-Gunn, & Clewell, 1992), child-focused interventions by child care staff as part of EI child care programs appear to be primarily responsible for any gains in children's intellectual development in families at high environmental risk.

The contention that the EI-oriented child care and its child-focused orientation component is the critical feature of the intervention for high environmental risk children is strengthened by observations that intervention's effects tend to be reduced when control group children take advantage of community child care. Scarr and McCartney (1988) offered this as a possible explanation for the absence of differences for their

2-year home-visiting program because a substantial proportion of mothers in their study were employed with nearly 50% of the children being enrolled in community care full-time during the course of the study. That is, child care, presumably quality child care, can make a difference. Similarly, experience in quality child care programs (i.e., programs meeting federal and state standards) for control group children in the Abecedarian project was associated positively with children's intellectual development. Even when controlling for the possible confounding factors of maternal IQ, maternal education, marital status, and the quality of the home environment, children enrolled in community child care performed better than children with minimal child care experience, although children in the EI child care group continued to outperform community child care groups (Burchinal, Lee, & Ramey, 1989). Finally, analyses of Project CARE, which compared a group receiving EI child care plus family support, a group receiving family support only, and a control group, provided additional evidence for the unique benefits of EI child care (Wasik et al., 1990). In this study, no independent benefits for the family support only group were obtained, and the group receiving EI child care and family support outperformed all others at 12, 18, 24, and 36 months of age. Again, no differences in the quality of the home environment were observed. Perhaps most relevant, however, was the finding that, after the occurrence of substantial declines in children's intellectual development observed at 18 months of age for the family support-only and control groups, a trend toward *increased* intellectual development for children in these two groups was noted at 24 months; a trend that continued for at least 2 years (Wasik et al., 1990). Wasik et al. (1990) pointed out that a reasonable, but by no means certain, explanation for this trend toward increased intellectual development is the participation of the family support-only and control-group children in quality child care, as the amount of child care participation was correlated with children's intellectual development. Of note, the mean age for entry into community child care for children in these two groups was approximately 20 months (more than 50% of the children had attended for at least 1 year by 54 months of age).

Taken together, it appears that quality child care, particularly EI child care with its systematic child-focused activities, is the primary contributor to preventing the overall decline in intellectual development for children at environmental risk, and those children at extreme risk benefit most. Furthermore, evidence suggests that neither family characteristics nor family interaction patterns are substantially altered (other than parents enrolling their children in the interventions) by involvement in the EI child care or through moderately intensive home-visiting interventions.

Biological Risk

The contribution of EI child care to minimizing the decline in children's intellectual development has also been examined in preventive interventions for children at risk due to biological factors, primarily low birth weight and prematurity. Most notable is the Infant Health and Development Program (IHDP, 1990). This comprehensive 3-year intervention program consisted of home visits beginning during the first year of the child's life (with specified curricula to foster child development and to support parents' management of self-identified problems) as well as parent groups beginning at 1 year (to provide information and social support). Of considerable significance was the EI child care component. A well-designed curriculum (Sparling & Lewis, 1984; Sparling, Lewis, & Neuwirth, 1988) was implemented in a full 5-day per week child care by highly trained staff beginning when the child was 1 year of age (Gross, 1993). At the end of 3 years, children receiving the comprehensive intervention scored substantially higher on tests of intellectual development in comparison to a control group (IHDP, 1990). In general, the intervention was less effective for children at greater biological risk (i.e., birth weight of less than 2,000 grams).

More detailed analyses revealed that premature low birth weight children who benefited most from the intervention were those who were also at high risk due to environmental factors. In fact, with either maternal intelligence or maternal education as the index of risk, the greater the risk, the more powerful the effect of the EI program (Blair, Ramey, & Hardin, 1995; Brooks-Gunn, Gross, Kraemer, Spiker, & Shapiro, 1992; Ramey & Ramey, 1992). That is, doubly vulnerable (i.e., extremely high risk) children benefited most. No impact whatsoever of the intervention was found for families at the highest educational levels.

To what extent can these comprehensive intervention effects be attributed to child-focused activities implemented in the EI child care component? After all, evidence suggests that for children at high biological risk (though low environmental risk), family interaction patterns can in fact be altered, and associated benefits with respect to children's intellectual development can clearly result from even low intensity EI home-based programs, including intervention components provided in the neonatal intensive care unit (Rauh, Achenbach, Nurcombe, Howell, & Teti, 1988). Some evidence even suggests that family interaction patterns can be altered in a similar manner through home intervention programs for doubly vulnerable children, at least for the child's first year of life (Resnick, Armstrong, & Carter, 1988). However, the fact remains that only relatively small differences between intervention and control groups have been found with respect to parent–child interactions in the IHDP sample for toddlers (Bradley et al., 1994; Spiker, Ferguson, & Brooks-Gunn, 1993). Moreover, beyond the first year of life, home visiting similar in intensity to that provided by the IHDP has not proven to be particularly effective for other risk groups (e.g., Scarr & McCartney, 1988).

Although teasing out the unique contributions of components from a comprehensive intervention cannot be achieved easily, evidence does suggest that the intensity of the interventions in the form of participation in all three components of the IHDP (i.e., home visits, parent group meetings, EI child care) does matter (Ramey et al., 1992). In this analysis, greater overall participation in the program was strongly associated with higher levels of children's intellectual development, but participation was unrelated to initial status characteristics of children and families (e.g., birth weight, maternal education, neonatal health). Clearly, days in which children participated in the EI child care contributed to this association, along with the other two components. However, what may be the most significant factor is the total amount of child-focused activities specified in the curricula that occurred both during home visits (home visitors assisted parents to carry out the activities) and by child care staff at the EI child care. Related evidence suggests that the rate at which the direct child-focused activities are implemented in the home and the EI child care is associated with better child developmental outcomes, above and beyond the effects of overall participation (Sparling et al., 1991). Accordingly, the number of implemented child-focused activities that involved trained interventionists may be the critical element of the comprehensive intervention.

In summary, it appears that doubly vulnerable infants and toddlers can reap important benefits from early intervention programs carried out during the first 3 years of life. The success of those interventions may be linked directly to child-focused activities carried out in an EI child care by highly trained staff or by parents under the direct supervision of intervention staff. However, only limited evidence is available to suggest that families alter their interaction patterns apart from the presence of intervention staff. Although the impact of EI on family characteristics for this extremely high-risk group has not been systematically evaluated, there is little reason to expect substantial changes based on results involving high environmental risk groups only.

Children with Established Disabilities

Infants and toddlers with established disabilities are often enrolled by their parents in formal early intervention programs in connection with their participation in the Education of the Handicapped Act Amendments of 1986. An individualized family service plan (IFSP) is developed in conjunction with the families and may include home visits, center-based services, parent groups, and other supports and services as agreed upon. Center-based activities include interventions involving the child or parent only or parents and children together. Groups of children or parent–child groups also participate in center-based services. When all components of the official EI program are combined, despite a relatively wide range of involvement, the average level of service is only 7 hours per month (Shonkoff, Hauser-Cram, Krauss, & Upshur, 1992). Consequently, center-based interventions as intensive as those described above for infants and toddlers at risk are a rare occurrence, and no comparable intervention studies for infants and toddlers with established disabilities have been conducted to determine the unique contributions of specific EI components. Moreover, many families seek out additional therapeutic support (e.g., physical, speech-language, or occupational therapy), family support (e.g., counseling, respite care), financial support (e.g., supplemental security income), and related services.

Analyses of available research suggest that this array of comprehensive EI services and supports is also capable of minimizing the decline in intellectual development that may occur in the absence of EI. This is certainly the case for children with Down syndrome (see Guralnick, 1998; Guralnick & Bricker, 1987; Spiker & Hopmann, 1997). Of course, significant delays in children's intellectual development remain but, as noted earlier, further declines can be minimized through EI, with effect sizes ranging from .50 to .75 SDs.

Although the intensity of center-based interventions is quite modest, it appears that it is the comprehensiveness of the EI program that is capable of addressing the many stressors facing families of children with established disabilities. Extensive information networks function well (often through parent-to-parent groups that have been established); various support groups and counseling programs are capable of minimizing interpersonal and family distress; well trained professionals are available to provide guidance with respect to developmental issues and to foster parenting strategies that encourage a child's development; and health professionals can readily provide state-of-the-art care drawing upon an extensive knowledge base directly linked to disability concerns (Cooley & Graham, 1991; Guralnick & Bricker, 1987; Spiker & Hopmann, 1997). As a consequence of these EI supports and services (see Figure 2), the three family patterns of interaction, particularly parent–child transactions (McCollum & Hemmeter, 1997), are better organized to promote optimal child developmental outcomes.

Out-of-home child care of limited intensity is usually provided in the form of the formal EI program. However, even when children participate alone in child-directed, center-based activities, other forms of out-of-home care, such as family child care, are also often sought by parents. Similar to the community child care effects for children at risk, this form of child-focused care can produce some positive effects on child development for children with established disabilities in the absence of a formal EI program (Neser, Molteno, & Knight, 1989). However, there is a limited conceptual basis and no empirical information to suggest that an intensive EI child care program, such as that discussed for children at extremely high-risk, will yield benefits greater than those achieved through existing comprehensive EI programs for children with established disabilities. This is certainly the case in the absence of stressors created by high-risk family characteristics for this group of children. What is a potential danger, however, is that the child's participation in out-of-home care that is not connected to an EI program can be detrimental. This is especially a concern if out-of-home care is used extensively, thereby limiting time available for parents to participate in the larger EI program. Although some stressors generated by either family characteristics or their child's disability may be eased through extensive out-of-home care, addressing other stressors becomes far more difficult. Because extensive out-of-home care may assume a more important role in fostering child development, it would appear that out-of-home child care must become closely integrated with the various components of the larger EI system in order to achieve benefits for children with established disabilities.

Producing Long-Term Benefits

For children at biological and environmental risk, especially those at extreme risk, the evidence reviewed above suggests that EI child care can serve an important preventive function during the first 3 years of life by helping to minimize the decline in intellectual development that occurs in the absence of systematic early intervention. But, in many ways, reliance upon primarily center-based, well directed, and often compensatory-focused (Bailey, 1997) interventions carried out by specialists seems inconsistent with the developmental model of EI presented earlier. If, as has been suggested, EI child care does not substantially alter the three family interaction patterns for children at risk (i.e., parent–child transactions, family-orchestrated child experiences, and health and safety provided by the family), how is it possible for optimal child development to result in the long term? Unquestionably, some stressors associated with family characteristics (see Figure 1) are addressed through EI child care. As noted earlier, EI child care can give families confidence that their child is consistently well cared for while they are seeking employment or are employed, and social networks can be extended through connections established in the EI child care setting.

Similarly, home-visiting features added to some EI child care programs may contribute to improving parent–child transactions or aspects of the other two components of family interaction patterns to at least some degree (see Benasich et al., 1992; Bradley et al., 1994). Nevertheless, despite the modest changes in family interaction patterns that have been found, it is reasonable to expect that should EI child care no longer be provided after 3 years of age, child developmental progress will again decline. After all, especially for families at extreme environmental risk, either with or without a child who has a biological risk as well, stressors are likely to be chronic and pervasive, continuing to affect family interaction patterns adversely over time.

Available evidence suggests that this is precisely what happens in the absence of continued EI. For the IHDP program, only small residual benefits remain 2 years after the program has ended (Brooks-Gunn, McCarton, Casey et al., 1994), and no delayed effects appear to be emerging (McCarton et al., 1997). The relatively rapid dissipation over time following the termination of EI programs designed for children from high environmental risk circumstances has been well documented (Barnett, 1995). Accordingly, for children at extreme risk, if it is the expectation that EI programs provided only during the infant and toddler periods that are primarily child focused will result in long-term benefits, including those that rely extensively on EI child care, there is little evidence to indicate that this will occur.

How, then, can longer-term benefits be achieved? It is possible that more intensive efforts designed to influence chronic and pervasive stressors related to family characteristics during the first 3 years of the child's life may be of value, but this has proven to be extremely difficult to accomplish. Unquestionably, some radical re-conceptualization or re-structuring of the entire system of community supports to children and families needs to be considered. Perhaps innovative home visiting strategies can be developed that, although child-focused, have a more lasting effect on specific features of parent–child transactions, family-orchestrated child experiences, and health and safety matters. Alternatively, comprehensive EI programs can be extended beyond 3 years of age. In so doing, additional time is available to address complex chronic family stressors; episodic stressors associated with transitions across developmental periods can be mitigated through supports and services provided by the comprehensive EI program. The EI child care feature can be particularly critical in preventing declines in development prior to entering school programs. This relationship among stressors, family interaction patterns, and duration of intervention in relation to children's development over time is illustrated in Figure 3. A critical transition point can be seen at age 3 years.

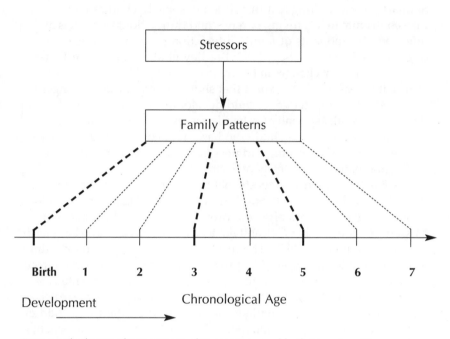

Figure 3.   The duration of intervention in relation to stressors and family interaction patterns.

By extending the EI program over time, it is anticipated that major declines in children's intellectual development can be avoided. In fact, available evidence suggests that programs of longer duration for high-risk families do have more lasting effects. For example, children in the Abecedarian program received 5 years of EI child care and continue to benefit years after the program has ended (Campbell & Ramey, 1994). It may well be that the long-term benefits of this extended birth-through-5-years program can be attributed to children's higher developmental levels when entering school, as well as more optimal family interaction patterns that gradually emerge over time (see Benasich et al., 1992). Accordingly, a major goal of the EI system for children at risk that includes an extensive EI child care component during the first 3 years of a child's life should be to ensure that parents seek out and enroll their child, at minimum, in a high-quality child care program during the pre-school years. Most preferable, of course, would be an EI child care pro-gram. Opportunities for improving family interaction patterns as part of these preschool programs may also be beneficial. In fact, large-scale, community-based, government-financed programs of this type for preschool-age children have proven to be effective, with long-term gains attributed to children's improved cognitive abilities and to the family's support of developmental and educational goals for their child (Reynolds, 1997).

As we have seen, center-based activities occupy a less prominent position for children with established disabilities. Nevertheless, center-based activities are often the "home base" for EI programs and a place where families seek guidance and support. Most of the children receiving services under Part H of the Education of the Handicapped Act Amendments of 1986 (now Part C of the Individuals with Disabilities Education Act Amendments [IDEA] of 1997 [PL 105-17]) during the infant and toddler years will continue to receive services during the preschool period. Such preschool programs are usually center based and are offered for only part of the day. Consequently, they must be coordinated with any other out-of-home care arrangements, and steps should be taken to ensure that appropriate family participation can be maintained.

Unfortunately, conditions under which long-term benefits result for children with established disabilities have not been well established (e.g., Gibson & Harris, 1988; McCollum & Hemmeter, 1997). As such, based on the available research literature, no specific recommendations can be made with regard to altering the existing EI system for children with established disabilities during the child's first 3 years of life that would maximize longer lasting benefits or influence out-of-home care decisions. However, stressors related to a child's disability can be anticipated to continue challenging families at various points in time, as numerous issues related to transitions or health and developmental concerns are likely to emerge. For certain groups of children, evidence for the importance of these supports continuing across transitions and resulting in long-term benefits is in fact available (Lovaas, 1987; McEachin, Smith, & Lovaas, 1993). Child-related difficulties that may be responsive to continuing services and supports from the EI system will certainly be apparent in most if not all of the settings in which the child participates. Therefore, a set of coordinated interventions that include both the preschool and child care environments is likely to be essential in achieving long-term benefits.

OPTIMIZING CHILD DEVELOPMENT IN THE CONTEXT OF OUT-OF-HOME CARE

With this background, it is now possible to return to the central questions regarding the compatibility of the early intervention system and out-of-home care for infants and toddlers at risk and for those with established disabilities. What are the optimal forms of out-of-home care during the infant and toddler periods? How can the need for out-of-home care and the need for early intervention be integrated? Of equal importance, how can the long-term benefits of early intervention be assured? Consideration of these and related issues have implications for research, practice, training, and policy.

Children at Risk

Children at extremely high risk due to environmental circumstances, with or without co-occurring biological risks, clearly benefit from the child-focused features provided by EI child care. Consistent findings suggest that children from the highest risk circumstances benefit most and that the more intensive the program, the better the outcome. Accordingly, to maximize development for these children, out-of-home care should be in the form of extensive EI child care. From both a practice and policy perspective, this will require that considerable effort be devoted to defining risk factors carefully (presumably based on a cumulative risk index) in order to identify highly vulnerable risk groups of children appropriately. Although much is known about highly vulnerable populations, additional epidemiological studies are warranted. The number of these families, how to establish cut-off points or ranges on risk indices, and the degree to which the families cluster geographically will help address cost and practice issues. In addition, many cultural and ethical issues surround the assessment process required to identify such high-risk families and must be thoughtfully considered. Expecting existing community child care options to function as EI child care is not realistic at this time. In fact, out-of-home care available to children from very high-risk environments is often of unusually poor quality (Burchinal, Roberts, Nabors, & Bryant, 1996; Howes, Phillips, & Whitebook, 1992; NICHD Early Child Care Research Network, 1997; Zigler & Gilman, 1993), despite the fact that subsidized, center-based community child care for low-income families in particular can improve the quality of the child care setting (NICHD Early Child Care Research Network, 1997). Indeed, some evidence exists to suggest that high-quality community child care can be beneficial, but it is not as effective as EI child care.

A correspondingly important research and practice issue is how to make the option of enrolling their child in an EI child care attractive to parents. One way to structure the EI child care is to set up entirely separate center-based programs in appropriate community settings, similar to the research models described, paralleling other child care options in the community. Although this plan has some merit, principally the ability to ensure a quality program, separating children based on their extremely high risk status can be isolating and clearly constrains both family and child social networks. Alternatively, a larger number of high-quality child cares can be established (or existing child care options can be supplemented to improve quality) to serve a wider range of children varying in risk status in the community. Within this model, special resources can be set aside to target the highest risk children. One advantage of this approach is that it can further enhance the overall quality of center-based child care in communities, perhaps producing more widespread benefits. Additional research on the feasibility and efficacy of these and related models is clearly needed.

For children with both environmental and biological risks, a variety of other options may need to be considered during the first year of the child's life. Due to their likely increased susceptibility to infections, EI child care may not be appropriate for these children (Gross, 1993). Accordingly, either arrangements need to be made for in-home care or families must receive support for their child to be cared for at home. Clearly, welfare reform provisions must somehow consider these potential health issues as they are likely to be related to child developmental outcomes. Admittedly, from a research perspective, the unique contributions of beginning EI during the first 18 months of life require clarification. Assuming that such benefits exist seems reasonable, however, and intensifying home-visiting programs during the first year of life for doubly vulnerable children should be strongly considered. Nevertheless, a number of important research and policy issues remain to be explored.

Evidence further suggests that EI child care for these at-risk populations should continue beyond the infant and toddler periods, extending through the child's first 5 years of life in order to achieve long-term benefits. As noted, home visiting programs of modest intensity and family support programs have not yet proven to be effective in either altering family characteristics or family interaction patterns to a substantial degree. However, the opportunity exists to build on the EI child care context to develop innovative services and supports for families that may ultimately yield long-term effects. Services and supports could include linking work options for mothers with parenting activities; enhancing the EI child care center's role as a focal point for community activities involving parents and children (family-orchestrated activities); creating a "co-parenting" option or "mentoring" system, drawing upon skilled parents in the community to help strengthen family interaction patterns and perhaps even alter certain family characteristics. All of these options carry important implications for research, policy, and training. It is within this context as well that arrangements can be made to ensure that parents enroll their children in some form of EI child care or quality EI program when they reach preschool age. The Child and Parent Centers (Reynolds, 1997) provide one such model, but even these excellent programs may need to be supplemented with good quality child care.

Children with Established Disabilities

Families of infants and toddlers with established disabilities must contend with a different set of issues. One problem is ensuring that the out-of-home care selected can be integrated with their child's formal EI programs. The hazard is that child care concerns can easily overwhelm EI concerns, and the demonstrated ability of EI programs to address stressors created by a child's disability will be lost. Accordingly, circumstances must be arranged such that needed resource supports, social supports, and information and services can be provided as part of the EI system.

That many families of children with established disabilities rely on family child care as a main out-of-home care placement poses additional problems. A large proportion of family child care centers are unregulated, providers are poorly paid, and staff turnover is often high (Golbeck & Harlan, 1997). Compounding these issues are the additional skills required by child care staff to accommodate the special needs of children with established disabilities. Although training programs and consultation models can be effective in some ways, they are usually of limited intensity and have limited availability (Jones & Meisels, 1987; Wesley, 1994).

Ideally, parents can enroll their child in an "inclusive child care" that provides early intervention services and supports as well as quality child care (O'Brien, 1997). In these all too rare settings, staff include well trained specialists, as well as child development generalists. The benefits that result in terms of continuity, quality, and parental confidence of such an inclusive program cannot be overemphasized. These settings can easily accommodate families at high and low environmental risk but, within the context of the general EI systems model, would certainly be recommended for children with established disabilities who are also at high risk due to environmental factors. As such, these programs would constitute a form of EI child care for children with established disabilities and who are from high environmental risk families.

In the absence of an inclusive child care option, the EI "home base" can function as a resource for information, services, and training for the child's out-of-home placement. Although continuing to work directly with families to address stressors as they arise or are anticipated, staff must also coordinate in the child's out-of-home care environments. How effectively the models that now exist or will emerge within the EI home base framework are able to integrate critical EI and out-of-home care functions remains an important research question. Moreover, available research suggests that both the quality of child care settings and the comprehensiveness of the EI programs found in these arrangements may be of concern (Bruder, Staff, & McMurrer-Kaminer, 1997). A lack of comprehensiveness (i.e., a focus on interventionist–child interactions and not family support or parent–child interactions) is also seen in home-visiting programs (McBride & Peterson, 1997).

As noted, family child care may pose a unique set of problems. In fact, much more work is needed to articulate models that reflect the range of out-of-home child care options, define how they should operate, and clarify responsibilities. Policy implications are considerable with regard to coordination of service. Whether it is reasonable to mandate some level of consultative services as part of the Individuals with Disabilities Education Act constitutes an important issue. Similarly, the extraordinary training issues that exist due to the diverse array of out-of-home placements available to young children with disabilities must also be considered. Clearly, as pressures to locate early and extensive out-of-home care for young children with disabilities increase, the need to identify effective models that are well integrated with the EI system will become even more critical.

REFERENCES

Bailey, D.B., Jr. (1997). Evaluating the effectiveness of curriculum alternatives for infants and preschoolers at high risk. In M.J. Guralnick (Ed.), *The effectiveness of early intervention* (pp. 227–247). Baltimore: Paul H. Brookes Publishing Co.

Barnett, W.S. (1995). Long-term effects of early childhood programs on cognitive and school outcomes. In R.E. Behrman (Ed.), *The future of children: Vol. 5. Long-term outcomes of early childhood programs* (pp. 25–50). Los Altos, CA: The Center for the Future of Children, The David and Lucile Packard Foundation.

Belsky, J. (1984). The determinants of parenting: A process model. *Child Development, 55,* 83–96.

Benasich, A.A., Brooks-Gunn, J., & Clewell, B.C. (1992). How do mothers benefit from early intervention programs? *Journal of Applied Developmental Psychology, 13,* 311–362.

Bendersky, M., & Lewis, M. (1994). Environmental risk, biological risk, and developmental outcome. *Developmental Psychology, 30,* 484–494.

Black, M.M., Nair, P., Kight, C., Wachtel, R., Roby, P., & Schuler, M. (1994). Parenting and early development among children of drug-abusing women: Effects of home intervention. *Pediatrics, 94,* 440–448.

Blair, C.B., Ramey, C.T., & Hardin, J.M. (1995). Early intervention for low birth weight, premature infants. Participation and intellectual development. *American Journal on Mental Retardation, 99,* 542–554.

Booth, C.B., & Kelly, J.F. (1998). Child-care characteristics of infants with and without special needs: Comparisons and concerns. *Early Childhood Research Quarterly, 13,* 603–622.

230   GURALNICK

Bowe, F.G. (1995). Population estimates: Birth-to-5 children with disabilities. *The Journal of Special Education, 20,* 461–471.

Bradley, R.H., Whiteside, L., Mundfrom, D.J., Casey, P.H., Caldwell, B.M., & Barrett, K. (1994). Impact of the Infant Health and Development Program (IHDP) on the home environments of infants born prematurely and with low birthweight. *Journal of Educational Psychology, 86,* 531–541.

Bradley, R.H., Whiteside, L., Mundfrom, D.J., Casey, P.H., Kelleher, K.J., & Pope, S.K. (1994). Early indications of resilience and their relation to experiences in the home environments of low birthweight, premature children living in poverty. *Child Development, 65,* 346–360.

Breslau, N., DelDotto, J.E., Brown, G.G., Kumar, S., Ezhuthachan, S., Hufnagle, K.G., & Peterson, E.L. (1994). A gradient relationship between low birth weight and IQ at age 6 years. *Archives of Pediatric and Adolescent Medicine, 148,* 377–383.

Brody, D.J., Pirkle, J.L., Kramer, R.A., Flegal, K.M., Matte, T.D., Gunter, E.W., & Paschal, D.C. (1994). Blood lead levels in the U.S. population. Phase 1 of the Third National Health and Nutrition Examination Survey (NHANES III, 1988 to 1991). *Journal of the American Medical Association, 272,* 277–283.

Brooks-Gunn, J., Gross, R.T., Kraemer, H.C., Spiker, D., & Shapiro, S. (1992). Enhancing the cognitive outcomes of low birth weight, premature infants: For whom is the intervention most effective? *Pediatrics, 89,* 1209–1215.

Brooks-Gunn, J., Klebanov, P.K., Liaw, F., & Spiker, D. (1993). Enhancing the development of low-birthweight, premature infants: Changes in cognition and behavior over the first 3 years. *Child Development, 64,* 736–753.

Brooks-Gunn, J., McCarton, C.M., Casey, P.H., McCormick, M.C., Bauer, C.R., Bernbaum, J. C., Tyson, J., Swanson, M., Bennett, F.C., Scott, D.T., Tonascia, J., & Meinert, C.L. (1994). Early intervention in low-birth-weight premature infants. *Journal of the American Medical Association, 272,* 1257–1262.

Brooks-Gunn, J., McCarton, C.M., & Hawley, T. (1994). Effects of *in utero* drug exposure on children's development. *Archives of Pediatric Adolescent Medicine, 148,* 33–39.

Bruder, M.B., Staff, I., & McMurrer-Kaminer, E. (1997). Toddlers receiving early intervention in childcare centers: A description of a service delivery system. *Topics in Early Childhood Special Education, 17,* 185–208.

Burchinal, M.R., Campbell, F.A., Bryant, D.M., Wasik, B.H., & Ramey, C.T. (1997). Early intervention and mediating processes in cognitive performance of children of low-income African American families. *Child Development, 68,* 935–954.

Burchinal, M.R., Follmer, A., & Bryant, D.M. (1996). The relations of maternal social support and family structure with maternal responsiveness and child outcomes among African American families. *Developmental Psychology, 32,* 1073–1083.

Burchinal, M.R., Lee, M.W., & Ramey, C.T. (1989). Type of day-care and preschool intellectual development in disadvantaged children. *Child Development, 60,* 128–137.

Burchinal, M.R., Roberts, J.E., Nabors, L.A., & Bryant, D.M. (1996). Quality of center child care and infant cognitive and language development. *Child Development, 67,* 606–620.

Caldwell, B., & Bradley, R. (1979). *Observation for measurement of the environment.* Unpublished manuscript, University of Arkansas, Little Rock.

Campbell, F.A., & Ramey, C.T. (1994). Effects of early intervention on intellectual and academic achievement: A follow-up study of children from low-income families. *Child Development, 65,* 684–698.

Chasnoff, I.J., Landress, H.J., & Barrett, M.E. (1990). The prevalence of illicit-drug or alcohol use during pregnancy and discrepancies in mandatory reporting in Pinellas County, Florida. *The New England Journal of Medicine, 322,* 1202–1206.

Children's Defense Fund. (1996). *The state of America's children.* Washington, DC: Author.

Cooley, W.C., & Graham, J.M. (1991). Common syndromes and management issues for primary care physicians. *Clinical Pediatrics, 30,* 233–253.

Education of the Handicapped Act Amendments of 1986, PL 99-457, 20 U.S.C. §§ 1400 *et seq.*

Feldman, M.A. (1997). The effectiveness of early intervention for children of parents with mental retardation. In M.J. Guralnick (Ed.), *The effectiveness of early intervention* (pp. 171–191). Baltimore: Paul H. Brookes Publishing Co.

Fewell, R.R. (1993). Child care for children with special needs. *Pediatrics, 91* (Suppl.), 193–198.

First, L.R., & Palfrey, J.S. (1994). The infant or young child with developmental delay. *The New England Journal of Medicine, 330,* 478–483.

Furstenberg, F.F., Jr., Nord, C.W., Peterson, J.L., & Zill, N. (1983). The life course of children of divorce: Marital disruption and parental contact. *American Sociological Review, 48,* 656–668.

Garmezy, N., & Masten, A.S. (1994). Chronic adversities. In M. Rutter, E. Taylor, & L. Hersov (Eds.), *Child and adolescent psychiatry* (4th ed., pp. 191–208). Oxford, England: Blackwell Scientific Publications.

Gibson, D., & Harris, A. (1988). Aggregated early intervention effects for Down's syndrome persons: Patterning and longevity of benefits. *Journal of Mental Deficiency Research, 32,* 1–17.

Golbeck, S.L., & Harlan, S. (1997). Family child care. In S.K. Thurman, J.R. Cornwell, & S.R. Gottwald (Eds.), *Contexts of early intervention: Systems and settings* (pp. 165–189). Baltimore: Paul H. Brookes Publishing Co.

Gross, R.T. (1993). Day care for the child born prematurely. *Pediatrics, 91* (Suppl.), 189–192.

Guralnick, M.J. (1988). Efficacy research in early childhood intervention programs. In S.L. Odom & M.B. Karnes (Eds.), *Early intervention for infants and children with handicaps: An empirical base* (pp. 75–88). Baltimore: Paul H. Brookes Publishing Co.

Guralnick, M.J. (1993). Second generation research on the effectiveness of early intervention. *Early Education and Development, 4,* 366–378.

Guralnick, M.J. (Ed.). (1997a). *The effectiveness of early intervention.* Baltimore: Paul H. Brookes Publishing Co.

Guralnick, M.J. (1997b). Second-generation research in the field of early intervention. In M.J. Guralnick (Ed.), *The effectiveness of early intervention* (pp. 3–20). Baltimore: Paul H. Brookes Publishing Co.

Guralnick, M.J. (1998). The effectiveness of early intervention for vulnerable children: A developmental perspective. *American Journal on Mental Retardation, 102,* 319–345.

Guralnick, M.J., & Bricker, D. (1987). The effectiveness of early intervention for children with cognitive and general developmental delays. In M.J. Guralnick & F.C. Bennett (Eds.), *The effectiveness of early intervention for at-risk and handicapped children* (pp. 115–173). New York: Academic Press.

Hack, M., Taylor, H.G., Klein, N., Eiben, R., Schatschneider, C., & Mercuri-Minich, N. (1994). School-age outcomes in children with birth weights under 750 g. *The New England Journal of Medicine, 331,* 753–759.

Howes, C., Phillips, D.A., & Whitebook, M. (1992). Thresholds of quality: Implications for the social development of children in center-based child care. *Child Development, 63,* 449–460.

Huston, A.C., McLoyd, V.C., & Garcia Coll, C.G. (1994). Children and poverty: Issues in contemporary research. *Child Development, 65,* 275–282.

Individuals with Disabilities Education Act (IDEA) Amendments of 1997, PL 105-17, 20 U.S.C. §§ 1400 *et seq.*

Infant Health and Development Program (IDHP). (1990). Enhancing the outcomes of low-birth-weight, premature infants: A multisite, randomized trial. *Journal of the American Medical Association, 263,* 3035–3042.

Jones, S.N., & Meisels, S.J. (1987). Training family day care providers to work with special needs children. *Topics in Early Childhood Special Education, 7,* 1–12.

Kelly, J.F., Morisset, C.E., Barnard, K.E., & Patterson, D.L. (1995). Risky beginnings: Low maternal intelligence as a risk factor for children's intellectual development. *Infants and Young Children, 8,* 11–23.

Keltner, B., & Tymchuk, A. (1992). Reaching out to mothers with mental retardation. *American Journal of Maternal Child Nursing, 17*(3), 136–140.

Kontos, S. (1988). Family day care as an integrated early intervention setting. *Topics in Early Childhood Special Education, 8,* 1–14.

Landis, L.J. (1992). Marital, employment, and childcare status of mothers with infants and toddlers with disabilities. *Topics in Early Childhood Special Education, 12,* 496–507.

Lipkin, P.H. (1996). Epidemiology of the developmental disabilities. In A.J. Capute & P.J. Accardo (Eds.), *Developmental disabilities in infancy and childhood: Vol. 1. Neurodevelopmental diagnosis and treatment* (2nd ed., pp. 137–156). Baltimore: Paul H. Brookes Publishing Co.

Lombardi, J. (1993). Looking at the child care landscape. *Pediatrics, 91* (Suppl.), 179–181.

Lovaas, O.I. (1987). Behavioral treatment and normal educational and intellectual functioning in young autistic children. *Journal of Consulting and Clinical Psychology, 55,* 3–9.

Martin, S.L., Ramey, C.T., & Ramey, S. (1990). The prevention of intellectual impairment in children of impoverished families: Findings of a randomized trial of educational day care. *American Journal of Public Health, 80,* 844–847.

McBride, S.L., & Peterson, C. (1997). Home-based early intervention with families of children with disabilities: Who is doing what? *Topics in Early Childhood Special Education, 17,* 209–233.

McCarton, C.M., Brooks-Gunn, J., Wallace, I.F., Bauer, C.R., Bennett, F.C., Bernbaum, J.C., Broyles, S., Casey, P.H., McCormick, M.C., Scott, D.T., Tyson, J., Tonascia, J., & Meinert, C.L. (1997). Results at age 8 years of early intervention for low-birth-weight premature infants. The Infant Health and Development Program. *Journal of the American Medical Association, 277,* 126–132.

McCollum, J.A., & Hemmeter, M.L. (1997). Parent–child interaction intervention when children have disabilities. In M.J. Guralnick (Ed.), *The effectiveness of early intervention* (pp. 549–576). Baltimore: Paul H. Brookes Publishing Co.

McCormick, M.C., Workman-Daniels, K., & Brooks-Gunn, J. (1996). The behavioral and emotional well-being of school-age children with different birth weights. *Pediatrics, 97,* 18–25.

McEachin, J.J., Smith, T., & Lovaas, O.I. (1993). Long-term outcome for children with autism who received early intensive behavioral treatment. *American Journal on Mental Retardation, 97,* 359–372.

McGauhey, P.J., Starfield, B., Alexander, C., & Ensminger, M.E. (1991). Social environment and vulnerability of low birth weight children: A social-epidemiological perspective. *Pediatrics, 88,* 943–953.

Meisels, S.J., & Shonkoff, J.P. (Eds.). (1990). *Handbook of early childhood intervention.* New York: Cambridge University Press.

Morgan, S.B. (1979). Development and distribution of intellectual and adaptive skills in Down syndrome children: Implications for early intervention. *Mental Retardation, 17,* 247–249.

Neser, P.S.J., Molteno, C.D., & Knight, G.J. (1989). Evaluation of preschool children with Down's syndrome in Cape Town using the Griffiths Scale of Mental Development. *Child: Care, Health and Development, 15,* 217–225.

NICHD Early Child Care Research Network. (1997). Poverty and patterns of child care. In J. Brooks-Gunn & G. Duncan (Eds.), *Consequences of growing up poor* (pp. 100–131). New York: Russell-Sage.

NICHD Study of Early Child Care. (1997, April). *Results of NICHD study of early child care.* Paper presented at the biennial meeting of the Society for Research in Child Development, Washington, DC.

O'Brien, M. (1997). *Inclusive child care for infants and toddlers: Meeting individual and special needs.* Baltimore: Paul H. Brookes Publishing Co.

Olsen, H.C., & Burgess, D.M. (1997). Early intervention for children prenatally exposed to alcohol and other drugs. In M.J. Guralnick (Ed.), *The effectiveness of early intervention* (pp. 109–145). Baltimore: Paul H. Brookes Publishing Co.

Osofsky, J.D. (1995). The effects of violence exposure on young children. *American Psychologist, 50,* 782–788.

Osofsky, J.D., Hann, D.M., & Peebles, C. (1993). Adolescent parenthood: Risks and opportunities for mothers and infants. In C.H. Zeanah, Jr. (Ed.), *Handbook of infant mental health* (pp. 106–119). New York: Guilford Press.

Palfrey, J.S., Singer, J.D., Walker, D.K., & Butler, J.A. (1987). Early identification of children's special needs. A study in five metropolitan communities. *Journal of Pediatrics, 111,* 651.

Parker, S., Greer, S., & Zuckerman, B. (1988). Double jeopardy: The impact of poverty on early child development. *The Pediatric Clinics of North America, 35,* 1227–1240.

Paulozzi, L.J., Shapp, J., Drawbaugh, R.E., & Carney, J.K. (1995). Prevalence of lead poisoning among 2-year-old children in Vermont. *Pediatrics, 96,* 78–81.

Ramey, C.T., Bryant, D.M., Wasik, B.H., Sparling, J.J., Fendt, K.H., & LaVange, L.M. (1992). Infant health and development program for low birth weight, premature infants: Program elements, family participation, and child intelligence. *Pediatrics, 89,* 454–465.

Ramey, C.T., & Campbell, F.A. (1984). Preventive education for high-risk children: Cognitive consequences of the Carolina Abecedarian Project. *American Journal of Mental Deficiency, 88,* 515–523.

Ramey, C.T., & Ramey, S.L. (1992). Effective early intervention. *Mental Retardation, 30,* 337–345.

Rauh, V.A., Achenbach, T.M., Nurcombe, B., Howell, C.T., & Teti, D.M. (1988). Minimizing adverse effects of low birthweight: Four-year results of an early intervention program. *Child Development, 59,* 544–553.

Resnick, M.B., Armstrong, S., & Carter, R.L. (1988). Developmental intervention program for high-risk premature infants: Effects on development and parent-infant interactions. *Journal of Developmental and Behavioral Pediatrics, 9,* 73–78.

Reynolds, A.J. (1997, April). *Long-term effects of the Chicago Child-Parent Center Program through age 15.* Paper presented at the biennial meeting of the Society for Research in Child Development, Washington, DC.

Sameroff, A.J., Seifer, R., Barocas, R., Zax, M., & Greenspan, S. (1987). Intelligence quotient scores of 4-year-old children: Social-environmental risk factors. *Pediatrics, 79,* 343–350.

Scarr, S., & McCartney, K. (1988). Far from home: An experimental evaluation of the mother-child home program in Bermuda. *Child Development, 59,* 531–543.

Shonkoff, J.P., Hauser-Cram, P., Krauss, M.W., & Upshur, C.C. (1992). Development of infants with disabilities and their families. *Monographs of the Society for Research in Child Development, 57*(6, Serial No. 230).

Sparling, J., & Lewis, I. (1979). *Learningames for the first 3 years: A guide to parent–child play.* New York: Walker & Co.

Sparling, J., & Lewis, I. (1984). *Learningames for threes and fours: A guide to adult–child play.* New York: Walker & Co.

Sparling, J., Lewis, I., & Neuwirth, S. (1988). *Early partners: Curriculum kit.* Lewisville, NC: Kaplan Press.

Sparling, J., Lewis, I., Ramey, C.T., Wasik, B.H., Bryant, D.M., & LaVange, L.M. (1991). Partners: A curriculum to help premature, low birthweight infants get off to a good start. *Topics in Early Childhood Special Education, 11,* 36–55.

Spiker, D., Ferguson, J., & Brooks-Gunn, J. (1993). Enhancing maternal interactive behavior and child social competence in low birth weight, premature infants. *Child Development, 64,* 754–768.

Spiker, D., & Hopmann, M.R. (1997). The effectiveness of early intervention for children with Down syndrome. In M.J. Guralnick (Ed.), *The effectiveness of early intervention* (pp. 271–305). Baltimore: Paul H. Brookes Publishing Co.

Taylor, L., Zuckerman, B., Harik, V., & Groves, B.M. (1994). Witnessing violence by young children and their mothers. *Journal of Developmental and Behavioral Pediatrics, 15,* 120–123.

U.S. Department of Health and Human Services, National Center on Child Abuse and Neglect. (1995). *Child maltreatment 1993: Reports from the states to the National Center on Child Abuse and Neglect.* Washington, DC: U.S. Government Printing Office.

Wasik, B.H., Ramey C.T., Bryant, D.G., & Sparling, J.J. (1990). A longitudinal study of two early intervention strategies: Project CARE. *Child Development, 61,* 1682–1696.

Wesley, P.W. (1994). Innovative practices: Providing on-site consultation to promote quality in integrated child care programs. *Journal of Early Intervention, 18,* 391–402.

Zeanah, C.H., Jr. (Ed.). (1993). *Handbook of infant mental health.* New York: Guilford Press.

Zigler, E., & Gilman, E. (1993). Day care in America: What is needed. *Pediatrics, 91* (Suppl.), 175–178.

Section III

❖

Ecological Perspectives on Infant and Toddler Care

❖

9

The Cultural Context
of Infant and Toddler Care

◆❖◆

Judith K. Bernhard
and Janet Gonzalez-Mena

The determination of appropriate caregiving practices is central to the consideration of quality out-of-home care for infants and toddlers. A growing body of literature documents the diverse practices that exist in infant and toddler caregiving. For example, Caudill and Frost (1974) found that by 3–4 months of age, there were differences in behavior between infants growing up in Japanese and American homes. In the area of sleep study, a number of researchers working in diverse areas such as Kenya (Super & Harkness, 1986), Mexico and Central America (Morelli, Rogoff, Oppenheim, & Goldsmith, 1992) Japan (Shwalb, Shwalb, & Shoji, 1996; Wolf, Lozoff, Latz, & Paludetto, 1996) and Italy (New, 1992) have contributed to an understanding of how sleeping arrangements result in fundamental shifts in the child's physical and social development. Similarly diverse practices have been noted in areas such as feeding (e.g., Gonzalez-Mena, 1992, 1995, 1997a; Phillips & Cooper, 1992) and maternal attention patterns (Bateson, 1994; Fajardo & Freedman, 1981; Field & Widmayer, 1981).

Research on cultural differences comes from a number of different bodies of literature including psychology, anthropology, pediatrics, ethno-pediatrics, and sociology. It is difficult to focus on culture alone because culture, biology, race, class, ethnicity, and adult educational level are related and are all part of the context in which development, and therefore the caregiving intended to support it, takes place. Some of the literature focuses directly on caregiving practices, such as anthropologist Meredith Small's (1998) study of the role of biological and cultural influences on parenting. Other studies focus on milestones and guidelines demonstrating how race, class, ethnicity, and educational level define the context of *normal* (Block & Popkewitz, 1998; Cole & Holland, 1994; Garcia Coll et al., 1996; Spencer, 1990; Young, 1974). Furthermore, within a given culture, social class origins play an important part in shaping families' value systems, which relate to the probability of future academic success for the infants and toddlers raised in those families (e.g., Laosa, 1978, 1980). There has been an ongoing debate regarding which factor is the primary determinant in explaining child outcomes. It is not our intention to attempt a settlement of the varying viewpoints. We will not attempt to link child outcomes with specific caregiving practices. Instead, we will concentrate on culture as one of the primary factors that affects caregiving practices, but we recognize that it is not the only one.

The purpose of this chapter is to highlight the key role of culture in the process of arriving at optimal practices. One's view of development is intimately connected with practice, and for trained caregivers, practice has been codified in textbooks and manuals that are generally based on a normative view of developmental appropriateness (Bernhard, 1995; Block & Popkewitz, 1998; Dahlberg, Moss, & Pence, 1999; McLoyd & Randolph, 1985; Sleeter & Grant, 1987; Walkerdine, 1984; Walsh, 1989). Both development and recommended practices for encouraging it are often described as universals in these books and in training programs. Our aim is to encourage those in the field of early childhood education to rethink their assumptions about what is appropriate care for infants and toddlers.

After the introductory definition and demographic sections, there is a brief literature review, in which a theoretical groundwork is set out. This chapter focuses its examples of cultural contextual approach on the particular issue of interdependence–independence. That issue has sufficient scope to provide serious discussions of a number of issues in infant/toddler care and to represent possible recurrent conflicting values and perceptions among caregivers and families. Caregivers working with infants and toddlers are often directly faced with issues of interdependence–independence in respect to caregiving practices, for instance, in communication with families, in children's treatment of one another, and in children's cooperation with caregivers' efforts to foster contextually appropriate skill development (Gonzalez-Mena, 1997a; Kim & Choi, 1996; Rogoff, 1990; Rothstein-Fisch, 1998).

DEFINITION OF KEY CONSTRUCTS

It is at this point appropriate to define the basic terms used in this chapter.

Culture

In the 1980s and 1990s, numerous books and articles have been written on the controversies that exist in attempting to arrive at a common definition for culture. One major controversy is the issue of how detailed the definition needs to be and whether it should be objective or subjective (Baunard & Spencer, 1996). Some writers have taken an integrative view of culture and see it as a process rather than as a collection of things (Cole, 1996). As noted by Hutchings,

> The things that appear on list-like definitions of culture are residua of the process. Culture is an adaptive process that accumulates the partial solutions to frequently encountered problems.... Culture is a human cognitive process that takes place both inside and outside the minds of people. It is the process in which our everyday cultural practices are enacted. (1995, p. 354)

Our view is that cultural differences penetrate to the core and are fundamental. One cannot, for instance, understand manual dexterity—a biologically shaped ability—apart from tool use, and tools are cultural artifacts. The argument for the centrality of culture in development was eloquently made by Geertz:

> We are, in sum, incomplete or unfinished animals who complete or finish ourselves through culture—and not through culture in general but through highly particular forms of it: Dobuan and Javanese, Hopi and Italian, upper-class and lower-class. (1973, p. 49)

This use of the term follows those uses that refer to the knowledge people must have in order to function acceptably as members of an interacting group in the contexts in which they interact. That includes the knowledge base that people can articulate as well as the knowledge that lies below the level of consciousness. An important part of culture is the particular system of shared meanings. Cognitive psychologists have focused on cultural models as a way of understanding the organization of shared meaning systems: "Cultural models are presupposed, taken-for-granted models of the world that are widely shared (although not necessarily to the exclusion of other, alternative models) by the members of a society and that play an enormous role in their understanding of that world and their behavior in it" (Holland & Quinn, 1987, p. 8).

A second area of controversy regards whether it is possible to say that any intact cultures are left in the world (Barfield, 1997). Whereas some earlier definitions assumed that cultures were traditional, static, and unchanging, beginning in the 1980s writers have increasingly recognized that more than half of the world's people are multilingual and members of at least two cultures. Our notion of culture does not assume that any cultural entity is homogeneous but rather acknowledges that people belong to many competing categories often involving power and subordination. Furthermore, features of culture are constantly being modified and changed to fit the contexts of people's lives (Gallimore & Goldenberg, 1996). People also use this knowledge to adapt to and transform their worlds.

Culture is a vast subject made even more complex by the fact that, because everyone is embedded in culture, it is difficult to stand apart and explain culture outside of one's own context. Culture shapes worldview, perception of reality, indeed every facet of human life (Bernhard, 1995; Chang, 1993; Cole, 1992; Gonzalez-Mena, 1992; Hall, 1977; Kagitcibasi, 1996; Kitayama, Markus, & Matsumoto, 1995; Phillips, 1995; Whiting & Edwards, 1988). Although culture is taught, the teaching is seldom done directly through actual lessons, planned or spontaneous. Culture is not simply information transmitted to infants and toddlers. Very young children are not merely passive recipients of disembodied cultural knowledge; rather, culture is co-constructed by caregiver and child through what has been called *guided participation* (Rogoff, 1990), situated learning in peripheral participation (Lave & Wenger, 1994), and mediated learning (Berk & Winsler, 1995; Vygotsky, 1987; Wertsch, McNamee, McLane, & Budwig, 1980). It is recognized that the North American situation represents a mixture and integration of cultures. Cultures never remain static but continually change, and it often happens that what was once true no longer is. Further, we note that everyone in a particular culture is not alike. There is wide individual and sub-group variation within cultures.

In sum, we recognize that ethnicity, socioeconomic status, gender, migrant status, and culture are highly confounded and stress that, in this chapter, our focus is on the ethno-cultural aspects of infant and toddler caregiving. It is beyond the scope of this chapter to discuss the culture of child care or the culture of different socioeconomic groups.

Ethnicity

Another ongoing area of debate relates to the difference between ethnicity and culture. These terms were originally used as a substitute for older terms such as *tribe* and *race*. In the broadest sense, the terms *ethnic groups* and *ethnicity* have been used in anthropology to refer to any group of people who have common histories and share the same culture and, especially, the same language (Barfield, 1997). Our use of the term *eth-*

nicity corresponds to a narrower definition, referring to a sub-group of people within a nation who are identified as having certain characteristics and a self-identify as being part of the group.

The way an ethnic group interacts within a nation is structured according to various patterns of dominance (e.g., ethnicity, class, race). Beginning in the 1960s, some anthropologists have focused on how modern states or movements attempting to capture state power have constructed dominant narratives about those who are assumed to form the national community. Migrants with different narratives are often ignored or marginalized. Even those who are not immigrants are defined as outsiders (e.g., indigenous peoples in North America). Depending on the context and institutional responses, an ethnic group can be part of the dominant narrative, diffuse itself and try to assimilate to the mainstream, or continually occupy a subordinate position in society.

Context

Any given situation is located in a particular setting or environment and so must be understood relationally (Bruner, 1990; Cole, 1996). The notion of *context* as something that surrounds the practice in focus has been applied by numerous theorists (e.g., Baltes, 1987; Bronfenbrenner, 1979; Cole, Griffin, & LCHC, 1987; Lerner, 1988, 1991). *Context*, then, is proposed as a useful abstraction for discussion of the larger environment in which people are embedded. Contexts, furthermore, are nested: A person's context is his or her family; the family's context is the community. What is called *context* is to some extent arbitrary, and, in any case, it is important to conceive of boundaries as permeable. We are taking a contextual developmental view that culture, or any other aspect of context, cannot be regarded as merely a variable to consider as an influence on development; rather, the two, development and context, come as a package. The contextual background of infants and toddlers who enroll in child care includes their family, which in turn is embedded in an even larger context with dimensions of race, class, language, and gender (Harkness & Super, 1996; Koch, 1985; McAdoo, 1993; Sameroff & Fiese, 1990; Sue & Sue, 1990). The family is located in a particular time and place with a particular history, which is in turn influenced by the larger social context (Bronfenbrenner, 1979; Cole, 1985, 1992; Lerner, 1988, 1991).

Context and Subordination   For some groups in North America, the mainstream culture may be conceived as neutral or friendly. These groups may be described as fitting more easily into a mosaic of cultures or melting pot. In many cases, however, a person, regardless of whether she or he is a newcomer, is constructed by the mainstream as being part of a group that historically has been in a subordinate position. Thus an Aboriginal person faces a much less friendly context than a

Swedish or Finnish person; black immigrants from African or Caribbean countries are likely to experience some of the institutional discrimination to which African Americans have been historically subjected.

A number of social theorists have proposed that the structure of U.S. and Canadian societies cannot be understood without taking into account subordination of particular cultural and racial groups by the majority culture (Giroux, 1983; Miles, 1989; Ng, 1993). Here, *subordination* is intended to refer to all means by which groups become *socially disadvantaged* through the operation of institutional processes. The term does not necessarily denote the presence of discriminatory or biased personal attitudes in those of the dominant groups. We are not simply speaking of cases in which those of a dominant group often say (or think) "those people in group X are inferior." Where various cultures live together, one should inquire instead whether there is a dominant group whose definitions of appropriateness are taken for granted by all (Bourdieu, 1977, 1986; Cannella, 1997; Corson, 1998; Foucault, 1972; Giroux, 1983; Smith, 1990). Associated with the dimension of dominance and subordination is the dimension of relative wealth and relative poverty, which is why social class plays an important role.

No child or family is culture-free even though some in the dominant culture see themselves as normal or standard and consider that only other people have culture (Darder, 1991; Delpit, 1988; Derman-Sparks & the ABC Task Force, 1989; Miles, 1989).

DEMOGRAPHICS

The United States and Canada have always been multicultural and multilingual (Takaki, 1993), but now there is a new and rapid increase of immigrants from countries outside of Europe (Grant, 1995).

The United States

Between 1960 and 1990, according to the 1995 census, 11.5 million people immigrated to the United States (U.S. Department of Health and Human Services, 1996). The immigrants are no longer predominately single men as in the historical waves of migration around the turn of the century. They are families with children. The percentage of foreign-born children in the United States is steadily increasing. Ethnic minorities now make up almost one third of the younger population (U.S. Department of Health and Human Services, 1996). If trends continue, there will no longer be a dominant racial group in the United States, a phenomenon that has already occurred in groups of children younger than 5 in California and also in some urban centers across the country (Chang, Muckelroy, & Pulido-Tobiassen, 1996). Changing demographics have profoundly affected child care centers. In 435 randomly surveyed California centers, 96% cared for children from more than one racial group and 80% from more than one language group (Chang, 1993).

Canada

Since the 1970s, Canada, a nation of approximately 30 million people, has witnessed significant changes in the ethnocultural characteristics of its population. In 1991, 1.9 million visible minority adults in Canada represented 9% of the population 15 years and older, a doubling of the 1981 proportion; 78% of these adults were immigrants. The diversity in the Canadian population is illustrated in the variety of languages represented. According to Statistics Canada (Citizenship and Immigration Canada, 1995), 32% of the total population of 27 million people report a home language other than English or French. Partly responsible for these changes is the ongoing immigration rate that now proceeds at about 225,000 immigrants and refugees per year (Statistics Canada, 1999). These annual figures, typical of the 1990s, include about 28,000 children who are younger than 10 years of age (Citizenship & Immigration Canada, 1993, 1994, 1995).

Implications of Changing Demographics

Under present global migration patterns, the racial, cultural, and linguistic diversity of the North American population is expected to continue to increase. Children from all continents form substantial minorities in child care populations in the United States and Canada. In some cases, the various groups constitute a majority of children in early childhood education (ECE) centers. Yet, there is often a lack of match among the cultural, linguistic, and racial backgrounds of caregivers and children in both the United States and Canada (Bernhard, Lefebvre, Chud, & Lange, 1995, 1996; Chang, 1993). Hence, ECE centers face a variety of challenges and are called on to respond in new ways.

Because of the rapid growth in the number of infant programs, it is important to think about what may happen to an infant in unfamiliar cultural settings that offer child care. Infants are just beginning to learn their own culture and to incorporate all those unwritten rules and shared meaning systems. Consider what happens when infants not of the dominant culture find themselves spending days with people not of their home culture. The challenge for the field is to figure out how to ensure that they remain firmly rooted in their own culture, continue to develop in their home language, and stay connected with their family. Furthermore, eventually the child must become a member of both cultures, not as a marginalized person, but as a fully bicultural one. A number of complex factors are at play, including unspoken messages by the members of the dominant culture and the stereotypes in the media about the worth of nondominant cultures to society. If children absorb negative images about their home culture, they may take in a negative view of themselves, especially if they are also poor. Some turn their backs on their home culture. This subtractive effect often results in the rejection of aspects of themselves and their families. Richard Rodriguez's (1981) auto-biography *Hunger of Memory* shows how the subtractive effect can work.

WHAT IS APPROPRIATE CARE?

To address the topic of appropriate care, a number of issues involving culture and development must first be considered.

Relation Between Culture and Development

It is important to think of culture and development together. Culture defines what constitutes development, what behavior is appropriate, and suitable ways of living (Aptekar, 1990; Cole, 1985; Harkness, 1980; Heath, 1982; Kagitcibasi, 1996; Kessen, 1979; Lerner, 1991; Sameroff & Fiese, 1990; Shweder & Sullivan, 1993; Sinha, 1988). That is, it is not only descriptive but also prescriptive. The relation between culture and development summarized here has been extensively documented (Greenfield & Cocking, 1994; Harkness, 1980; Kagitcibasi, 1996; LeVine, 1980; Minick, Stone, & Forman, 1993; Misra & Gergen, 1993) and argued (Bernhard, 1995; Gonzalez-Mena, 1997a; McLoyd, 1990; Walkerdine, 1984, 1990).

Development, as defined in a given culture, includes the skills val-ued in that culture. Cultural priorities may differ widely, from reading and academic pursuits, to artistic and practical skills such as weaving, to spiritual exercises such as worship or healing, to the social skills involved in managing people. The culture's values shape what matters for the individuals within it. If individual achievement is stressed more than interpersonal harmony, the usual developmental pathway is more likely to emphasize the former (Misra & Gergen, 1993; Rogoff, Mosier, Mistry, & Goncü, 1993; Sagi, van IJzendoorn, & Koren-Karie, 1991). Sim-ilar differences exist in discourse norms such as structuring of attention and regulation of talk and turn taking (Corson, 1998; Crago, 1992; Oakes, 1988). The idea of the dominant culture as normal is an often unac-knowledged problem that results in specific cultural information being mistaken as universal.

To discuss infant/toddler care, one must acknowledge the cultural context in which it is embedded and recognize the contextual nature of every aspect of care and education. Nothing that happens in a young child's day is separate from cultural context. The way an infant is cared for is a major factor in ongoing socialization and future adult personal-ity. Who the baby is (self-identity), how she or he relates to others, and even the course of development itself are all influenced by the early months and years. Caregivers should be sensitive to cultural differences and aware of the possible effects of cross-cultural versus culturally consistent caregiving, especially for infants who are not part of the dominant culture (Bernhard & Freire, 1995; Chang & Pulido, 1994; Gonzalez-Mena, 1992; Lally, 1996; Mistry, 1995; Williams, 1994).

FIRST- AND SECOND-LANGUAGE CONSIDERATIONS

Language loss can be illustrative of cultural loss. In a large-scale study of 1,000 families across the United States, Wong Fillmore and her colleagues (1991a, 1991b) investigated the experiences of 3- and 4-year-old children who spoke English as a second language. The findings indicate that children who attended English-only early childhood programs used English increasingly at home even when their families did not speak English. Nearly two thirds of the children (64.4%) no longer used the family language at home, and many lost their first language altogether. This was in contrast to their older siblings who were firmly established in their own language when they first encountered an English-only institution. The authors concluded that the younger the child is at the time of initial exposure to a child care center where only English is spoken, the greater the probability of losing the family language. Further, this work has documented the long-term devastating effects on families that resulted from parents and children lacking a common language for deep-level communication.

Whereas studies of mismatch and poor outcomes have rarely focused on infants and toddlers, the data on children ages 3–15 suggest the possibility that the problem is worth considering from infancy. Given the institutionalization of infant care, it seems plausible that this is part of a larger problem beginning in infancy, with the first contact with English-immersion child care. The negative effects for children ages 3–15 and their families are richly documented (Fine, 1990; Kozol, 1991; McLoyd, 1990; Mehan, 1997).

Accepted practices of the field may put some infants and toddlers who are not of the dominant culture at risk for losing their home language and culture and thus work against pluralistic integration (Wong Fillmore, 1997). Furthermore, there is evidence that children who maintain their home language past the early childhood years benefit cognitively and socially (Cummins, 1991, 1996; Cummins & Corson, 1997; Dolson, 1985; Gunnar, 1996; Hagman & Lahdenpera, 1988; Minami & Ovando, 1995; Shore, 1997). Although honoring the mother culture is emphasized, the goal is a bicultural citizen (Au, 1980; Darder, 1991; Pease-Alvarez & Hakuta, 1993).

The Role of Consistency in Caregiving Practices

Problems can occur as the families' values and priorities conflict with the policies and practices of the program (Bernhard & Freire, 1995; Gonzalez-Mena, 1997a; LeVine et al., 1994; O'Loughlin, 1992). Certain institutional practices result in negative outcomes in situations involving poor segments of the population (Corson, 1993; Delpit, 1988; Fine, 1990; Giroux, 1983; Portes & Bernhard, 1996; Smith, 1993). Under those circumstances, the culture that children of the nondominant culture learn in child care is not consistent with that at home, and adults involved are not sufficiently aware of the possible culture clash and its implications (Gonzalez-Mena, 1997a; LaGrange, Clark, & Munroe, 1994).

INTERDEPENDENCE AND INDEPENDENCE

This section focuses on two major themes to illustrate areas in which cultural differences sometimes surface; differences that manifest themselves in the day-to-day care of infants and toddlers. Although independence has generally been a cultural priority of the dominant culture, sometimes priorities cross cultural boundaries. Some members of the dominant culture emphasize interdependence more than independence, and conversely people who are not of the dominant culture sometimes stress independence. We are not claiming that one is the exclusive goal of any particular culture. What we want to examine is how the strong emphasis on independence built into the structure of most early childhood programs sometimes lies in opposition to the goals of parents not of the dominant culture.

Infants and toddlers are faced with the beginnings of many major and ongoing tasks of childhood, two of which are becoming independent individuals and establishing connections with others. The parents' job is to help their children with both these tasks, but most parents, either consciously or unconsciously, give higher priority to one than the other. Their choice depends on their goals, which often reflect the cultural context (Kitayama et al., 1995).

Independence as a goal is based on the idea that infants are born dependent and must be helped gradually toward being independent individuals who stand on their own two feet and will someday leave home and make a life for themselves. Many of the practices of parents and caregivers relate to this goal, for example, encouraging self-feeding and other self-help skills. Encouraging curiosity, initiative, and motoric exploration are other examples of how adults help children toward the goal of eventual independence.

The focus on the benefits of independence has led to a situation in which many educators assume this is the goal for all families. From this perspective they may erroneously label certain children as being excessively dependent or immature. Educators may not be aware that the children may simply be more closely tied to their families than is prescribed by mainstream American culture due to their family's emphasis on interdependence instead of independence. Starting at birth, some families see developing sparks of independence as a threat to family ties. They may be less interested in self-help skills than in maintaining closeness. They may teach their children to put others before self, to willingly accept help, and to put respect for elders and group harmony before assertiveness and self-expression. Interdependence goals sometimes are in direct conflict to independence goals and this has implications for what is considered to be appropriate caregiving. Both goals take a different form in early life than in later life and, both can, and usually do, result in functional individuals who are independent yet interconnected, though the quality of the independence and the interconnections may be different depending on the family's priorities.

Parents' decisions about whether to encourage independence in their children may be made not primarily because of a cultural value but rather as a response to oppression. Some African American parents decide to try to prepare their children for the harsh realities of racism by stressing interdependence so their children have the group to support them. The group provides not only support but also validation of a reality that is more benign than one they find outside the group. Other African American parents may go the opposite direction and stress independence in order to make a sturdy, self-reliant individual that can stand up to the negative effects of oppression (I. Shareef, personal communication, June 16, 1997).

The idea of interdependence may bring to some people's minds the old cliché, "tied to mother's apron strings." As Edward Hall noted, this is a culturally relevant judgment:

> The world is divided into those cultures who cut the apron strings and those who do not.... In many cultures, the bonds with the parents, grandparents and even ancestors are not severed but are maintained and reinforced. I'm thinking of China, Japan, the traditional Jewish family of central Europe, the Arab villagers, the Spanish of North and South America, and the Pueblo Indians of New Mexico, to mention only a few. (1977, p. 226)

Strong parent–child ties are seen as permanent and immutable in a number of cultures (for work in China, see Hsu, 1981). We stress again that all of the people in the cultures mentioned are not alike. Individual, familial, generational, and intergroup differences are part of most cultural groups. Furthermore, we note that culture is dynamic and changing, especially when one culture comes in contact with another.

Parents who do cut the apron strings often see their job as promoting their children's ever-increasing autonomy. The goal is to help each child stand on his or her own feet and be self-reliant. Given the push for independence, there is the danger of dependence being labeled as dysfunctional. That is the opposite view of parents who see independence as dysfunctional, as something to be avoided or restrained. If the aim is to keep the family and all its members together for a lifetime, independence must be downplayed.

Both goals, independence and interdependence, make sense, and which is emphasized is determined by the context. But the interdependence goal is rarely talked about by many U.S. early childhood educators. Many who teach about childrearing assume that every family values independence as much as they do.

Most children, no matter how they were raised, do grow up to become both independent individuals and people who create and maintain relationships. There is no culture in the world in which adults cannot feed themselves, regardless of how long they were spoon-fed as children. There is no culture in which people are so separate from each other that all the members decline cooperation. Children, when they become adults, accomplish both the major tasks even if their parents focused mainly on one.

The following examples are based on research and meant to illustrate the extent of cultural variation that can play out through the themes of independence and interdependence.

Example 1: Sleeping

In North America, the length the child sleeps is often used as a sign of maturity. Mothers want their infants to sleep throughout the night as soon as possible. Super and Harkness (1986) conducted research on the sleep/wake patterns of Kipsigis babies in Kenya and found wide variations from Western norms. During the day, the Kipsigis babies are often carried on their mothers' backs and sleep when they can. At night, they sleep with their mothers and can nurse whenever they wake up. There are many periods of sleep sprinkled throughout day and night, and even as adults, Kipsigis are more flexible than Americans in their sleeping patterns.

Hale-Benson (1986) reported similar flexible sleeping patterns among some African American families in which a baby who is constantly with mother or caregiver may sleep and eat in a rhythmic pattern day and night with frequent repetition of each activity. This is in contrast to the expectation that the baby will be awake during the day except for naps and sleep for long periods at night. The point is that these are not just variations from a norm but are equally valid approaches to caregiving (Bhavnagri & Gonzalez-Mena, 1997; Gonzalez-Mena, 1997a; Rogoff, 1990).

Example 2: Self-Control

Indirect teaching provides a set of unwritten and unspoken rules babies learn. Bateson (1994) provided the following example from observations of two mothers and their 10-month-old daughters. One mother was European American and the other Iranian American. The setting was a college classroom in Iran; the students sat in chairs in a circle around the mother–daughter pair in the center. The European American mother brought toys and put the baby down on a small rug near the toys. She sat on a chair looking down at her daughter. The baby explored the toys, then, enticed by all the students sitting out there watching, scooted off the rug, crawling on her belly out to explore. The students attracted the baby's attention by making noises and dangling keys and other things they had with them. The mother let the baby go. She also let her have what the students offered. This child was learning to be an independent individual who could make choices.

The Iranian American mother–daughter pair provided quite a contrast. The mother sat down on the rug with the baby, leaving the chair empty. The edges of the rug seemed to be clear boundaries to the baby and although she could crawl well, she never went off the rug. The students called out to her, trying to entice her the way they had the first baby. She stayed where she was.

Then the mother invited the baby to go play with the students, while at the same time holding her arms around her and offering her a bite of banana to stay. Bateson, an American anthropologist who has studied this Iranian culture, explained that the mother was teaching her child several important lessons. One was to stay close to her and avoid strangers. Another was about contradictions and invitations: "Iranian courtesy is full of invitations that are not meant to be accepted, but Iranians enjoy the tension this creates" (Bateson, 1994, p. 35).

At 10 months of age, both those little girls were learning important cultural lessons. If those two girls were in child care centers in which the caregivers were not aware of the variety of parental goals regarding self-control, the lessons learned would be confused. Similar confusion may arise daily in infant/toddler care across this continent as children of one culture are cared for by caregivers of another; many caregivers have not sufficiently questioned their assumptions about appropriateness.

In the United States, the issue of maternal attention to children according to socioeconomic status and ethnicity has been investigated (Field & Widmayer, 1981). Results indicate that Latino and African American mothers gave different objectives for their interactions. The Latino mothers encouraged responsivity, whereas the African Americans expressed a desire not to spoil their children with too much attention. These findings indicate that it is not possible simply to postulate universally desirable patterns of interaction apart from cultural values. (See also Fajardo and Freedman, 1981, and Chisholm, 1983, on Navajo and African American mothers.)

Example 3: Harmony and Authority

Diana Baumrind's (1971) classic research on parenting styles is an example of research often considered to have universal application. In Baumrind's research, an authoritarian parenting style was found to be predictive of poor school achievement. Chao (1994), however, pointed out that, in spite of the fact that normative psychological literature tends to portray Chinese parents as authoritarian, studies show that their children perform very well in school. They do not fit the pattern that Baumrind found. Chao looked to see if Chinese parents were indeed more controlling than a group of European American counterparts. She studied 50 Chinese immigrant mothers and 50 European American mothers using a standardized measure of parental control. The Chinese mothers scored significantly higher on authoritarian parenting style. They also were significantly higher on a scale of Chinese childrearing ideologies, which involved gentle training and gave a different meaning to parental control and authoritarian style than that held by European Americans. When compared with authoritarian European American mothers, the Chinese authoritarian mothers showed several differences, all of which related to a high level of maternal involvement and closeness. Having the child physically close to the mother, even sleeping with the mother, was part of this pattern. Chao explained that *authoritarian* has a different meaning for Chinese families. The roots of Chinese childrearing practices go back to Confucius who taught the fundamental importance of social harmony. Chinese families embrace authority because it brings harmony. Their concept of control contains the idea of training children in the appropriate expected behaviors. Their child-training literature is based on beliefs about the inherent goodness of the child and the role of the environment. European Americans have a different historical and sociocultural context and are more likely to see the need to use control to dominate the child because of a belief about weaknesses and flaws of human nature (Chao, 1994).

A related study by Lin and Fu (1990) focused on Taiwanese, Chinese, and European American parents and found that both groups of Asian parents rated higher on parental control (authority). Furthermore, they were simultaneously focusing on independence and achievement more than were the European American parents. In some of our research (Bernhard, Freire, Torres, & Nirdosh, 1998), we too have found cases in a Central American population in which very strong parental authority has been associated with high academic performance. It is worth noting, however, that the teachers we interviewed expected that such strong authority would produce opposite results, presumably based on their experience with children in other cultures. The issue of how parents are to exercise their authority so as to ensure the best outcomes for their children requires much further investigation (for discussion see Ballenger, 1992; Grieshaber, 1996; Shor, 1998).

VIEWS OF DEVELOPMENT

Since the 1970s, Kessen (1979) and others have documented the construction of the North American child and how the educational system molds children in accordance with that unitary construction. Griffith expressed a similar view of normative practice:

> The child development discourse is a historically developed conception of children's maturation. It stands as the scientific ground of knowledge about children's development and therefore the knowledge base for strategies and activities to facilitate children's maturation in many settings.... Child development, as discourse, is a set of claims about children's maturational processes, understood to be facilitated or hindered by the child's environment. It asserts that all children have their own developmental pace which is normal for them and that they proceed through sequential stages in the developmental process. Children are conceptualized as naturally spontaneous, inquiring, purposeful, requiring direction, not force, and so on. (1995, pp. 110–111)

This particular, official construction of the child, however, may not coincide with parents' views of how children are, how they are supposed to be, and what they need. Researchers throughout the world have documented that often parents and teachers have significant differences in values and expectations regarding the development of children (Bernhard, Freire, & Pacini-Ketchabaw, 1998; Okagaki & Sternberg, 1993; Robinson, Robinson, Wolins, Bronfenbrenner, & Richmond, 1973). Furthermore, a number of thinkers have written on the resulting theoretical and practical considerations (Gonzalez-Mena, 1995, 1997a, 1997b, 1998; Kagitcibasi, 1996; Sjölund, 1973; Valsiner & Litvinovic, 1996; West, Hausken, & Collins, 1993).

Cultural differences penetrate to the core and are fundamental. We propose that such an approach is most likely to contribute to a deeper understanding of human development. Yet professionals in child care have sometimes given too little attention to issues of heterogeneity and diversity. Documentation regarding caregivers' differential perceptions of individual strengths and problem areas of children's behavior was provided in a Canadian research study involving 77 randomly chosen child care centers. Two hundred caregivers were asked to characterize one randomly chosen pair of children in which one was a child of a minority race or culture and the other a child of the majority race or culture. Operationally, *minority background* was defined as the child having either a family language other than English or French or being of non-Caucasian racial background (e.g., Asian, African, Latina/Latino, Aboriginal). *Majority background* included all other children. The labels used in interviews, respectively, were *focal* and *paired* child. The two children were matched for age and sex, and the interviewer was blind to the selection process and the names of the children. Results indicated that minority children were often described as lacking assertiveness and being immature without regard to their families' cultural expectations for these children (Bernhard, Lefebvre, Kilbride, Chud, & Lange, 1998). These findings suggest that the practices of many child care professionals are consistent with the hypothesis that they believe in universal homogeneous patterns.

There is a link between the goal of routinized institutional functioning and the universalistic assumptions of child care personnel about developmental patterns. Routine pressures on teachers demand elaboration of rules of thumb and handy generalization across cultural groups. We stress the need for educators to consider pluralism in views of optimal child development and to honor equally valid ways in which children develop (Chang et al., 1996; Gonzalez-Mena, 1997a; Holloway, Rambaud, Fuller, & Eggers-Piérola, 1995).

Consider a contextual and pluralistic approach to understanding specific, common developmental challenges. Understanding the goals and skills valued in communities in which children live is essential for defining what is considered appropriate development in a particular context. It is also necessary for examining children's cognitive skills and the specific practices of guided participation used by children and their caregivers and companions (Durret, O'Bryant, & Pennebaker, 1975; Harkness & Super, 1996; Rogoff, 1990; Valsiner & Litvinovic, 1996). The rest of the chapter will set out implications for researchers, practitioners, policy makers, and teacher trainers.

IMPLICATIONS FOR RESEARCHERS

Based on the literature reviewed, we now summarize issues that need to be considered by all those seeking deeper understanding of children in situations of cultural diversity:

1. Further research is needed to document the long-term effects of early English immersion on children and families.
2. Further research is needed to document successful efforts at maintaining continuity between the practices of families and out-of-home caregivers.
3. Longitudinal studies are needed that follow children who receive home-language out-of-home care during infancy to investigate the effects on later English learning and academic proficiency.
4. Documentation is needed on the effects of programs that do make extensive efforts to seek family input and collaboration.

IMPLICATIONS FOR PRACTITIONERS

One overall recommendation is for the field to work to gain a deeper understanding of cultural issues as they play out in infant/toddler care. More specifically, there are three areas of need: increased collaboration with families and communities, increased skills and understanding of deep cultural issues, and increased numbers of bilingual/bicultural staff.

Programs should strive to increase collaboration with families and the community. Parallel with the National Association for the Education of Young Children (1995), a collaborative model for ECE should be held as an ideal for all programs. Such a model improves communication and problem solving and ensures that attempts to honor diversity go beyond words and become realized in practice. The model offers one way for parents to become valued partners in children's care and education. Through collaboration, it is also easier for both stakeholders to remain conscious of the fact that they both care deeply about the children, and all are acting for the best as they see it. Structural and institutional changes are required to actively find ways to give parents control and to find opportunities to work together in order to support parental goals for children.

Practitioners need to increase their skills in understanding and responding to deep cultural issues as they play out in day-to-day practice. Practitioners need to increase their knowledge of diverse patterns, values, goals, and practices. They must seek insights into their own unarticulated cultural practices and try to gain a genuine understanding of each child's developmental context as well. Caregivers will profit by having multiple viewpoints. They can gain those by moving away from an "expert model." Caregivers can be more responsive to differences when they see themselves as both holders of knowledge and also as learners. Only then can they take a serious look at how practices may need to change to be more responsive to differences. We are not saying that practices always need to change, but sometimes change is best for the child, family, and program.

Not only should caregivers become familiar with variations in goals and practices, but they would profit from training in how to handle the person-to-person conflicts around specific issues of infant care practices that arise when goals, values, beliefs, and practices clash. Creating a dialogue instead of a lecture, lesson, or argument is the first step to managing cultural differences. A key component of establishing a collaborative relationship with families is developing an understanding of families' cultures and concerns and of obtaining practical experience in working with parents.

Programs should recruit and hire more bilingual/bicultural staff when appropriate. In order to improve appreciation of different practices and values, as well as to facilitate parent–caregiver collaboration, most centers can benefit from the presence of bilingual and bicultural teachers. More specifically, however, the children's family languages will likely be more safeguarded in centers in which, for as many children as possible, at least one teacher or staff person matches the child's linguistic background. Centers would do well to recruit qualified staff accordingly. Such recruited staff would be in a position to support children's developing competence as members of their own community.

Although active measures to maintain home language are advocated here, it is true that newcomer parents themselves are divided on the issue. Some, seeing optimal outcomes for their children through assimilation into the mainstream, simply want their children to learn English as quickly as possible. Others recognize the home language may be better for their children's deeper thoughts. According to the bilingual/bicultural position adopted here, this is a chicken-and-egg situation. It is argued that, if parents from language groups other than English believe the children can succeed being bilingual and bicultural, they would be less likely to seek (in their view) to disencumber the children of the home language.

Although a strong presence of home language in out-of-home care is stressed, the goal is still bilingualism/biculturalism. Ideally, children at risk of losing their language and culture because of subordination factors should be bathed in their own language and culture as infants and toddlers. Cultural consistency is important. When caregivers are of a different culture, they must become competent in culturally responsive care, that is, understanding the parents' goals, values, beliefs, and practices in order to provide at least a measure of cultural consistency.

Practitioners, in addition to informing themselves about the benefits of home language and culture retention, must take steps to convey to parents that their languages and cultures are valuable constituents of the social mosaic. Where minority cultures are devalued or ignored by the mainstream, many people of these cultures will seek to eliminate all marks of difference. Yet, as the society becomes more tolerant of diversity, the formation of bicultural citizens will be appreciated. Our position here is consistent with the concept of additive bilingualism (Cummins, 1996) endorsed by NAEYC:

> The development of children's home language does not interfere with their ability to learn English. Because knowing more than one language is a cognitive asset... early education programs should encourage the development of children's home language while fostering the acquisition of English. (1995, p. 5)

IMPLICATIONS FOR PERSONNEL PREPARATION

1. All preparation, preservice and in-service, should seriously consider the impact of culture. Also to be considered is information on how socioeconomic status, race, and educational level define the context in which normal milestones and guidelines apply.
2. Preparation should include information on cultural differences within North America, as well as those that relate to immigrants from other countries, taking demographic shifts into account so that the information is relevant or potentially relevant.
3. Personnel preparation should include making students/trainees aware of the effects of cross-cultural infant/toddler care especially for children not of the dominant culture. Those responsible for the training of caregivers may have to become more adequately prepared to support students when working in diverse situations.

4. An anti-bias approach should be taken so that caregivers learn to be culturally sensitive, self-reflective, and responsive to diverse patterns of interactions. In particular, caregivers should acquire skills in interacting equitably and respectfully in all areas of diversity, including race, ethnicity, class, language, gender, ability, and sexual orientation.

5. It is not enough to just talk about diversity, but students need to be in contact with people who are different from themselves. In some situations, that comes about naturally. In others, it must be built into personnel preparation. For example, practicum supervisors can arrange for exposure to diverse practices and values for practicum students who need that exposure.

A reason for exposing students to families of diverse backgrounds can be stated in terms of the work of Moll and Greenberg (1990); student-trainees are encouraged to see the "funds of knowledge" in children's households. Each household requires and assembles such knowledge in order to ensure its survival. The desirability of caregivers visiting children's households is not only a matter of observation but also of learning. The caregiver does not simply transmit knowledge but needs to gain something from the household and culture. The idea of learning from households could be an essential component of the practicum experience. Until students learn to look at the child in a family context, rather than studying children in general or as unique individuals, they do not have the whole picture (Corson, Bernhard, & Gonzalez-Mena, 1998). It is also important to consider how well prepared and supported students are when undertaking these field experiences. In order to avoid reinforcing stereotypes and prejudices, it is essential to devote significant resources to preparing, supervising, and debriefing students' experiences. These conditions of learning are crucial to avoid negative consequences.

We want to highlight two programs as examples of how to take diversity into account in personnel preparation. The first is the Program for Infant/Toddler Caregivers, which is collaboratively operated by WestEd's Center for Child and Family Studies and the California Department of Education. This training program considers being responsive to cultural issues as essential in the care of the very young. Their training of trainers, which started in 1990, now includes an emphasis on cultural perspectives in all four modules, covering topics such as early learning and cognitive development, group care environments, and caregiving routines. Large numbers of participants, many coming from culturally diverse backgrounds, have completed the requirements to become certified trainers of the program. The effectiveness of this approach was demonstrated in a recent evaluation of family child care providers trained by program-certified trainers. Using the *Family Day Care Rating Scale* (Harms & Clifford, 1989), the evaluators found that program-trained child care providers were rated an average of 5.93, with 89% of the caregivers in the good range or better (Brown, 1997). This result differs dramatically from the average rating of 3.39 found in a large-scale study of family child care and relative care in California, North Carolina, and Texas, in which only 9% of the caregivers fell in the good range or better (Galinsky, Howes, Kontos, & Shin, 1994).

The second example comes from Wisconsin. As a way of ensuring that every student has experiences with people from diverse backgrounds, the Wisconsin teacher education programs have the following Human Relations Code Point requirement (Grant, 1993). Every teacher candidate must complete eight Human Relations Code Points before receiving a teaching license. Code Point 5 describes the field experience required:

> A minimum of 50 documented hours of direct involvement with adult and pupil members of a group whose background the student does not share. (University of Wisconsin–Madison, 1990, p. 3)

This unusually broad-based practice experience was of some value, but one researcher found that graduates of these training programs had difficulty implementing such multicultural content in their classrooms (Sleeter, 1989). It is not sufficient to simply put people together. Something more has to happen. Training must include reflection on cross-cultural experiences and discussion on the implications for practice. We need to find ways to ensure every student has extended experience with diverse groups as well as assistance in understanding and using those experiences.

IMPLICATIONS FOR POLICY

The field of infant/toddler care needs continued recognition and support from government at all levels. Historically, child care has been on the bottom of the list of social priorities. The health of children and their long-term functioning as productive members of society is at stake. Child care has been low on the educational ladder in status and funding, yet recent research shows that the first year may be the most important of all for brain development, and the 2 years following also have an impact on later cognitive functioning, as well as later school success. Affordable, high-quality infant/toddler care should be made available to everyone who needs it. Furthermore, parents should have a wide range of choices so that, if they so desire, they can put their children in programs that are culturally specific. In this way infants and toddlers can be steeped in their own language and culture. There should also be programs available for parents who want to expose their children to cultures beyond their own.

Social policy must affirm the values of diversity and biculturalism. These values are supported and enhanced when there is close collaboration with families and community. Programs, licensing agencies, and other regulating bodies must examine their policies, standards, and practices with the goal of increased collaboration with the people being served and the communities to which they belong. At issue are not just individual interactions between caregivers and parents, but also institutional changes. It is important to not only write policies that increase collaboration but to examine existing ones for barriers that get in the way of a collaborative approach to early care and education for infants and toddlers. A focus on involvement of parents and communities in the education of the youngest members of society would support a collaborative model for education and care of all children. Policies regarding parental rights would support the collaborative model allowing parents individually and as a group to have more input in the education and care of their children. Parents who feel respected and empowered are more likely to take a long-term view of goals for their children. Also they are more likely to ask for what they want than make decisions based solely on survival issues.

Monocultural/English-only programs for some parents represent survival in a society that puts a low priority on bilingualism/biculturalism. More training dollars are vital if practitioners are to become knowledgeable, sensitive, responsive, and skilled in cultural issues. Too many people think that anybody can take care of infants and toddlers, especially if they have had children of their own. The beginning of a child's life is too important a time to leave children in the hands of the untrained and hope the caregivers will do a good job. The training must include multiple perspectives on appropriate practice.

CONCLUSION

Culture, the subject of this chapter, is not simply one of many issues to be examined when discussing infant/toddler care. Culture is not a separate issue, but the context in which all issues related to infant/toddler care are embedded. Without taking cultural context into consideration, there can be no deep or informed discussion of the central issues.

Our purpose here has been to highlight the contextual nature of every aspect of care and education of infants and toddlers and look at the key role that cultural context plays when considering optimal practices. Our goal has been not to merely broaden horizons into anthropology but to bring many cultures from the margins into the mainstream, forming a unified whole. We do not mean unity to imply uniformity, but rather diversity. We envision a pluralistic integration in which cultures relate closely to each other, but their members retain their unique flavor and identity. The key to a pluralistic model is that no single culture dominates another. The pluralism we hope for, and the formation of future bicultural citizens, must begin with research-based, strong pro-diversity policies based on parental input and collaboration and diverse, well trained, and sensitive early childhood professionals.

REFERENCES

Aptekar, L. (1990). How ethnic differences within a culture influence child rearing: The case of Colombian street children. *Journal of Comparative Family Studies, 2*, 67–79.

Au, K.H. (1980). Participation structures in a reading lesson with Hawaiian children: Analysis of a culturally appropriate instructional event. *Anthropology and Education Quarterly, 11*(2), 91–95.

Ballenger, C. (1992). Because you like us: The language of control. *Harvard Educational Review, 62*(2), 199–208.

Baltes, P.B. (1987). Theoretical propositions of life-span developmental psychology: On the dynamics between growth and decline. *Developmental Psychology, 23*(5), 611–626.

Barfield, T. (Ed.). (1997). Cultural pluralism. In *Dictionary of Anthropology* (pp. 100–101). Oxford, England: Blackwell Scientific Publications.

Bateson, M.C. (1994). *Peripheral visions.* New York: HarperCollins.

Baumrind, D. (1971). Current patterns of parental authority. *Developmental Psychology Monographs, 4*(1), 2.

Baunard, A., & Spencer, J. (Eds.). (1996). *Encyclopedia of cultural anthropology.* London: Routledge.

Berk, L., & Winsler, A. (1995). *Scaffolding children's learning: Vygotsky and early childhood education* (Vol. 7 of the NAEYC Research into Practice Series). Washington, DC: National Association for the Education of Young Children.

Bernhard, J.K. (1995). The changing field of child development: Cultural diversity and the professional training of early childhood educators. *Canadian Journal of Education, 20*(4), 415–436.

Bernhard, J.K., & Freire, M. (1995). Latino refugee children in child care: A study of parents and caregivers. *Canadian Journal of Research in Early Childhood Education, 5*(1), 59–71.

Bernhard, J.K., Freire, M., & Pacini-Ketchabaw, V. (1998). A Latin American parents' group participates in their children's schooling: Parent involvement reconsidered. *Canadian Ethnic Studies Journal, 30*(3), 77–98.

Bernhard, J.K., Freire, M., Torres, F., & Nirdosh, S. (1998). Latin Americans in a Canadian primary school: Perspectives of parents, teachers, and children on cultural identity and academic achievement. *Journal of Regional Studies, 19*(3), 217–236.

Bernhard, J.K., Lefebvre, M.L., Chud, G., & Lange, R. (1996). Linguistic match between children and caregivers in Canadian early childhood education. *Canadian Journal of Research in Early Childhood Education, 5*(2), 5–18.

Bernhard, J.K., Lefebvre, M.L., Chud, G., & Lange, R. (1995). *Paths to equity: Cultural, linguistic, and racial diversity in Canadian early childhood education.* Toronto, Ontario, Canada: York Lanes Press.

Bernhard, J.K., Lefebvre, M.L., Kilbride, K., Chud, G., & Lange, R. (1998). Troubled relationships in early childhood education: Parent–teacher interactions in ethno-culturally diverse settings. *Early Education and Development, 9*(1), 5–28.

Bhavnagri, N., & Gonzalez-Mena, J. (1997). The cultural context of infant caregiving. *Childhood Education, 74*(1), 2–8.

Block, M., & Popkewitz, T. (1998, January). *Child development, knowledge/power, truth and certainty in early childhood education.* Paper presented at the Reconceptualizing Early Childhood Education conference, Honolulu, HI.

Bourdieu, P. (1977). *Outline of a theory of practice.* New York: Cambridge University Press.

Bourdieu, P. (1986). The forms of capital. In J.C. Richardson (Ed.), *Handbook of theory and research in the sociology of education* (pp. 241–257). New York: Greenwood Press.

Bronfenbrenner, U. (1979). *The ecology of human development: Experiments by nature and design.* Cambridge, MA: Harvard University Press.

Brown, A. (1997). Child care initiative project. *Bridges, 3*(1), 19–21.

Bruner, J. (1990). *Acts of meaning.* Cambridge, MA: Harvard University Press.

Cannella, G. (1997). *Deconstructing early childhood education.* New York: Peter Lang Publishing Co.

Caudill, W., & Frost, L. (1974). A comparison of maternal care and infant behavior in Japanese-American, American, and Japanese families. In W.P. Lebra (Ed.), *Mental health research in Asia and the Pacific: Youth socialization and mental health* (Vol. 3). Honolulu: University Press of Hawaii.

Chang, H.N. (1993). *Affirming children's roots: Cultural and linguistic diversity in early care and education.* San Francisco: California Tomorrow.

Chang, H.N., Muckelroy, A., & Pulido-Tobiassen, D. (1996). *Looking in, looking out: Redefining child care and early education in a diverse society.* San Francisco: California Tomorrow.

Chang, H.N., & Pulido, D. (1994). The critical importance of cultural and linguistic continuity for infants and toddlers. *ZERO TO THREE Bulletin, 15*(2), 13–17.

Chao, R. (1994). Beyond parental control and authoritarian parenting style: Understanding Chinese parenting through the cultural notion of training. *Child Development, 65,* 1111–1119.

Chisholm, J.S. (1983). *Navajo infancy.* Albuquerque: University of New Mexico Press.

Citizenship and Immigration Canada (1993). *Immigration statistics (Table IM3).* Toronto, Ontario: Supply and Services Canada.

Citizenship and Immigration Canada. (1994). *A broader vision: Immigration and citizenship plan 1995–2000.* Toronto, Ontario: Supply and Services Canada.

Citizenship and Immigration Canada (1995). Immigrants to Canada: Preliminary statistics for 1993. In *Statistics Quarterly Update.* Toronto, Ontario: Supply and Services Canada.

Cole, M. (1985). The zone of proximal development: Where culture and cognition create each other. In J.V. Wertsch (Ed.), *Culture, communication, and cognition: Vygotskian perspectives* (pp. 146–161). New York: Cambridge University.

Cole, M. (1992). Context, modularity, and the cultural constitution of development. In L.T. Winegar & J. Valsiner (Eds.), *Children's development within social context: Vol. 2. Research and methodology* (pp. 5–31). Mahwah, NJ: Lawrence Erlbaum Associates.

Cole, M. (1996). *Cultural psychology: A once and future discipline.* Cambridge, MA: Harvard University Press.

Cole, M., Griffin, P., & the Laboratory of Comparative Human Cognition (LCHC). (1987). *Contextual factors in education.* Madison: Wisconsin Center for Education Research.

Cole, M., & Holland, D. (1994, April). *Between discourse and schema: Reformulating a cultural-historical approach to culture and mind.* Paper presented in invited session, "Vygotsky's Cultural-Historical Theory of Human Development," at the meeting of the American Anthropological Association, Atlanta, GA.

Corson, D. (1993). *Language, minority education and gender: Linking social justice and power.* Toronto, Ontario, Canada: OISE Press.

Corson, D. (1998). *Changing education for diversity.* Philadelphia: Open University Press.

Corson, P., Bernhard, J.K., & Gonzalez-Mena, J. (1998). Culturally situated explorations of child development: A home visit project in an early childhood education preparation program. *Journal of Early Childhood Teacher Education, 19*(3), 245–258.

Crago, M.B. (1992). Communicative interaction and second language acquisition: An Inuit example. *TESOL Quarterly, 26*(3), 487–505.

Cummins, J. (1991). Language development and academic learning. In M. Malave & G. Duquette (Eds.), *Language, culture and cognition* (pp. 161–175). Clevedon, England: Multilingual Matters.

Cummins, J. (1996). *Negotiating identities: Education for empowerment in a diverse society.* Los Angeles: National Association for Bilingual Education.

Cummins, J., & Corson, D. (Eds.). (1997). *Bilingual education.* Norwell, MA: Kluwer Academic Publishers.

Dahlberg, G., Moss, P., & Pence, A. (1999). *Beyond quality in early childhood education and care: Postmodern perspectives.* London: Falmer Press.

Darder, A. (1991). *Culture and power in the classroom: A critical foundation for bicultural education.* Toronto, Ontario, Canada: OISE Press.

Delpit, L.D. (1988). The silenced dialogue: Power and pedagogy in educating other people's children. *Harvard Educational Review, 58*(3), 280–298.

Derman-Sparks, L., & the ABC Task Force. (1989). *Anti-bias curriculum: Tools for empowering young children.* Washington, DC: National Association for the Education of Young Children.

Dolson, D.P. (1985). The effects of Spanish home language use on the scholastic performance of Hispanic pupils. *Journal of Multilingual and Multicultural Development, 6*(2), 135–155.

Durret, M.E., O'Bryant, S., & Pennebaker, J.W. (1975). Childrearing report of white, black, and Mexican-American families. *Developmental Psychology, 2,* 871–879.

Fajardo, B.J., & Freedman, D.G. (1981). Maternal rhythmicity in three American cultures. In T.M. Field, A.M. Sostek, P. Vietze, & P.H. Leiderman (Eds.), *Culture and early interactions* (pp. 133–146). Mahwah, NJ: Lawrence Erlbaum Associates.

Field, T.M., & Widmayer, S.M. (1981). Mother–infant interactions among lower SES black, Cuban, Puerto Rican, and South American immigrants. In T.M. Field, A.M. Sostek, P. Vietze, & P.H. Leiderman (Eds.), *Culture and early interactions* (pp. 41–60). Mahwah, NJ: Lawrence Erlbaum Associates.

Fine, M. (1990). *Framing dropouts.* Albany: State University of New York Press.

Foucault, M. (1972). *The archeology of knowledge.* London: Tavistock.

Gallimore, R., & Goldenberg, C. (1996). Accommodating cultural differences and commonalities in educational practice. *Multicultural Education, 4*(1), 16–19.

Galinsky, E., Howes, C., Kontos, S., & Shin, S. (1994). *The study of children in family child care and relative care: Highlights of findings.* New York: Families and Work Institute.

Garcia Coll, C.T., Lamberty, G., Jenkins, R., McAdoo, H.P., Crnic, K., Wasik, B.H., & Vázquez García, H. (1996). An integrative model for the study of developmental competencies in minority children. *Child Development, 67,* 1891–1914.

Geertz, C. (1973). *The interpretation of cultures.* New York: Basic Books.

Giroux, H.A. (1983). Theories of reproduction and resistance in the new sociology of education: A critical analysis. *Harvard Educational Review, 53*(3), 257–293.

Gonzalez-Mena, J. (1992). Taking a culturally sensitive approach in infant/toddler programs. *Young Children, 47*(2), 4–9.

Gonzalez-Mena, J. (1995). Cultural sensitivity in routine caregiving tasks. In P. Mangione (Ed.), *Infant/toddler caregiving: A guide to culturally sensitive care* (pp. 12–19). Sacramento: Far West Laboratory and California Department of Education.

Gonzalez-Mena, J. (1997a). *Multicultural issues in child care.* Mountain View, CA: Mayfield Publishing Co.

Gonzalez-Mena, J. (1997b). *The child in the family and in the community.* New York: Merrill.

Gonzalez-Mena, J. (1998). *Foundations: Early childhood education in a diverse society.* Mountain View, CA: Mayfield Publishing Co.

Grant, C.A. (1993). The multicultural preparation of U.S. teachers: Some hard truths. In G.K. Verma (Ed.), *Inequality and teacher education* (pp. 41–57). London: Falmer.

Grant, R. (1995). Meeting the needs of young second language learners. In E.E. Garcia, B. McLaughlin, B. Spodek, & O.N. Saracho (Eds.), *Meeting the challenge of linguistic and cultural diversity in early childhood education* (pp. 1–17). New York: Teachers College Press.

Greenfield, P.M., & Cocking, R.R. (1994). *Cross-cultural roots of minority child development.* Mahwah, NJ: Lawrence Erlbaum Associates.

Grieshaber, S. (1996, October). *Beating mum: How to win the power game.* Paper presented at the 6th annual Reconceptualizing Early Childhood Education Conference, Madison, WI.

Griffith, A. (1995). Mothering, schooling, and children's development. In M. Campbell & A. Manicom (Eds.), *Knowledge, experience, and ruling relations: Studies in the social organization of knowledge* (pp. 108–121). Ontario, Canada: University of Toronto Press.

Gunnar, M. (1996, December). *Quality of care and the buffering of stress physiology: its potential role in protecting the developing human brain.* From a speech given at the ZERO TO THREE Eleventh National Training Institute, Washington, DC.

Hagman, A., & Lahdenpera, A. (1988). Nine years of Finnish-medium education in Sweden: What happens afterwards? The education of minority children. In T. Skutnabb-Kangas & J. Cummins (Eds.), *Minority education: From shame to struggle.* (pp. 328–335). Clevedon, England: Multilingual Matters.

Hale-Benson, J. (1986). *Black children: Their roots, culture and learning styles.* Baltimore: Johns Hopkins University Press.

Hall, E.T. (1977). *Beyond culture.* New York: Anchor Books.

Harkness, S. (1980). The cultural context of child development. In C.M. Super & S. Harkness (Eds.), *Anthropological perspectives on child development* (pp. 7–15). San Francisco: Jossey-Bass.

Harkness, S., & Super, C. (1996). *Parental cultural belief systems: Their origins, expressions, and consequences.* New York: Guilford Press.

Harms, T., & Clifford, R. (1989). *The family day care rating scale.* New York: Teachers College Press.

Heath, S.B. (1982). Questioning at home and at school: A comparative study. In G. Spindler (Ed.), *Doing the ethnography of schooling.* New York: Holt, Rinehart, and Winston.

Holland, D., & Quinn, N. (Eds.). (1987). *Cultural models in language and thought.* Cambridge: MIT Press.

Holloway, S.D., Rambaud, M.F., Fuller, B., & Eggers-Piérola, C. (1995). What is "appropriate practice" at home and in child care? Low-income mothers' views on preparing their children for school. *Early Childhood Education Quarterly, 10,* 451–473.

Hsu, F. (1981). *Americans and Chinese: Passage to differences* (3rd ed.) Honolulu: University Press of Hawaii.

Hutchings, E. (1995). *Cognition in the wild.* Cambridge: MIT Press.

Kagitcibasi, C. (1996). *Family and human development across cultures.* Mahwah, NJ: Lawrence Erlbaum Associates.

Kessen, W. (1979). *The American child and other cultural inventions. American Psychologist, 34*(10), 815–820.

Kim, U., & Choi, S.H. (1996). Individualism, collectivism, and child development: A Korean perspective. In P.M. Greenfield & R.R. Cocking (Eds.), *Cross-cultural roots of minority child development* (pp. 227–258). Mahwah, NJ: Lawrence Erlbaum Associates.

Kitayama, S., Markus, H.R., & Matsumoto, H. (1995). Culture, self, and emotion: A cultural perspective on "self-conscious" emotions. In J. Tangney & K. Fischer (Eds.), *Self-conscious emotions: The psychology of shame, guilt, embarrassment, and pride* (pp. 439–463). New York: Guilford Press.

Koch, S. (1985). The nature and limits of psychological knowledge: Lessons of a century qua "science." In S. Koch & D.E. Leary (Eds.), *A century of psychology as science* (pp. 75–97). New York: McGraw-Hill.

Kozol, J. (1991). *Savage inequalities: Children in America's schools.* New York: Crown.

LaGrange, A., Clark, D., & Munroe, E., (1994). *Culturally sensitive child care: The Alberta study.* Edmonton: Alberta Association for Young Children.

Lally, J.R. (1996). The impact of child care policies and practices on infant/toddler identity formation. *Young Children, 51*(1), 58–67.

Laosa, L.M. (1978). Maternal teaching strategies in Chicano families of varied educational and socioeconomic levels. *Child Development, 49,* 1129–1135.

Laosa, L.M. (1980). Maternal teaching strategies in Chicano and Anglo-American families: The influence of culture and education on maternal behavior. *Child Development, 51,* 759–765.

Lave, J., & Wenger, E. (1994). *Situated learning: Legitimate peripheral participation.* New York: Cambridge University Press.

Lerner, R.M. (1988). Personality development: A life-span perspective. In E.M. Hetherington, R.M. Lerner, & M. Perlmutter (Eds.), *Child development in life-span perspective* (pp. 21–46). Mahwah, NJ: Lawrence Erlbaum Associates.

Lerner, R.M. (1991). Changing organism-context relations as the basic process of development: A developmental contextual perspective. *Developmental Psychology, 27*(1), 27–32.

LeVine, R.A. (1980). Anthropology and child development. In C.M. Super & S. Harkness (Eds.), *Anthropological perspectives on child development* (pp. 87–90). San Francisco: Jossey-Bass.

LeVine, R.A., Dixon, S., LeVine, S., Richman, A., Leiderman, P.H., Keefer, C.H., & Brazelton, T.B. (1994). *Child care and culture: Lessons from Africa.* New York: Cambridge University Press.

Lin, C.C., & Fu, V.R. (1990). A comparison of child-rearing practices among Chinese and Caucasian-American parents. *Child Development, 61*(2), 429–433.

McAdoo, H. (1993). The social cultural contexts of ecological developmental family models. In P.G. Boss, W.J. Doherty, R. LaRossa, W.R. Shumm, & S.K. Steinmetz (Eds.), *Sourcebook of family theories and methods: A contextual approach* (pp. 298–301). New York: Plenum Publishing.

McLoyd, V. (1990). The impact of economic hardship on black families and children: Psychological distress, parenting, and socioemotional development. *Child Development, 61*(2), 311–346.

McLoyd, V.C., & Randolph, S. (1985). Secular trends in the study of Afro-American children: A review of child development. In A.B. Smuts & J.W. Hagen (Eds.), History and research in child development. *Monographs of the Society for Research in Child Development, 50*(4–5, Serial No. 211).

Mehan, H. (1997). Tracking untracking: The consequences of placing low-track students in high-track classes. In P. Hall (Ed.), *Race, ethnicity, and multiculturalism: Policy and practice* (pp. 65–81). New York: Garland Publishing.

Miles, R. (1989). *Racism.* London: Routledge.

Minami, M. & Ovando, C.J. (1995). Language issues in multicultural contexts. In J.A. Banks & C.A.M. Banks (Eds.), *Handbook of multicultural education* (pp. 427–444). New York: Macmillan.

Minick, N., Stone, C.A., & Forman, E.A. (1993). Integration of individual, social, and institutional processes in accounts of children's learning and development. In E.A. Forman, N. Minick, & C.A. Stone (Eds.), *Context for learning: Sociocultural dynamics in children's development* (pp. 3–18). New York: Oxford University Press.

Misra, G., & Gergen, K.J. (1993). On the place of culture in psychological science. *International Journal of Psychology, 28*(2), 225–243.

Mistry, J. (1995). Culture and learning in infancy. In P. Mangione (Ed.), *Infant/toddler caregiving: A guide to culturally sensitive care* (pp. 20–27). Sacramento: Far West Laboratory and California Department of Education.

Moll, L., & Greenberg, J.B. (1990). Creating zones of possibilities: Combining social contexts. In L. Moll (Ed.), *Vygotsky and education* (pp. 319–348). New York: Cambridge University Press.

Morelli, G.A., Rogoff, B., Oppenheim, D., & Goldsmith, D. (1992). Culture variation in infants' sleeping arrangements: Questions of independence. *Developmental Psychology, 28,* 513–604.

National Association for the Education of Young Children (NAEYC). (1995). *Position statement: Responding to linguistic and cultural diversity: Recommendations for effective early childhood education.* Washington, DC: Author.

New, R. (1992, April). *Babies and bathwater: Uses and abuses of child development research and developmentally appropriate practice.* Paper presented at the meeting of the American Educational Research Association, San Francisco.

Ng, R. (1993). Racism, sexism, and nation building in Canada. In C. McCarthy & W. Crichlow (Eds.), *Race, identity and representation in education* (pp. 50–59). New York: Routledge.

Oakes, J. (1988). Culture: From the Igloo to the classroom. *Canadian Journal of Native Education, 15*(1), 41–47.

Okagaki, L., & Sternberg, R.J. (1993). Parental beliefs and children's school performance. *Child Development, 64,* 36–56.

O'Loughlin, M. (1992, September). *Appropriate for whom?: A critique of the culture and class bias underlying developmentally appropriate practice in early childhood education.* Paper presented at the conference on Reconceptualizing Early Childhood Education, Chicago.

Pease-Alvarez, L., & Hakuta, K. (1993). Perspectives on language maintenance and shift in Mexican-origin students. In P. Phelan & A.L. Davidson (Eds.), *Renegotiating cultural diversity in American schools,* (pp. 89–107). New York: Teachers College.

Phillips, C.B. (1995). Culture: A process that empowers. In P. Mangione (Ed.), *Infant/toddler caregiving: A guide to culturally sensitive care* (pp. 2–9). Sacramento: Far West Laboratory for Educational Research and Development and California Department of Education.

Phillips, C.B., & Cooper, R.M. (1992). Cultural dimensions of feeding relationships. *ZERO TO THREE Bulletin, 12*(5), 10–13.

Portes, P., & Bernhard, J.K. (1996, April). *Socio-psychological factors in immigrant students' achievement: Ethnocultural differences across social contexts.* Paper presented at the meeting of the American Educational Research Association, New York.

Robinson, H.B., Robinson, N.W., Wolins, M., Bronfenbrenner, U., & Richmond, J.B. (1973). *Early child care in the United States of America.* New York: Gordon & Breach.

Rodriguez, R. (1981). *Hunger of memory: The education of Richard Rodriguez.* Boston: David R. Godine Publisher Inc.

Rogoff, B. (1990). *Apprenticeship in thinking: Cognitive development in social context.* New York: Oxford University Press.

Rogoff, B., Mosier, C., Mistry, J., & Goncü, A. (1993). Toddlers' guided participation with their caregivers in cultural activity. In E.A. Forman, N. Minick, & C.A. Stone (Eds.), *Context for learning: Sociocultural dynamics in children's development* (pp. 203–253). New York: Oxford University Press.

Rothstein-Fisch, C. (1998, November). *Bridging home and school cultures: Recognizing and understanding cultural value differences.* Paper presented at the conference of the National Association for Education of Young Children, Toronto, Ontario, Canada.

Sagi, A., van IJzendoorn, M.H., & Koren-Karie, N. (1991). Primary appraisal of the strange situation: A cross cultural analysis of pre-separation episodes. *Developmental Psychology, 27*(4), 587–596.

Sameroff, A.J., & Fiese, B.H. (1990). Transactional regulation and early intervention. In S.J. Meisels & J.P. Shonkoff (Eds.), *Handbook of early childhood intervention* (pp. 119–191). New York: Cambridge University Press.

Shor, R. (1998). *Inappropriate child rearing practices as perceived by Jewish immigrant parents from the former Soviet Union.* Unpublished document. Hebrew University of Jerusalem, Israel.

Shore, R. (1997). *Rethinking the brain: New insights into early development.* New York: Families and Work Institute.

Shwalb, D.W., Shwalb, B.J., & Shoji, J. (1996). Japanese mothers' ideas about infants and temperament. In S. Harkness & C. Super (Eds.), *Parental cultural belief systems: Their origins, expressions, and consequences* (169–191). New York: Guilford Press.

Shweder, R.A., & Sullivan, M.A. (1993). Cultural psychology: Who needs it? *Annual Review of Psychology, 44,* 497–523.

Sinha, J.B.P. (1988). Reorganizing values for development. In D. Sinha & H.S.R. Kao (Eds.), *Social values and development: Asian perspectives* (pp. 275–284). Newbury Park, CA: Sage Publications.

Sjölund, A. (1973). *Day care institutions and children's development.* Lexington, MA: D.C. Heath.

Sleeter, C. (1989). Doing multicultural education across the grade levels and subject areas: A case study of Wisconsin. *Teaching and Teacher Education, 5*(3), 189–203.

Sleeter, C.E., & Grant, C.A. (1987). An analysis of multicultural education in the United States. *Harvard Educational Review, 57,* 421–444.

Small, M.F. (1998). *Our babies ourselves: How biology and culture shape the way we parent.* New York: Doubleday.

Smith, D. (1990). *The conceptual practices of power: A feminist sociology of knowledge.* Toronto, Ontario, Canada: University of Toronto Press.

Smith, D. (1993). The standard North American family. *Journal of Family Issues, 14*(1), 50–65.

Spencer, M.B. (1990). Development of minority children: An introduction. *Child Development, 61,* 267–269.

Statistics Canada (1999). *The daily for 1999-02-17.* Ottawa: Supply and Services.

Sue, D.W., & Sue, D. (1990). *Counseling the culturally different.* New York: John Wiley & Sons.

Super, C.M., & Harkness, S. (1986). The developmental niche: A conceptualization at the interface of child and culture. *International Journal of Behavioral Development, 9,* 545–569.

Takaki, R. (1993). *A different mirror: A history of multicultural America.* Boston: Little, Brown & Company.

U.S. Department of Health and Human Services (1996). *Trends in the well-being of America's children and youth.* Washington, DC: General Accounting Office.

University of Wisconsin, Madison, School of Education. (1990). *Recommended guideline for course listing documentation.* Madison: Author.

Valsiner, J., & Litvinovic, G. (1996). Processes of generalization in parental reasoning. In S. Harkness & C.M. Super (Eds.), *Parental cultural belief systems: Their origins, expressions, and consequences* (pp. 56–82), New York: Guilford Press.

Vygotsky, L.S. (1987). *Collected works: Vol. 1.* New York: Plenum.

Walkerdine, V. (1984). Developmental psychology and the child-centered pedagogy: The insertion of Piaget into early education. In J. Henriques, W. Holloway, C. Urwin, C. Venn, & V. Walkerdine (Eds.), *Changing the subject: Psychology, social regulation and subjectivity* (pp. 153–202). London: Methuen.

Walkerdine, V. (1990). Theories of development and effective learning. *Educational and Child Psychology, 7*(2), 23–28.

Walsh, D.J. (1989). Changes in kindergarten: Why here? Why now? *Early Childhood Research Quarterly, 4,* 377–391.

Wertsch, J.V., McNamee, G.D., McLane, J., & Budwig, N.A. (1980). The adult–child dyad as problem-solving system. *Child Development, 51*, 1215–1221.

West, J., Hausken, E.G., & Collins, M. (1993). *Readiness for kindergarten: Parent and teacher beliefs* (National Center for Education Statistics Report No. 93-257). Washington, DC: U.S. Department of Education, Office of Educational Research and Improvement.

Whiting, B., & Edwards, C. (1988). *Children of different worlds: The formation of social behavior.* Cambridge, MA: Harvard University Press.

Williams, L.R. (1994). Developmentally appropriate practice and cultural values: A case in point. In B.L. Mallory & R.S. New (Eds.), *Diversity and developmentally appropriate practices: Challenges for early childhood education* (pp. 155–165). New York: Teachers College Press.

Wolf, A.W., Lozoff, B., Latz, S., & Paludetto, R. (1996). Parental theories in the management of sleep routines in Japan, Italy and the United States. In S. Harkness & C.M. Super (Eds.), *Parents' cultural belief systems* (pp. 364–385). New York: Guilford Press.

Wong Fillmore, L. (1991a). Language and cultural issues in the early education of language-minority children. In S.L. Kagan (Ed.), *The care and education of America's young children: Obstacles and opportunities In Ninetieth Yearbook of the National Society for the Study of Education* (pp. 30–49). Chicago: University of Chicago Press.

Wong Fillmore, L. (1991b). When learning a second language means losing the first. *Early Childhood Research Quarterly, 6*, 323–346.

Wong Fillmore, L. (1997). Luck, fish seeds, and second-language learning. In C. Pearson Casanave, & S. Schecter (Eds.), *On becoming a language educator: Personal essays on professional development.* Mahwah, NJ: Lawrence Erlbaum Associates.

Young, V.H., (1974). A Black American socialization pattern. *American Ethnologist, 1*, 405–413.

10

Supporting
Infants and Toddlers

The Nascent Policy Agenda

◆❖◆

*Sharon Lynn Kagan
and Kathryn Taaffe McLearn*

Never the beneficiaries of pro-natalist policies that characterized post-World War II European countries, America's infants and toddlers have been largely disregarded as policy candidates in their own right. Rather, their policy fate has been inextricably enmeshed with general policies for children and families. What results are infant and toddler policies that, unfortunately, are limited in quantity, bereft of scope, and only marginally effective in producing quality. Why this is so and why these trends are beginning to be reversed are the subjects of this chapter. Suggesting that the United States is now at a major precipice regarding infant and toddler policy, the chapter draws examples from the fields of health, child care, family support, and home visiting to show why past policy has existed and why and how future policies for America's infants and toddlers may be more promising.

BACKGROUND

Seasoned observers of the policy scene have noted that three ingredients are necessary for policy construction (Richmond & Kotelchuck, 1984): 1) a well honed knowledge base, 2) clear public will, and 3) a coherent social strategy. By examining these three conditions in turn, it is a bit more clear why infants and toddlers have remained remote from durable services and policy attention. First, with regard to the knowledge base, there was only a limited body of research to refute these beliefs. Clarke-Stewart (1977) pointed out that although the research community knew something about the initial impact of early care on children's contemporaneous behavior, less was known about long-term effects. Little was known then about how mothers—other than those from small, intact middle-class families—actually cared for their children; even less was known about fathers and fathers' care. Literature on families as social networks was only beginning to emerge, as was information on the impact of cultural and ethnic variation on the developing child. Outcome research focused heavily on IQ, a metric that was regarded as limited and largely suspect for infants and toddlers.

Second, with regard to public will, policy has the most viable chance for enactment when a compelling case can be made for it. In the case of infants and toddlers, until the 1990s, there was little public need and less of a public constituency for it. Most mothers of infants and toddlers across the income spectrum were not in the workforce; health care—although always important—was less sophisticated and less costly; and family support was provided by less mobile and geographically proximate family members. Parents, extended families, and existing social services seemed to have filled the need; demographics of past eras did not compel policy action.

Beyond demographics, prevailing attitudes prevented the coalescence of a public will to enact policy for infants and toddlers. Steeped in a national ethos that rewards self-sufficiency and autonomy, American child and family policy is predicated on a noninterventionist approach that presumes families are able to care for themselves and nurture their young. This attitude dates back to the settlement of this country, when the architects of American democracy brought with them the strong belief that families should bear the greatest responsibility for nurturing children, with government playing only secondary roles, if any. Social services were designed as supports of last resort, only to be used when families "failed" or could not otherwise meet their familial obligation.

Other connected attitudes have further complicated this issue of public will. Americans believe that parents, particularly of the very young, are the most influential in advancing their children's development. And beyond this, there is a belief not simply that mothers provide optimal care for their infants and toddlers, but that young children suffer irreparably when served out of the home. Out-of-home services, where children are not typically cared for by consistent or well trained personnel, are thought to provide little opportunity for the kind of parental attachment or nurturing necessary to optimize development. So, attitudinal values about the primacy of mothers' roles and the inadequacy of out-of-home care conspired to delimit public will.

Finally, even if such beliefs had not prevailed and even if the research base had been strong, there was little thought about a social strategy. America was all but a neophyte in enacting public policy specifically for young children. Our nation's Head Start program—never then intended to serve infants and toddlers, except in several of its allied demonstration efforts (e.g., Child and Family Resource Program)—was one of only a handful of examples of programs designed especially for very young children. Its existence, and that of the limited few other efforts, never coalesced into an organized policy strategy known routinely in other European countries; what emerged was a set of awkward and unrelated policy gestures lacking integration, coherence, and systemic intentionality.

CURRENT SITUATION

Despite these conditions, a new era for infants and toddlers is being ushered in, with the Richmond and Kotelchuck (1984) conditions being more clearly addressed. First, from the perspective of knowledge, the understanding of development is increasing, as countless chapters in this book have noted. The prominence of research on the brain is bringing about dramatic changes in how America thinks about the early years, so much so that the topic has received considerable foundation, media, and White House attention with a White House Conference on Brain Development taking place in 1996. Specifically, evidence from the neurological and behavioral sciences continues to show that there is much more "plasticity" than was previously thought in the brain's capacity to reorganize itself and respond to environmental nutrients. This means that the child's environment and experiences—in utero and during the early years of life—directly affect how the brain learns, adapts, and stores information. It is everyday social interactions with adults who are consistently nurturing and caring that physically shape the brain and become the building blocks for future brain functioning and behavior (Shore, 1997). Researchers are also learning more about the provision of quality care for infants and toddlers (National Institute of Child Health and Human Development, 1997) and about the impacts of various interventions on infants and toddlers.

Second, public will is being altered as more women are driven into the workforce. In the period from World War II to the 1970s, women with young children tended to remain home until their children reached kindergarten. By 1987, this had changed dramatically: Half of children younger than age 3 had mothers who worked out of the home, and this number had risen to 57% by 1993 (Kamerman & Kahn, 1994). More recent data confirm that this trend has continued (Young, Davis, & Schoen, 1996). Child care, once considered a social amenity, is now regarded as a necessity.

Simultaneously, public pressure for better health care, parental education, home visitation, and family support is escalating as parents, who increasingly recognize the importance of the early years, say they want to know more about fostering their children's well-being (Young, Davis, & Schoen, 1996). A 1996 national survey of mothers and fathers revealed parents are eager for information and services to help them rear their infants and toddlers. Nearly 80% of parents said they would like more information in at least one of six areas of childrearing with more than 50% wanting specific information on helping their young child learn. Parents also value enhanced services such as home visits, telephone information lines, and written information to track their children's health and development information.

Third and finally, although no coherent social strategy currently exists for infants and toddlers, more programs and services for young children are being established. Adding to the 1986 Congressional legislation that mandated services for infants and toddlers with disabilities, now 21 states are funding one or more statewide programs for infants and toddlers (Knitzer & Page, 1998). These take the form of outreach and screening initiatives, supports for healthy infant care, parenting education, and family support services, along with initiatives that respond to special needs. Despite the importance of these efforts, they often remain isolated initiatives, rarely connecting with one another. Mirroring history, public or governmental efforts usually are born from discrete agencies, each with a primary and distinct mission so that, despite rhetorical admonitions to the contrary, policy for infants and toddlers remains effectively segregated by discipline. Health efforts are spawned by health agencies and child care by child care agencies. On the child care front, countless pieces of child care legislation are being proposed with only limited attention to how these efforts will relate to education services. This reflects past practice where, for example, the federal Even Start Program, a U.S. Department of Education effort first funded in 1989, provides home-based instruction to parents and children together in an effort to help parents become partners in their children's early development. Though some ancillary services are provided, Even Start is primarily an educational program.

Several exceptions to these more discipline-bound efforts are emerging. For example, in 1988, Congress enacted the Comprehensive Child Development Act (later repealed by the Human Services Amendments of 1994), which establishes a two-generation family support program that offers comprehensive services to children from birth to elementary school age from low-income families and provides supports for their parents. Recently, the U.S. Congress provided support to launch Early Head Start, an effort to provide Head Start–like services to infants and toddlers in programs throughout the nation. The Community Integrated Service Systems Action enabled communities to develop comprehensive coordinated family-centered services to address health and related needs for pregnant women, children, and adolescents. In 1994, the Commonwealth Fund, in partnership with local funders and health care providers across the nation launched Healthy Steps, a program based within primary pediatric care that offers parents information, home visits, and other services that support families in rearing their young children. The Starting Points Initiative, launched by Carnegie Corporation of New York, is another example of a more comprehensive effort to reform the systems that serve young children.

Hardly a complete list, these efforts suggest that a totally new momentum for infant and toddler social policy is emerging in this nation. It is not yet coherent, but the fact that so much action is taking place suggests that the nation is at a critical juncture, a turning point where it is imperative to coalesce policy knowledge and to consolidate lessons that are germane to future policy. To do so, we examine three discrete policy domains (health care, including children with special health needs; child care and early education; and home visiting and family support) and then draw conclusions from the analysis.

HEALTH CARE

All children need health and medical care if they are to grow and develop optimally. Health care for children encompasses both health promotion and disease prevention strategies that are necessarily broad and that increasingly demand multisector approaches that integrate medical, public health, educational, and social services (Fielding & Halfon, 1994). Even healthy children need a full spectrum of health care services. This care must begin before birth with comprehensive prenatal care and continue after birth, with regular and specialized care that is both preventive and curative. In all cases, comprehensive services must be appropriate to the child's age and must take into account developmental and dependency needs.

Scope of Health Care for Young Children

Infants' and toddlers' health needs and risks fundamentally differ from those of older children and adults and thus require special consideration in the structure, organization, and delivery of health services. As with adults, children's health is defined not only by physiological well-being but by the psychosocial dimensions of experience. This is especially so in the first 3 years of life when physiological, emotional, and cognitive development are so tightly interwoven and services or treatments that address only one domain of child functioning, usually the physical, represent a relatively limited and often substandard form of care.

Furthermore, infants' and toddlers' unique needs also arise from their developmental vulnerability and the degree to which they are dependent on others—parents, social and governmental institutions—for their health care (Halfon, Inkelas, & Wood, 1995; Wehr & Jameson, 1994). During critical developmental periods, infants and toddlers face windows of opportunity to master particular cognitive and physical tasks, which can have compounding effects upon their long-term health and development. A young child's developmental trajectory should direct the organization of a child's health care, including assessing development and risk, planning clinical interventions, monitoring improvement, measuring quality of care, and constructing appropriate risk adjustment for capitation (i.e., a fixed monetary fee for a defined package of clinical health services).

Young children also have complex and changing dependency relationships that affect their health development and utilization of health services. Infants and toddlers depend upon their parents or other caregivers to recognize and respond to their health care needs, to organize their care and authorize treatment, and to comply with recommended treatment regimens (Halfon, Hochstein, & Inkelas, 1996).

In addition, comprehensive care for young children must be two-generational and include maternal and family health (Zuckerman & Parker, 1995). Child health services need to provide parents with counseling about their own health care behaviors and circumstances such as maternal depression, domestic violence, and household smoking that are known to affect child health and well-being adversely. For instance, mothers of infants and toddlers who are depressed are twice as likely to say they become frequently frustrated with their child's behavior during the day, are less likely to establish a daily routine or read to their child, and are more likely to yell at their young child (Young, Davis, & Schoen, 1996). Studies suggest that prolonged maternal depression adversely affects how the mother nurtures and interacts with the child, resulting in adverse functional and structural changes in the child's developing brain and causing the child to become withdrawn (Dawson, Hessl, & Frey, 1994). In addition, household smoking is known to increase a young child's vulnerability to ear infections and bronchial asthma.

For the promotion of child health and development, numerous national commissions of leading health care experts recommend the following (Carnegie Task Force on Meeting the Needs of Young Children, 1994; Durch, 1994; National Commission on Children, 1991; Select Panel for the Promotion of Child Health, 1981):

- Health care services that provide an ongoing "medical home" for the child and that are comprehensive, preventive, and primary, including well-child and acute care visits; immunizations; health screening; counseling and anticipatory guidance; dental care; home visits; vision and hearing tests; and developmental and behavioral assessments
- Specially designed services and supports for children with chronic conditions and disabilities.
- Comprehensive services that include parental education and counseling
- Access to health care ensured through services such as transportation to the health facilities and translators who can speak with parents and children in their own language

Consequences of Poverty on the Health of Young Children

As of 1995, nearly one quarter of all children younger than age 3 in the United States are growing up in poverty, and poverty can adversely influence the health and development of young children (Brooks-Gunn & Duncan, 1997; Duncan & Brooks-Gunn, 1997). A large body of research suggests that children growing up in poverty are at increased risk of compromised physical health and cognitive development and are more likely to experience behavioral difficulties than children growing up in families who do not live in poverty. According to a 1996 survey, parents with less than $20,000 annual income report that their young child was two thirds as likely to be in excellent health and twice as likely to be in fair or poor health as young children from families living above the poverty level (Young, Davis, & Schoen, 1996).

Specifically, young children born to families in poverty are more likely to have experienced low birth weight and infant mortality, malnutrition, and lead poisoning than children who are not poor (Brooks-Gunn & Duncan, 1997). Low birth weight and malnutrition are important indicators of children's health. Low birth weight is associated with an increased likelihood of infant mortality, serious physical disabilities, cognitive and emotional problems that can result in learning disabilities, lower levels of academic achievement, and grade retention.

Malnutrition in the first 2 years of life has much more devastating consequences than at any other time, inhibiting normal growth and development. Unfortunately, children growing up in poverty suffer from higher rates of malnutrition, anemia, being severely underweight, and being a lower height for age than other children (Carnegie Task Force on Meeting the Needs of Young Children, 1994; Brooks-Gunn & Duncan, 1997).

Finally, in impoverished neighborhoods, families with infants and toddlers are more likely to live in old apartments and homes that have hazards, such as toxic levels of lead that can compromise a growing child's health and development. Research shows that lead exposure for infants and toddlers is linked to stunted growth, hearing loss, vitamin D metabolism damage, anemia, and a decreased IQ score (Brooks-Gunn & Duncan, 1997). In addition, toxic lead levels appear to increase a young child's risk of having a reading disability sixfold and of later dropping out of school sevenfold (Carnegie Task Force on Meeting the Needs of Young Children, 1994). And children in low-income neighborhoods all too often have an inadequate supply of health professionals and the poorest prenatal and child health services (Carnegie Task Force on Meeting the Needs of Young Children, 1994).

The Role of Private Health Insurance in Children's Health

Since the end of World War II, private health insurance has been the primary means of financing health care for America's young children and pregnant women, and most often coverage has been provided through employer plans. This type of insurance is primarily for medical conditions with co-payments, eliminating any real financial assistance for the minor problems faced by most families with children (Halfon, Hochstein, & Inkelas, 1996). Well-child visits, immunizations, and other preventive services—the types of services used most heavily by families with infants and toddlers—generally are not covered.

Since the 1980s, the extent of private insurance coverage has declined for children largely because of an increase in health care costs and a rise in the number of children in poverty. The percent of children with employer-based insurance declined from 66% in 1980 to 63% in 1990, and at the same time, the amount of cost sharing by families has increased (Sheils & Wolfe, 1992). A 1996 survey reports that only 59% of infants and toddlers currently have employer-based health care coverage, 28% have Medicaid coverage, and 7% have private nonemployer coverage (Young, Davis, & Schoen, 1996). Unfortunately, most young children's parents must pay at least part of their child's health care expenses themselves, even when the child has private health insurance coverage. Fewer than half of these infants and toddlers with private insurance are covered by plans that provide full reimbursement for such expenses as well-child care (42%), immunizations (49%), and visits when the child is ill (37%)—a major expense in these early years. For one quarter of all young children who come from families with incomes less than $40,000, parents have some difficulty paying for their child's health and medical expenses.

Children without Health Insurance

Children living in poverty are not the only children receiving inadequate health care. Many young children receive substandard care because they have no health insurance. In 1992, 10.5 million children younger than age 5 lacked access to health care because they had no health insurance, even though the majority of these children had parents who were employed (Data User Services Division, Data Access and Use Staff, Bureau of the Census, 1993). Trends indicate that employer-based coverage is eroding, leaving greater gaps than before in health benefits for children. Survey data from the U.S. Bureau of Census indicate that from 1988 through 1992, an estimated 3 million children lost private health insurance due to losses of employer-based health insurance (Newacheck, Hughes, & Stoddard, 1996; Newacheck, Hughes, English, et al., 1995).

Evidence suggests that children without health insurance are more likely to go without basic health care, which puts them at risk for potentially poor health outcomes. Uninsured children are less likely than insured children to have physician contact, a regular source of care, or access to regular doctor visits after business hours in a given year (Newacheck, Stoddard, Hughes, & Pearl, 1998). They are less likely to receive preventive care, be adequately immunized, and be seen by physicians for a variety of acute or chronic illnesses such as ear infections, injuries, or asthma (National Maternal and Child Health Policy Consortium, 1997). Unfortunately, when their families do seek care for these young uninsured children, it is more likely to be in an emergency room (Newacheck, Hughes, & Stoddard, 1996; Young, Davis, & Schoen, 1996).

The Vital Role of Medicaid in Children's Health

Created in 1965 as Title XIX of the Social Security Act, the Medicaid program has long been the primary program supporting the provision of health care services to low-income pregnant women and children. Medicaid is jointly administered by federal and state governments and operates as a financing program rather than as a service delivery system. Medicaid is an open-ended entitlement program. Thus, rather than operating within a specified annual budget, it is required to extend all medically necessary services to all individuals who qualify (Sheils & Wolfe, 1992).

State Medicaid programs are required to extend to pregnant women and young children a rich set of benefits that include comprehensive prenatal care, as well as preventive, primary, and acute care services. In addition, under the Early and Periodic Screening, Diagnostic and Treatment (EPSDT) Program, the federal government mandates that all states provide early and periodic screening programs to eligible children. States have the option of adding a broad range of diagnostic and treatment services to this package that can include, but is not limited to, case management, prescription drugs, and physical or occupational therapy.

With the increases in the numbers of young children in poverty and the shrinkage of employer-based coverage for children, Medicaid has served a central role in providing a safety net for the financing of children's health services. Legislation in 1986 severed the link between Medicaid and AFDC maintenance payments and expanded the coverage to include pregnant women and children up to age 6 with incomes up to 133% of the poverty level. States have the option of further expanding the coverage for pregnant women and young children up to 185% of the poverty level, and, using federal funds, some states have received federal Medicaid waivers to extend coverage to other children near poverty (Davis, 1997). Data indicate that 33% of infants younger than 1 year of age and 29% of toddlers are covered by Medicaid (Henry J. Kaiser Family Foundation, 1997). The gains in Medicaid coverage in the 1990s have largely offset the losses that occurred in private health insurance coverage. The net result is that the number and proportion of young children without insurance essentially remained the same (Newacheck, Hughes, & Cisternas, 1995).

Even so, Medicaid plays a central role in providing continued access to health care for millions of infants and toddlers in families who are poor or near poor (Newacheck, Hughes, English, et al., 1995). For example, poor children with Medicaid coverage have been shown to use preventive care at significantly higher rates than poor children without Medicaid coverage and at rates similar to nonpoor children. Children who have Medicaid coverage are also more likely to receive physician care for acute conditions such as acute and recurrent ear infections and pharyngitis. Medicaid coverage is also helpful for low-income young children with chronic conditions such as asthma. Additionally, studies indicate that poor children with disabilities who have Medicaid coverage use physician services at a rate almost comparable to those of nonpoor children with disabilities.

State Initiatives to Provide
Health Care to Uninsured Children

Since the early 1990s, states have taken the lead in expanding health care coverage for the growing number of children in low-income families or families living in poverty who need health insurance (Gauthier & Schrodel, 1997). These innovative programs that are currently operating in 19 states can be grouped into four basic approaches: 1) expanding Medicaid coverage, both through increased enrollment and through broader eligibility limits; 2) using state-designed child health programs based on public–private partnerships; 3) subsidizing employer-based coverage; and 4) providing tax incentives or vouchers directly to families to purchase private insurance (see side bar).

Most states establish a separate, usually nonprofit corporation to administer benefits and to determine eligibility. Generally, state-designed programs obtain most of their funding through state financing streams. Funds may come from a variety of sources such as general state revenues; special taxes on tobacco, alcohol, or employers; proceeds from the sale or conversion of not-for-profit hospitals; or contributions from

---

HOW STATES PROVIDE HEALTH INSURANCE TO CHILDREN

State initiation and financing of child health coverage programs is relatively new. Many states have developed innovative programs that use subsidies to individuals (e.g., Florida); provide subsidies to employers (e.g., New York); or establish public–private partnerships (e.g., California).

Florida's Healthy Kids program is available to all uninsured children enrolled in grades kindergarten through 12th grade and their preschool siblings regardless of income. A family's eligibility for the school lunch program confirms eligibility for a reduced premium in Healthy Kids. The program is financed through a combination of state revenues, contributions from local communities or counties and premiums paid by participants on a sliding scale.

The **New York** Child Health Plus program uses managed care to provide comprehensive primary, preventive, and inpatient care to children of the working poor. The program began in 1990 as a partnership between the state government and private insurers. The program currently reaches 260,000 children. With the addition of federal S-CHIP funds, by the year 2000 enrollment will increase to 360,000 children. An evaluation of the program shows that it reduces hospitalization by 4%, increases all types of primary care and specialty care visits, and satisfies most parents with its quality and ease of use.

In **California** Kaiser Permanente will donate $100 million to provide subsidized health insurance for up to 50,000 uninsured children from low income families. Children in the Kaiser Permanente Cares for Kids program will receive the full range of benefits offered to all other Kaiser families. This initiative will work with the state and Medicaid to enroll children into Medicaid and is part of a larger initiative that is scheduled to go nationwide in 1999 and increase funding for uninsured children to $80 million a year.

private sources such as foundations or corporations (Gauthier & Schrodel, 1997; National Governors' Association, 1997). Given that there is no funding from the federal government, states have maximum flexibility to define and operate the programs, and families are less likely to experience the stigma associated with "welfare" programs.

The benefits and services provided to families with young children vary by state. However, the majority of programs provide coverage for preventive and primary care for services such as routine well-baby care, immunizations, and primary and acute care visits, as well as prescription drug diagnostic tests and emergency room visits. Although frequently more limited than Medicaid coverage, these groundbreaking state programs have helped millions of low-income families secure health care for their infants and toddlers.

New Federal Legislation

In August 1997 President Clinton signed into law the most significant funding increase for children's health coverage since the original enactment of Medicaid in 1965 (National Governors' Association, 1997). As part of the Balanced Budget Act of 1997, this Title XXI legislation provides states with $20.3 billion in new federal block grant funding over the next 5 years to provide health insurance coverage to uninsured "gap" children—children who have family incomes too high to qualify for Medicaid but too low to afford private health insurance. Children in families may qualify in one or two ways depending on which enables eligibility: Incomes below 200% of the federal poverty level can qualify, or children could be covered up to 50% above the state's Medicaid eligibility. States cannot use these new dollars to replace or supplant existing coverage, and states must continue to maintain the Medicaid eligibility for children that was in effect in June 1997.

Beginning October 1997, the law allows states to apply voluntarily to use this money to expand coverage under the existing Medicaid program, to create a new state children's health program, the State Children's Health Insurance Program (S-CHIP), or to implement a combination of both. States that choose to establish or expand their children's health insurance program have broad flexibility on how to determine benefits and deliver care. However, states must adopt benefits from one of the following benchmark benefit packages: The HMO with the largest commercial enrollment; a state employees' health plan, the federal employees' health benefit program by Blue Cross and Blue Shield, or a package approved by the secretary of Health and Human Services.

The federal funding arrives in the form of a block grant with few strings attached or requirements for what should be included in a "benefits" package for children. As states make important decisions about how to use the new federal block grant funds, child health professionals, parents, and advocates will need to work with governors, key legislators, and managed care organizations to make certain that the new funds are being used to provide young children with a benefits package that includes health and medical services that are comprehensive, preventive, and developmentally appropriate.

Young Children with Special Health Care Needs

Advances in medicine and surgery have improved life expectancies of young children with a wide range of chronic illnesses and disabilities. The same advances have created outpatient and community-based options for much of the care of children with special needs. Yet, for clinicians and policy makers, there has been difficulty in developing a standard definition of children with special health needs and thus identifying the size of this population. Current estimates are that 15–20 million children have some kind of chronic condition, and between 1 and 2 million children have severe health conditions that are likely to require extensive daily caregiving (Palfrey, Haynie, & American Academy of Pediatrics Medical Home Program for Children with Special Needs, 1996).

In the 1990s definitions have been developed that tend to have a broader focus than just chronic conditions. One of the many working definitions that reflect the diversity of this target population states is, "Children with special health needs are those who have or are at increased risk for chronic physical, developmental, behavioral, or emotional conditions and who also require health and related services of a type and mount beyond that required of children generally." To complicate the situation even further, children with special needs not only vary in the type of disabling situation, but also vary in degree ranging from mild to moderate and severe. Especially for children younger than age 3, whose development often appears in spurts, it is not always easy to determine who has developmental delays or to identify mild problems such as articulation disorders, mild learning disabilities, or behavior problems (Gallagher, 1994).

Children with special health care needs, including infants and toddlers, require a broad range of primary, specialized, and related services. In addition to well-child care, health promotion, and disease prevention, children with special health care needs often require specialty care, diagnostic and intervention strategies, therapies and ongoing ancillary services such as occupational therapy, physical therapy, speech-language therapy, and individual and family counseling, as well as long-term management of ongoing medical complications. For many children with special needs, health services are frequently delivered at home, in school, and in the community. Successfully managing the various components requires a more collaborative role between parents, health professionals, social services, and other related services.

Since the 1960s, the design of federal policy for children with disabilities has been a disparate set of programs that has been based in either health or education without ample linkage between the two systems. In the case of low-income young children covered by Medicaid, those identified with special health needs could be served through the Early Periodic Screening Diagnosis and Treatment (EPSDT) Program that provides services for diagnosis and treatment of physical and mental problems. However, the identification of children with special health needs is usually limited to these who qualify for Supplemental Security Income (SSI) program. Although this approach offers some consistency across states, it is limited in that SSI only includes a small subset of young children with chronic diseases (Maternal and Child Health Bureau, 1996). In addition, a limited number of young children with special health care needs have been eligible for services through state-run Title V programs. This program serves children with complex physical conditions; children with either mental conditions or who are at risk for chronic conditions are seldom included.

In the 1960s, the Education for All Handicapped Children Act, PL 94-142, was passed to bring structural changes to the educational system to guarantee that there would be 1) services available for all children with disabilities; 2) fairness in diagnosis and treatment, particularly for minority children and families; 3) a clear set of educational objectives to ensure that the children were not merely being put aside by the educational community; and 4) an opportunity for the family to have some say in their child's educational planning (Gallagher, 1989). Although the original mandate of PL 94-142 was to ensure that all children with disabilities were served, it did not provide services to children younger than age 3.

The passage of the Education of the Handicapped Act Amendments (PL 99-457) in 1986 attempted to complete the mandate of PL 94-142 by serving children younger than age 3 and to direct attention to the chaotic circumstances created when many different service providers from many different disciplines operate independently (Gallagher, 1989). The purposes of PL 99-457 are fourfold: 1) to enhance the development of infants and toddlers with disabilities; 2) to minimize the need for special education costs after infants and toddlers with disabilities reach school age; 3) to enhance the capacity of families to meet the needs of their infants and toddlers with disabilities; and 4) to increase the capabilities of individuals with disabilities so they can live more independently (Harbin, Gallagher, Lillie, & Eckland, 1992).

The law provides the states with planning money from the federal government to design a comprehensive interagency, multidisciplinary program of services for children with disabilities. The expectation has been that the lion's share of the funds to operate the program would come from existing federal funding streams such as Medicaid, Title V, and SSI. The challenge of this legislation at the federal, state, and local levels has been to design and implement a system to serve a heterogeneous group of children from diverse families, treated by a multidisciplinary set of professionals in various settings (Gallagher, 1994). All 50 states participate and are developing a comprehensive, coordinated service system consisting of 14 separate requirements (see Table 1). Each

Table 1.   Minimum components of PL 99–457, Part H

1. Definition of developmentally delayed

2. Timetable for serving all in need in the state

3. Comprehensive multidisciplinary evaluation of needs of children and families

4. Individualized family service plan and case management services

5. Child find and referral system

6. Public awareness

7. Central directory of services, resource, experts, research and demonstration projects

8. Comprehensive system of personnel development

9. Single line of authority in a lead agency designated or established by the governor for implementation of:

   a. General administration and supervision

   b. Identification and coordination of all available resources

   c. Assignment of financial responsibility to the appropriate agency

   d. Procedures to ensure the provision of services and to resolve intra- and interagency disputes

   e. Entry into formal interagency agreements

10. Policy pertaining to contracting or making arrangements with local service providers

11. Procedure for timely reimbursement of funds

12. Procedural safeguards

13. Policy and procedures for personnel standards

14. System for compiling data on the early intervention programs

From Harbin, G., Gallagher, J.J., Lillie, T., & Eckland, J. (1992). Factors influencing state progress in the implementation of Public Law 99–457, Part H. *Policy Sciences, 25,* 104; reprinted by permission.

governor has chosen a lead agency that takes responsibility for bringing together state and federal resources to serve infants and toddlers with disabilities. Among the states, the lead agency varies and includes state departments of health, education and social welfare.

Recognizing the diversity of young children, families, and professionals that PL 99-457 is designed to affect, major changes and flexibility in the service delivery system are required that differ from past programs serving children with disabilities. First, PL 99-457 requires the establishment of a state interagency coordinating council, including parent representatives to promote interagency agreements among service providers. Second, the law requires that an individualized family service plan (IFSP) is developed for each child and that the services be multidisciplinary in nature, calling upon the participation, where appropriate, of 10 separate disciplines (e.g., medicine, social work, nursing, nutrition, occupational therapy, physical therapy, psychology, special education, speech-language pathology, audiology) to conduct a multidisciplinary assessment. Third, the law clearly mandates greater parental involvement at all levels—from participation on interagency councils to involvement in the development and periodic review of the IFSP.

One of the essential systems involved in caring for young children with special health care needs has been and will continue to be the health care system. Under fee-for-service arrangements, special needs children have access to specialty care, specialized university programs, regional treatment centers, and delivery organizations developed to meet the specialized needs of this population. These services have been financed through commercial insurance plans, Medicaid, the federal and state maternal and child health programs, and special education. In addition, young children's care often is coordinated through public health, educational, or social service providers.

Increasingly, young children with special health needs are being enrolled in managed care arrangements. Although in theory managed care organizations can be well suited to meeting the needs of young children with special health care needs, the empirical literature suggests managed care organizations are often not suited for caring for this population. With managed care arrangements, infants and toddlers with special health needs, like other young children, will receive their care in a system that is designed to control the use of specialists, especially outside of the plan's network. Managed care plans cannot assume that one size fits all of these children. Currently, no operational definition exists for identifying children with special needs served by managed care organizations. Plan policies and procedures often ignore the specialized needs of this population.

Studies suggest that children enrolled in fully capitated managed care may be receiving equivalent or better levels of preventive and primary care than children receiving care under fee for service; however, studies of utilization of specialty care suggest that families enrolled in managed care experience difficulty obtaining intensive levels of certain specialty services such as ancillary therapies and mental health care for their children. Although parents reported their child's basic medical needs were met by the managed care plan, they often had to rely on services and financing outside the plan for health-related services. Families also reported difficulty coordinating services in and out of the plan, and using parents as liaisons with plan providers is not common (Fox & McManus, 1996; Newacheck, Hughes, Halfon, & Brindis, 1997).

Recognizing that children with special health care needs require a broad range of primary, specialized, and related services, managed care systems face a critical issue: Can they control costs and still offer the full range of appropriate services? In striving to control costs, managed care plans may or may not include in their benefits package a broad range of service options that are necessary to the health and development of infants and toddlers with special health needs. And as managed care plans strive to constrain utilization, they may tend to limit the number of pediatric specialists or use adult rather than pediatric specialists. Even if the managed care system has contractual language to cover needed services, the route to establish "medical necessity" may be complex, prolonged, and controlled by nonpediatric decision makers. In addition, the risk of taking care of young children with chronic illnesses or disabilities is not well defined and often is subject to change with potentially costly additions.

In sum, the dependency of infants and toddlers with special health needs requires caregivers from a wide variety of health and related institutions. The concept of service integration and family participation is the foundation of PL 99-457, yet the reality is that it is difficult to accomplish. It remains to be seen.

The Challenge

Amidst the changing environment in the health care industry, the innovative state programs and new federal legislation on children's health coverage provide a unique opportunity to marry the strong political interest in children's health and well-being with the best wisdom in the field about the types, quality, and range of health care services that young children need and deserve. National and state leadership is necessary to bring the key forces to the table to establish quality assurance guidelines and benefits packages so that infants and toddlers have access to an ongoing "medical home." A medical home should provide comprehensive, preventive, and primary health care that includes enhanced services that emphasize cognitive and emotional development as well as managing disease and illness.

Although the United States remains the only industrialized nation except South Africa not to support policies that promote universal primary and preventive health care for children, incremental steps are being taken to build on achievements, to bring better health care to the nation's young children, and to provide newborns with the opportunity for a good start in life.

CHILD CARE AND EARLY EDUCATION

As noted previously, the status of infant and toddler policy is enmeshed with broader child and family policy. Nowhere is this more true than in child care. Gormley summed up the status of American child care policy succinctly: "Despite occasional bursts of attention, child care has not yet secured a firm niche on the public agenda. Child care remains a private headache, only fitfully addressed by public policies" (1995, p. 1). The dilemma is that America is not certain who is responsible for child care: parents who need the service; corporations who would like to offer it, but deem themselves constrained by fiscal realities; or the government, who is uncertain of how much support to provide to whom.

Such lack of clarity wreaks havoc for child care. Access to services is limited, particularly for children living in poverty (U.S. Department of Education, NCES, 1995) who are deemed to benefit most from high-quality programs. But quality is also a problem; stated simply, quality services are in short supply. A national study found that 86% of all child care centers provided poor or mediocre services, with 12% of this care being of poor quality (Cost, Quality, and Child Outcomes [CQCO] Study Team, 1995). Though still poor to mediocre, the quality of care in preschool classrooms far outstripped that found in infant and toddler classrooms. In infant/toddler classrooms, 40% of the care was described as poor, a condition that actually threatened the health and safety of infants and toddlers. Similar weaknesses were found in family child care settings. Although family child care has been less studied by researchers than other early care and education programs, existing data suggest that the quality of care in these settings is as varied as that of centers, and that unregulated family child care and relative care offer somewhat lower-quality care than regulated home-based programs (Fosberg, 1981; Galinsky, Howes, Kontos, & Shinn, 1994).

Many factors conspire to make the care of infants and toddlers so weak—inadequate regulatory provisions, inadequate provider training and certification, and inadequate compensation and funding. Each is discussed below and sheds light on the major policy challenges facing child care for infants and toddlers.

Inadequate Regulatory Provisions

With regard to regulatory provision, there is mounting evidence that the stringency of regulatory policy is linked to the provision of quality. The Cost, Quality, and Child Outcomes Study (1995) of both nonprofit and for-profit care in four states found that states with more demanding licensing standards had fewer poor-quality centers than those with comparatively more relaxed standards. This finding is consonant with those reported by Howes, Smith, and Galinsky (1995) indicating that the quality of child care in Florida improved when the regulatory standards were strengthened.

Despite the evidence that standards establish the preconditions for quality child care, government policy lags behind. With the exception of Head Start's Performance Standards (and later, Early Head Start's Performance Standards), the federal government has vacillated in its involvement with regulation affecting young children. Since 1968, experts have proposed, revised, and reproposed federal regulations for child care. Because of cost and the anti-regulatory propensity, the proposed federal regulations have set forth only minimal standards. Today, the federal role is still ambiguous. The 1980 Federal Interagency Day Care Requirements (FIDCR), while repeatedly serving as a guideline for minimum standards of quality, have been withdrawn, and the 1985 Model Child Care Standards Act fell short of providing a useful set of guidelines for states (Phillips, 1996; Young & Zigler, 1986). The Model Act limited its scope to the prevention of child abuse and failed to assert minimum standards or thresholds of quality care in areas that have been empirically linked to positive child outcomes.

At present, child care regulations rest largely with state governments, and these standards are varied, weak, and sometimes even nonexistent. In reviewing these standards, a 1997 study of state regulations for center-based infant and toddler child care found that current regulations do not require child care centers to meet acceptable minimal standards of quality for infant and toddler care (Young, Marsland, & Zigler, 1997). Specifically, they fall short of the recommended standards set forth by experts in the field (e.g., Bredekamp, 1987; Federal Register, 1980; Hayes, Palmer, & Zaslow, 1990).

Based on recommended standards, the Young, Marsland, and Zigler (1997) analysis rated each state on nine quality indices grouped into three domains: 1) grouping (e.g., staff-to-child ratios and group size); 2) caregiver qualifications (e.g., general education, specialized and

in-service training); and 3) the program (e.g., physical facilities, equipment and toys, orientation, developmental appropriateness) to determine if they met basic standards of appropriate practice. Overall, not a
single state met the criteria across the three domains for "optimal" or
"good" standards, and only 17 states (33%) had regulations rated as
"minimally acceptable" for infants and toddlers. Specifically, 67% of the
states received overall ratings of "poor" or "very poor," indicating that
they failed to require even minimally acceptable care that assures the
safe and healthy development of very young children. Looking at the
three domains, the findings revealed the following:

Groupings   Thirty-seven states (73%) received ratings of either
"poor" or "very poor," indicating that they failed to regulate staff-to-
child ratios and group size adequately. Only 28% of states had "good"
or "minimally acceptable" ratings, and no state received an "optimal"
rating in this domain. This means that 18 states allow ratios of 1:5 to 1:8
for infants and 1:6 to 1:8 for toddlers. Moreover, 23 states failed to regulate group size.

Caregiver Qualifications   Almost all of the states (98%) had
"poor" or "very poor" ratings for caregiver education and for pre- and
in-service training. As such, most state regulations permit infants and
toddlers to be cared for by staff who on average have not completed
high school, have had only some general training in child development,
and have had fewer than 5 hours of in-service training annually.

Program   The data revealed that 88% of the states had at least
broad language requiring centers to provide developmentally appropriate programs of care for infants and toddlers. Twenty-eight states
were rated as either "good" or "optimal," indicating that they required
centers to operate a developmentally appropriate program of care in the
areas of social, intellectual, emotional, and physical development.

In sum, the majority of state child care regulations continue to allow
infants and toddlers to be cared for in environments that do not meet
basic standards of appropriate practice and that do not assure the safe
and healthy development of very young children. Although state policymakers have improved regulations for staff-to-child ratios and developmentally appropriate practice, policymakers still fail to see the
importance of keeping group size small and requiring staff to be educated and trained in the care of infants and toddlers. Despite advances
in the understanding of how environmental factors influence early development and repeated calls for more stringently regulated child care, a
majority of states continue to fall short of "minimally acceptable" levels
across all three quality domains. Furthermore, minimal standards are
just that—minimal. No states' regulations require or actively promote the
provision of optimal care as defined by experts in the field.

In the protracted absence of federal child care regulations, energies must continue to be directed toward strengthening regulations at the state level. This is especially true in the late 1990s, given the push for greater state autonomy and responsibility in areas not constitutionally designated to the federal government. Yet, state policymakers have discussed relaxing staff-to-child ratios and group size guidelines. Proponents of this view argue that staff-to-child ratios and group size regulations unnecessarily restrict providers, thereby reducing the costs of child care (Passell, 1996; Scarr, 1996). Although this argument may be worthy of debate with respect to preschool- and school-age children, it is inappropriate with respect to infants and toddlers who require individualized care, particularly in combination with more exacting requirements for training and education.

The importance of ongoing oversight and monitoring must also be considered. Although the specifics of quality oversight vary from state to state, little monitoring actually occurs once a center is licensed. In the best cases, licensed facilities are subject to periodic inspections, unannounced visits, and specified procedures for licensing renewal. In fact, the most stringent oversight occurs as infrequently as every 3 years (Gazan, 1997).

In addition, efforts must be made to assist parents to be better informed and more effective consumers of child care. Parents need to understand that having a state child care license does not guarantee that their child is being cared for in a safe and healthy environment that promotes social, emotional, cognitive, and physical development.

Inadequate Provider Training and Certification

Research is unequivocal that the most important single ingredient of overall program quality is the nature of the relationship between the provider and the child (Galinsky et al., 1994; Willer et al., 1991). This relationship is dramatically affected by the level of training and education that a caregiver obtains. The more training and education practitioners have—both general education and specialized early childhood training and education—the more adept they are at helping children to thrive and to develop the secure attachments that are so critical to healthy development (Arnett, 1989; CQCO Study Team, 1995; Fosberg, 1981; Phillips & Howes, 1987; Ruopp, Travers, Glantz, & Coelen, 1979; Schweinhart, Barnes, Weikart, Barnett, & Epstein, 1993; Whitebook, Howes, & Phillips, 1989). Practitioners who receive ongoing training tend to be more responsive and sensitive to young children's needs (Howes, Smith, & Galinsky, 1995) and are less harsh and restrictive than staff with lower levels of specialized training (Arnett, 1989; Ruopp et al., 1979; Whitebook et al., 1989). The value of such training is rendered even more important because children who experience such supportive relationships and secure child care attachments perform well cognitively (Galinsky, Howes, & Kontos, 1995). Studies show, for example, that children in centers with higher turnover rates of staff (and therefore less opportunity for forming durable attachments) have less developed language skills and social skills (Whitebook et al., 1989).

Yet, despite the evidence that caregiver training and education is inextricably linked to the quality of care for young children and the outcomes they derive from child care, training requirements and opportunities for ongoing professional development in the United States are inadequate; entry-level, pre-service training is the norm, with few opportunities for intermediate or advanced training geared toward practitioners already working with children (Kagan & Cohen, 1997). The facts speak for themselves: 40% of early care and education teachers in center-based programs have high school degrees or less, and about 10% have 2-year college degrees (Willer et al., 1991). Center-based teachers receive, on average, only 10 hours of ongoing training annually (Kisker, Hofferth, Phillips, & Farquhar, 1991). The situation is worse for assistant teachers; about half of those in centers have high school degrees or less (Whitebook et al., 1989). Among regulated family child care providers, the average education is 1 year of college, although the course work is not necessarily related to young children; one third of regulated providers have never received any specialized training (Kisker et al., 1991).

The problem of limited training and professional development opportunities exists in part because the field does not impose certification requirements that require more training. Other industrialized countries where the quality of care is considered much higher than the United States have far more stringent professional development and licensing requirements for early childhood workers (Pritchard, 1996). For example, Finland requires preschool teachers to have at least 3 years of related college-level training (Ojala, 1989); Japan requires 2 years of college-level training (Lassegard, 1993); Sweden requires 2.5 years at the college level (Gunnarsson, 1993); and in the United Kingdom the standard is 4 years of college-level preparation (Pascal, Bertram, & Heaslip, 1991). France requires the same masters-level preparation for teachers in preschools that they require for teachers in elementary schools (Richardson & Marx, 1989). Gormley's observation is illustrative of the difference between U.S. standards and other nations' standards for early care and education practitioners: the United States sets its requirements in terms of hours, but other industrialized countries set their requirements in terms of years (Gormley, 1995).

The more rigorous standards for qualification of early care and education caregivers found in other countries are accompanied by more

coordinated training delivery systems, and, in some countries, requirements are being adjusted to coordinate multiple routes into the profession (Pritchard, 1996). For example, Sweden has generalized a training
base for early care and education practitioners in a variety of roles (such
as preschool teachers and infant nurses) who work in various programs
(Gunnarsson, 1993), and the United Kingdom has developed alternate
paths to meeting requirements (Pascal et al., 1991) in an effort to enhance
the availability of relevant training and to increase the number of qualified practitioners (Kagan & Cohen, 1997).

Other industrialized nations, however, do not provide the only
sophisticated models of licensing and professional development; the
approaches of other fields in the United States also offer important lessons for early care and education (Kagan & Cohen, 1997). State governments across the country require licenses for many professionals and
nonprofessionals working with the public (Mitchell, 1996), including
helping professionals (e.g., social workers, registered nurses, licensed
practical nurses, teachers), technical professionals (e.g., architects, engi-
neers), tradespeople (e.g., electricians), and service workers (e.g., cos-
metologists). The rationales for requiring licensing for individuals in
other fields include protecting consumers from harm, ensuring a minimum quality of services, and protecting the public at large (Kagan &
Cohen, 1997).

The structures that support individual licensure in other fields are
also well established, including state-level individual licensing laws;
state-level boards to administer examinations and grant licenses; standard examinations developed by the profession; national organizations
that accredit the schools that prepare individuals for the occupation;
professional organizations that play key roles in setting entry-level standards and offering advanced levels of individual certification; and training that is integrated into higher education (Mitchell, 1996).

The U.S. military has also developed a coherent and coordinated
professional development system, specifically for their early care and
education staff (Army Child Development Services). All personnel working with children in the military either have a bachelor's or master's
degree in fields related to young children and families or participate in
the military's "basic training" during their first year. Ongoing training
is required of all personnel, and training is organized sequentially and
builds toward certificates and academic degrees (Kagan & Cohen, 1997).

Given the lack of training requirements and limited ongoing
professional development opportunities in early care and education, it
is unrealistic to expect high performance from practitioners and, in turn,
high-quality programs in which infants and toddlers receive the
individualized and expert care they need to thrive. Building on the

examples of other industrialized nations, other professions in the United States, and the U.S. military, the report emanating from the Quality 2000 Initiative, *Not By Chance* calls for a coherent, coordinated credentialing system for early care and education practitioners nationwide. The Quality 2000 approach calls for a series of three licenses for early care and education workers by the year 2010 (Kagan & Cohen, 1997):

- First, all center directors and directors of family child care support services would be required to have early childhood administrator licenses. To obtain this license, an individual must have at least a master's or bachelor's degree in early childhood education or child development from an accredited institution, including at least 15 credits in early childhood administration; certification in pediatric first aid; and demonstrated competency in management and in working with children and families.
- Second, all teachers in centers and public teachers for children ages 3 and 4 must obtain an early childhood educator license. This license requires an associate's or bachelor's degree in early childhood education or child development from an accredited institution; practicum experience with the age of children with whom individuals would work; certification in pediatric first aid; and demonstrated competency in working with children and families.
- Third, lead providers in large family child care homes and center assistant teachers would be required to have an early childhood associate educator license. To obtain this license, an individual would need at least a child development associate (CDA), revised National Association for Family Child Care (NAFCC) accreditation, or an equivalent, meaning at least 120 hours of formal education in child development/early childhood education and demonstrated competency in working with children and families; practicum experience with the age of children with whom individuals would work; and certification in pediatric first aid.

Individuals who do not have training or education in child development or early childhood education, but who have an interest in working with young children and families, would have access to entry-level jobs as supervised assistants in child care centers or large family child care homes provided that they participate in ongoing training leading to licensure (Kagan & Cohen, 1997).

Inadequate Compensation and Funding

Perhaps the most significant policy issue facing child care for infants and toddlers is that of inadequate public investment in services for this population. In the United States, about one quarter of program revenues are generated from government sources (CQCO Study Team, 1995; U.S. Department of Commerce, 1993), while parents, community organizations, and practitioners (through their foregone wages) pick up the remainder of the costs. Contrast this to Italy and France, where parents rarely pay more than a quarter to one third of the cost of programs for infants and toddlers (Gormley, 1995; Kamerman & Kahn, 1994). This comparative discrepancy bodes poorly for child care, highlighting the underinvestment that characterizes U.S. policy. This underinvestment directly affects the compensation afforded workers in the field, and adequate compensation is critical to the quality of programs (CQCO Study Team, 1995; Galinsky et al., 1994; Whitebook et al., 1989; Whitebrook, Howes, & Phillips, 1993). In the current system, there are few financial incentives for program staff to pursue professional development, and salaries are so low that most staff cannot afford to pay for training and education themselves. The average annual income for early care and education practitioners working in centers and family child care homes is less than $13,000 a year (CQCO Study Team, 1995; Modigliani, Helburn, Morris, & Culkin, 1996). This, in part, contributes to high staff turnover rates, which fortifies a pernicious cycle of poor quality.

To redress this, early care and education staff must be compensated at least at levels comparable to what personnel with similar experience and education earn in other fields. One way to precipitate increased salaries and benefits for staff would be to require higher levels of training and education. Creating a system for licensing individuals, as discussed previously, may hold the best promise for increasing the compensation of the staff and therefore increasing the professionalism of the field. Other possible approaches include raising wages through subsidies to parents, allocating funds earmarked for wages directly to programs, and instituting a refundable tax credit for early care and education staff.

Poor compensation significantly contributes to an inadequately skilled provider workforce, but this is not the sole financial problem that undermines early care and education services for infants and toddlers. The lack of funding also affects who has access to services. In many cases, children from low-income families are unable to attend early care and education programs because there are limited subsidies, and often parents are not able to afford program fees (Kagan & Cohen, 1997). Although program fees are a strain on many families, the problem is particularly acute for families with infants. A study conducted in six communities across the country found that a full-time worker earning the minimum wage would have to contribute at least 50% of her or his earnings to pay for infant care at five of the six sites, and even if she or he managed to enroll the infant in the community's lowest-priced program, she or he would have to contribute 35% of her or his income in four of the six communities (Clark & Long, 1995).

From a policy perspective, however, there are analytic issues related to the inability to generate the requisite revenue. Although scholars estimate that reform will be costly, they disagree on the precise amounts of funding needed. For example, Barnett (1993) designed a unified federal subsidy approach at an estimated government cost of $63 billion. This estimate is based on four factors: the age of the child, family income, maternal employment, and child disability. All parents of 3- to 5-year-olds, working parents of children from birth to age 3, and all parents of children with disabilities from birth to age 5 would receive assistance paying for child care, but families in which parents or the only parent work would receive more assistance than families with an at-home parent, and low-income parents would receive more than middle- and upper-income families. Parents of children with disabilities would also receive additional funds.

Regenstein, Silow-Carroll, and Meyer (1995) offered an approach to expanding quality early care and education programs to 3- and 5-year-olds that would cost, in their estimation, $25.5 billion annually in 1994 dollars. Their approach involves making part-day, high-quality programs available free of charge to all 3- and 4-year-olds through programs based in public schools, and making full-day wraparound programs available to children with working parents. The wraparound programs would be free to impoverished parents and subsidized for low-income parents, while middle- and upper-income families would be required to pay the full price of wraparound programs that enable them to work. Bergmann (1994) offered another view, estimating that if the government provided free programs to those parents whose incomes fall in the bottom fifth, and partially subsidized programs on a sliding scale to parents in the next two fifths, the annual cost would be $36 billion for children younger than age 5. It is clear that there is no agreement on the costs of funding early care and education services to date.

In addition to being unclear about *how much* is needed to create a quality early care and education system, a second challenge that limits the ability to generate adequate revenue is that it is unclear *how* to go about raising funds. Several options are receiving attention (Kagan & Cohen, 1997):

- Individual and corporate income taxes: Increasing federal individual income tax receipts by approximately 10% or increasing federal individual and corporate income tax receipts by approximately 8.5% would generate about 50 billion new dollars a year. The use of income taxes to generate revenue is attractive because they are familiar to taxpayers and they would not require the creation of a new tax collection mechanism. Income taxes are, however, one of the least popular and most visible taxes, making them extremely difficult to increase.

- Federal payroll taxes and trust funds: Increasing the current social security payroll tax (the largest and best known payroll tax) by about 2% would generate approximately $50 billion new dollars a year, and by putting the funds directly into a trust fund, it would be assured that the revenues would in fact be used for early care and education services.
- New sales or excise tax: Increasing federal excise taxes by 50% and imposing a 10% surcharge on state sales tax receipts would generate about $50 billion in new funds a year. Another option would be to create a new excise tax dedicated to early care and education.

Other approaches include new savings and loan strategies, increasing the populations eligible to receive the school aid formula, and cutting other government expenditures to raise some of the needed new funds. Although these present potential mechanisms for generating new revenue for early care and education, it is important to note that no single strategy will yield sufficient funds and that each has advantages, as well as disadvantages, that must be carefully considered (Kagan & Cohen, 1997).

The Challenge

The three themes just discussed—regulation, training and certification, and funding—represent critical policy issues that must be addressed in order to promote quality infant and toddler child care. Although they are certainly not the only variables amenable to policy, if these three were suitably addressed, America would be well on its way to optimizing quality care for infants and toddlers. Though far from this goal presently, the analytic and practical work needed to move this agenda is emerging. The time is appropriate to convert this nascent policy agenda to reality.

HOME VISITING AND FAMILY SUPPORT

Because infants and toddlers are so dependent on their families, policies affecting them must focus on the programs and services that are provided to parents and their children. America has not been blind to this need. Indeed, there is evidence that the nation has been and remains more willing to provide direct and indirect services that enable parents to parent more effectively than to provide direct services for infants and toddlers. This section explores reasons why this is so, by beginning with a brief history of parenting. We, then, move to a discussion of the current situation and discuss two promising strategies that have evolved in the private and public sectors to support the parents of infants and toddlers: home visiting and family support.

Parenting in Perspective

Over the course of America's history, it has been the expectation not only that parents would be the primary caregivers and nurturers of their children but that parenting expertise was either inherited magically from the elders of past generations or was learned informally from the institutions that encase the family, notably the church and the neighborhood. Formal parenting education and preparental training was deemed unnecessary because parenting was a natural act that would unfold as the situation demanded. Early on, only when parents were deemed unable or unfit were more structured parenting education supports offered. For example, when the early infant schools were formed for children of the indigent and poor, they were predicated on the belief that such families could not provide adequate and appropriate care and as a result were somehow more morally dependent for parenting wisdom than more affluent members of society (Infant School Society of Boston, 1828). The earliest seeds of parenting education and support—like services for children—began with a deficit orientation.

Later, as more middle-class families encountered the challenges of rearing young children in an increasingly socially and geographically mobile society and as the benefits of parent engagement in children's development were scientifically documented, the need for parenting education and support began to expand across classes. Child development study groups and parenting discussion groups emerged with the child study movement. Parent cooperatives—typically aligned with child study groups—were born. And with the advent of Mothers Aid Societies and the national Parent–Teachers Association, opportunities for parents to learn about young children became popular across classes.

It should be noted that, historically, the majority of these efforts were rooted in the private sector: There was little dedication to formalizing parenting education efforts within policy or the public sector. Only in the 1960s, when a cascade of programs to support the economically disadvantaged were developed, was a commitment to parent involvement, parent education, and parent support ensconced in public policy—and then, for low-income families. Today, as parents across the income spectrum are creating a demand for parenting education, and as the need for and benefits of parenting education and family support services are increasingly being manifest, support is growing. Today, parenting education efforts are often funded either privately or with public dollars as discrete efforts or linked with health initiatives such as Healthy Families America. Similarly, family support programs, launched in the private sector, are now receiving public support at the federal level through the 1993 Family Preservation and Family Support Act and countless state-supported efforts.

These changes, though appearing subtle, actually bespeak a revolution that is taking place—quietly and incrementally. There is a growing understanding on the part of policy makers that supporting parents remains a good way to support the positive nurturance of young children. The question at hand is whether this surge of interest is sufficient to create the ground-swell of support needed to convert specific programs to a cogent policy—making parenting education and family support a durable part of the policy agenda.

Current Situation:
Information Gaps and Misunderstandings

There is good reason for the growth of interest in parenting education. Today's parents appear to lack information about normative development and how such knowledge relates to their own parenting practices. A 1997 survey indicates that although 53% of parents say they are sure of signs to watch for in their child's physical development, fewer express understanding about the course of emotional (38%), social (37%), and intellectual (44%) development (Peter D. Hart Research Associates, 1997). Furthermore, parents seem generally aware of the importance of the early years, but most do not understand the direct connection between healthy child development and their own parenting practices (Peter D. Hart Research Associates, 1997). In particular, parents do not understand the extent of their influence on their infants' or toddlers' long-term intellectual capacity and social development. Even among parents who do understand the depth of their influence during the early years, there is evidence that many remain misinformed about how parenting practices can promote the emotional, social, and intellectual development of infants and toddlers (Peter D. Hart Research Associates, 1997).

The current state of parents' knowledge fortifies parents' call for support and demonstrates a need to broaden strategies to support families with infants and toddlers. Moreover, the overwhelming body of new research demonstrating the significance of early childhood to long-term healthy development adds urgency to this need. The issue is what form should such support take, given the nature of our national history relative to the matters of family autonomy and the role of the public and private sectors. Two strategies have emerged that bear examination: home visiting and family support.

Home Visiting   Home visiting as a specific form of parenting education in which visitors go into the homes of families is not a new idea (Gomby, Larson, Lewit, & Behrman, 1993). It began in the late 19th century when private charities sent volunteers into the homes of poor families in urban centers to disseminate "moral and behavioral guidance" (Weiss, 1993, p. 115). Like the deficit orientation of other children's services, these efforts were based on the premise that poverty was the result of personal failings and could be remedied through friendship and guidance from a volunteer visitor (Weiss, 1993). As the plight of the urban poor became more evident and it was recognized that poverty could not be reduced through moral guidance, the home visitor also became an advocate and provider of information about other services. With the emergence of the profession of social work in the early 20th century, ventures into the home were curtailed somewhat as services were dispensed in office settings (Weiss, 1993). Then, in the 1960s, a reemergence of home visiting aided disadvantaged children and families by providing parents with support and information about how to improve their homes as environments that encourage children's healthy development (Gomby et al., 1993).

The 1960s press for home visiting came initially from a common sense notion that home visits provided a unique opportunity to reach individual families and tailor services to match their needs. In addition, it was thought that home-visiting strategies could touch families who might not seek out services (Gomby et al., 1993). Espousing these values, home visiting was often initially pioneered by one or two dedicated individuals at the local level. As the concept gained momentum, programs were expanded first to the state and then to the federal level, often through legislation. Parents as Teachers (PAT) is one such example. In 1981, PAT was established in Missouri with the goal of improving children's readiness for school by connecting parents of preschool children and schools. Since then, more than 1,000 PAT programs have been established in 42 states, and some programs have expanded from serving children from birth to 3 years old to serving children up to 5 years of age.

Home visiting programs have also emerged as part of child care, health, education, child abuse, substance abuse, and community development programs. For example, in 1988, Congress enacted the Comprehensive Child Development Center Act (PL 100-297) that included home visiting as a required component. (This act was later repealed under the Human Services Amendments of 1994 [PL 103-252].) Federal Even Start programs, first funded in 1989, are required to provide home-based instructional services to parents and children together in an effort to help parents become full partners in the education of their children and to help children reach their full potential as learners. In addition, the Services for Children of Substance Abusers Act (PL 103-43) was incorporated into the ADAMHA (Alcohol, Drug, and Mental Health Administration) Reorganization Act of 1992 (PL 103-321) with a component that establishes a home-visiting program for pregnant women who are at risk of delivering an infant with health or developmental complications. In 1991, the U.S. Advisory Board on Child Abuse and Neglect recommended the development of a national, universal, voluntary neonatal home visiting program with the aim of preventing the maltreatment of children. Finally, maternal and infant home visiting programs are required as part of the 1992 Community Integrated Service Systems.

Interestingly, home visiting programs have a broad base of public support and have been amenable to legislative action by policy makers even though the data supporting their efficacy are not consistent. New Parents as Teachers of Missouri (NPAT) is illustrative. On the one hand, an evaluation of NPAT showed that parents who participated in the program demonstrated significantly greater knowledge in four of six areas of parenting than did parents in a comparison group (Pfannenstiel & Seltzer, 1989). Parents' participation in NPAT also significantly increased children's intellectual achievement and language ability at age 3, and NPAT children ranked higher in four of six dimensions of social development (Pfannenstiel & Seltzer, 1989). On the other hand, an evaluation of the Texas PAT found no differences in cognitive development between the PAT participants and a control group when the participants were children of more highly educated mothers (Barnes, Goodson, & Layzer, 1995).

Similarly, when examining the impact of home visiting programs, ambivalence exists. One study of a home visiting program located in Memphis, Tennessee, found that at the end of a 2-year period of home visiting during infancy, mothers in the treatment group expressed greater empathy, fewer unrealistic expectations of their infants, and diminished belief in the value of physical punishment than their counterparts in the comparison group (Kitzman et al., 1997). However, there are virtually no reliable studies of long-term effects of home visit programs for infants and toddlers that are environmentally at risk (Barnes et al., 1995). Similar ambivalence exists when looking at children's cognitive development. For example, in a review of 15 home visiting programs aimed at improving the cognitive development of children of low-income families, six programs had significant positive results (Olds & Kitzman, 1993). More recent research (Olds et al., 1997; Olds et al., 1998) has found positive long-term effects on children's criminal and anti-social behaviors and on maternal life course, and reductions in child abuse and neglect.

These mixed results may be attributed to several factors. Home visiting programs are difficult to evaluate because they aim to provide a holistic approach to services, which results in ambiguity of quantifiable outcomes (Barnes et al., 1995). Furthermore, it is difficult to generalize findings across studies because there are great differences in characteristics of the programs themselves. They vary in the staff training requirements, the families they serve, the frequency and duration of services, and whether home visits are the primary form of service or if they are provided in conjunction with other programs (Gomby et al., 1993; Olds & Kitzman, 1993). They also have varying goals, such as preventing health problems; preventing child abuse; promoting prenatal health; promoting healthy social, physical, or intellectual development; or a combination of these. Finally, it is difficult to assess the efficacy of home-visiting efforts because the instruments used to collect data may not be sufficiently attuned to family culture and diversity, and to the intricacies of family interactions.

Given this ambivalence in the research, several next steps should be considered. First, a more consolidated, dedicated research agenda is needed to determine which types of programs are best suited for which children and families. Such an agenda must address program variation and must allow for the development of appropriate instrumentation. Second, although it is advisable to maintain a diversity of program options, legislation could promote linkages between home visiting efforts, and among home-visiting and community-based services (e.g., health, mental health) for young children and families. Home visits may gain potency when integrated into larger networks of services for families and children (Weiss, 1993). Third, it is necessary to consider carefully the nature of training that is necessary to derive optimum benefits from home visiting. Preliminary evidence suggests that programs employing professionals may be more likely to benefit parents' caregiving skills and children's intellectual development than those staffed by paraprofessionals (Olds & Kitzman, 1993). Fourth, as noted by ZERO TO THREE (1999), home visitation programs need to have clearly defined goals, stable and adequate funding, and evaluations and continuous quailiy improvement effects.

Family Support   Like home visiting, family support began as a grassroots movement that spawned statewide initiatives and ultimately led to the creation of national legislation. Unlike home visitation, the development of family support policy, however, has gone beyond programmatic change to encompass a multitude of institutions and agencies and has catalyzed a shift in social service strategies in this country. A brief review of the history of family support helps explain its growth and impact.

The family support movement has historical antecedents in three distinct schools of American social services practice: the settlement house, self-help, and parent education movements (Weissbourd, 1987). Located within neighborhoods, the settlement house movement of the late 19th century aimed to provide aid to families with direct services, always respecting the specific character of a community and the conditions of daily life. From the settlement movement, the family support movement derives a commitment to working with a holistic understanding of families and communities (Weissbourd, 1987). The proliferation of self-help groups of the 1960s reflected the empowerment agenda of the era. Individuals joined together around common issues and were connected in sharing experiences and engendering action. From the self-help movement, the family support movement draws an emphasis on empowerment of the individual through mutual support and interdependence (Weissbourd, 1987). And continuing in the tradition of the parent education movement, family support is dedicated to informing parents on the principles of child development and maintains that all families benefit from parent education (Weissbourd, 1987). These three antecedents were each engaged in a type of social reform that, when blended, possessed unique synergy and new potential.

Although the family support movement draws from this rich history of thought, it is also shaped by demographic and sociopolitical forces that have emerged since the 1960s. First, partly in response to the increasing mobility and fragmentation of American families and communities, family support has emerged as one way to serve children, families, and communities (Bronfenbrenner & Neville, 1994). Second, as the public has become increasingly dissatisfied with the perceived ineffectiveness of human service bureaucracies, it has demanded services that are more family focused, accessible, and responsive to client needs— characteristics of family support. Third, because an emphasis on personal responsibility and the role of the family has resurfaced from diverse political quarters, family support has been incorporated into legislation with political support from both sides of the political aisle. In short, family support is both a blend of several historic social service traditions, as well as a response to the changing character of the needs of families with young children.

Grounded in movements of social thought of the past, and propelled by demographic and sociopolitical realties, the family support movement has evolved through several stages, from the individual, often informal, community-based programs of the 1970s into a full-fledged national movement. Motivated by the lack of available services, the first small programs of the 1970s proved remarkably successful in addressing the social services problems of the time (Weissbourd, 1994). In this early period, it was hoped that family support programs would sprout up "on every corner" (Weissbourd, 1994). During this period, the focus remained on developing new program models and improving older ones, each based on the needs of individual families and communities. The terminology of the time also emphasized providing resources to enable families to take an active role in helping themselves.

Recognizing the changing face and changing needs of America's families and communities, the professional, public, academic, and political communities turned their attention to the emerging family support movement. This marked the second stage in the development of family support, characterized by the adoption of family support by mainstream institutions, leading to two distinct types of institutional change. The first type of institutional change was the incorporation of family support programs and principles into existing services—health clinics, schools, hospitals, and social welfare—prompting these institutions to change their internal approaches to service delivery. The second type of institutional change was the application of the concepts of family support to develop new community-wide approaches. Family support programs, aiming to provide families with comprehensive support, served as links, integrating the social services provided by disparate agencies and organizations in the community. In this second stage, programs were incorporated into mainstream settings and the ideas of family support were used as a springboard for institutional reform.

The third and most dramatic stage in the development of family support was ushered in with the passage of the Family Preservation and Support Services Program of 1993. This legislation, which represents the single largest effort to date to fund community-based family support programs, mandated a more integrated, cross-system approach to planning. Under the initiative, states were required to develop comprehensive plans for using new funds to create or expand family support services in conjunction with all other existing services for children and families. Plans were developed with the participation of families, local community groups, and nongovernmental service providers. This sweeping policy initiative has transformed human services by mandating that states and mainstream institutions become involved in community-based, integrated service efforts. The principles and goals of family support—promoting healthy development of children and their parents; respecting the contributions of parents, communities, and different cultures; and a holistic approach aimed at providing comprehensive universal services—are being integrated as a standard in service delivery.

Policy Conclusions from Home Visiting and Family Support Although family support and home visiting began as isolated local programs, they have each occasioned major policy shifts on both the state and national levels. Home visiting has enjoyed success at the programmatic level through dramatic expansion in the number of existing programs. Family support policy, however, has gone beyond a model of programmatic expansion, aiming to transform human services. In this sense, the development of both home visiting and family support are instructive not simply as a means of service delivery, but as prototypes for how American policy emerges—from grassroots, through the states, to the federal government—and how it is transformed, beginning in one sector and flourishing in another. What has emerged is a uniquely American approach to serving the parents of very young children.

CONCLUSION

A review of the three domains of policy summarized in this chapter demonstrates clearly that services for infants and toddlers linked to health seem to garner considerable policy support. Parenting services for the families of infants and toddlers are also supported, though child care services for infants and toddlers are less robustly funded. Clearly, greater support is needed within all domains. It is also needed across the three domains. Yet, the funding experience to date indicates that services for infants and toddlers are legislated and provided in a categorical fashion, with different programs targeting different children and with only a few programs considering the total child within the context of family and community.

This review has clearly indicated that although policy for infants and toddlers has not been coherent, it has been incremental. Now, the United States must strive to adopt a long-term vision and not be daunted by the inevitable episodic setbacks. The nation must also recognize that policies for infants and toddlers are framed by deep-seated values and attitudes as well as historic policy practices, making change all the more challenging. Finally, the nation needs to recognize the policy distance that has been traveled. Although the journey has been periodically halted, a new horizon is emerging. Our responsibility is to create a new policy vista by capitalizing on analytic and strategic capabilities and on the current policy momentum—one that affords countless opportunities.

REFERENCES

ADAMHA Reorganization Act, PL 102-321, 42 U.S.C. §§ 201 *et seq.*
Army Child Development Services. (n.d.). *A staff development and compensation initiative for caregiving personnel.* Alexandria, VA: U.S. Army Child and Family Services Center.
Arnett, J. (1989). Caregivers in day care centers: Does training matter? *Journal of Applied Developmental Psychology, 10,* 541–552.

Barnes, H.V., Goodson, B.D., & Layzer, J.I. (1995). *National evaluation of family support programs: Review of research on supportive interventions for children and families (Vol. 1)*. Cambridge, MA: Abt Associates.

Barnett, W.S. (1993). New wine in old bottles: Increasing the coherence of childhood care and education policy. *Early Childhood Research Quarterly, 8*, 519–558.

Bergmann, B.R. (1994). Curing child poverty in the United States. *AEA Papers and Proceedings, 84*(2), 76–80.

Bredekamp, S. (Ed.). (1987). *Developmentally appropriate practice in early childhood programs serving children from birth through age 8*. Washington, DC: National Association for the Education of Young Children.

Bronfenbrenner, U., & Neville, P.R. (1994). America's children and families: An international perspective. In S.L. Kagan & B. Weissbourd (Eds.), *Putting families first: America's family support movement and the challenge of change*. (pp. 3–27). San Francisco: Jossey-Bass.

Brooks-Gunn J., & Duncan, G.J. (1997). The effects of poverty on children. *The Future of Children, 7*(2), 55–71.

Carnegie Task Force on Meeting the Needs of Young Children. (1994). *Starting points: Meeting the needs of our youngest children*. New York: The Carnegie Corporation of New York.

Clark, S.J., & Long, S.K. (1995). *Child care prices: A profile of six communities*. Washington, DC: The Urban Institute.

Clarke-Stewart, A. (1977). *Child care in the family*. New York: Academic Press.

Comprehensive Child Development Center Act of 1988, PL 100-297, 42 U.S.C. §§ 2501 *et seq.*

Cost, Quality, & Child Outcomes Study Team. (1995). *Cost, quality, and child outcomes in child care centers*. Denver: Department of Economics, University of Colorado.

Data User Services Division, Data Access and Use Staff, Bureau of the Census. (1993). *Current population survey, March 1993 technical documentation*. Washington, DC: U.S. Bureau of the Census.

Davis, K. (1997, February). *Meeting the health needs of America's children: Paper presented at the Aspen Institute conference*. New York: The Commonwealth Fund.

Dawson, G., Hessl, D., & Frey, K. (1994). Social influences on early developing biological and behavioral systems related to risk for affective disorder. In D. Cicchetti (Ed.), *Development and Psychopathology* (pp. 759–779). New York: Cambridge University Press.

Duncan, G.L., & Brooks-Gunn, J. (Eds.). (1997). *Consequences of growing up poor*. New York: Russell Sage Foundation.

Durch, J. (Ed.). (1994). *Protecting and improving quality of care for children under health care reform: Workshop highlights*. Washington, DC: Institute of Medicine.

Education for All Handicapped Children Act of 1975, PL 94-142, 20 U.S.C. §§ 1400 *et seq.*

Education for All Handicapped Act Amendments of 1986, PL 99-457, 20 U.S.C. §§ 1400 *et seq.*

Federal Register. (1980). *Federal interagency day care requirements*. Washington, DC: Department of Health, Education, and Welfare.

Fielding, J.E., & Halfon, N. (1994). Where is the health in health reform? *Journal of the American Medical Association, 272*, 1292–1296.

Fosberg, S. (1981). *Family day care in the United States: Summary of findings: Final report of National Day Care Home Study* (Vol. 1). Cambridge, MA: Abt Associates.

Fox, H.B., & McManus, M.A. (1996). *Medicaid managed care for children with chronic or disabling conditions: Improved strategies for states and plans.* Washington, DC: Maternal and Child Health Policy Research Center.

Galinsky, E., Howes, C., & Kontos, S. (1995). *The family child care training study: Interim Report.* New York: Families and Work Institute.

Galinsky, E., Howes, C., Kontos, S., & Shinn, M. (1994). *The study of children in family child care and relative care.* New York: Families and Work Institute.

Gallagher, J.J. (1989). A new policy initiative: Infants and toddlers with handicapping conditions. *American Psychologist, 44*(2), 387–391.

Gallagher, J.J. (1994). Policy designed for diversity: New initiatives for children with disabilities. In D. Bryant (Ed.), *Implementing early intervention* (pp. 336–350). New York: Guilford Publications, Inc.

Gauthier, A.K., & Schrodel, S.P. (1997). *Expanding children's coverage: Lessons from state initiatives in health care reform.* Washington, DC: Alpha Center.

Gazan, H. (1997). *Emerging trends in child care regulation.* St. Paul, MN: National Association of Regulatory Administration.

Gomby, D.S., Larson, C.S., Lewit, E.M., & Behrman, R.E. (1993). Home visiting: Analysis and recommendations. In R.E. Behrman (Ed.), *The future of children: Home visiting* (Vol. 3, pp. 6–22). Los Altos, CA: Center for the Future of Children, The David and Lucile Packard Foundation.

Gormley, W.T. (1995). *Everybody's children: Child care as a public problem.* Washington, DC: Brookings Institution.

Gunnarsson, L. (1993). Sweden. In M. Cochran (Ed.), *International handbook of child care policies and programs* (pp. 491–514). Westport, CT: Greenwood Press.

Halfon, N., Hochstein, M., & Inkelas, M. (1996). *Models for assuring children's health security: Why children are different.* Unpublished manuscript, UCLA Center for Healthier Children, Families, and Communities.

Halfon, N., Inkelas, M., & Wood, D. (1995). Nonfinancial barriers to care for children and youth. *Annual Review of Public Health, 16*, 447–72.

Harbin, G., Gallagher, J.J., Lillie, T., & Eckland, J. (1992). Factors influencing state progress in the implementation of Public Law 99-457, Part H. *Policy Sciences, 25*, 103–115.

Hayes, C.D., Palmer, J.L., & Zaslow, M.J. (Eds.). (1990). *Who cares for America's children? Child care policy for the 1990's.* Washington, DC: National Academy Press.

Henry J. Kaiser Family Foundation. (1997). *Medicaid's role for children fact sheet.* Washington, DC: Author.

Howes, C., Smith, E., & Galinsky, E. (1995). *The Florida child care quality improvement study.* New York: Families and Work Institute.

Human Services Amendments of 1994, PL 103-252, 42 U.S.C. §§ 1 *et seq.*

Infant School Society of Boston. (1828). *Constitution and by-laws.* Boston: T.R. Marvin.

Kagan, S.L., & Cohen, N.E. (1997). *Not by chance: Creating an early care and education system for America's children.* New Haven, CT: The Bush Center in Child Development and Social Policy, Yale University.

Kamerman, S.B., & Kahn, A.J. (1994). *A welcome for every child: Care, education, and family support for infants and toddlers in Europe.* Arlington, VA: ZERO TO THREE: National Center for Infants, Toddlers, and Families.

Kisker, E., Hofferth, S., Phillips, D., & Farquhar, E. (1991). *A profile of child care settings: Early education and care in 1990* (Vol. I). Princeton, NJ: Mathematica Policy Research, Inc.

Kitzman, H., Olds, D.L., Henderson, C.R., Hanks, C., Cole, R., Tatelbaum, R., McConnochie, K.M., Sidora, K., Luckey, D.W., Shaver, D., Engelhardt, K., James, D., & Barnard, K. (1997). Effect of prenatal and infancy home visitation by nurses on pregnancy outcomes, childhood injuries, and repeated child-bearing. *Journal of the American Medical Association, 278*(8), 644–652.

Knitzer, J., & Page, S. (1998). *Map and track: State initiatives for young children and families, 1998 edition.* New York: National Center for Children in Poverty.

Lassegard, E. (1993). Japan. In M. Cochran (Ed.), *International handbook of child care policies and programs* (pp. 313–332). Westport, CT: Greenwood Press.

Maternal and Child Health Bureau. (1996). *National agenda for children with special health care needs in managed care organizations: Summaries of expert work group meetings.* Rockville, MD: Author, Health Resources and Services Administration.

Mitchell, A. (1996). Licensing: Lessons from other occupations. In S.L. Kagan & N.E. Cohen (Eds.), *Reinventing early care and education: A vision for a quality system* (pp. 101–123). San Francisco: Jossey-Bass.

Model Child Care Standards Act of 1985, PL 98-473, 42 U.S.C. §§ 1397b *et seq.*

Modigliani, K., Helburn, S., Morris, J., & Culkin, M. (1996). *The economics of family child care project.* Unpublished manuscript. Boston: Wheelock College.

National Commission on Children. (1991). *Beyond rhetoric: A new American agenda for children and families.* Washington, DC: U.S. Government Printing Office.

National Governors' Association. (1997). *Children's health: Implementing the balanced budget act of 1997: A resource notebook.* Washington, DC: Author.

National Institute of Child Health and Human Development Early Child Care Research Network (1997, April). *Mother–child interaction and cognitive outcomes associated with early child care: Results of the NICHD study.* Paper presented at the biennial meeting of the Society for Research in Child Development. Washington, DC.

National Maternal and Child Health Policy Consortium. (1997). *Facts about uninsured children.* Virginia: Author.

Newacheck, P.W., Hughes, D.C., & Cisternas, M. (1995). Children and health insurance: An overview of recent trends. *Health Affairs, 14,* 244–254.

Newacheck, P.W., Hughes, D.C., English, A., Fox, H.B., Perrin, J., & Halfon, N. (1995). The effect on children of curtailing Medicaid spending. *Journal of the American Medical Association, 274*(18), 1468–1471.

Newacheck, P.W., Hughes, D.C., Halfon, N., & Brindis, C. (1997). Social HMOs and other capitated arrangements for children with special health care needs. *Maternal and Child Health Journal, 1*(2), 111–119.

Newacheck, P.W., Hughes, D.C., & Stoddard, J.J. (1996). Children's access to primary care: Differences by race, income, and insurance status. *Pediatrics, 97*(1), 26–32.

Newacheck, P.W., Stoddard, J.J., Hughes, D.C., & Pearl, M. (1998). Health insurance and access to primary care for children. *The New England Journal of Medicine, 338*(8), 513–519.

Ojala, M. (1989). Early childhood training, care, and education in Finland. In P.P. Olmsted & D.P. Weikart (Eds.), *How nations serve young children: Profiles of child care and education in 14 countries* (pp. 87–118). Ypsilanti, MI: High/Scope Press.

Olds, D.L., & Kitzman, H. (1993). Review of research on home visiting for pregnant women and parents of young children. In R.E. Behrman (Ed.), *The future of children: Home visiting* (Vol. 3, pp. 53–92). Los Altos, CA: Center for the Future of Children, The David and Lucile Packard Foundation.

Olds, D.L., Eckenrode, J., Henderon, C.R. Kitzman, H., Powers, J., Cole, R., Sidora, K., Morris, P., Pettitt, L.M., & Luckey, D. (1997). Long-term effects of nurse home visitation on maternal life course and child abuse and neglect. *Journal of the American Medical Association, 278*(8), 637–643.

Olds, D.L., Henderon, C.R., Cole, R., Eckenrode, J., Kitzman H., Luckey, D., Pettitt, L., Sidora, K., Morris, P., & Powers, J. (1998). Long-term effects of nurse home visitation on children's criminal and anti-social behavior. *Journal of the American Medical Association, 208*(14), 1238–1244.

Palfrey, J., Haynie, M., & the American Academy of Pediatrics Medical Home Program for Children with Special Needs. (1996, February). Strategies for managed care: Managed care and children with special health care needs: Creating a medical home. *AAP News* (Insert).

Pascal, C., Bertram, T., & Heaslip, P. (1991). *Comparative directory of initial training for early years teachers.* Worcester, England: Association of Teacher Education in Europe, Early Years Working Group.

Passell, P. (1996, December 25). Three strategies to help families in the United States. *The New York Times*, p. D2.

Peter D. Hart Research Associates. (1997). *Key findings from a nationwide survey among parents of zero to three-year-olds.* Report prepared for ZERO TO THREE: National Center for Infants, Toddlers, and Families. Washington, DC: Author.

Pfannenstiel, J.C., & Seltzer, D.A. (1989). New Parents as Teachers: Evaluation of an early parent education program. *Early Childhood Research Quarterly, 4,* 1–18.

Phillips, D.A. (1996). Reframing the quality issue. In S.L. Kagan & N.E. Cohen (Eds.), *Reinventing early care and education: A vision for a quality system* (pp. 43–64). San Francisco: Jossey-Bass.

Phillips, D.A., & Howes, C. (1987). Indicators of quality in child care: Review of research. In D. Philips (Ed.), *Quality in child care: What does research tell us?* (pp.1–19). Washington DC: National Association for the Education of Young Children.

Pritchard, E. (1996). Training and professional development: International approaches. In S.L. Kagan & N.E. Cohen (Eds.), *Reinventing early care and education: A vision for a quality system* (pp. 124–141). San Francisco: Jossey-Bass.

Regenstein, M., Silow-Carroll, S., & Meyer, J.A. (1995). *Early childhood education: Models for expanding access.* Washington, DC: The Economic and Social Research Institute.

Richardson, G., & Marx, E. (1989). *A welcome for every child: How France achieves quality in child care—Practical ideas for the United States.* New York: The French-American Foundation.

Richmond, J., & Kotelchuck, M. (1984). Commentary on changed lives. In J.R. Berrueta-Clement, L.J. Schweinhart, & D.P. Weikart, (Eds.), *Changed lives: The effects of the Perry Preschool Program on youths through age 19* (pp. 204–210). Ypsilanti, MI: High/Scope Press.

Ruopp, R., Travers, J., Glantz, F., & Coelen, C. (1979). *Children at the center: Final results of the National Day Care Study.* Cambridge, MA: Abt Associates.

Scarr, S. (1996, April). *Child care research, social values, and public policy.* Paper presented at the State Meeting of the American Academy of Arts and Sciences. Cambridge, MA.

Schweinhart, L.J., Barnes, H.V., Weikart, D.P., Barnett, W.S., & Epstein, A.S. (1993). *Significant benefits: The High/Scope Perry Preschool Study through age 27.* Ypsilanti, MI: High/Scope Press.

Select Panel for the Promotion of Child Health. (1981). *Better health for our children: A national strategy. Volume 1: Major findings and recommendations.* Washington, DC: U.S. Department of Health and Human Services.

Services for Children of Substance Abusers of 1993, PL 103-43, 42 U.S.C.A.§§ 2008(i)(2)(B)(ii) *et seq.* (West 1993).

Sheils, J.F., & Wolfe, P.R. (1992). The role of private health insurance in children's health care. *The Future of Children, 2*(2), 115–133.

Shore, R. (1997). *Rethinking the brain: New insights into early development.* New York: Families and Work Institute.

U.S. Department of Commerce. (1993). *Statistical abstract of the United States, 1992.* Washington, DC: U.S. Government Printing Office.

U.S. Department of Education, National Center for Education Statistics. (1995). *Approaching kindergarten: A look at preschoolers in the United States.* Washington, DC: Author.

Wehr, E., & Jameson, E.J. (1994). Beyond benefits: The importance of a pediatric standard in private insurance contracts to ensuring health care access for children. *The Future of Children, 5*(3), 115–133.

Weiss, H.B. (1993). Home visits: Necessary but not sufficient. In R.E. Behrman (Ed.), *The future of children: Home visiting* (Vol. 3, pp. 113–128). Los Altos, CA: Center for the Future of Children, The David and Lucile Packard Foundation.

Weissbourd, B. (1987). A brief history of family support programs. In S.L. Kagan, D.R. Powell, B. Weissbourd, & E. Zigler (Eds.), *America's Family Support Programs* (pp. 38–56). New Haven, CT: Yale University.

Weissbourd, B. (1994). The evolution of the family resource movement. In S.L. Kagan & B. Weissbourd (Eds.), *Putting families first: America's family support movement and the challenge of change.* (pp. 28–48). San Francisco: Jossey-Bass.

Whitebook, M., Howes, C., & Phillips, D. (1989). *Who cares? Child care teachers and the quality of care in America: Final report of the National Child Care Staffing Study.* Oakland, CA: Child Care Employee Project.

Whitebook, M., Howes, C., & Phillips, D. (1993). *National Child Care Staffing Study revisited: Four years in the life of center-based care.* Oakland, CA: Child Care Employee Project.

Willer, B., Hofferth, S., Kisker, E., Divine-Hawkins, P., Farquhar, E., & Glantz, F. (1991). *The demand and supply of child care in 1990: Joint findings from the National Child Care Survey 1990 and A Profile of Child Care Settings.* Washington, DC: National Association for the Education of Young Children.

Young, K.T., Davis, D., & Schoen, C. (1996). *The commonwealth fund survey of parents with young children.* New York: The Commonwealth Fund.

Young, K.T., Marsland, K.W., & Zigler, E. (1997). The regulatory status of center-based infant and toddler child care. *American Journal of Orthopsychiatry, 67*(4), 535–544.

Young, K.T., & Zigler, E. (1986). Infant and toddler day care: Regulation and policy implications. *American Journal of Orthopsychiatry, 56*(1), 43–55.

ZERO TO THREE/National Center for Infants, Toddlers, and Families. (1999). *Home visitation: Reaching babies and families "where they live."* Washington, DC: Author.

Zuckerman, B., & Parker, S. (1995). Preventive pediatrics: New models of providing needed health services. *Pediatrics, 5,* 758–762.

11

Supporting Families as Primary Caregivers

The Role of the Workplace

◆ ❖ ◆

Ellen Galinsky and James T. Bond

Over the past 150 years, employers have provided work–family supports for families whenever women's labor was crucial either to addressing a national crisis or to ensuring business success. The first employer-supported child care centers on record were created during the Civil War to help women participate in the war effort. In 1910, the Association of Day Nurseries noted the existence of 450 child care centers in working-class neighborhoods, some of which were sponsored by factories that employed the children's mothers. And both world wars saw increases in employer involvement. During the Second World War, Congress passed the Lanham Act to encourage the development of child care programs so women could work in industries critical to the national defense. During that time, there were many innovations that would look novel 50 years later, such as laundry service and hot dinners sent home with the children (Galinsky & Friedman, 1993; Tentler, 1979).

The growing number of women entering the labor force in the 1970s renewed employers' interest in addressing child care needs of employees, though it was thought that these efforts would be a passing fad and would disappear in the first business downturn (Feinstein, 1979). At the same time, a new field of research on work and family life began to emerge that drew from developmental, industrial, and community psychology; sociology; anthropology; economics; and public policy research, among other fields. Overall, there have been five strands in this research: 1) research on work and family life among adults, 2) research on the impact of parental employment on children, 3) research on the prevalence of work–family supports, 4) research on employees' access to work–family supports, and 5) research on the impact of work–family supports on employees and on business productivity. These five strands of research are briefly reviewed below.

RESEARCH ON
WORK AND FAMILY LIFE AMONG ADULTS

The research on work and family life has its origins in a study on dual-career couples in Britain conducted by Rapoport and Rapoport in the 1970s (Rapoport & Rapoport 1971, 1976; Rapoport, Rapoport, Strelitz, & Kew, 1977). Kanter (1977) also wrote a seminal paper on why there had been scant attention to this new reality in people's lives, stating that work and family were seen as separate, nonoverlapping worlds. She issued a call for research to help elucidate this new phenomenon.

The most well-known study that brought public attention to work and family life in the 1970s was the *Quality of Employment Survey* (QES). This study consisted of representative samples of employed American adults and was conducted by the Institute for Social Research at the University of Michigan at three points in time (Quinn et al., 1971; Quinn & Shepard, 1974; Quinn & Staines, 1979). The 1977 QES and other studies identified the work and family factors most significantly associated with various outcomes, including:

- Work–family conflict (Burke, Weir, & DuWors, 1979; Crouter, 1984; Hughes & Galinsky, 1988; Keith & Schafer, 1980; Piotrkowski & Katz, 1983; Voydanoff, 1988)
- Role strain (Bohen & Viveros-Long, 1981)
- Job satisfaction (Repetti & Cosmas, 1991)
- Psychological well-being (Barnett & Baruch, 1985; Barnett & Marshall, 1991; Repetti, 1987)
- Marital relations (Hughes, Galinsky, & Morris, 1992; Repetti, 1989)
- Parenting satisfaction and children's development (Greenberger, Goldberg, Hamill, O'Neil, & Payne, 1989; Greenberger, O'Neil, & Nagel, 1994; Howes, Sakai, et al., 1995; Kohn, 1969; Kohn & Schooler, 1973; Lerner & Galambos, 1985; Menaghan & Parcel, 1990; O'Neill, 1992; Piotrkowski & Crits-Cristoph, 1981; Piotrkowski & Katz, 1983)

The Department of Labor discontinued its funding of the QES in the late 1970s. This study was picked up and elaborated by the Families and Work Institute, which conducts a nationally representative study of work and family life, the *National Study of the Changing Workforce* (Bond, Galinsky, & Swanberg, 1998; Galinsky, Bond, & Friedman, 1993) every 5 years.

Many work–family studies focused on work–family conflict because it has been seen as the psychological point at which work roles and family roles intersect. Voydanoff (1988) defined this concept as the inter-role conflict in which the demands of one role interfere with fulfilling the demands of the other. Piotrkowski (1979) differentiated structural and psychological conflict or interference. Structural conflict is the extent to which the demands of one role promote practical difficulty in managing the demands of the other, and psychological conflict is the transfer of moods from one domain to the other. Studies have examined the workplace antecedent of work–family conflict and psychological well-being. Among the factors that recur as significant are the amount and scheduling of work time, job autonomy, supportive supervisors, supportive coworkers, and lower job demands (Greenberger et al., 1989; Hoffman, 1989; Karasek, 1979; Repetti & Cosmas, 1991; Repetti & Wood, 1995; Staines & Pleck, 1983; Voydanoff, 1988).

A number of researchers are now questioning the "separate spheres" model of work–family research, in which work and family are still seen as competing domains with clear boundaries and demands, which, when they intersect, give rise to conflict and tension, particularly for women. Barnett (1997) called for an "overlapping spheres" model of work–life in which the boundaries are less clear and there are positive effects of operating in both spheres for women and for men. Thus, the emphasis is on integration rather than conflict and interference. A study on parental employment and on how children see their working parents by Ellen Galinsky (1999) postulated a new conceptual framework that looks at the overlapping domains of work and family life and poses an integration as well as a conflict model.

RESEARCH ON THE IMPACT OF PARENTAL EMPLOYMENT ON CHILDREN[1]

Studies of the impact of parental employment on children have taken three different approaches. First, there are numerous studies comparing the children of employed and nonemployed parents. The vast majority of these studies have concentrated on assessing how the regular absence of mothers during working hours affects children's development. A second approach includes both mothers and fathers. These studies probe how the nature of parents' jobs and work–family stress affect children.

[1]This section draws heavily on a research review conducted in 1996 by the Families and Work Institute: *The Impact of Parental Employment on Children* by Alison Sidle Fuligni, Ellen Galinsky, and Michelle Poris (1996).

The third approach also explores the nature of parents' jobs, concentrating on how the skills and competencies that are valued in the workplace affect parents' child-rearing values and styles.

Approach 1: Comparing the Children of Employed and Nonemployed Parents

The earliest studies compared the children whose mothers were at home full time with those whose mothers were employed. Underlying these studies was the implicit or explicit assumption that maternal employment would be harmful to the mother–child attachment, to the family relationship, and to children's subsequent development.

Attachment Research   These studies have focused on infants and on the mother–child attachment for two reasons. First, secure attachments have been found in study after study to predict later successful development (Ainsworth, 1979; Bowlby, 1969). Infants with secure attachments to their mothers are found to be better able to solve problems, to explore, and to be independent in the toddler years. In the preschool years, securely attached children tend to be more constructively involved at school, to play better with other children, and to be cooperative and compliant with adults. In their school years, these children fare better as well (Arend, Gove, & Sroufe, 1979; Egeland, Carlson, & Sroufe, 1993; Erickson, Kormarcher, & Egeland, 1992; Londerville & Main, 1981;Vaughn, Gove, & Egeland, 1980). Second, there is no evidence that mother–child separation after infancy affects the mother–child attachment (Gamble & Zigler, 1988).

In the 1980s, two studies created a stir around the country because they concluded that a small but statistically significant number of infants who were away from their mothers for more than 20 hours per week during their first year were more likely to have insecure attachments to their mothers than infants who did not experience this separation (Barglow, Vaughn, & Molitor, 1987; Belsky & Rovine, 1987). The finding that infants are potentially at risk for later developmental problems was obviously of great concern because it was speculated that insecure attachments in infancy might be expressed as anger, aggression, or withdrawal during the preschool years.

The preponderance of studies of infants does not find differences in the security of attachment relationships for the children of employed and nonemployed mothers (Clarke-Stewart, 1988; Goldberg & Easterbrooks, 1988; Owen, Easterbrooks, Weintraub, Jaeger, & Hoffman, 1988). The most comprehensive study to date, sponsored by National Institute of Child Health and Human Development (NICHD) Early Childhood Network (1997) and conducted by 10 research teams in 10 communities, likewise did not find that mother–child attachment is affected by maternal employment and the early use of child care, except in cases in which the mother was less sensitive and responsive to begin with.

In sum, it has become clear that maternal employment in the first year of the child's life is not directly linked to an insecure attachment relationship between the mother and the child. When studies find this outcome, other interrelated factors seem to come into play (Fuligni et al., 1996). Children are found to develop more positively when both the mother and father believe that the mother should work and when both the mother and father support each other emotionally (Gottfried, Gottfried, & Bathurst, 1988). The income that mothers and fathers contribute to the family tends to make a positive difference in children's development (Brooks-Gunn, Guo, & Furstenberg, 1993; Dubow & Ippolito, 1994; Duncan, Brooks-Gunn, & Klebanov, 1994; Hoffman, 1989). Furthermore, the quality of child care also affects children. Put simply, high-quality child care is good for children, whereas low-quality child care is potentially harmful (Cost, Quality, and Child Outcomes Study Team, 1995; Galinsky, Howes, Kontos, & Shinn, 1994; Kontos, Howes, Shinn, & Galinsky, 1994). Lois Hoffman and Lise M. Youngblade, leading theorists in the debate on maternal employment, sum it up this way: "The existing data reviewed here suggest that mothers' employment may have effects, both positive and negative, on the child's social and academic competencies, but these effects are not direct ones" (1999, p. 26). They suggest that "the father's role, the mother's sense of well-being, and parental orientations toward independence and autonomy" all make a difference (1999, p. 26).

Quality and Quantity of Time Spent Apart   Another issue these studies have probed is how the amount of time mothers and fathers (here fathers were also studied) spend with or away from their children affects children's development. A review of these studies leads to the conclusion that simply looking at the amount of time does not present a complete picture of family relationships. The quality of parent–child interactions also plays a role in the overall effect on children's development. For example, one study that examined father–toddler interaction found that child outcomes, such as attachment security, positive affect, and attention, are more strongly related to qualitative aspects of fathering, such as sensitivity, than to measures of the amount of time fathers spend with toddlers (Easterbrooks & Goldberg, 1984). When parents are responsive and warm with their children, the children are more socially competent in kindergarten (Pettit, Harrist, Bates, & Dodge, 1991) and perform better in school (Paulson, 1994).

Social Development of Young Children   Research on the social development of children with employed and nonemployed mothers generally supports the conclusion that maternal employment does not harm—and may even benefit—children's development of self-esteem, independence, peer relationships, and egalitarian views. There are several issues such as maternal role satisfaction, child care arrangements, and the home environment, which are important to consider and require further exploration in explaining the relationship between maternal employment and children's social development (Fuligni et al., 1996).

Cognitive Development of Young Children Small studies of infants, ranging from birth to 18 months, find no difference between children of employed and nonemployed mothers on measures of mental and motor development (Hock, 1980; Weintraub, Jaeger, & Hoffman, 1988). For toddlers, language development does not differ according to maternal employment, although some toddlers of nonemployed mothers may score higher on IQ measurements (Cohen, 1978; Schachter, 1981). Maternal employment has the most positive effect on cognitive development when children are from low-income families and when they receive stimulating experiences at home and in their child care experience (Baydar & Brooks-Gunn, 1991).

Impact of Child Care on Children These studies on the impact of child care have emerged in four divergent waves. The first of these compares children cared for in child care settings with children who have only experienced parental care. Without examining the quality of the child care, there are no clear-cut results (Hayes, Palmer, & Zaslow, 1990; Phillips, 1987). Although there was some concern that the children's relationships with teachers or child care providers might diminish the mother–child relationship, this is not the case. As Gamble and Zigler said, the chance that child care can "prevent the formation of primary attachment to parents, or cause them to be directed elsewhere seems small indeed" (1988, p. 81).

The second wave of research on the impact of child care addresses the question, How do children, particularly low-income children, fare in model high-quality early childhood intervention programs? The results reveal that low-income children make some short-term improvements in intellectual performance, as well as in language and mathematical achievements. Although these early gains tend to fade away in the elementary school years, longitudinal studies find that children in high-quality intervention programs often have fewer placements in special education. In addition, some longitudinal studies show that children in exemplary early childhood programs have higher rates of graduating from high school, fewer juvenile-delinquency offenses, lower adolescent pregnancy rates, higher employment rates, less reliance on welfare, more commitment to marriage, and higher property ownership (Campbell & Ramey, 1994; Consortium for Longitudinal Studies, 1983; Haskins, 1989; Lally, Mangione, Honig, & Wittmer, 1988; Lazar &

Darlington, 1982; McKey et al., 1985; Schweinhart, Barnes, & Weikart, 1993; Weikart, 1990).

Because most children don't have the opportunity to attend high-quality intervention programs, however, the third wave in the research on child care examines the experiences of children in typical community-based child care settings. Three multisite observational studies of both center care and family child care conducted between 1988 and 1995 reveal a more dismal picture of the quality of child care available to most families. These studies indicate that only 12%–14% of children are in child care arrangements that are likely to promote their growth and learning, whereas 12%–21% are in child care arrangements that are unsafe and potentially harmful to their development. For infants and toddlers, the proportion in unsafe settings is even higher: 35%–40% (Cost, Quality, and Child Outcomes Study Team, 1995; Galinsky et al., 1994; Kontos et al., 1994; Whitebook, Phillips, & Howes, 1990).

This third wave of child care research has uncovered the characteristics associated with high-quality education and care. Children in center-based arrangements fare better emotionally, socially, and cognitively when they are in arrangements that have a sufficient number of adults for each child in several ways:

- High staff-to-child ratios
- Smaller group sizes
- Higher levels of staff education and specialized training
- Low staff turnover and administrative stability
- Higher levels of staff compensation

Studies of center-based arrangements also reveal that these characteristics of quality are interrelated (Cost, Quality, and Child Outcomes Study Team, 1995; Phillips, Mekos, Scarr, McCartney, Phillips, & Abbott-Shim, 1999; Whitebook & Howes, 1993).

In family child care (i.e., care in the home of the provider), children fare better emotionally and cognitively when their providers

- Are committed to taking care of children and are doing so from a sense that this work is important and is what they want to be doing
- Seek out opportunities to learn about children's development and child care, have higher levels of education, and participate in family child care training
- Think ahead about what the children are going to do and plan experiences for them
- Seek out the company of others who are providing care and are more involved with other providers
- Are regulated

- Have slightly larger groups (three to six children) and slightly higher numbers of adults per child, charge higher rates, and follow standard business and safety practices

As in center-based arrangements, studies find that these characteristics of quality go together. Providers who have one of these characteristics are likely to have others. In other words, providers who are "intentional" in their approach provide more sensitive and responsive education and care than providers who are not intentional (Galinsky et al., 1994).

Given the concern that relatively few existing child care arrangements promote young children's optimal development, a fourth wave in research on child care is currently emerging. Studies in this genre ask the question: How effective are efforts designed to improve quality? Several new studies offer some hopeful news about quality. One is a study of family child care training that reveals that the children were more likely to be securely attached to their providers following training, and that the quality of the caregiving environments improved (Galinsky, Howes, & Kontos, 1995). In another study, where a state improved its staff-to-child ratios and instituted higher educational requirements for staff, the changes in children's development are impressive: The children are more securely attached, exhibit better cognitive and social development, are more proficient with language, and have fewer behavior problems (Howes, Galinsky, Shinn, Sibley, & McCarthy, 1998; Howes, Smith, & Galinsky, 1995).

Approach 2:
Research on How Work–Family Factors Affect Children

Another approach in this area of research examines the impact that stress, work–family conflict, role strain, and role satisfaction have on children's development. Studies find that parents who experience higher levels of stress and strain have children who are not developing as well as the children of parents with less stress and strain. For example, when mothers see their multiple roles interfering with each other, their children have less self-control, their sons have conduct problems, and their daughters are less mature (Barling & VanBart, 1984).

Yet, fulfilling multiple roles can lead to enhanced role satisfaction in parents and positive outcomes for children. When mothers are satisfied with their jobs, their daughters show higher levels of self-control and fewer conduct problems (Barling & VanBart, 1984); the mothers also are more available (Piotrkowski & Katz, 1983) and provide more cognitive stimulation for their daughters (O'Neil, 1992).

Studies are beginning to identify the personal, family, job, and workplace factors that contribute to stress or satisfaction (Galinsky, 1999).

One of the more significant factors is having a demanding job, which has been linked to parenting behavior and, in turn, to children's development. One study found that parents who experience more time pressure at work exhibit harsher discipline of their children than parents who experience less time pressure (Greenberger et al., 1994), and another study reported that on days when mothers have high workloads, they are less emotionally and behaviorally available to their children than on days when the workload is lighter (Repetti & Wood, 1995). The impact of job demands, however, can be both positive and negative for children. O'Neil (1992) observed that when parents have highly demanding jobs and experience the high role strain that can be associated with such jobs, they may not provide as much cognitive stimulation to their children. In contrast, another study found that mothers in highly demanding jobs may have children who are more geared to succeed (Piotrkowski & Katz, 1982).

Approach 3:
Research on Work as a Socialization Influence

Another way that parental employment may influence children's development is by affecting parents' values and child-rearing styles. The nature of employment, and employment itself, may influence parents' ways of thinking and behaving, which may have an effect on how they socialize their children. Drawing on the work of Kohn (1969; Kohn & Schooler, 1973), many researchers have examined the relationship between parents' education and job characteristics and their child-rearing practices and values. For example, the skills and method of thinking required by different jobs can affect the degree of independence or conformity that parents believe is important and reinforce in their children (Hoffman, 1989). Furthermore, those parents who hold higher positions in the social structure are more likely to value self-direction in their children (Spade, 1991) and expect their children to achieve similar positions in society.

One characteristic of jobs—job complexity—is repeatedly linked to the way that parents interact with their children as well as to specific child outcomes. Parents whose jobs are highly complex are more likely to value self-direction in their children; to encourage autonomy and intellectual flexibility (Menaghan & Parcel, 1990); to provide cognitive stimulation and affective warmth (Greenberger et al., 1994; Menaghan & Parcel, 1990) to use child-rearing practices that are firm but flexible, not harshly controlling, as well as to be less strict about discipline than parents with less complex jobs (Greenberger et al., 1994).

Parents' level of commitment to and absorption in both work and parenting can affect their relationships with their children. A high level of job absorption may affect the quality and quantity of time that parents spend with children, which may have different effects at different ages (Bronfenbrenner & Crouter, 1982). Fathers who are more involved in their work are more supportive of their young children's autonomy and affiliation than fathers who are less involved in their work (Grossman, Pollack, & Golding, 1988). However, the commitment of both men and women to parenting is a stronger predictor of their expectations of children's maturity and their positive perceptions of children than is their commitment to work (Greenberger & Goldberg, 1989).

Overall, studies on the impact of parental employment on children have come a long way from examining mothers' work as harmful to children. Research is beginning to show the importance of examining the broader context surrounding parental employment by studying parents' attitudes, job conditions, economic needs, and resources. Although there is much to learn from more robustly defining these variables and from conducting longitudinal research, it is clear that mothers' and fathers' employment has the potential to affect children's development in both positive and negative ways.

RESEARCH
ON THE PREVALENCE OF WORK–FAMILY SUPPORTS

Although employers have increasingly addressed the work–family concerns of employees in the 1980s and 1990s, there have been few attempts to track the prevalence and trends in employers' response. Most of the studies to date have been conducted on nonrepresentative samples (e.g., Buck Consultants, 1990; Christensen, 1989; Conference Board, 1994; Hewitt Associates, 1990, 1993; Scharlach & Stanger, 1994).

Data, however, are now available for a representative sample of employers with 100 or more employees from the 1998 Business Work–Life Study (Galinsky & Bond, 1998). This study found that 68% of companies with 100 or more employees allow employees to periodically change starting and quitting times, while 24% allow employees to change starting and quitting times on a daily basis. As for maternity leave, 9% permit fewer than 12 weeks off, while 33% allow more than the federally mandated 12 weeks. More than half (53%) offer at least some replacement pay for maternity leave, and 13% for paternity leave. One half (50%) provide dependent care assistance plans (DCAPs) that help employees pay for child care with pretax dollars, 33% give employees access to information to locate child care in their community, and 9% sponsor child care at or near the worksite.

The major predictors of companies' providing work–life assistance are 1) industry, 2) company size, 3) the proportion of top executive positions filled by women, and 4) the proportion of top executive positions filled by minorities. The Families and Work Institute will repeat the Business Work–Life Study every 5 years, enabling researchers to trace the prevalence and trends among employers in supporting the personal and family needs of employees.

RESEARCH ON EMPLOYEES' ACCESS TO WORK–FAMILY SUPPORTS

There are several studies that have examined the access to what Titmuss (1959) termed occupational welfare—that is, human services provided as a condition of employment. Most of these studies have focused on health insurance and fringe benefits (Miller, 1992).

In considering work–family assistance, there are many needs assessments conducted on specific employee populations (e.g., Families and Work Institute, unpublished data; Fernandez, 1986), but until the early 1990s, there were few studies on representative groups of employees. One study of a representative sample of women was the *National Child Care Survey* (Hofferth, Brayfield, Deitch, & Holcomb, 1991). Although focused on child care, it included a broad array of employer-provided child care supports and services. Miller (1992) re-analyzed these data and found that the distribution of child care benefits was not at all equitable. Fourteen percent of women with children younger than 13 were offered at least one form of child care assistance. The women with the greatest access were more likely to earn high wages, to work more hours per week, or to work in professional or administrative jobs. Although more than half of the women in this study had access to flexible time policies, again the distribution was not equitable. Women in professional, technical, and administrative support occupations and with high educational levels had more access than other women.

Continuing this line of research, *The 1997 National Study of the Changing Workforce* (Bond, Galinsky, & Swanberg, 1998) provides the most recent comprehensive view of employees' access to work and family supports among a representative sample of employees in the United States. Data from the 1997 study are presented later in this chapter.

RESEARCH ON THE IMPACT OF EMPLOYER SUPPORTS ON EMPLOYEES AND ON THE BOTTOM LINE: A HISTORICAL PERSPECTIVE[2]

The process of responding to employees' personal and family needs has been one of broadening focus. Initially, employers focused on women

---

[2]This section draws heavily from *The New Business Case for Addressing Work–Life Issues* by Ellen Galinsky and Arlene A. Johnson, a 1998 paper published by Families and Work Institute.

and their child care concerns. Then, as more employers began to provide child care assistance, the focus was enlarged to encompass all workers and a broader array of programs to meet their needs, including elder
care and time flexibility. As such programs and policies became more
widespread, employers recognized that if the culture frowned upon or
if supervisors penalized employees who took leaves or worked flexible
schedules, then these policies might as well not exist. Thus, employers
initiated efforts to train supervisors in how to manage work–family
issues at the workplace and took steps to create more family-responsive
environments. More recently, the focus has broadened again to include
attention to work structure and work processes based on research that
shows these factors are crucial to employees' effectiveness at work as
well as to their health and well-being. Finally, the focus has moved
beyond the organization doors, to forge stronger connections between
the employer and the community.

As with attempts to map any social transformation, the boundaries
between these periods are not neat or distinct. They overlap, blur, and
blend, one into another. Furthermore, individual employers may start
with any one or more of these set of issues. Despite such ambiguities,
there has been a historical progression that can be described, and there
is research during each of these time periods on the impact of employers' support on employees' well-being and on the bottom line.

A Focus on Women and Child Care   The issue of employed
mothers and child care dominated the attention of employers in the
1970s and 1980s and remains of concern today. The trigger for this interest has been, and continues to be, the growing number of women in the
workforce, including those with children younger than 3 years. As of
1995, 46% of the workforce was female. Increasingly, working women
have children and need to arrange child care for their children.

Much of the early research on the impact of employer support
revolves around the question: What is the cost of not responding to
employees' child care needs? Employees are likely to miss work when
they spend long hours trying to locate child care or when they deal with
the often tenuous arrangements they have, especially when these
arrangements collapse and their child care provider is sick, moves away,
or takes another job. When employees with child care problems show up
at work, they may not be very productive because they feel so worried
and stressed (Fernandez, 1986; Galinsky et al., 1993; Galinsky & Hughes,
1987; Shinn, Phillips, Howes, Galinsky, & Whitebook, 1991). In addition,
employers who don't help employees with child care may be losing out
because they are not attracting the best and the brightest.

To address these concerns, employers typically help employees find
child care through child care resource and referral services; help employ-

ees pay for child care through discounts, Dependent Care Assistance Plans, or vouchers; and sometimes provide on- or near-site child care.

A Focus on All Employees, Dependent Care, and Flexible Time and Leave In the late 1980s, a number of employers began to broaden their focus to include all employees, both women and men; to broaden the range of family and personal life issues addressed; and to expand their definition of family. The changing demographics that stimulated these changes relate to the increasing diversity of the workforce. In addition, employers recognize that all employees have personal or family concerns that they must attend to at every stage in their life cycle. The research during this period addressed the question: What are the benefits of work–family solutions? The following are some results of that research.

Before 1988, AEtna experienced a 23% turnover among new mothers following childbirth. They found that those most likely to leave were their highest performers. In response, AEtna extended its parental leave to 6 months, allowed a part-time return, and trained supervisors in managing leaves. The company found that turnover was reduced by 50%—to between 9% and 12%. Because AEtna had done a cost of turnover study, it was able to calculate savings at approximately $1 million per year (AEtna, internal research by Work/Life Strategies department). Another study at AT&T found that leaves that are managed with supervisors with the least family-supportive attitudes are the most costly (Marra & Lindner, 1992; Staines & Galinsky, 1992).

A study at Johnson & Johnson by the Families and Work Institute (1993) found that the average number of days absent among all Johnson & Johnson workers declined over the 2-year period following the introduction of much more generous flexible time and leave policies. Furthermore, users of the company's flexible time program were more likely to recommend Johnson & Johnson as an employer to prospective employees and more likely to want to remain at the company than nonusers. A nationally representative study of the U.S. workforce conducted by the Families and Work Institute in 1992 found that workers with access to flexible time and leave were more satisfied with their jobs, more likely to want to remain on the job, and showed more initiative than workers with no access to these policies (Galinsky & Bond, 1996). The study at Johnson & Johnson found that users of their on-site child care were more satisfied with the quality of their child care and worried less about child care than a comparable group of nonusers at Johnson & Johnson.

A study of an integrated array of work–life programs and policies conducted at Fel-Pro, an auto gasket company headquartered in Skokie, Illinois, by researchers at the University of Chicago (Lambert & Hopkins,

1993) found that the employees who used the most benefits at Fel-Pro had the highest performance evaluations and the lowest intention of leaving the company. Furthermore, they had fewer disciplinary actions against them. Similarly, IBM found that among their top performers, the second most important reason given for staying at the company was IBM's work–family program and policies (IBM internal survey, 1991).

Thus, the business case for a packaged or integrated response to work–family—either for adding new programs or consolidating existing company programs—revolves around improvements in recruitment, retention, and other indicators of job performance such as higher performance ratings and fewer disciplinary actions. In response, employers typically enhance alternative work arrangements, including longer leaves, part-time return to work, greater work time flexibility, and less punitive absence control policies; expand dependent care supports, including elder care; and develop communication strategies to promote understanding and use of programs.

A Focus on Supervisors and Culture   In the early 1990s, there was a shift in how a number of employers began thinking about work–life issues. In the early days of responding to these issues, employers focused on increasing worker productivity and availability for work by reducing work–family conflict at work. Family was seen as a "problem," and the idea was to keep family concerns out of the workplace. But in the 1990s, some employers began to re-evaluate their approach. Instead of dwelling on the conflict between work and family, they thought about the synergy between these domains of life. Their emphasis shifted from how to reduce the negative impact of family life on productivity (e.g., absenteeism) to how to increase discretionary effort and improve organizational effectiveness. The initial impetus for this transformation was a growing sense that company programs would only be able to achieve their intended effects if they existed within a supportive culture.

The most important trend affecting this new vision was widespread downsizing, with some estimates concluding that 43 million jobs were lost to downsizing between 1979 and 1996. The survivors of downsizing became dispirited, committed to doing their own jobs well but not to helping their organizations succeed (Bond, 1999). Thus, there was a need for efforts to rekindle the relationship between employer and employee and to assure that employees would go that extra mile for their employers. As in every period, these changes in perspective called well established business assumptions into question:

- Programs are all that are needed to bring about change (not change in manager/supervisor behavior).
- Work–life is a program (not a culture change effort).

- People are motivated by a sink-or-swim atmosphere (not a supportive one).

The justification for moving to a culture-change perspective was based on the findings of several studies, including the *1997 National Study of the Changing Workforce* (Bond et al., 1998), which revealed that workers with supportive supervisors and a family-friendly culture were more willing than workers without this support to go that extra mile to help their companies succeed. Employers are beginning to focus on communication: publicizing managers' commitment to work–life issues, finding managers to serve as role models, removing the mixed messages within the organization, and trying to align practice with policy ("walk the talk") by improving the way front-line supervisors address work–life concerns of employees.

A Focus on Work Processes and Work Structure   In the late 1990s, mounting pressure at the workplace—caused by fewer employees in downsized organizations doing more work, increased use of technology creating for some workers the "everytime, everyplace" office, and the rush to market in a fast-paced, global economy—created widespread feelings of burnout. In the wake of re-engineering, some employers began to ask, "How does the way we organize work influence workers' effectiveness on the job, health, and well-being?"

Recent work–life studies reveal that the work environment as well as the way that jobs are structured are crucial to employee productivity, well-being, and the fit between work and home. Among the factors that are most significant are job autonomy, job demands, schedule control, supervisor and co-worker support, work–family culture, equal opportunity, and a lack of discrimination (Bond et al., 1998; Galinsky et al., 1993). The findings from such studies provide a "business case" to support bringing together efforts to create organizational change and to improve work–life balance of employees.

With a grant from the Ford Foundation, researchers from MIT worked at Xerox to discover assumptions about the way employees do their work that make their lives difficult and to work with them to improve these work practices. In one worksite, employees were unhappy because of constant interruptions. Their experimental intervention consisted of setting aside specified periods of the day with no interruptions. This resulted in their first on-time product launch as well as less stress and pressure on workers. At another Xerox site, the workgroup experimented with alternative schedules. The result was a 30% reduction in absenteeism. In addition, customer responsiveness and hours of coverage increased (Rapoport et al., 1996).

A Focus on Community   Recognizing that they are not insular, employers have begun to focus more systematically on the connections between themselves and their communities. Community life must be good in order to attract employees and customers as well as to provide needed services to employees. Employers have become involved in work–life endeavors in the community in several different ways (Dombro, Sazer O'Donnell, Galinsky, Gilkeson, Melcher, & Farber, 1996).

Creating Communitywide Networks   One example of a communitywide network is One Small Step in the San Francisco Bay area, an initiative in which community employers agree to take at least one small step to respond to their employees' family and personal needs with a new or expanded program, policy, or practice.

Developing Efforts to Increase the Supply of Quality Dependent Care   In October 1997, 38 leading foundations and corporations announced their support for more than 100 projects across the nation to improve the quality of early care and education programs with an investment of $11.8 million. In Florida, a public/private partnership has raised more than $2 million to help working poor families afford child care.

Participating in Community Mobilization Efforts   In North Carolina, employees—with support from their employers—participate in county- and state-level partnerships that determine the needs for their locations, then develop and implement plans for improving the quality and delivery of services for young children and their families.

Using Business Expertise to Develop Strategies to Finance the Early Childhood System   In Colorado, 25 leaders in business and finance developed a long-term plan to finance early care and education.

Working on Community Projects   Activities range from tutoring children to mentoring young adults, repairing neighborhoods to building housing or recreational centers, and staffing homeless shelters to working in soup kitchens.

ACCESS TO EMPLOYER SUPPORTS FOR THE PARENTS OF YOUNG CHILDREN: FINDINGS FROM THE 1997 NATIONAL STUDY OF THE CHANGING WORKFORCE

Despite such movement toward employer support of families with young children, the latest research, compiled from the *1997 National Study of the Changing Workforce,* shows that supports are not equally accessible for all employees (Bond et al., 1998). In past studies examining workplaces, supports for parents have generally been defined as supports for those with children younger than 13 or 18 years old. The findings presented here, however, pertain to parents with children younger than 6. These findings are particularly important given current attention to promoting young children's health development and school readiness stimulated by brain research on young children (Shore, 1997).

Data from the *1997 National Study of the Changing Workforce* are used to address two questions:

- To what extent do working parents with young children have access to traditional benefits, family-friendly workplace programs and policies, supportive supervisors and a supportive culture, and a better quality workplace environment?
- Which working parents are more likely to have such access?

The *National Study of the Changing Workforce,* conducted every 5 years by the Families and Work Institute, examines the work, personal, and family lives of the U.S. workforce. No other ongoing study investigates these issues with a nationally representative sample, and no other study is as comprehensive as this one.

In 1997, telephone interviews were conducted with a randomly selected national sample of 3,552 employed men and women ages 18 and older. The findings in this chapter concern only the 2,877 wage and salaried workers in this sample. Furthermore, because we needed a sample large enough to permit reliable estimates for subgroups of parents with young children for this chapter, we focus on the 536 employed mothers and fathers with children younger than 6 rather than the much smaller sample of 287 employed parents with children younger than 3—the main focus of this volume. Nonetheless, most child-related concerns are common to both groups of parents.

The response rate for the survey was 52% (completed interviews divided by known eligibles plus unknown but estimated eligibles). The final sample was weighted by key demographics to match the entire U.S. labor force based on data from the March 1996 Current Population Survey (CPS).

Access to Health Insurance with Family Coverage

Health insurance coverage for one's family is by far the most important traditional work–family benefit offered by employers. This is especially true for families with infants or toddlers in child care, as these children tend to become sick with greater frequency than their peers who are not in child care (see Chapters 6 and 7).

As shown in Table 1, more than four in five workers (84%) with children younger than 6 have access to family health insurance coverage from their employers. Employed parents who are men, who have higher hourly wages, who have higher family incomes, who are married or living with a partner, who work full time, and who work for larger employers are more likely to have access to family health insurance through their employers than other groups. Employees who are more traditionally at risk—women, workers with lower-wage jobs and in lower-income

Table 1.   Access to family health insurance by employed parents with children younger than 6

Employee group	Access	No access	Significance (df, test)
All parents (N=533)	84%	16%	
Gender			
Men (n=304)	89	11	***
Women (n=229)	78	22	(df=1, P χ²)
Hourly earnings			
$7.70 or less (n=119)	66	34	***
$7.71–$19.25 (n=254)	87	13	(df=1, M-H χ²)
More than $19.25 (n=125)	95	5	***
Family income			
Less than $28.7K (n=112)	69	31	***
$28.7K–$71.5K (n=280)	86	14	(df=1, M-H χ²)
$71.6K or more (n=120)	93	7	***
Marital status			
Married/partnered (n=453)	86	14	***
Single (n=78)	73	27	(df=1, P χ²)
Work status			
Full time (n=461)	89	11	***
Part time (n=69)	56.5	43.5	(df=1, P χ²)
U.S. employees			
Fewer than 50 (n=161)	71	29	***
50-999 (n=150)	89	11	(df=1, M-H χ²)
1000 or more (n=209)	91	9	***

Source: Galinsky, Bond, and Friedman (1993).

Significance Levels: * p<.05; ** p<.01; *** p<.001. *Tests:* P χ² = Pearson χ²; M-H χ² = Mantel-Haenszel χ².

families, and workers raising children by themselves—are less likely to have access to family health insurance than other groups.

The number of employees whose employers fully pay their family health insurance costs is small: 16%. However, 76% of employees receive at least partially paid family coverage (Table 2).

In sum, more advantaged workers have greater access to family health insurance through their employers and are more likely to have that insurance paid for in part or in full by their employers than are other workers.

Table 2.   Access to fully or partly paid family health insurance by employed parents with children younger than 6

Employee group	Fully/ partly paid	Not paid/ not available	Significance (df, test)
All parents (N=532)	76%	24%	
Gender			
Men (n=303)	84	16	***
Women (n=229)	66	34	(df=1, P χ²)
Hourly earnings			
$7.70 or less (n=119)	56	44	***
$7.71–$19.25 (n=255)	79	21	(df=1, M-H χ²)
More than $19.25 (n=125)	86	14	
Family income			
Less than $28.7K (n=113)	58	42	***
$28.7K–$71.5K (n=280)	79	21	(df=1, M-H χ²)
$71.6K or more (n=120)	86	14	
Marital status			
Married/partnered (n=453)	78	22	*
Single (n=78)	65	35	(df=1, P χ²)
Work status			
Full time (n=461)	80	20	***
Part time (n=70)	50	50	(df=1, P χ²)
U.S. employees			
Fewer than 50 (n=161)	60	40	***
50-999 (n=151)	77	23	(df=1, M-H χ²)
1000 or more (n=208)	87.5	12.5	

Source: Galinsky, Bond, and Friedman (1993).
*Significance Levels: * p<.05; ** p<.01; *** p<.001. Tests: P χ² = Pearson χ²; M-H χ² = Mantel-Haenszel χ².*

Because workers may have access to health insurance from other sources other than their employers, we also investigated the extent to which wage and salaried workers have any source of health insurance for their children. Overall, 5% of wage and salaried workers do not have health insurance coverage for their children younger than 18 years old from any source (Table 3). The percentage of workers who are uncovered from any source rises to 11% among single parents and 12% among workers in low-income households.

Table 3.   Access to family health care from any source by employed parents with children younger than 6

Employee group	Access from own job	Access from other source	Not covered	Significance (df, test)
All parents (N=536)	62%	33%	5%	
Gender				
Men (n=305)	73	22	5	***
Women (n=231)	47	49	4	(df=1, M-H χ²)
Hourly earnings				
$7.70 or less (n=122)	40	52	8	***
$7.71–$19.25 (n=254)	63	32	5	(df=1, M-H χ²)
More than $19.25 (n=126)	79	21	1	
Family income				
Less than $28.7K (n=116)	40	48	12	***
$28.7K–$71.5K (n=280)	65	31	3	(df=1, M-H χ²)
$71.6K or more (n=120)	73	27	1	
Marital status				
Married/partnered (n=457)	64	32	4	**
Single (n=79)	48	41	11	(df=1, M-H χ²)
Work status				
Full time (n=463)	67	28	5	***
Part time (n=72)	25	72	3	(df=1, M-H χ²)
U.S. employees				
Fewer than 50 (n=163)	44	49	8	***
50–999 (n=151)	66	31	3	(df=1, M-H χ²)
1000 or more (n=210)	74	23	3	

Source: Galinsky, Bond, and Friedman (1993).

Significance Levels: * $p<.05$; ** $p<.01$; *** $p<.001$. *Tests:* P χ² = Pearson χ²; M-H χ² = Mantel-Haenszel χ².

Access to Paid Vacation Days

Vacations are important to families. Vacations seem to reduce parents' sense that life is too hectic and rushed, that they are pressed for time (Families and Work Institute, 1995; Galinsky, 1999), and that they don't have enough time together as a family (Galinsky et al., 1993).

More than four in five employees with young children have access to paid vacation days (Table 4). Importantly, 22% of mothers with young children and 31% of low-wage workers do not have access to paid vacations. Working parents who are men, who earn more on an hourly basis, who work full time, and who work for larger organizations have greater access to paid vacation days than other workers.

Table 4. Access to paid vacation days by employed parents with children younger than 6

Employee group	Access	No access	Significance (df, test)
All parents (N=535)	84.5%	15.5%	
Gender			
Men (n=306)	89	11	***
Women (n=229)	78	22	(df=1, P χ²)
Hourly earnings			
$7.70 or less(n=121)	69	31	***
$7.71–$19.25 (n=254)	88	12	(df=1, M-H χ²)
More than $19.25 (n=126)	90.5	9.5	
Family income			
Less than $28.7K (n=114)	78	22	*
$28.7K–$71.5K (n=278)	86	14	(df=1, M-H χ²)
$71.6K or more (n=120)	88	12	
Marital status			
Married/partnered (n=453)	89	11	***
Single (n=78)	58	42	(df=1, P χ²)
Work status			
Full time (n=461)	89	11	***
Part time (n=71)	58	42	(df=1, P χ²)
US employees			
Fewer than 50 (n=161)	74.5	25.5	***
50-999 (n=151)	84	16	(df=1, M-H χ²)
1000 or more (n=210)	94	6	

Source: Galinsky, Bond, and Friedman, (1993).

Significance Levels: * p<.05;** p<.01; *** p<.001. Tests: P χ² = Pearson χ²; M-H χ² = Mantel-Haenszel χ².

Access to Paid Holidays

Studies in child development reveal that ritual and tradition are important to children's development, school readiness, and family functioning (Powell, 1992). For many families, the most memorable rituals take place around the celebration of holidays.

As with vacations, more than four in five employed parents with young children have access to paid holidays (Table 5). However, one third of low-wage parents and 29% of single parents in the labor force have no access to paid holidays. Working parents who are men, who earn more hourly, who have higher family incomes, who are married or living with a partner, who work full time, and who work for larger organizations have greater access to paid holidays than other workers.

Table 5. Access to paid holidays by employed parents with children younger than 6

Employee group	Access	No access	Significance (df, test)
All parents (N=533)	84%	16%	
Gender			
Men (n=305)	88	12	*
Women (n=228)	80	20	(df= 1, P χ^2)
Hourly earnings			
$7.70 or less(n=121)	67	33	***
$7.71–$19.25 (n=253)	87	13	(df= 1, M-H χ^2)
More than $19.25 (n=126)	93	7	
Family income			
Less than $28.7K (n=114)	74	26	***
$28.7K–$71.5K (n=279)	85	15	(df= 1, M-H χ^2)
$71.6K or more (n=121)	93	7	
Marital status			
Married/partnered (n=456)	86	14	***
Single (n=77)	71	29	(df= 1, P χ^2)
Work status			
Full time (n=462)	87	13	***
Part time (n=71)	63	37	(df= 1, P χ^2)
U.S. employees			
Fewer than 50 (n=161)	77	23	***
50-999 (n=151)	83	17	(df= 1, M-H χ^2)
1000 or more (n=209)	91	9	***

Source: Galinsky, Bond, and Friedman (1993).

Significance Levels: * $p<.05$; ** $p<.01$; *** $p<.001$. Tests: P χ^2 = Pearson χ^2; M-H χ^2 = Mantel-Haenszel χ^2.

Access to Paid Time Off to Care for Sick Children

Surveys of workers indicate that having sick children is one of the most stressful aspects of being an employed parent (Fernandez, 1986). Estimates from other studies vary about the access that parents have to taking time off for their sick children, but it is evident that this issue is of major concern to parents and policy makers alike (Heymann, Earle, & Egleston, 1996).

Overall, almost one in two wage and salaried workers with young children (49%) is able to take time off for sick children without losing pay (Table 6). For families with fewer resources, however, access is much lower: only 36% of parents with lower family incomes, 37% of single

Table 6.   Allowed to take time off for sick children without losing pay:
Employed parents with children younger than 6

Employee group	Allowed	Not allowed	Significance (df, test)
All parents (N=522)	49%	51%	
Hourly earnings			
$7.70 or less (n=121)	37	63	***
$7.71–$19.25 (n=247)	48	52	(df=1, M-H χ²)
More than $19.25 (n=124)	61	39	
Family income			
Less than $28.7K (n=115)	36	64	***
$28.7K–$71.5K (n=274)	48	52	(df=1, M-H χ²)
$71.6K or more (n=116)	65.5	34.5	
Marital status			
Married/partnered (n=443)	51	49	*
Single (n=78)	37	63	(df=1, P χ²)
Work status			
Full time (n=450)	51	49	**
Part time (n=71)	34	66	(df=1, P χ²)

Source: Galinsky, Bond, and Friedman (1993).
Significance Levels: * p<.05; ** p<.01; *** p<.001. Tests: P χ² = Pearson χ²; M-H χ² = Mantel-Haenszel χ².

parents, and 34% of part-timers can take time off to care for sick children without lost pay.

Access to Flextime

When employees are asked what would most help them balance work and family life, time flexibility is typically at the top of the list (Families and Work Institute, unpublished data). Employees who have access to traditional flextime are allowed to select their starting and quitting times, but must stick to the times they choose, while employees with daily flextime can change their starting and quitting times whenever they choose. Overall, 44% of employed parents with young children have access to traditional flextime (Table 7). Not unexpectedly, women, lower wage workers and workers with lower family incomes have less access than other workers. It is important to note that workers at smaller organizations have no less access to traditional flextime than workers at larger organizations.

Table 7.   Access to traditional flextime by employed parents with children younger than 6

Employee group	Access	No access	Significance (df, test)
All parents (N=535)	44%	56%	
Gender			
Men (n=305)	48	52	*
Women (n=230)	39	61	(df= 1, P χ²)
Hourly earnings			
$7.70 or less (n=122)	42	58	**
$7.71–$19.25 (n=254)	35	65	(df= 1, M-H χ²)
More than $19.25 (n=126)	61	39	
Family income			
Less than $28.7K (n=112)	31	69	***
$28.7K–$71.5K (n=293)	41	59	(df= 1, M-H χ²)
$71.6K or more (n=106)	62	38	

Source: Galinsky, Bond, and Friedman (1993).

*Significance Levels: * p<.05; ** p<.01; *** p<.001. Tests: P χ² = Pearson χ²;* M-H χ² = Mantel-Haenszel χ².

Far fewer working parents (26%) have access to daily flextime (Table 8). As is the case with many work–family policies, women, lower wage workers, and workers from lower income families have less access than other workers. Only 13% of workers from lower income families can change their start and finish time daily.

Difficulty Taking Time Off to Address Family Needs

As other studies have shown, the offering of flexible time and leave policies does not necessarily indicate that employees can or will use them. Sometimes supervisors stand in the way or the company culture disapproves of their usage. Likewise, employees with no access to formal policies may, in fact, take time off work when they need to. Thus, we asked employees a question that reflects the practice at their organization: "How hard is it for you to take time off during your work day to take care of personal or family matters?"

Among parents with children younger than 6 years of age, 36% report that it is either very or somewhat hard to take time during the day for family or personal issues. Employees from lower income households (Mantel-Haenszel (χ^1=5.79; df=1; p<.05) and larger companies (Mantel-Haenszel [χ^1=4.74; df=1; p<.05]) find this more difficult than other groups of employees.

Table 8.   Access to daily flextime by employed parents with children younger than 6

Employee group	Access	No access	Significance (df, test)
All parents (N=535)	26%	74%	
Gender			
Men (n=305)	31	69	**
Women (n=230)	20	80	(df=1, P χ²)
Hourly earnings			
$7.70 or less (n=121)	18	82	***
$7.71–$19.25 (n=254)	19	81	(df=1, M-H χ²)
More than $19.25 (n=126)	44	56	
Family income			
Less than $28.7K (n=114)	13	87	***
$28.7K–$71.5K (n=280)	22	78	(df=1, M-H χ²)
$71.6K or more (n=120)	47	53	

Source: Galinsky, Bond, and Friedman (1993).

Significance Levels: * p<.05; ** p<.01; *** p<.001. Tests: P χ² = Pearson χ²; M-H χ² = Mantel-Haenszel χ².

Employees were also asked whether they agreed or disagreed with the following statement: "At the place where you work, employees who ask for time off for family reasons or try to arrange different schedules or hours to meet these needs are less likely to get ahead in their jobs or careers." Forty-three percent of workers with children younger than 6 strongly or somewhat agreed that the use of flexibility impedes advancement. Parents with children younger than 6 who work in large companies are more likely to feel this way (Mantel-Haenszel [χ^1=4.34; df=1; p<.05]). Otherwise there are no differences among employee groups in the extent to which they believe that using flexibility impedes advancement.

Access to Parental Leave for Childbirth

The Family and Medical Leave Act (FMLA) of 1993 provided 12 weeks of job-guaranteed leave for childbirth or adoption for employees who had worked at least 1,250 hours over the preceding year for an employer with 50 or more employees within a 75-mile radius of her or his worksite. Applying these requirements, data from the *1992 National Study of the Changing Workforce* (Galinsky, Bond, & Friedman, 1993) were used to estimate how many employed mothers and fathers with children younger than the age of 18 at home have access to parental leave under

FMLA. The results indicate that 41% of employed mothers and 49% of employed fathers meet the eligibility requirements and are covered by FMLA (Galinsky & Bond, 1996).

It is well known, however, that employer policy and practice exceed these requirements. Thus the *1997 National Study of the Changing Workforce* (Bond, Galinsky, & Swanberg, 1998) provides an opportunity to ascertain how many women and men with young children think that they can take time off from work for childbirth or for becoming a father without endangering their jobs.

Overall, 93% of employees with children younger than 6 think that women can take time off from work for childbirth without endangering their jobs. Perhaps surprisingly, there are no differences among employee groups on this question, including women and men, those who have lower and higher family incomes or those who work for small, mid-size, or large organizations.

A smaller proportion of working parents (81%) think that men can take time off work when they become fathers without endangering their jobs. Single employees (including those who are divorced or widowed) with young children report that men have less access to paternity leave without job jeopardy than do workers with young children who are married or living with a partner (Pearson [$\chi^1=4.13$; df=1; $p<.05$]).

Access to Child Care Resource and Referral

Another important way in which employers can help employees with young children manage their work and family responsibilities is by providing assistance with dependent care. An increasing number of employers are providing a service called child care resource and referral to help employees find child care for their children (Galinsky, Friedman, & Fernandez, 1991).

One in five employees with children younger than 6 works for an employer who offers a program or service that helps employees find child care (Table 9). Access is higher for workers from households with incomes in the top quartile and for those who work for large companies (1,000 or more employees).

Access to On- or Near-Site Child Care

When many people think of assistance with child care, an on- or near-site center comes to mind. Generally, however, it has been found that not many employees want child care at work and not many employers want to provide it. Where it is feasible and desired, child care at the workplace is highly appreciated and has been linked to less worry about child care while at work and greater satisfaction with the quality of

Table 9. Access to child care resource and referral by employed parents with children younger than 6

Employee group	Access	No access	Significance (df, test)
All parents (N=535)	20%	80%	
Family income			
Less than $28.7K (n=112)	16	84	*
$28.7K–$71.5K (n=293)	18	82	(df=1, M-H χ²)
$71.6K or more (n=106)	26	74	
U.S. employees			
Fewer than 50 (n=161)	11	89	***
50–999 (n=151)	8	92	(df=1, M-H χ²)
1000 or more (n=208)	35.5	64.5	

Source: Galinsky, Bond, and Friedman (1993).
Significance Levels: * $p<.05$; ** $p<.01$; *** $p<.001$. Tests: P χ² = Pearson χ²; M-H χ² = Mantel-Haenszel χ².

child care that the employee's child receives (Families and Work Institute, 1993).

Twelve percent of employees with children younger than 6 report that they have access to a child care center operated or sponsored by their employer at or near their work location. Parents employed by larger companies are more likely to have access to employer sponsored or operated child care at or near their work site (Mantel-Haenszel [$\chi^1=7.52$; df=1; $p<.01$]).

Access to Financial Assistance for Child Care

The cost of child care is of great concern to employed parents who typically spend about 10% of their family income on child care. Low-income families, however, often pay a much greater share of their family income for child care. Families earning less than $15,000 per year—who pay for child care services—pay 23% while families earning $50,000 or more pay 6% (Hofferth et al., 1991).

Twelve percent of employed parents with children younger than 6 work for employers who provide employees with direct financial assistance—vouchers, cash, or scholarships—to help defray the cost of child care (Table 10). Full-time employees and those who work for larger employers are the most likely to receive financial assistance for child care.

Table 10.   Access to financial assistance for child care by employed
parents with children younger than 6

Employee group	Financial assistance	No financial assistance	Significance (df, test)
All parents (N=522)	12%	88%	
Work status			
Full time (n=450)	13	87	*
Part time (n=69)	4	72	(df=1, P χ²)
U.S. employees			
Fewer than 50 (n=163)	4	96	***
50–999 (n=147)	9.5	90.5	(df=1, M-H χ²)
1000 or more (n=200)	19.5	80.5	

Source: Galinsky, Bond, and Friedman (1993).
Significance Levels: * p<.05; ** p<.01; *** p<.001. Tests: P χ² = Pearson χ²;
M-H χ² = Mantel-Haenszel χ².

Another way that employers help employees pay for child care is
by setting up Dependent Care Assistance Plans allowed under federal tax
law. Under these plans, employees set aside part of their pretax wages
in an account that can be used to pay for child care.

Thirty-one percent of employees with children younger than 6 have
access to DCAPs (Table 11). Those more likely to have access are employees who have higher hourly earnings, who have higher family income,
who are married, and who work for larger employers. In fact, 47% of
employees with young children who work for large companies have
access to DCAPs. Although the relative tax advantages of DCAPs for
lower income families can be debated, it is ironic that those most in need
of financial assistance for child care have the least access to this benefit.

Support by Supervisor and Workplace Culture

Studies conducted by the Families and Work Institute reveal the importance of support by both the supervisor and the workplace culture.
Employees with supervisors and a workplace culture that are supportive when the employee has a work–life issue feel less stressed and more
successful at balancing work and family life. In addition, they are more
loyal, more satisfied with their jobs, and more likely to recommend their
employer as a place to work (Families and Work Institute, 1993; Galinsky & Bond, 1996).

Between six and seven of every ten employed parents with children younger than 6 strongly agree that their supervisor accommodates
them and is understanding when work–family issues arise (Table 12).

Table 11. Access to dependent care assistance plans (DCAPs) by employed parents with children younger than 6

Employee group	Access to DCAPs	No access to DCAPs	Significance (df, test)
All parents (N=513)	31%	69%	
Hourly earnings			
$7.70 or less (n=115)	20	80	***
$7.71–$19.25 (n=242)	28	72	(df=1, M-H χ^2)
More than $19.25 (n=123)	43	57	
Family income			
Less than $28.7K (n=109)	13	87	***
$28.7K–$71.5K (n=269)	30	70	(df=1, M-H χ^2)
$71.6K or more (n=116)	45	55	
Marital status			
Married/partnered (n=438)	32	68	*
Single (n=73)	20.5	79.5	(df=1, P χ^2)
U.S. employees			
Fewer than 50 (n=159)	13	87	***
50–999 (n=143)	27	73	(df=1, M-H χ^2)
1000 or more (n=200)	47	53	

Source: Galinsky, Bond, and Friedman (1993).

Significance Levels: * $p<.05$; ** $p<.01$; *** $p<.001$. Tests: P χ^2 = Pearson χ^2; M-H χ^2 = Mantel-Haenszel χ^2.

Fewer (approximately two fifths) strongly agree that they are comfortable raising work–family issues or that their supervisor really cares about the effect that work demands have on their personal or family life.

The only findings of note were differences related to the size of local worksites. Employed parents at smaller work sites were more likely to view their supervisors as accommodating of family/personal business (Mantel-Haenszel [$\chi^1=7.30$; df=1; $p<.01$]), to feel comfortable raising personal or family business with their supervisors (Mantel-Haenszel [$\chi^1=6.63$; df=1; $p<.05$]), and to feel their supervisors really care about the impact of work demands on family and personal life (Mantel-Haenszel [$\chi^1=4.43$; df=1; $p<.05$]).

Between one fourth and one third of workers with young children perceive their workplace culture as not supportive of their personal and family concerns (Table 13). The only differences found were that employed parents at smaller local worksites were more likely to perceive the cultures of their workplaces as supportive. They were less likely to agree that putting family or personal needs ahead of jobs was not viewed favorably (Mantel-Haenszel [$\chi^1=4.67$; df=1; $p<.05$]) and that

Table 12.   Perceived work–family supportiveness of supervisor on the job among employees with children younger than 6

My supervisor...	Strongly agree	Somewhat agree	Somewhat disagree	Strongly disagree	Sample size
... accommodates me when I have family or personal business to take care of	72%	22%	2%	4%	474
... is understanding when I talk about personal or family issues that affect my work	61	29	5	5	460
... really cares about the effects that work demands have on my personal and family life	40	38	10	12	476
I feel comfortable bringing up personal or family issues with my supervisor	43	29	14	14	466

Source: Galinsky, Bond, and Friedman (1993).

employees have to choose between job advancement and devoting attention to their personal or family lives (Mantel-Haenszel [χ^1=9.59; df=1; p<.01]). This pattern of findings also held for employees at companies with different numbers of workers nationwide, suggesting that large corporations may push unfriendly cultures down the line to competing plants and offices around the country.

Quality of Job Conditions and the Work Environment

Analyses of the *1992 National Study of the Changing Workforce* (Galinsky et al., 1993) have consistently revealed that the quality of job conditions and the work environment are significant predictors of employees' well-being and effectiveness at work. Specifically, workers with more job autonomy and reasonably—not overly—demanding jobs experience less work–family conflict, less stress, and better coping than other workers (Galinsky & Bond, 1996). Similarly, these and other job and workplace characteristics are predictive of workers' willingness to go that extra mile to help their organizations succeed (Galinsky & Johnson, 1998).

To measure job autonomy in the *1997 National Study of the Changing Workforce* (Bond et al., 1998), respondents were asked how strongly they

Table 13. Perceived supportiveness of the workplace culture among employees with children younger than 6

At my place of employment	Strongly agree	Somewhat agree	Somewhat disagree	Strongly disagree	Sample size
... employees who put their family or personal needs ahead of their jobs are not looked on favorably	13%	19.5%	31.5%	36%	532
... if you have a problem managing your work and family responsibilities, the attitude is "You made your bed, now lie in it."	61	29	5	5	460
... employees have to choose between advancing in their jobs or devoting attention to their family or personal lives.	11	22	30	37	527

Source: Galinsky, Bond, and Friedman (1993).

agreed or disagreed with the following items: "I have the freedom to decide what I do on my job"; "It is basically my own responsibility to decide how my job is done"; and "I have a lot of say about what happens on my job." The job autonomy index represents the average of these three items, with 1 indicating low job autonomy and 4 indicating high job autonomy. One-way analyses of variance were conducted on the sample of workers with children younger than 6 to determine which groups of employees have greater job autonomy. The mean rating for the total sample of workers with children younger than 6 is 2.98.

Employed mothers, workers with lower hourly wages, and those in lower-income households experience less job autonomy than other groups of employees (Table 14). To measure job pressures, respondents were asked how strongly they agreed or disagreed with the following items: "My job requires that I work very hard;" "I never seem to have enough time to get everything done on my job;" and "My job requires that I work very fast." The job pressure index represents the average of these three variables, with 1 indicating low job pressures and 4 indicating high job pressures. The mean rating for the total sample of workers with children younger than 6 is 3.07.

Table 14.   Perceived job autonomy by characteristics of employed parents with children younger than 6

Job autonomy by	Means (standard deviations)	Significance, F ratio, df (contrasts)
Gender		
Men (*n*=305)	3.06 (.726)	**, F=7.80, df=1
Women (*n*=229)	2.88 (.744)	(Men>Women)
Hourly earnings		
Q1: $7.70 or Less (*n*=122)	2.81 (.852)	***, F=11.35, df=2
Q2&Q3: $7.71–$19.25 (*n*=254)	2.91 (.694)	(Q4>Q1; Q4>Q2&3)
Q4: More than $19.25 (*n*=125)	3.22 (.640)	
Family income		
Q1: Less than $28.7K (*n*=115)	2.77 (.739)	***, F=10.71, df=2
Q2&Q3: $28.7K–$71.5K (*n*=279)	2.97 (.740)	(Q2&3>Q1; Q4>Q1;
Q4: $71.6K or more (*n*-120)	3.21 (.666)	Q4>Q2&3)

Source: Galinsky, Bond, and Friedman (1993).

Employees with hourly wages or family incomes in the top quartile and in the middle two quartiles experience higher pressure on the job than other workers. In addition, working parents who are married or living with partners experience higher pressure on the job than single parents (Table 15).

DISCUSSION OF FINDINGS FROM THE *1997 NATIONAL STUDY OF THE CHANGING WORKFORCE*

These findings lead to several important conclusions. First, although work–family assistance on the job grew dramatically in the 1980s and 1990s, workers who are socioeconomically advantaged benefit more than others. For example,

- Workers with higher hourly wages are more likely than their lower wage counterparts to have greater access to family health insurance from their employer, family health insurance that is fully or partly paid by their employer, health insurance for their children from any source, paid vacations, paid holidays, paid time off to care for sick children, traditional flextime, daily flextime, DCAPs, and job autonomy.
- Workers with higher family income are more likely than their lower family income counterparts to have greater access to family health insurance from their employer, family health insurance that is fully for partly paid by their employer, health insurance for their children from any source, paid holidays, paid time off for sick children,

Table 15. Perceived job pressures by characteristics of employed parents with children younger than 6

Job pressures by	Means (standard deviations)	Significance, F ratio, df (contrasts)
Hourly earnings		
Q1: $7.70 or Less (*n*=122)	2.83 (.747)	***, F=9.93, *df*=2
Q2&Q3: $7.71–$19.25 (*n*=254)	3.09 (.653)	(Q4>Q1; Q2&3>Q1)
Q4: More than $19.25 (*n*=125)	3.19 (.579)	
Family income		
Q1: Less than $28.7K (*n*=115)	2.83 (.756)	***, F=9.66, *df*=2
Q2&Q3: $28.7K–$71.5K (*n*=279)	3.09 (.650)	(Q4>Q1; Q2&3>Q1)
Q4: $71.6K or more (*n*-120)	3.19 (.574)	
Marital status		
Married/partnered (n=456)	3.10 (.739)	**, F=7.09, *df*=1
Single (*n*=77)	2.88 (.7448)	(Married/partnered>single)

Source: Galinsky, Bond, and Friedman (1993).

traditional flextime, daily flextime, less difficulty arranging time off, child care resource and referral, DCAPs, and job autonomy.
• Married workers or workers living with a partner are more likely than their single, divorced, or separated counterparts to have greater access to fully or partly paid health insurance for their children from their employer, health insurance for their children from any source, paid holidays, paid time off to care for sick children, paternity leave, and DCAPs.

Second, despite the fact that employed mothers are known to have greater responsibility for managing work and family concerns, employed fathers have greater access to work–family assistance. Employed fathers with young children are more likely than employed mothers with young children to have access to family health insurance from their employer, family health insurance that is fully paid by their employer, family health insurance that is fully or partly paid by their employer, health insurance for their children from any source, paid vacations, paid holidays, traditional flextime, daily flextime, and job autonomy.

Third, employed parents who work for larger employers have greater access to work–family programs and policies that require expenditures by employers, but not to time and leave flexibility. Moreover, there is greater supervisor support and a more supportive workplace culture at small local work sites than larger ones.

• Employed parents who work for large organizations nationwide are more likely than employed parents at smaller organizations to have access to family health insurance from their employer, health insurance for their children from any source, paid vacations, paid holidays, child care resource and referral, on- or near-site child care, financial assistance for child care, and DCAPs.

- There are no differences by employer size in access to time and leave flexibility.
- Employed parents who work at smaller local work sites have more supportive supervisors and workplace cultures, and those employed by companies with fewer employees nationwide also have more supportive workplace cultures.

Finally, we are left with a few startling statistics:

- Only 16% of employed parents with young children have family health insurance that is fully paid by their employers.
- 24% of employed parents with young children from low-income households do not have access to family health insurance that is fully or partly paid by their employers.
- 12% of employed parents with young children from low-income households and 11% of single parents with young children do not have health insurance for their children from any source.
- 31% of employed parents with young children whose earnings fall in the bottom quartile and 22% of employed mothers with young children do not have access to paid vacations.
- 33% of employed parents with young children whose earnings fall in the bottom quartile and 29% of single parents with young children do not have access to paid holidays.
- 64% of employed parents with young children from low-income households and 63% of single parents with young children do not have access to paid time off to care for sick children.
- 56% of all parents with young children, 69% of employed parents in low-income households, and 61% of employed mothers do not have access to traditional flextime.
- 74% of all parents with young children, 87% of employed parents in low-income households, and 80% of employed mothers with young children do not have access to daily flextime.
- 57% of employed parents with young children from low-income households find it difficult to take time off during the day to care for family issues.
- 87% of employed parents with young children from low-income households do not have access to DCAPs.
- Between one fourth and one third of employed parents with young children report that the work–family culture of their workplaces is not supportive of them as family members.

RECOMMENDATIONS

This review of research on employer supports for parents leads to several recommendations for research. Studies of the impact of work and family among adults should experiment with new conceptual models that emphasize the overlapping domains of work and family life and examine work–life integration as well as work–life conflict. These studies should examine the antecedents and consequences of work–life integration and work–life conflict.

Studies of the impact of parental employment on children should identify the work and family conditions most strongly associated with children's optimal development. These constructs should be rigorously defined, and careful attention should be paid to factors that mediate the effects of work and family factors on children. Finally, longitudinal studies are essential. Studies that examine young children's growth and development in families or in child care should include an assessment of parents' work environment and work experience as it affects parents, then children's development. There is a need for new studies on representative samples of employees that document the prevalence, trends, and predictors of the provision of employer supports for families. These studies should examine small and mid-size employers as well as large employers. The Families and Work Institute is undertaking studies that address each of these recommendations, though clearly much more research than ours will be required. In terms of policy and practice concerning the positive development of all infants and toddlers, we suggest the following.

There should be a broad-scale public effort to raise public awareness of the importance of employers supporting the parents of young children. These efforts should emphasize the win/win nature of work–life assistance: There are benefits for the employer in enhancing productivity, and there are benefits for families and young children in reducing family stress and providing better quality services and supports to young children. This public awareness effort should address all employers, but special efforts should be made to reach those that employ low-wage parents and single-parent families. Smaller employers should be targeted as well. Such public awareness efforts should include respected public spokespersons and respected business leaders speaking out on behalf of the needs of young children. A business-to-business approach could be very effective.

Accompanying the public awareness would be incentives to employers. Because employers express reservations about the efficacy of tax credits to motivate increased family-friendliness, a national panel of employers should be convened to determine what public-sector incentives would be most effective.

Technical assistance should be available to employers in implementing a family-friendly agenda. Technical assistance can come from state and local government, other businesses, or consultants. The government's role in promoting a family-friendly agenda for parents is as a

1. Regulator, such as the expansion of FMLA and provision of wage replacement or health insurance for uninsured or underinsured children
2. Service-provider, improving the supply of quality affordable community services and programs
3. Partner, fostering public–private partnerships to benefit young children and their employed parents
4. Leader, speaking out about the importance of these issues, convening business leaders, holding conferences, and so forth

Business expertise should be used by states and communities to improve services for young children such as community task forces on the financing of child care.

CONCLUSION

In the 1960s, the role of the workplace in supporting the families of young children was on the sidelines, if in the picture at all. As of 2000, the workplace is beginning to be considered in research, policy, and practice. In the coming decade, the workplace should move more to the front and center as the United States considers efforts to improve the development of young children. For good or for ill, managing work and family responsibilities is a major concern of all families today who are trying to support their children economically as well as love, teach, and care for them.

REFERENCES

Ainsworth, M. (1979). Infant–mother attachment. *American Psychologist, 34,* 932–937.

Arend, R.A., Gove, F.L., & Sroufe, L.A. (1979). Continuity of individual adaptation from infancy to kindergarten: A predictive study of ego-resiliency and curiosity in preschoolers. *Child Development, 50,* 950–959.

Barglow, P., Vaughn, B.E., & Molitor, N. (1987). Effects of maternal absence due to employment on the quality of infant–mother attachment in a low-risk sample. *Child Development, 58,* 945–954.

Barling, J., & VanBart, D. (1984). Mothers' subjective employment experience and the behavior of their nursery school children. *Journal of Occupational Psychology, 57,* 49–56.

Barnett, R.C. (1997, September). *The shape of things to come: A new view of work/life for the next century.* Paper presented at the 1997 Work/Family Congress, New York.

Barnett, R.C., & Baruch, G.K. (1985). Women's involvement in multiple roles and psychological distress. *Journal of Personality and Social Psychology, 49,* 135–145.

Barnett, R.C., & Marshall, N. (1991). The relationship between women's work and family roles and their subjective well-being and psychological distress. In M. Frankenhaeuser, V. Lundberg, & M.A. Chesney (Eds.), *Women, work, and health: Stress and opportunities* (pp. 111–136). New York: Plenum.

Baydar, N., & Brooks-Gunn, J. (1991). Effects of maternal employment and child-care arrangements on preschoolers' cognitive and behavioral outcomes: Evidence from the children of the National Longitudinal Survey of Youth. *Developmental Psychology, 27,* 932–945.

Belsky, J., & Rovine, M. (1987). Temperament and attachment security in the Strange Situation: An empirical rapprochement. *Child Development, 58,* 787–795.

Bohen, H.H., & Viveros-Long, A. (1981). *Balancing jobs and family life: Do flexible work schedules help?* Philadelphia: Temple University Press.

Bond, J.T. (1999). *The impact of downsizing on employees.* Unpublished paper, Families and Work Institute, New York.

Bond, J.T., Galinsky, E., & Swanberg, J.E. (1998). *The 1997 national study of the changing workforce* (2nd ed.). New York: Families and Work Institute.

Bowlby, J. (1969). *Attachment and loss: Vol. 1. Attachment.* New York: Basic Books.

Bronfenbrenner, U., & Crouter, A.C. (1982). Work and family through time and space. In S.B. Kamerman & C.D. Hayes (Eds.), *Families that work: Children in a changing world* (pp. 39–83). Washington, DC: National Academy Press.

Brooks-Gunn, J., Guo, G., & Furstenberg, F.F. (1993). Who drops out of and who continues beyond high school? A 20-year follow-up of black urban youth. *Journal of Research on Adolescence, 3,* 271–294.

Buck Consultants, Inc. (1990). *Parental leave: An employer view.* New York: Author.

Burke, R.J., Weir, T., & DuWors, R.E. (1979). Type A behavior of administrators and wives' reports of marital satisfaction and well-being. *Journal of Applied Psychology, 64,* 57–65.

Campbell, F.A., & Ramey, C.T. (1994). Effects of early intervention on intellectual and academic achievement: A follow-up study of children from low-income families. *Child Development, 65,* 684–698.

Christensen, K. (1989). *Flexible staffing and scheduling in U.S. corporations (Research Bulletin No. 240).* New York: The Conference Board.

Clarke-Stewart, K.A. (1988). The "effects" of infant day care reconsidered. *Early Childhood Research Quarterly, 3,* 293–318.

Cohen, S.E. (1978). Maternal employment and mother–child interaction. *Merrill-Palmer Quarterly, 24*(3), 189–197.

Conference Board. (1994). Family and medical leave. *Work-Family Roundtable, 4*(4), 7.

Consortium for Longitudinal Studies. (1983). *As the twig is bent: Lasting effects of preschool programs.* Mahwah, NJ: Lawrence Erlbaum Associates.

Cost, Quality, & Child Outcomes Study Team. (1995). *Cost, quality, and child outcomes in child care centers.* Denver: Economics Department, University of Colorado at Denver.

Crouter, A.C. (1984). Spillover from family to work: The neglected side of the work–family interface. *Human Relations, 37,* 425–442.

Dombro, A.L., Sazer O'Donnell, N., Galinsky, E., Gilkeson Melcher, S., & Farber, A. (1996). *Community mobilization: Strategies to support young children and their families.* New York: Families and Work Institute.

Dubow, E.F., & Ippolito, M.F. (1994). Effects of poverty and home environment on changes in the academic and behavioral adjustment of elementary school-age children. *Journal of Clinical Child Psychology, 23,* 401–412.

Duncan, G., Brooks-Gunn, J., & Klebanov, P. (1994). Economic deprivation and early childhood development. *Child Development, 65,* 296–318.

Easterbrooks, M.A., & Goldberg, W.A. (1984). Toddler development in the family: Impact of father involvement and parenting characteristics. *Child Development, 55,* 740–752.

Egeland, B., Carlson, E., & Sroufe, L.A. (1993). Resilience as process. *Development and Psychopathology, 5,* 517–528.

Erickson, M.F., Kormarcher, J., & Egeland, B. (1992). Attachments past and present: Implications for therapeutic intervention with mother–infant dyads. *Development and Psychopathology* (pp. 495–507). New York: Cambridge University Press.

Families and Work Institute. (1993). *An evaluation of Johnson & Johnson's work-family initiative.* New York: Author.

Families and Work Institute. (1995). *Women: The new providers (Whirlpool Foundation study, part one).* New York: Author.

Family and Medical Leave Act (FMLA) of 1993, PL 103-3, 5 U.S.C. §§ 6381 *et seq.,* 29 U.S.C. §§ 2601 *et seq.*

Feinstein, K.W. (1979). *Working women and families.* Newbury Park, CA: Sage Publications.

Fernandez, J. (1986). *Child care and corporate productivity: Resolving family/work conflicts.* Lexington, MA: Lexington Books, D.C. Heath Co.

Fuligni, A.S., Galinsky, E., & Poris, M. (1996). *The impact of parental employment on children.* New York: Families and Work Institute.

Galinsky, E. (1999). *Ask the children.* William Morrow & Company.

Galinsky, E., & Bond, J.T. (1998). *The 1998 Business Work-Life Study.* New York: Families and Work Institute.

Galinsky, E., & Bond, J.T. (1996). Work and family: The experiences of mothers and fathers in the U.S. labor force. In C. Costello & B.K. Krimgold (Eds.), *The American woman, 1996-97: Women and work* (pp. 79–103). New York: W.W. Norton & Company.

Galinsky, E., Bond, J.T., & Friedman, D.E. (1993). *National study of the changing workforce.* New York: Families and Work Institute.

Galinsky, E., & Friedman, D.E. (1993). *Education before school: Investing in quality child care.* New York: Scholastic Inc.

Galinsky, E., Friedman, D.F., & Hernandez, C.A. (1991). *The corporate reference guide to work-family programs.* New York: Families and Work Institute.

Galinsky, E., Howes, C., & Kontos, S. (1995). *The family child care training study: Highlights of findings.* New York: Families and Work Institute.

Galinsky, E., Howes, C., Kontos, S., & Shinn, M. (1994). *The study of children in family child care and relative care: Highlights of findings.* New York: Families and Work Institute.

Galinsky, E., & Hughes, D. (1987, August). *The Fortune magazine child care study.* Paper presented at the annual convention of the American Psychological Association, New York.

Galinsky, E., & Johnson, A.A. (1998). *The new business case for addressing work-life issues.* New York: Families and Work Institute.

Gamble, T.J., & Zigler, E. (1988). Effects of infant day care: Another look at the evidence. In E. Zigler & M. Frank (Eds.), *The parental leave crisis: Toward a national policy* (pp. 77–99). New Haven, CT: Yale University Press.

Goldberg, W.A., & Easterbrooks, M.A. (1988). Maternal employment when children are toddlers and kindergartners. In A.E. Gottfried & A.W. Gottfried (Eds.), *Maternal employment and children's development: Longitudinal research* (pp. 121–154). New York: Plenum Press.

Gottfried, A.E., Gottfried, A.W., & Bathurst, K. (1988). Maternal employment, family environment, and children's development: Infancy through the school years. In A.E. Gottfried & A.W. Gottfried (Eds.), *Maternal employment and children's development: Longitudinal research* (pp. 11–58). New York: Plenum.

Greenberger, E., & Goldberg, W.A. (1989). Work, parenting, and the socialization of children. *Developmental Psychology, 25,* 22–35.

Greenberger, E., Goldberg, W.A., Hamill, S., O'Neil, R., & Payne, C.K. (1989). Contributions of a supportive work environment to parents' well-being and orientation to work. *American Journal of Community Psychology, 17,* 755–783.

Greenberger, E., O'Neil, R., & Nagel, S.K. (1994). Linking workplace and homeplace: Relations between the nature of adults' work and their parenting behaviors. *Developmental Psychology, 30,* 990–1002.

Grossman, F.K., Pollack, W.S., & Golding, E. (1988). Fathers and children: Predicting the quality and quantity of fathering. *Developmental Psychology, 24,* 82–91.

Haskins, R. (1989). Beyond metaphor: The efficacy of early childhood education. *American Psychologist, 44*(2), 274–282.

Hayes, C., Palmer, J., & Zaslow, M. (1990). *Who cares for America's children? Child care policy for the 1990's.* Washington, DC: National Academy Press.

Hewitt Associates. (1990). *Work and family benefits provided by major U.S. employers in 1990.* Lincolnshire, IL: Hewitt Associates.

Hewitt Associates. (1993). Employer response to family and medical leave legislation. In *On employee benefits.* Lincolnshire, IL: Hewitt Associates.

Heymann, J., Earle, A., Egleston, B. (August, 1996). Parental availability for the care of sick children. *Pediatrics, 98*(2), 228–230.

Hock, E. (1980). Working and non-working mothers and their infants: A comparative study of maternal caregiving characteristics and infant social behavior. *Merrill-Palmer Quarterly, 26,* 79–101.

Hofferth, S.L., Brayfield, A., Deitch, S., & Holcomb, P. (1991). *National child care survey, 1990.* Washington, DC: The Urban Institute.

Hoffman, L.W. (1989). Effects of maternal employment in the two-parent family. *American Psychologist, 44,* 283–292.

Hoffman, L.W., & Youngblade, L.M. (1999). *Mothers at work: Effects on children's well-being.* New York: Cambridge University Press.

Howes, C., Galinsky, E., Shinn, M., Sibley, A., & McCarthy, J. (1998). *The Florida Child Care Quality Improvement Study: 1996 Report.* New York: Families and Work Institute.

Howes, C., Sakai, L.M., Shinn, M., Phillips, D., Galinsky, E., & Whitebook, M. (1995). Race, social class, and maternal working conditions as influences on children's behavior in child care. *Journal of Applied Developmental Psychology, 16,* 107–124.

Howes, C., Smith, E., & Galinsky, E. (1995). *The Florida child care quality improvement study: Interim Report.* New York: Families and Work Institute.

Hughes, D., & Galinsky, E. (1988). Balancing work and family life: Research and corporate application. In A.E. Gottfried & A.W. Gottfried (Eds.), *Maternal employment and children's development: Longitudinal research* (pp. 233–268). New York: Plenum.

Hughes, D., Galinsky, E., & Morris, A. (1992). The effects of job characteristics on marital quality: Specifying linking mechanisms. *Journal of Marriage and Family, 54,* 31–42.

Kanter, R.M. (1977). *Work and family in the United States: A critical review and agenda for research and policy.* New York: Russell Sage Foundation.

Karasek, R.A. (1979). Job demands, job decision latitude, and mental strain: Implications for job redesign. *Administrative Science Quarterly, 24,* 285–314.

Keith, P., & Schafer, R. (1980). Role strain and depression in two-job families. *Family Relations, 29,* 483–488.

Kohn, M.L. (1969). *Class and conformity: A study in values.* Homewood, IL: Dorsey Press.

Kohn, M.L., & Schooler, C. (1973). Occupational experience and psychological functioning: An assessment of reciprocal effects. *American Sociological Review, 38,* 97–118.

Kontos, S., Howes, C., Shinn, M., & Galinsky, E. (1994). *Quality in family child care and relative care.* New York: Teachers College Press.

Lally, J.R., Mangione, P., Honig, A., & Wittmer, D. (1988, April). More pride, less delinquency: Findings from the ten-year follow-up study of the Syracuse University Family Development Research Program. *ZERO TO THREE Bulletin, 8,* 13–17.

Lambert, S.J., & Hopkins, K. (1993). *Added benefits: The link between family-responsive policies and work performance at Fel-Pro, Inc.* Chicago: University of Chicago.

Lazar, I., & Darlington, R. (1982). Lasting effects of early education: A report for the Consortium for Longitudinal Studies. *Monographs of the Society for Research on Child Development, Vol. 47*(2-3), No. 195.

Lerner, J.V., & Galambos, N.L. (1985). Mother role satisfaction, mother–child interaction, and child temperament: A process model. *Developmental Psychology, 21,* 1157–1164.

Londerville, S., & Maine, M. (1981). Security of attachment, compliance, and maternal training methods in the second year of life. *Developmental Psychology, 17*(3), 289–299.

Marra, R., & Lindner, J. (1992). The true cost of parental leave: The parental leave cost model. In D.E. Friedman, E. Galinsky, & V. Plowden (Eds.), *Parental leave and productivity: Current research* (pp. 55–78). New York: Families and Work Institute.

McKey, R.H., Condelli, L., Ganson, H., Barrett, B.J., McConkey, C., & Plantz, M. (1985). *The impact of Head Start on children, families, and communities* (DHHS Publication NO. OHDS 85-31193). Washington, DC: U.S. Government Printing Office.

Menaghan, E.G., & Parcel, T.L. (1990). Parental employment and family life: Research in the 1980's. *Journal of Marriage and the Family, 52,* 1079–1098.

Miller, B.M. (1992). *Private welfare: The distributive equity of family benefits in America.* Unpublished dissertation, Brandeis University, Waltham, MA.

NICHD Early Child Care Research Network. (1997). The effects of infant child care and attachment security: Results of the NICHD study of early child care. *Child Development, 68*(5), 860–879.

O'Neil, R. (1992). *Maternal work experiences, psychological well-being and achievement-fostering parenting.* Unpublished manuscript, University of California, Los Angeles.

Owen, M.T., Easterbrooks, M.A., Chase-Lansdale, L., & Goldberg, W. (1984). The relation between maternal employment status and the stability of attachments to mother and to father. *Child Development, 55*, 1894–1901.

Paulson, S.E. (1994). Relations of parenting style and parental involvement with 9th grade students' achievement. *Journal of Early Adolescence, 14*(2), 250–267.

Pettit, G.S., Harrist, A.W., Bates, J.E., & Dodge, K.A. (1991). Family interaction, social cognition, and children's subsequent relations with peers at kindergarten. *Journal of Social and Personal Relationships, 8*(3), 383–402.

Phillips, D. (Ed.). (1987). *Quality in child care: What does research tell us?* Washington, DC: National Association for the Education of Young Children.

Phillips, D.A., Mekos, D., Scarr, S., McCartney, K., & Abbott-Shim, M. (1999). *Within and beyond the classroom door: Assessing quality in classroom centers.* Unpublished manuscript. University of Virginia, Charlottesville.

Piotrkowski, C.S. (1979). *Work and the family system.* New York: Macmillan.

Piotrkowski, C.S., & Crits-Cristoph, P. (1981). Women's jobs and family adjustment. *Journal of Family Issues, 2*, 126–147.

Piotrkowski, C.S., & Katz, M.H. (1982). Indirect socialization of children: The effects of mothers' jobs on academic behaviors. *Child Development, 53*, 1520–1529.

Piotrkowski, C.S., & Katz, M.H. (1983). Work experience and family relations among working-class and lower-middle-class families. *Research in the Interweave of Social Roles: Jobs and Families, 3*, 187–200.

Powell, D.R. (1992). *Making it in today's world: Options for strengthening parents' contributions to children's learning.* West Lafayette, IN: Purdue University.

Quinn, R.P., Seashore, S., Kahn, R., Mangione, T., Campbell, D., Staines, G.L., & McCollough, M. (1971). *Survey of working conditions: Final report on univariate and bivariate tables* (Document No. 2916-0001). Washington, DC: U.S. Government Printing Office.

Quinn, R.P., & Shepard, L. (1974). *The 1972-73 quality of employment survey: Descriptive statistics, with comparison data from the 1969-70 survey of working conditions.* Ann Arbor: University of Michigan: Survey Research Center, Institute for Social Research.

Quinn, R.P., & Staines, G.L. (1979). *The 1977 quality of employment survey: Descriptive statistics with comparison data from the 1969-1970 and the 1973-1974 surveys.* Ann Arbor, MI: Survey Research Center, Institute for Social Research.

Rapoport, R., Bailyn, L., Kolb, D., Fletcher, J., Friedman, D.E., Eaton, S., Harvey, M., & Miller, B. (1996). *Relinking life and work: Toward a better future.* New York: Ford Foundation.

Rapoport, R., & Rapoport, R.N. (1971). *Dual-career families.* New York: Penguin.

Rapoport, R., & Rapoport, R.N. (1976). *Dual-career families re-examined.* New York: Harper/Colophon.

Rapoport, R., Rapoport, R.N., Strelitz, Z., & Kew, S. (1977). *Fathers, mothers, and society.* New York: Vintage.

Repetti, R.L. (1987). Individual and common components of the social environment at work and psychological well-being. *Journal of Personality and Social Psychology, 52*, 710–720.

Repetti, R.L. (1989). Effects of daily workload on subsequent behavior during marital interaction: The roles of social withdrawal and spouse support. *Journal of Personality and Social Psychology, 57*(4), 651–659.

Repetti, R.L., & Cosmas, K.A. (1991). The quality of the social environment at work and job satisfaction. *Journal of Applied Psychology, 21*, 840–854.

Repetti, R., & Wood, J. (1995). *The effects of daily stress at work on mother–child interactions*. Poster presented at the Biennial Meetings of the Society for Research on Child Development. Indianapolis, IN.

Schachter, F.F. (1981). Toddlers with employed mothers. *Child Development, 52,* 958–964.

Scharlach, A.E., & Stanger, J. (1994). *Mandated family and medical leave: Boon or bane?* Unpublished manuscript, University of California, Berkeley.

Schweinhart, L.J., Barnes, H.V., & Weikart, D.P. (1993). Significant benefits: The High/Scope Perry Preschool Study through age 27. *Monographs of the High/Scope Educational Foundation, 10.*

Shinn, M., Phillips, D., Howes, C., Galinsky, E., & Whitebook, M. (1990). *Correspondence between mothers' perceptions and observer ratings of quality in child care centers.* New York: Families and Work Institute.

Shore, R. (1997). *Rethinking the brain: Research and implications of brain development in young children.* New York: Families and Work Institute.

Spade, J.Z. (1991). Occupational structure and men's and women's parental values. *Journal of Family Issues, 12,* 343–360.

Staines, G.L., & Galinsky, E. (1992). Parental leave and productivity: The supervisor's view. In D.E. Friedman, E. Galinsky, & V. Plowden (Eds.), *Parental leave and productivity: Current research* (pp. 21–32). New York: Families and Work Institute.

Staines, G., & Pleck, J. (1983). *The impact of work schedules in the family.* Ann Arbor, MI: Survey Research Center, Institute for Social Research.

Tentler, L.W. (1979). *Wage earning women: Industrial work and family life in the U.S., 1900-1930.* New York: Oxford University Press.

Titmuss, R.M. (Ed.). (1959). *Essays on the welfare state.* New Haven, CT: Yale University Press.

Vaughn, B.E., Gove, F.L., & Egeland, B. (1980). The relationship between out-of-home care and the quality of infant–mother attachment in an economically disadvantaged population. *Child Development, 51,* 1203–1214.

Voydanoff, P. (1988). Work role characteristics, family structure demands, and work/family conflict. *Journal of Marriage and the Family, 50,* 749–761.

Weikart, D.P. (1990, February 26.). *Testimony at the U.S. Congressional Subcommittee on Education and Health, Joint Economic Committee.* Washington, DC.

Whitebook, M., Phillips, D., & Howes, C. (1990). *National child care staffing study.* Oakland, CA: Child Care Employee Project.

Whitebook, M., Phillips, D., & Howes, C. (1993). *National child care staffing study revisited: Four years in the life of center-based child care.* Oakland, CA: Child Care Employee Project.

12

The Whole Child

Transdisciplinary Implications for Infant and Toddler Care

◆❖◆

Debby Cryer

Each of the preceding chapters has allowed the reader to view a specific aspect of infant/toddler development and care. In the first section of this book, chapters focused on what research has told us about basic development during the first 3 years of life—cognitive, language, and social development were presented in terms of what happens and what is needed by the child. In the second section, areas related to out-of-home care were examined, specifically within the context of defining quality of child care for infants and toddlers, health-related issues, and early intervention programs. Finally, broader environmental issues were portrayed, in terms of the cultural context in which infants and toddlers are raised and the resources that are available to families and child care programs to support the care and education of infants and toddlers within our society.

In summarizing, it helps to consider the chapters as a totality, not as 10 separate pieces. As separate pieces, each chapter presents its own discipline-specific information for the reader. If the reader considers information presented across chapters, he or she can see that there are recurring ideas woven throughout the fabric of the book. These recurring threads are some of the basics for ensuring that infants and toddlers begin life with the supports they need to optimize their chances for later success in society. These are the requirements that emerge when infants and toddlers are considered as whole beings, rather than from the perspectives of specific disciplines.

This summary chapter highlights five tenets that cut across the individual disciplines represented in the chapters. The implications of these basic cross-cutting themes are presented in terms of practice in out-of-home child care, preparation for personnel in these programs, public policy, and future research. The basic recurring ideas to be discussed in this summary chapter are:

- Positive development requires that the health of infants and toddlers be optimized, not only after they are born, but through prenatal care for their mothers as well.
- Infants and toddlers require caring adults who are responsive and sensitive to the child's initiations.
- Infants and toddlers require environments that are interesting and responsive to the children's initiations.
- Infants and toddlers benefit when the interrelationship between family and out-of-home care is positive and constructive.
- The primary contexts in which the child is embedded, both in family and in child care, often require societal supports to ensure children's success.

INFANT/TODDLER HEALTH

Positive development requires that the health of infants and toddlers be optimized, not only after they are born, but through prenatal care for their mothers as well. Encouraging the health of infants and toddlers is necessary if caring adults are to optimize chances for children's developmental success. The importance of prenatal health care for mothers as well as health care for infants and toddlers is brought up in several of the preceding chapters. In addition, health care for infants and toddlers is a policy issue that has received significant attention in the United States.

Importance of Sanitary
Precautions in Out-of-Home Child Care

The two chapters on health issues (Chapters 6 and 7) are clear about the additional risks to which infants and toddlers are exposed when they attend out-of-home care. There are many implications for practice in the information provided, although it appears that practice can affect diarrheal diseases more readily than respiratory diseases. Because sanitary practices can decrease the spread of diarrheal diseases in child care programs, consistent sanitary precautions should be implemented, such as sanitation of toys that are shared among children; frequent, thorough hand washing for both children and adults at all necessary times; excluding children with diarrhea from the classroom; and the maintainence of a clean environment. In terms of personnel preparation, this indicates that all staff working with this age group need training in this area. The content of the training should not only cover what must be done to protect children's health, but also must include the rationale for these practices so that teachers truly understand the implications of what they do. Because of frequent staff turnover, training must be repeated for all new employees. Promoting relationships between child care programs and community health care resources is one possible avenue towards better personnel preparation. Administrative practices should consist of continued monitoring to ensure that the required sanitary precautions are consistently implemented.

Child care practices should also ensure that infant/toddler environments are designed to encourage implementation of the required sanitary precautions that prevent the spread of disease. For example, to make implementation of appropriate handwashing procedures more likely, child care classrooms should be equipped with appropriate numbers of conveniently located sinks with warm water, and foot pedals or automatic faucets to prevent recontamination of hands. Rooms where toilet training is taking place should be equipped with child-sized toilets or toilets with adaptive seats, so that potty chairs are not needed, because of the additional sanitary problems associated with their use. In addition, rooms should be designed to encourage care for smaller rather than larger groups of children, as larger groups represent higher chances for exposure to disease from more sources. Only toys that can be sanitized should be used. There should be sufficient space so that children are not crowded together, and cribs or cots can be placed a sufficient distance from one another, so that germs are not easily transmitted during nap times.

From the policy perspective, licensing regulations in some states require classrooms to be equipped adequately, and groups of infants/toddlers to be small in size. But regulation is often weak or poorly enforced (i.e., many programs are exempt from regulation for a variety of reasons, licensing visits are infrequent, or only some of the comprehensive sanitation requirements are required). Therefore many programs are not required by governmental policy to consistently meet sanitation standards that would better protect infants and toddlers. Obviously the implication here is for policy makers to tighten up on health-related infant/toddler regulation, basing rules on the latest research. However, because the child care system in the United States is generally underfunded, policy would have to be supplemented with the means to pay for the upgraded regulation.

Handling Sick Children

Even in a child care program where sanitary precautions are well implemented in practice, very young children in child care will still become sick quite often, more so than their stay-at-home peers. Thus, personnel preparation and practice need to emphasize how staff should care for sick children, both in terms of their health and emotional needs. Child care policies (both regulatory and within individual child care programs) need to be explicit on what steps will be taken when a child is ill. Clear communication is needed between child care providers and families so that the priorities of both are understood and respected, without endangering the children in the program. For example, the parent's need to be at work must be balanced against the reality of how much attention the child care program is able to provide for a sick child, and the program's need to protect others from health risks. Flexibility, combined with well-informed caution, is necessary here. Also, it cannot be forgotten that children who are not feeling well must be handled with great sensitivity from their caregivers to ensure comfort and security.

Medically Vulnerable Children

Health-related practices are even more important when medically vulnerable children with disabilities are included in child care programs. Special attention is needed, both in personnel preparation and practice, to reduce the risk of disease. Children who are more likely to become severely ill, with greater consequences, should receive special consideration when child care placement is considered. Smaller groups, such as in family child care or home care, might well be more appropriate for fragile children.

The Child's Immature Immune System

Research on the development of the child's immune system helps us understand when infants and toddlers are most vulnerable to disease. Infants are especially vulnerable to disease between 6 and 9 months of age when their immune systems are no longer supported by their mother's contribution, but their own system has not yet been established. The question of whether infants at this stage of vulnerability should be placed in child care at all is often discussed. Actually, children are 2 years of age before their immune systems are fully functioning. However, it is a reality that mothers of children younger than 1 year of age must work, either to maintain their position in their place of employment or to help support their families.

The research on the development of the human immune system reminds us about the important benefits of breastfeeding of infants, because some immunity is passed from the mother to child during the period when the child's own defenses are just beginning. Thus, accommodating mothers who wish to continue breastfeeding their infants in child care should be encouraged. Positive communication with the mothers and cooperation with them to make breastfeeding work well should be part of the practice in child care programs. Child care personnel require training in this area so that they understand the importance of breastfeeding, know how to encourage it while respecting each mother's choice about how her baby should be fed, and can rid themselves of any preexisting biases that they have on the subject.

The health risks associated with infants younger than 1 year of age who are in out-of-home child care should be included when employers and governmental agencies consider family leave policies. To address the problems related to infants' health risks, policies need to be created that extend parental leave and provide adequate financial support and employer-friendliness, so that parents can actually take advantage of any leave that is offered.

Some Areas in Which Research Is Still Needed

Researchers have substantial information about health care for infants and toddlers in out-of-home care, in terms of what practices are needed, and why. Prior research allows constituents in the child care system to make relatively informed decisions in this area. However, less is known about how to best ensure that child care staff actually implement practices consistently. Informing child care staff is just the beginning of encouraging the desired practices, and research is still needed to clarify many issues. For example, we do not know what requirements are needed to ensure that sanitary practices will be carried out consistently. Strategies need to be designed, implemented, and evaluated in this regard. Experiments are also needed to help us more fully understand the effects of some child care structure variables (e.g., group size, size of available space, or the introduction of equipment that makes sanitary procedures easier to implement) on incidence of illness.

Finally, basic medical research is still needed to provide information that will affect the care of infants and toddlers in the future. Longitudinal studies are needed to examine whether the increase in infant/toddler illnesses has long-term effects on adults' health later in life. Further work is needed to develop immunizations to protect children from the troublesome diseases that are currently so prevalent in out-of-home care.

CARING AND RESPONSIVE ADULTS

Infants and toddlers require caring adults who are responsive and sensitive to the child's initiations. In the chapters on development (Chapters 2, 3, and 4), we found that infants are active, rather than passive, learners. They act on their world and the people in it, and learn from the responses they receive. In addition, their brains are going through the process of pruning synapses to make brain functioning more efficient, and what is not used is more likely to be eliminated. This information has numerous implications, especially for practice and personnel preparation. The primary implication is that adults in the lives of children must be responsive to the children's initiations, so that they receive stimulation and feedback that is most useful for what they are working on at the moment. Based on research, the implications for what is needed as infants and toddlers interact with the caring adults who provide out-of-home care should be considered.

Enough Adults to Provide Enough Attention

If adults are to be responsive and sensitive, they need to be able to give individual children enough attention. Then the adult will at least have the opportunity to notice that a child is initiating an interaction and be able to respond. To be able to give children sufficient attention, the ratio of children to adults must be low enough to allow for this. In infant/toddler care, just providing the quality of care that meets children's custodial needs, which includes all the sanitation requirements mentioned earlier, takes significant staff time. The attentive interactions that children need adds to the amount of time staff must put into the job. For example, the turn-taking conversations, which are so important to the development of a child's language, take time, as does providing hands-on affection through holding and cuddling individual children to encourage strong attachment to caring adults. The decisions made by child care constituents, including families, care providers and policy makers, must support the need for attentive care if optimal development can be expected for children in out-of-home care.

Enough Time to Create a Relationship

Creating a relationship that is sensitive and responsive to each child takes time. Therefore, practicing continuity of caregivers may be one way to encourage this, as opposed to having children experience many caregiver changes during the early years. Knowing children very well, over longer periods of time, might well make it more likely for caregivers to be able to read the subtle signs children show that require accurate responses from adults. Thus, program administrators may need to change traditional staffing patterns, and the child care field should work on methods for encouraging staff to remain in child care for longer periods.

Importance of the Teacher's Personal Characteristics

Although stringent ratios are associated with more appropriate caregiving behaviors by child care staff, and continuity of caregivers may provide the time needed to establish relationships, these do not ensure the attentive, intimate interactions required by very young children. Ratios and continuity of caregiver may be necessary, but insufficient, components for the types of interactions infants and toddlers need to be able to develop positively. Equally important is what the caregiver brings to the job in terms of personality and knowledge.

It is unlikely that caregivers will have much positive emotional energy to spare for children if their own lives are emotionally stressed. Nor will they remain in the lives of the children to support their emotional and intellectual development over any period of time—frequent turnover of staff eliminates children's chances to form important relationships in child care environments. In many cases, the stress of poverty is a reality for the nation's caregivers because wages are very low—so low that often teachers are unable to afford child care for their own children that matches the quality of child care they may be providing to the children of others. In addition, the low status of being a child care provider erodes a teacher's self-esteem. It is necessary to realize that if children are cared for by individuals who are depressed or dissatisfied with their jobs, the children will show the effects. Therefore, maintaining high morale through support of caregivers is as important in practice as is the careful selection of staff. From a political and societal perspective, it is imperative to recognize the need for child care teachers to be respected as educators and rewarded accordingly, in wages, benefits, and working conditions.

Teacher Education to Promote Appropriate Interactions

Preceding chapters have shown evidence of a relation between better educated child care providers and higher quality early child care and education. The education required for teachers of infants and toddlers needs to reflect the developmental requirements of the children, which differ, to some extent, from the needs of older children. Providing the appropriate content in the training of infant/toddler teachers will increase the likelihood that appropriate practices are implemented.

Helping teachers to understand the rationale for certain practices is the first step toward encouraging teachers to implement those practices in their own programs. Teachers will be more likely to facilitate children's learning when they know what children naturally have the capacity to learn and how they learn it. Topics to be stressed include how the brain develops, the active nature of infants' and toddlers' learning, and the importance of the caring adults' behavior to that learning.

It is nearly impossible to teach any person all of the specific practices that can be found in high-quality infant/toddler programs. But once the rational for practices is understood, teachers are more likely to be able to generalize their learning and produce the specific practices that are needed. For example, in helping infants and toddlers learn to communicate well, teachers will benefit from knowing that it is crucial for a child to frequently hear language about the things he or she is experiencing or interested in. In addition, teachers need to understand that conversations should be the primary means toward encouraging language development and that the conversations must incorporate any initiations and responses that the young children are able to make. Teachers also benefit from knowing that very young children respond well to higher tones and variation in pitch. Once teachers have this knowledge, even though they have not been taught what to do in each instance, they might be more likely to perform the necessary practices, such as incorporating conversations into both custodial care and play times, talking about what the child is focused on, and not feeling embarrassed about talking to babies or using "baby talk" or songs with the children.

Because attachment issues are so important at this stage of development, teachers require information that encourages the development of strong, secure attachment relationships in children. Once practitioners have the information they need to understand the development of relationships, they may be more likely to practice such methods as handling children as individuals instead of as a group, taking the extra steps needed to reach more difficult babies, using children's names frequently, and allowing children to choose their own primary caregivers. In addition, they might consider the benefits of keeping children in groups with familiar children to encourage friendships.

Teacher education can also be used to minimize the negative effects of cultural clashes that might occur between a child's home and the child care environment, as discussed in Chapter 9. Helping teachers to understand that children are most likely to be successful as bicultural individuals, secure and competent with both their home and other ways of living, requires serious in-depth discussions about preconceptions of child-rearing attitudes and other viable possibilities that exist. Important issues in this area include the various paths that can be taken to reach similar cognitive or language outcomes, the pros and cons of learning a second language during the very early years, communicating with families to understand cultural values and preferences, and ensuring that acculturation (not assimilation) of the child takes place. Without being awakened to the practices that are needed in this area, it would be very difficult for teachers to provide truly sensitive or responsive care.

Some Areas in Which Research Is Still Needed

There continue to be many areas in which research could inform practice with regard to the relationships between teachers and children in out-of-home child care. Research is needed to assess whether the implications that are represented here are valid when applied in practice (e.g., Does the content of teacher training, described in this section, actually improve chances that teachers and children will form secure attachments?). This research would need to both challenge assumptions and promote applications.

To answer some questions about the nature of adult–child relationships in out-of-home infant/toddler care, intervention studies would be useful in determining the best methods for fostering children's social development. For example, the effects of curricular approaches that use methods supported by the current research findings might be evaluated, especially for children who might be at risk for developing the social and emotional skills needed for success in society.

Making sense of the effects of child-rearing practices in different cultures will require many different studies. At present, there are many assumptions being made about the effects of cultural practices on children, few of which are supported by stringent research that has been replicated over time. For example, the best methods for bringing about the development of bicultural individuals are not known, nor are the effects of being bicultural on the development of various capabilities. Researchers must examine whether there are basic tenets in childrearing that are important across cultures. Child care specialists also lack information about relative effects of learning a second language, under varying conditions, in the very early years. All of these issues require research to inform personnel preparation, practice, and policy.

Various research methodologies will be needed to help clarify these types of issues, including both case studies and quantitative studies of varying sorts. It is likely that researchers will need to increase their acceptance of the different methodologies that are available, as well as broaden their definitions of developmental milestones to include those that are valued in a wider range of cultures. In addition, researchers will need to become more aware of their own cultural biases when designing studies and interpreting results.

INTERESTING AND RESPONSIVE ENVIRONMENTS

Infants and toddlers require environments that are interesting and responsive to children's initiations. The implications associated with recognizing the infant/toddler as an active learner are not only important with regard to the people with whom they interact, but also to aspects of the child's environment. Chapter 2 on cognitive development is clear in its explanation about how even the youngest infants observe the objects and actions in their environments and then learn from what they see happening. In a way, the infant makes demands upon the environment, using senses early on to figure out how things operate, and later on, manipulating objects to discover all of their properties.

The behavior of infants and toddlers is fascinating if adults know what to look for, and the children's learning can be enhanced by caring adults who know how to set up interesting spaces with lots of opportunities for children to experiment and explore safely. Teachers may be bored with infants and toddlers if they do not understand the developmental processes that are occurring and may see no reason for any actions that go beyond custodial care. However, personnel preparation can help teachers extend their teaching repertoires to increase children's opportunities for learning. This training should include topics such as observing children to assess their interests and then providing multiple ways for children to explore those interests. Young children give clues about their learning needs and interests. When teachers pay attention to these clues and facilitate what the child is trying to do by providing resources in many different ways, learning is encouraged. Thus, learning to observe children in their environments and to set up environments in response to what the children do is an important, necessary component of personnel preparation for teachers of infants and toddlers.

Personnel preparation should also include topics such as how to arrange spaces to provide access to the materials children need to move ahead in their learning. Teachers need to understand that young children develop rapidly, especially during the first 3 years, and require environments that change as children demand new challenges. Because children habituate to familiar stimuli, new materials must be regularly introduced into the environment to allow new learning to take place. These materials do not have to be expensive educational toys, but only safe objects in which children show interest. For example, frozen juice can lids that can be dropped into slots cut in a cardboard box can challenge toddlers during certain points in their development just as effectively as any commercially produced toy.

With regard to language development, teachers should also be taught the importance of introducing novelty into a young child's environment. The more things children experience, the more opportunities they have for learning new words, as long as those words are provided in a context the child can understand.

Providing teachers with the information they need to create environments that encourage learning for infants and toddlers is only part of moving what is known from research in this area into practice. Child care program administration must support teachers in creating the environments that children require for developmental progress. For example, financial resources should be allocated so that teachers have access to the materials and equipment they need to provide rich learning environments for the children in their care. Too often, resources are put into the environments for older children, while the younger groups are expected to "make do." The attitude is that older children have greater learning needs, while infants and toddlers require only custodial care and minimal learning materials. This attitude requires change if child care providers are to provide infants and toddlers the experiences they need to maximize their potential.

Some Areas in Which Research Is Still Needed

Although research is able to inform practice about how infants' and toddlers' physical environments encourage or discourage the development of social, communication, and intellectual abilities, many of the implications for these findings are still only assumptions. Further research is needed to test these assumptions. In terms of the basic research on how cognitive development progresses, there has been little done to ascertain whether results are consistent across cultural or socioeconomic groups.

There is an opportunity to study the effects of many environmental practices on young children's development. For example, the amount of stimulation found in the same infant/toddler child care environments is often criticized as being either over- or under-stimulating. In addition, the interplay between quality of interactions and environment is not understood.

POSITIVE INTERRELATIONSHIPS
BETWEEN FAMILY AND OUT-OF-HOME CARE

Infants and toddlers benefit when the interrelationship between family and out-of-home care is positive and constructive. In this book several chapters highlight the positive interrelationship that is needed between the important people in a child's family and their out-of-home care environment. Chapters 5 and 8 make strong arguments for comprehensive early childhood programs where significant effort is put into the parent and teacher aspects of raising infants and toddlers.

In practice, partnering with families is extremely important for the well-being of children. Parents and teachers need to share information to encourage understanding of the child and enthusiasm for what the child can do. Often, teachers need preparation to help them take on a professional attitude that is flexible and supportive with family members. Then they can provide parents of children in this age group with the special support required to validate their decision to use child care and to understand that having a child in child care need not ever compromise the parents' relationships with the child. In addition, parents might often need information about what children's developmental needs are and how they can be encouraged at home. Teachers require ongoing education themselves, so that the information they provide to parents is accurate and up-to-date, and also to help them realize that information sharing is not a one-way exchange.

Some Areas in Which Research Is Still Needed

It is clear from the research discussed in preceding chapters that the effects of the adult-focused components of early childhood comprehensive programs have not been well documented. Researchers are at the beginning of understanding how to evaluate these programs and to examine their effects. In many cases, the assumed goals for adult components of programs are unclear, and, thus, it is difficult to ascertain whether the methods used have produced expected outcomes. For example, home visiting is presented as a possibility for improving children's chances for developmental success. However, the objectives of this comprehensive program component are often unclear, and it is difficult to ascertain whether the home visiting has produced desired outcomes. In addition, the quality of the adult-focused program components have not been fully operationalized for measurement in research. So there remain many challenges to researchers to help policy makers and practitioners understand how and when adult aspects of comprehensive programs are most helpful for children.

The necessity of parent–teacher communication across cultures was mentioned earlier in this chapter, but it is important to revisit this issue. Certainly, there is much that remains unknown about how to best encourage communication among the adults in the lives of children to promote children's development and happiness. This issue becomes even more complicated when teachers and families are from different cultures. Studies are needed to help all constituents better understand how to share information and values without bias and to understand the best options for a child. Questions about what practices and behaviors are more likely to bring about the outcomes desired for children and their families need to be examined. Many passionately held beliefs are only based on assumptions.

SOCIETAL SUPPORTS FOR FAMILY AND CHILD CARE

The primary contexts in which the child is embedded, both family and child care, require societal supports to ensure children's success. Infants and toddlers need the basics discussed in this chapter to ensure their successful development. These basics, however, are dependent on societal support for both family and child care. Throughout this book, it has been shown that raising infants and toddlers to be developmentally successful requires families and child care programs that are strong in many ways—so that children can be given the attention and opportunities needed to optimize chances for success. Yet, under the present conditions, supports to encourage these strengths are too often lacking. Supports available to those who are raising America's infants and toddlers are inadequate and unreliable. For example, families with very young children are often insecure financially and sometimes ill prepared to optimize the development of a child. Out-of-home child care programs are generally underfunded, and regulation and staff wage issues create child care environments where even adequate custodial care is difficult to produce. Galinsky and Bond show that supports for families are more likely to exist for employed parents who are already raising their children under better conditions but tend to be less certain for parents in less advantaged positions. In Chapter 10, Kagan and McLearn describe the progress that has been made in directing public policy to meet the needs of infants and toddlers and are hopeful in the prospect of continued progress. The current societal reality does not appear to support the basics for all children.

If society requires that all children be given the best chance for success, then change is needed. To make informed decisions about how best to support the development of all of the youngest citizens, research might lead the way. For example, further policy research could help policy makers understand how to best direct scarce resources. Businesses could evaluate whether more family-friendly policies are cost effective and beneficial to enterprise. Information from research might provide a rationale for change. Yet, societal attitudes, such as those that create the conditions under which parents raise children, are not amenable to change without some severe shock to the system or without continual education that reaches and persuades the adults in the society.

Obviously the level of societal supports for families and child care programs that are now in place will allow the status quo to continue. If parents want more, for more children, and for the United States as a whole, then more will be required of society to meet this final basic need.

CLOSING THOUGHTS

In closing, it is important to return to the title of this chapter and remind ourselves that infants and toddlers should be considered "whole" beings. An overemphasis on any single aspect of development is likely to result in a lack of attention to other equally important aspects. The characteristics and needs of infants and toddlers are interrelated and are best viewed within the context of the whole child who is embedded within family, child care, and social/cultural environments.

Yet, continuing to study the various specific aspects of infants' and toddlers' development is necessary if we are to come to a more advanced understanding of how to optimize children's chances for developmental success. New information that is obtained will have further implications—for the practices used with infants and toddlers in child care and education, for the personnel preparation of those who care and teach, for the public policy that is enacted for the well-being of children, and for informing future research. Learning to understand the development of infants and toddlers through research is certainly a challenge in itself. However, the greatest challenge we face may well be transforming the information we have discovered into actual practices that positively affect infants and toddlers in their real world settings.

Index

Page numbers followed by *f* indicate figures; those followed by *t* indicate tables.

Abecedarian Project, 132–133, 141, 216–218
Abuse, *see* Child abuse; Substance abuse
Adenovirus, 166t, 167, 184t
Adult Attachment Interview, 105–107
Adult Involvement Scale, 128, 155
Advisory Committee on Services for Families with Infants and Toddlers, 137
Aeromonas, 182, 184t, 186t
Ætna, parental leave program, 321
African Americans
  independence *versus* interdependence, 247
  maternal attention, 250
  mother–child speech, 57
  quality of child care, 128–129
  sleeping patterns of infants, 249
Alcohol abuse, *see* Substance abuse
Antibiotic resistance
  diarrhea, infectious, 193–194
  respiratory disease, 171–172
Arithmetic operations, development of, 34–36, 35f
Arnett Scale of Caregiver Behavior, 147, 152, 155
Assessment Profile, 152
Astrovirus, 183, 184t, 186t
AT&T, parental leave program, 321
Attachment formation, theory of, 89
Attachment relationships
  caregiver–child, 96–97, 100
  conceptual model of, 88f, 89–90
  effect on later behaviors, 99–100
  effect on peer relationships, 100
  father–child, 96, 313, 318

mother–child, 97–98, 100, 105–107, 312–313, 314
  nonconcordance, 97–98
  parental employment and, 312–314
  quality of child care and, 127–128, 148
Audition, prenatal, 9
Auditory learning, 12–13
Autobiographical memory, 20

Bacillus cereus, 182
Bacterial respiratory disease, 171–172
Behaviorism, 14
Bilingual children
  child care considerations for, 77, 245–246, 254–255, 358–359
  language development in, 51–52, 77
  quality of care for, 139
  socialization in, 107–108
  vocabulary development in, 64
Biological risk
  development of children, optimizing, 226–227
  early intervention, 219–220
  health issues, 227
  long-term benefits of programs, 222–225
  risk factors, 213
Birth weights, low
  early intervention programs, 219–220
  home visiting programs, 134–135
  low-income families, 118, 275
  risk of developmental problems, 208–209

Book reading
   cognitive development, 36–38, 37f
   conversational skills, 59
   extended discourse with, 67
   vocabulary development, 66
Brain damage, potential for recovery, 9
Brain development, see Cognitive
      development
Breastfeeding, 355
Bronchitis, see Respiratory disease

Calicivirus, 184t, 186t
Campylobacter, 182, 184t, 197t
CARE program, see Project CARE
Caregivers
   caregiver–child relationships,
      96–100, 105–109, 356
   child development training, 107, 358
   cognitive development training, 41,
      358, 360
   compensation, 108, 292–293, 357
   cultural awareness of, 253–255,
      255–257, 358–359
   degree programs for, 107, 292
   illness of, 174
   second languages in, 52, 77,
      254–255, 358–359
   self-esteem of, 357
   training, general, 130, 288, 289–292,
      357–359, 362
   turnover, 108, 129–130, 290, 293, 357
   U.S. military, 291
Carnegie Corporation
   report on children, 118, 119, 146
   Starting Points Initiative, 273
Case management, quality indicators,
      144–145
Categorization, development of,
      31–34
CCDP, see Comprehensive Child
      Development Program
C–COS, see Child–Caregiver Obser-
      vation System
Center-based child care
   availability, 121–122
   compared to home visiting
      programs, 135
   defined, 165, 181
   quality, 124–125, 141–143, 315
   respiratory disease in, 165–174
   training of caregivers, 292

Central nervous system, see Cogni-
      tive development
Certification of child care providers,
      290–292, 293
CFRP, see Child and Family Resource
      Program
Child abuse
   after participation in intervention
      programs, 134
   prevention of, 298–299
   statistics, 207
Child and Family Resource Program
      (CFRP), 132
Child care practitioners, see Care-
      givers
Child care programs
   acceptance of infants and toddlers,
      122
   bilingualism, 51–52, 77, 245,
      254–255, 358–359
   for children with disabilities,
      210–211, 354
   cultural issues, 243–245, 253–258,
      358–359, 362–363
   effectiveness of, 126–130
   enrollment statistics, 118–119, 179
   for high-risk children, 210–211
   illegal, 120
   infection control, 174–176, 180–181
   licensure, 120, 121, 181, 287, 289
   need for, 118–120, 122, 210, 271–272
   quality, see Quality of care
   regulation of, 120, 121–122, 287–289
   sick children, handling of, 354
   see also Center-based child care;
         Employer-supported child
         care; Family care homes;
         Intervention programs
Child–Caregiver Observation System
      (C–COS), 155
Childhood amnesia, 18–20
Children of Substance Abusers Act of
      1992, 298–299
Classical conditioning, 14–15
Cleveland Family Study, respiratory
      disease, 166–167
Clostridium, 182, 184t, 186t
Cognitive development
   arithmetic operations, 34–36, 35f
   categorization, 31–34
   conceptual development, 31–34
   habituation, 10–11

influence of environmental stimulation on, 8, 356, 360–361
intervention programs, effect on, 132–133, 134, 135
learning, 9–18
maternal employment, effect on, 314
memory, 18–20
neurological bases, 8–9, 11, 271
object permanence, 24–31, 26f, 28f, 30f
object segregation, 20–24, 21f, 23f
perception, 12–14
quality of child care and, 128–129
recommendations for enhancing, 40–41
symbolization, 36–39, 37f
television, role in, 36, 38–39
training of caregivers in, 41, 358, 360
see also IQ
Colds, see Respiratory disease
Communication skills, see Language development
Community Integrated Service Systems Action, 273
Community-based child care, 142
Comprehensive Child Development Act of 1988, 272, 298
Comprehensive Child Development Program (CCDP), 134, 142, 143–144
Comprehensive intervention programs, see Intervention programs
Concepts, development of, 31–34
Conjugate reinforcement, 15
Context
    cultural, 241–242, 244–245
    in quality of care, 139–140, 147, 149f
Continuity, in quality of care, 129–130, 137, 138–139, 147, 148, 149f, 356–357
Conversational skills, development of
    intent of communication, 54, 61–62
    intersubjectivity, 54–55
    topic maintenance, 59–61
    turn taking, 55, 56–59
    vocabulary acquisition, 65–66
Costs
    of child care, 293–294
    of illness in child care, 174, 194
Cross-cultural studies
    extended discourse, 67, 70
    feeding, 237

independence versus interdependence, 247–248
infant behavior, 237
lack of, 40
maternal attention, 237, 250
mother–child speech, 57
parenting styles, 250–251
pictures as symbols, 37–38, 37f
self-control, 249–250
sleeping arrangements, 237
sleeping patterns of infants, 248–249
Cryptosporidium
    asymptomatic excretion of, 186, 186t, 187
    attack rates, 184t, 190t
    exclusion of children with, 197t
    inoculum size, 182t
    transmission, 189, 192
Cultural issues
    adaptive culture, 93
    attachment relationships, 90
    bicultural skills, 93–94, 107–108, 245–246, 254–255, 359
    caregiver training, 255–257, 358–359
    child care programs, 243–244, 253–258, 358–359, 362–363
    context, 241–242, 244–245
    definition of culture, 239–240
    demographics, North American, 242–243
    development, views of, 251–253
    ethnicity, 240–241
    independence versus interdependence, 246–251
    policies regarding, 257–258
    quality of care, 139
    second language considerations, 51–52, 77, 245, 254–255, 358–359
    social development, 93–94, 244–245
    subordination, 241–242, 243–244
    see also Bilingual children; Cross-cultural studies; Racism

DCAPs, see Dependent care assistance plans
Dependent care assistance plans (DCAPs), 318, 336, 337t, 340–342
Depression
    in caregivers, 106–107, 357

Depression—*continued*
　maternal, 106–107, 274
Development
　cultural issues, 244–245
　family interaction patterns, effects
　　on, 211–214, 212f, 215
　optimizing for children at high
　　risk, 225–227
　parental employment, impact on,
　　311–316
　risk factors, 207–209
　see also Cognitive development;
　　Language development; Social
　　development
Diarrhea, infectious
　antibiotics, 193–194
　asymptomatic excretion, 185–187,
　　186t
　attack rates of pathogens, 183,
　　184–185t, 190t
　contamination patterns, 188–189
　exclusion of ill children, 192,
　　196–197, 352–353
　pathogens, 181–183, 182t, 184–185t,
　　186t, 197t
　prevention and control, 191–192,
　　195–198, 352–353
　rates of occurrence, 181, 187–188
　transmission, 181–183, 189–191,
　　192–193
　vaccines, 197–198
Differentiation theory, sensory
　perception, 12–13
Disabilities, infants and toddlers with
　availability of services for, 123, 210
　early intervention, 210–211,
　　214–215, 214f, 220–222
　family stressors, 212f, 213–214, 225
　federal policy on, 282–285
　funding for child care, 294
　health care of, 281–285, 354
　long-term benefits of programs for,
　　225
　managed care, 284
　Medicaid, 278, 282
　out-of-home placement, 228–229
　Education for All Handicapped
　　Children Act of 1975, 282
　Education of the Handicapped Act
　　Amendments of 1986, 282–285,
　　283t

prevalence, 209
states' provision of services,
　282–285
Discourse
　adult support of, 67–69
　cultural differences, 67, 70, 244
　extended, 66–70, 76
　gender differences, 68
　in pretend play, 69–70
　reading, predictor of, 67
　shared, 95–96
Discrimination, *see* Racism
Dishabituation, *see* Habituation
Diversity, *see* Cultural issues
Domination, cultural, *see* Cultural
　issues
Dopamine, role in object permanence
　performance, 31
Drug abuse, *see* Substance abuse

E. coli
　antibiotic resistance, 190, 193–194
　asymptomatic excretion, 186t, 187
　attack rates, 184t, 190t, 192
　exclusion of children with, 197,
　　197t
　inoculum size, 182t
　symptoms, 183
　transmission, 183, 189–191, 192
Ear infections, *see* Otitis media
Early and Periodic Screening, Diag-
　nostic, and Treatment (EPSDT)
　Program, 277–278, 282
Early childhood programs, *see* Inter-
　vention programs
Early Head Start program
　description, 154–155
　establishment, 119, 273
　ingredients included in the pro-
　　gram, 137
　performance standards, 287
　quality controls, 142
Early intervention, *see* Intervention
　programs
Education, of caregivers, *see* Training,
　of caregivers
Education for All Handicapped Chil-
　dren Act of 1975 (PL 94-142), 282
Education of the Handicapped Act
　Amendments of 1986 (PL 99-

457), 282–285, 283t
Employer-supported child care
    access to, 319, 324–342
    benefits of, 321–322
    employer incentives, 344
    historical perspective, 309, 318–324
    prevalence, 318–319
    see also Workplace issues
Environmental risk
    development of children, optimiz-
        ing, 226–227
    early intervention, 216–218
    health issues, 227
    long-term benefits of programs,
        222–225
    risk factors, 213
EPSDT, see Early and Periodic Screen-
    ing, Diagnostic, and Treatment
    Program
ERPs, see Evoked response potentials
    (ERPs)
Ethnicity, defined, 240–241
Even Start Program, 272, 298
Evoked response potentials (ERPs),
    11
Expanded Child Care Options
    project, 140
Experience-dependent processes, 8–9
Experience-expectant processes, 8
Extended discourse, see Discourse

Faces, as visual stimuli, 11
Family care homes
    availability of, 121–122
    defined, 165, 181
    quality of, 125–126, 286, 315–316
    respiratory disease in, 173
    training of caregivers, 292, 316
Family Day Care Rating Scale
    (FDCRS), 152, 155, 257
Family Development Research
    Program (FDRP), 133
Family interaction patterns, 211–214,
    212f, 215, 217, 218
Family Preservation and Family Sup-
    port Act (1993), 297, 302
Family support programs
    described, 135–137
    historical perspective, 300–302
    social policy, 272–273, 302–303

see also Intervention programs
Father–child relationships, 96, 313,
    318
FDCRS, see Family Day Care Rating
    Scale
FDRP, see Family Development
    Research Program
Feeding, classical conditioning, 14
Fel-Pro, work-life programs, 321–322
Fetus, hearing ability in the womb, 9
Frank Porter Graham Child
    Development Center
    study of otitis media, 168–169
    study of respiratory disease,
        166–167, 171–172
Friendship relationships, 95, 103–104
Funding, of child care programs,
    293–295

Gender differences
    extended discourse skills, 68
    maternal stress and, 316
    social development, 129–130
Giardia lamblia
    asymptomatic excretion, 186, 186t,
        187
    attack rates, 185t, 190t, 192
    exclusion of children with, 197t
    inoculum size, 182t
    transmission, 189
    treatment, 197

Habituation, 10–11
    dishabituation to mother, 12
    memory and, 19
    in object permanence studies,
        25–29
    in object segregation studies, 21–24
    relation to IQ, 11
Haemophilus influenzae type B, 188
Hand washing for control of disease,
    174, 191, 195–196, 352–353
Head Start programs, 119, 271, 287
Health care
    chronic illnesses and disabilities,
        281–285, 354
    effects on development, 273–274
    immunizations, 119, 175–176,
        197–198, 276, 277

Health care—*continued*
  insurance, 276–286
  low-income families, 275–276
  programs, 274–275
  sick children in child care, 354
Health insurance
  coverage statistics, 276, 277, 278
  federal legislation, 280–281
  Medicaid, 277–278, 280
  private, 276
  state initiatives, 278–280
  workplace issues, 325–327, 326t,
    327t, 328t
Health, Education, and Welfare Day
    Care Requirements (HEWDCR),
    126
Healthy Steps program, 273
Hearing, in infants, 9
Hepatitis A virus, 192
HEWDCR, *see* Health, Education,
    and Welfare Day Care
    Requirements
High-risk children
  biological risk of, 219–220
  early intervention for, 210–211,
    214–215, 214f
  environmental risk, 216–218
  family stressors, 212f, 213–214
Hippocampus, evoked potential
    activity associated with visual
    stimuli, 11
Home visiting programs
  assessment of, 300
  availability of, 123
  compared to center-based
    programs, 135
  descriptions, 132–135
  in early intervention, 220, 223
  high-risk families, 216, 227
  historical perspective, 132–134,
    298–299
  need for, 272
  quality indicators, 143–144
  social policy, 272–273, 302–303
  success of, 134, 362
Hospitalization, for respiratory
    disease, 173–174
Hunger of Memory (Rodriguez), 244
Hygienic intervention for disease
    control, 174, 191–192, 195–196,
    352–353

IBM, work–family program, 321–322
IHDT, *see* Infant Health and
    Development Program
Imitation
  deferred, 19
  of adults, 17–18, 17f
Immune system, development of,
    163–165, 164f, 354–355
Immunizations
  diarrhea, infectious, 197–198
  insurance coverage, 276, 277
  low-income families, 119
  respiratory disease, 175–176
Independence of children, cultural
    differences, 246–251
Infant Health and Development
    Program (IHDP), 133–134,
    141–142, 219–220, 223
Infant/Toddler Environment Rating
    Scale (ITERS), 128, 146, 152, 155
Infantile amnesia, 18–20
Infectious diseases, *see* Diarrhea,
    infectious; Respiratory disease
Innate abilities
  cognitive development, 7
  number concepts, 34–36, 35f
  sensory perception, 13
Instrumental conditioning, 15–16
Insurance, *see* Health insurance
Interdependence of children, cultural
    differences, 246–251
International Reading Association,
    position statement on language,
    77
Intervention programs
  availability of, 123, 210
  children at high risk, 216–220,
    222–227
  cognitive development, effect on,
    132–133, 134, 135, 299
  disabilities, infants and toddlers
    with, 123, 220–222, 228–229
  Early Head Start program, 119, 137,
    142, 154–155
  early intervention, 209–211,
    214–215, 214f, 216–225
  family support programs, 135–137,
    300–302
  health care, 132, 135
  home visiting programs, 123,
    134–135, 298–300

language development, effect on, 74–75, 133, 134, 299
long-term benefits, 222–225, 314
prenatal services, 123
quality, 117–118, 141–145, 151, 155
two-generation programs, 131–135, 154–155
types of, 120–121
Intonation contours of speech, to infants, 56–57, 358
IQ
  in children at high risk, 208, 214
  in children with disabilities, 221
  early intervention for children at high risk , 217, 218, 220
  habituation rate as indicator, 11
  historical use of, 270
  intervention programs, effect on, 75, 133
  lead poisoning and, 276
  low birth weight and, 208–209
  maternal, 207, 208, 217, 218, 219
  maternal employment, effect on, 314
  see also Cognitive development
ITERS, see Infant/Toddler Environment Rating Scale

Johnson & Johnson, child care support, 321

Kibbutzim, 96, 100

Language development
  in bilingual children, 51–52, 77
  conversational skills, 53–66, 75–76
  cultural factors, 50, 55, 62, 70, 77
  environmental factors, 49, 52–53, 70–74
  extended discourse, 66–70, 76
  frequency of communicative attempts, 61–62
  intent of communication, 54, 61–62
  interactionist model, 49–50
  intersubjectivity, 54–55
  intervention programs, 74–75, 133, 134
  maternal employment, effect on, 314
  preschools, 71–74

quality of child care and, 128–129
recommendations for caregivers, 75–77, 360–361
topic maintenance, 59–61
turn taking, 55, 56–59
varying communication partners, 62–63
vocabulary development, 63–66, 76
Latinos, maternal attention, 250
Lead poisoning, 208, 275, 276
Learning
  arbitrary associations, perceptual, 13–14
  auditory, 9–10, 12–13
  classical conditioning, 14–15
  habituation, 10–11
  imitation, 17–18, 17f
  instrumental conditioning, 15–16
  observational, 17–18
  prenatal, 9
  synchronous associations, perceptual, 12–13
  visual, 9–10, 12–14
  see also Memory
Listening, see Hearing, in Infants
Listeria monocytogenes, 182–183, 185t
Localization, 9–10
Low birth weights, see Birth weights, low
Low-income families
  characteristics of, 118–119, 207–208
  children with disabilities from, 209
  cultural issues in, 93
  financial assistance for child care, 335–336, 336t, 337t
  flextime, 331–332, 332t, 333t
  funding for child care, 293–294
  health insurance, 278–280, 325–327, 326t, 327t, 328t
  health problems, 275–276
  intervention programs, 74–75, 314
  job quality, 340t, 341t
  language development, 74–75
  Medicaid, 277–278
  paid holidays, 330t
  paid vacations, 328, 329t
  parenting support, 296
  poverty rate, 118, 207, 275
  quality of child care, 92, 125–126, 127, 139, 140, 148
  sick children, time off for, 330, 331t

Low-income families—*continued*
  social development in, 91

Malnutrition, 275–276
Managed health care, 284–285
Maternal characteristics
  depression, 106–107, 274
  employment, 312–314
  intelligence, 207, 208
  mental illness, 213
Maternal role in language
    development
  topic maintenance, 60–61
  turn taking, 56–59
  vocabulary development, 65–66
Medicaid, health care services,
    277–278
Memory
  autobiographical, 20
  development, 18–20
  hippocampus, 11
  infantile amnesia, 18–20
  language as basis, 20
  see also Learning
Middle ear infections, *see* Otitis
    media; Respiratory disease
Model Child Care Standards Act of
    1985, 287
Mortality, infant, 275
Mother's voice, infant recognition of,
    9, 12
Mother–child interactions, quality of
    child care and, 127–128
Mother–child relationships, 97–98,
    105–107, 312–313, 314

Narrative skills
  extended discourse, 66–70
  memory and, 20
National Association for Education of
    Young Children (NAEYC)
  bilingualism, 255
  position statement on language, 77
  standards for group sizes, 125
National Child Care Staffing Study,
    125
National Child Care Survey, 319
National Day Care Study, 129
National Household Education

Survey, 118
NAEYC, *see* National Association for
    Education of Young Children
*National Study of the Changing Work-
    force* (1997), 311, 319, 323, 324–342
Nature/nurture, in development, 8–9
Neurological development
  evoked response potentials (ERPs),
    11
  plasticity, 271
  see also Cognitive development
Neurotransmitters, 31
Novelty, need for, 40, 360–361
  see also Habituation
Numbers, infants' learning of, 34–36,
    35*f*

Object permanence, 24–31
  A/not B error, 24–25, 27–29
  neural bases, 29, 31
  Piaget, 24–25, 27
  sequence of actions, 27, 29, 30*f*
  size of objects, 27, 28*f*
  solidity of objects, 25, 26*f*, 27
Object segregation, 20–24, 21*f*, 23*f*
Observational Ratings of the Caregiv-
    ing Environment (ORCE), 152,
    155
Operant conditioning, 15–16
OCRE, *see* Observational Ratings of
    the Caregiving Environment
Otitis media
  acute, incidence of, 164–165, 168,
    169*t*
  center-based care compared to
    home care, 170–171, 173
  effusion, prevalence of, 168–171
  smoking and, 274

Parent and Child Centers (PCCs), 132
Parent and Child Development
    Centers (PCDCs), 132
Parenting
  cross-cultural studies, 250–251
  historical perspective, 296
  support, 296–302
Parents as Teachers (PAT), 298, 299
Parents, programs for, *see* Interven-
    tion programs

PAT, *see* Parents as Teachers
Pattern recognition, prenatal, 9
Pavlov, classical conditioning, 14
PCCs, *see* Parent and Child Centers
PCDCs, *see* Parent and Child Development Centers
Peer Play Scale, 101–102
Peer relationships, 100
PEIP, *see* Prenatal/Early Infancy Project
Perceptual learning, *see* Learning
Personal Responsibility and Work Opportunity Reconciliation Act of 1996, 119
Pharyngitis, *see* Respiratory disease
Phenylketonuria (PKU), children with, 29, 31
Phonetic features of speech, 56–57
Piaget, Jean
    deferred imitation, 19
    egocentrism theory, 54, 59
    object permanence, 24–25, 27
    sensory integration theory, 12
Picturebooks, role in cognitive development, 36–38, 37f
Pictures, *see* Symbolization, role in cognitive development
PKU, *see* Phenylketonuria
PL 94-142, *see* Education for All Handicapped Children Act of 1975
PL 99-457, *see* Education of the Handicapped Act Amendments of 1986
Playmate relationships, 95, 100–104
Pneumonia, *see* Respiratory disease
Policies, social
    child care, 286, 363
    cultural issues, 257–258
    family leave, 94, 355
    family support programs, 272–273, 300
    health and sanitation standards, 195, 353
    health care services, 285–286
    historical perspective, 269–271
    home visiting programs, 298–299
    lack of, 94
    parenting support, 297
    welfare, 94
Poverty, *see* Low-income families

Practitioners, *see* Caregivers
Prefrontal cortex, role in object permanence, 29, 31
Prejudice, *see* Racism; Sexism
Premature births
    early intervention programs, 219–220
    home visiting programs, 134–135
    low-income families, 118
Prenatal care
    exposure to drugs and alcohol, 207–208
    impact on development, 352
    infant hearing in the womb, 9
    intervention programs, 123, 137
    low-income families, 118, 276
Prenatal/Early Infancy Project (PEIP), 134
Preschools
    early intervention programs, 224–225
    quality of, 286
    role in language development, 71–74
Pretend play
    adult–child play, 101
    extended discourse in, 69–70
    peer play, 102
Program for Infant/Toddler Caregivers, 256–257
Project CARE, 133, 142, 218
Prosodic features of speech, 56–57
Psychological attributes of caregivers, 105–107

Quality 2000 Initiative, Not By Chance, 292
Quality of care
    adult–child ratios, 72, 92, 124–125, 128, 129, 287–288, 315, 356
    attachment relationships, effect on, 127–128, 148, 314–316, 356
    case management issues, 144–145
    in center-based facilities, 124–125, 141–143, 315
    cognitive development, effect on, 128–129
    in comprehensive intervention programs, 141–145, 151, 154–155

Quality of care—*continued*
  continuity of caregivers, 129–130,
    137, 138–139, 147, 148, 149*f*,
    356–357
  cultural issues, 139, 147, 149*f*
  Early Head Start program, 154–155
  educational level of family, 92
  in family care homes, 125–126, 286,
    315–316
  goals, 139–140
  group sizes, 72, 92, 124–125, 129,
    287–288, 315
  in home visiting programs,
    143–144
  in infant/toddler classrooms, 286
  income and, 92, 125–126, 127, 139,
    140, 148
  individual children, focus on,
    140–141, 152
  language development, effect on,
    52, 71–74, 128–129
  longitudinal studies, 130
  measurement of, 128, 146–147, 152,
    155
  model, 148–151, 149*f*
  mother–child interactions, effect
    on, 127–128
  preschools, 71–74, 286
  process quality, 92, 124, 138, 146,
    149*f*
  relationships with caregivers,
    52–53, 127–128, 138, 147, 148,
    149f, 314–316, 356
  research recommendations, 148,
    150–153
  social development, effect on,
    129–130, 314
  structural quality, 72, 92, 124–126,
    139–140, 146, 149*f*
  training of caregivers, 72, 92, 130,
    288, 289–292, 315
  variables affecting, 148, 150–151
Quality of Employment Survey (QES),
  310

Racism, 93, 94, 147, 247
  see also Cultural issues
Ratios, caregiver–child
  attachment, effect on, 128
  language skills, effect on, 128–129

quality of care and, 72, 92, 124–125,
    128, 129, 287–288, 315, 356
  social skills, effect on, 129
Reading
  extended discourse and, 67
  lead poisoning and, 276
  vocabulary development and,
    63–64
Regulation of child care programs,
    120, 121–122, 287–289
Reinforcement, conjugate, 15
Relationships
  Adult Attachment Interview,
    105–107
  attachment relationships, 95–100,
    312–314
  biological contributions, 104–105
  caregiver–child, 52–53, 96–100,
    105–109, 138, 356
  development of, 95–104, 108–109
  effects on behavior, 99–100
  father–child, 96, 313, 318
  friendship relationships, 95,
    103–104
  mother–child, 97–98, 100, 105–107,
    312–313, 314
  Peer Play Scale, 101–102
  peer relationships, 100
  playmate relationships, 95, 100–104
  quality of care, 52–53, 127–128, 138,
    147, 148, 149f, 314–316, 356
  temperament of child, 104–105
Respiratory disease, *see also* Otitis
    media
  antibiotic resistance, 171–172
  bacterial, 171–172
  in child care settings, 167, 170, 173
  cost, 174
  hospitalization for, 173–174
  incidence, 163, 167
  pathogens, 166*t*
  prevention and control, 174–176,
    352–353
  vaccines, 175–176
  viral, 163, 167
Rotavirus
  asymptomatic excretion, 186*t*, 187
  attack rates, 185*t*, 190*t*, 192
  inoculum size, 182*t*
  transmission, 189, 192
  vaccine, 197–198

Salmonella, 182, 185*t*, 197, 197*t*
Sanitary precautions, *see* Hygienic
    intervention for disease control
S-CHIP, *see* State Children's Health
    Insurance program
School readiness
    extended discourse and, 67
    vocabulary development and,
        63–64
Second language learners
    cultural issues in child care, 51–52,
        77, 245, 254–255, 358–359
    language development in, 51–52
Self-control
    attachment relationships, effect on,
        99
    cross-cultural studies, 249–250
Sensory perception, theories, 12–13
Sexism, 94
Shigella
    antibiotic resistance, 193
    asymptomatic excretion, 186*t*, 187
    attack rates, 185*t*, 190*t*, 192
    exclusion of children with, 197,
        197*t*
    inoculum size, 182*t*
    symptoms, 183
    transmission, 183, 189, 191
Simultaneous bilingualism, 51–52
Single parents
    dependent care assistance plans
        (DCAPs), 337*t*
    health insurance, 325–327, 326*t*,
        327*t*, 328*t*
    job pressures, 341*t*
    paid holidays, 329, 330*t*
    paid vacations, 328, 329*t*
    sick children, time off for, 330–331,
        331*t*
    Sleeping patterns, cross-cultural
        studies, 248–249
Smoking, health of children and, 274
Social development
    cultural differences, 93–94
    family characteristics, 90–92
    parental employment, effect on,
        313–314, 317–318
    parents' educational level, effect
        on, 91
    quality of child care, effect on,
        129–130, 314

schedule of, 87
social context, 88*f*, 90–92
theoretical model, 87–88, 88*f*
Social policies, *see* Policies, social
State Children's Health Insurance
    program (S-CHIP), 280
State health insurance initiatives,
    278–280
Story telling, role in vocabulary
    development, 66
Streptococcus pneumoniae, 166t, 171–172
Study of Children in Family Child
    Care and Relative Care, 126
Study of Early Child Care, 148
Subitization, 36
Subordination, cultural, 241–242,
    243–244
Substance abuse
    in families at high risk, 216
    intervention program effectiveness,
        134
    prenatal, 207–208
    Services for Children of Substance
        Abusers Act of 1992, 298–299
Symbolization, role in cognitive
    development, 36–39, 37*f*
Synapses, elimination of, 8
Synaptogenesis, 8
Syracuse University Family Develop-
    ment Research Program, 133

Taxes
    dependent care assistance plans
        (DCAPs), 318, 336
    for funding child care, 294–295
Teachers, *see* Caregivers
Television and video pictures, role in
    cognitive development, 36, 38–39
Training, of caregivers
    in center-based child care, 292
    child development, 107, 358
    cognitive development, 41, 358, 360
    cultural issues, 255–257, 358–359
    degree programs, 107, 292
    effect on quality of care, 72, 92, 130,
        288, 289–292, 315
    in family care homes, 292, 316
    to promote appropriate interac-
        tions, 357–359, 362
    U.S. military, 291

Turn taking, 55, 56–59, 101, 356
Two-generation programs, *see* Inter-
    vention programs

Vaccines, *see* Immunizations
Videotapes, *see* Television and video
    pictures, role in cognitive
    development
Violence, family
    social development, 91
    statistics, 207
Viruses, *see* Diarrhea, infectious; Res-
    piratory disease
Visual learning, 12–13
Vocabulary development, 63–66, 76
Vocalizations of infants, turn taking,
    56–57
Voice recognition
    mother's voice, 12
    prenatal, 9

Welfare programs
    child care needs, 122
    health issues, 227
    social development of children, 94
White House Conference on Brain
    Development (1996), 271
White House Conference on Infants
    and Toddlers (1997), 146
Wisconsin teacher education pro-
    grams, training in cultural issues,
    257
Workplace issues
    community focus of employers,
        323–324
    dependent care assistance plans
        (DCAPs), 318, 336, 337t,
        340–342
    employer incentives, 344
    employers' views of family,
        322–323, 336–338, 338t, 339t,
        341, 342
    financial assistance for child care,
        35–336, 336t, 337t
    flextime, 318, 321, 331–333, 332t,
        333t, 340–342
    health insurance, 325–327, 326t,
        327t, 328t, 340–342
    historical perspective, 309–324
    job autonomy, 338–339, 340–341,
        340t
    job pressures, 339–340, 341t
    on-site or near-site child care, 318,
        334–335
    paid holidays, 329, 330t, 340–342
    paid vacations, 328, 329t, 340–342
    parental employment, impact on
        children, 311–318
    parental leave, 318, 321, 333–334,
        341
    public awareness of, 343
    resource and referrals, access to,
        318, 334, 335t
    sick children, time off for, 330–331,
        331t, 340–342
    work–family conflict, 310–311, 316
    see also Employer-supported child
        care; Single parents

Xerox, work–life experiment, 323